HOW THE IRISH WON
THE AMERICAN
REVOLUTION

HOW THE IRISH WON THE AMERICAN REVOLUTION

The Forgotten Heroes of America's War of Independence

BY PHILLIP THOMAS TUCKER, PHD

Skyhorse Publishing

Skyhorse Publishing books may be purchased in bulk at special discounts for sales promotion, corporate gifts, fund-raising, or educational purposes. Special editions can also be created to specifications. For details, contact the Special Sales Department, Skyhorse Publishing, 307 West 36th Street, 11th Floor, New York, NY 10018 or info@skyhorsepublishing.com.

Skyhorse® and Skyhorse Publishing® are registered trademarks of Skyhorse Publishing, Inc.®, a Delaware corporation.

Visit our website at www.skyhorsepublishing.com.

10 9 8 7 6 5 4 3 2 1

Library of Congress Cataloging-in-Publication Data is available on file.

Cover design by Brian Peterson
Cover photo credit: Getty Images

Print ISBN: 978-1-5107-5567-3
Ebook ISBN: 978-1-63450-387-7

Printed in the United States of America

Contents

Contents

To my Mother, Betty Jane Cox-Tucker, and my Father,
Willard Thomas Tucker

Cum nad chimhne ar sinnsre—ancient Gaelic for
"This in Remembrance of Our Fathers"

Introduction

The Forgotten Irish Contribution to Decisive Victory

One of the greatest mysteries of American history has revolved around the intriguing question of how General George Washington and his revolutionaries could have possibly prevailed over a mighty British empire at the height of its power and prosperity. Many explanations have been offered to explain this enduring mystery throughout the past, but none are entirely satisfactory for a variety of reasons. Can a more accurate and correct answer be found at this late date to better explain how and why England lost its thirteen colonies forever to change the course of history? Fortunately for America, it possessed a large population of colonists who were already militants, agitators, and rebels before they ever migrated to the New World.

For more than two centuries, what has been most forgotten about America's stirring creation story were the crucial and disproportionate contributions that the Irish people, especially the more numerous Scotch-Irish (compared to Irish Catholics) from Northern Ireland, played in the winning of the American Revolution. Largely because of Ireland's dark legacy of early subjugation by England and difficult economic times that caused a mass exodus of immigrants to colonial America, the Irish people became not marginal, but the leading players in America's struggle for liberty and creation.

While the importance of the role of the Celtic-Gaelic people in leading America's westward expansion has been widely acknowledged by historians, the comparable leading role of the Irish and Scotch-Irish (lowland Scots who had settled in Ulster Province, Northern Ireland) in serving as the vanguard of America's resistance effort throughout the War of Independence, as known in Europe, from 1775 to 1783 has been generally unrecognized or unappreciated. Even more, the Celtic-Gaelic people also made fundamental contributions in shaping the very essence and character of America: a classic case of the past dictating the future in a variety of significant ways. Therefore, to a surprising degree, even some of the struggle's most basic complexities and truths have been left unexplored, leaving gaps that need to be filled at this late date.

Unfortunately, this sanitization of the historical record has resulted in the popular New England-based stereotype of the yeoman farmer-soldier of British descent, or Anglo-Saxon, having led and won the Revolution largely on his own. This mythical portrayal of America's struggle for survival has overlooked the Revolution's most important players who were more responsible for leading the way in agitating for independence, sustaining the war effort, and leading the way to decisive victory than any other ethnic group in America from beginning to end. Therefore, as seen in every nation that defined its origins, what has been created is a highly romanticized view of America's creation story that is excessively congratulatory and self-aggrandizing.

The Irish and Scotch-Irish actually fought in more disproportionate numbers compared to colonists of British descent and served as the longest-lasting and most sturdy core foundation of General George Washington's Continental Army, especially during crucial periods, as well as important contributors on the political and economic fronts. Nevertheless, the Irish have become the forgotten players of America's struggle for independence as no other distinctive group of white colonists in America.

Occupying a rung of America's social ladder far lower than the stereotypical middle-class yeoman farmer-soldier, the mostly illiterate Irish Catholics were primarily members of the indentured servitude class, while the Scotch-Irish were only slightly socially and economically more elevated because of their greater literacy and Protestantism. These Emerald Islanders were motivated to overturn an inequitable hierarchical society because of harsh economic, social, and cultural realities that had long existed on both sides of the Atlantic.

Luckily for America's fortunes, the height of Irish immigration to America reached its peak during the first half of the decade of the 1770s to set the stage for the dramatic bolstering of the ranks of a new generation of highly motivated fighting men for America. A large percentage of Irish and Scotch-Irish common soldiers along with officers, including Washington's top generals, served as the reliable backbone of America's resistance effort, especially in Washington's Army, from beginning to end.

The standard interpretations of America's revolutionary struggle and the endless romance of the mythological American Revolution have obscured the undeniable truth of the all-important contributions of the Irish and Scotch-Irish people. Unfortunately, leading British, Irish, and American historians have not focused on the pivotal roles (military, economic, and political) played by the Irish and the Scotch-Irish primarily because of the scarcity of documentation and records of a diasporic people. Even Revolutionary War historian Thomas J. Fleming admitted as late as 2005 of a much-belated personal revelation that the "most surprising thing about the soldiers" at Valley Forge, Pennsylvania, during the winter of 1777–1778, was the high percentage of Irish soldiers (both Catholic and Scotch-Irish) who served in Washington's Army. So many Celtic-Gaelic soldiers filled the Pennsylvania Continental Line that it was widely known as the Line of Ireland at the time: one of America's largest and most distinguished combat units, which served as a solid foundation for the army.

This significant Irish and Scotch-Irish contribution has also been long obscured because the mythical revolution has presented America's struggle for liberty as primarily an Anglo-Saxon triumph won by colonists of English descent without Irish roots or contributions.

The Founding Fathers have garnered the lion's share for almost singlehandedly bestowing the enlightened concepts of liberty upon the less-educated common people (including hundreds of thousands of Irish and Scotch-Irish) as if they possessed no revolutionary heritage and egalitarian legacy of their own. In truth, the revolutionary tradition of rising up against abusive centralized authority was already deeply embedded in the hearts and minds of the average Irish immigrant who never needed to read Age of Enlightenment philosophers or pamphleteers to become fiery revolutionaries against the British in either Ireland or America.

Unfortunately, what traditional historians have presented to us has been basically an inverted and severely distorted interpretation of the American Revolution from the top down. Compared to the upper-class elites, the lowly Emerald Islanders, including those who still spoke Gaelic and worked in the gentry's expansive fields (including those owned by Founding Fathers) were the ones who actually made the most sacrifices for independence. However, the Irish have been long seen in America through the lens of negative stereotypes and ugly caricatures, including even distorted comic figures perpetuated for entertainment purposes. Therefore, any serious consideration of meaningful Irish contributions to America's creation story was almost entirely incomprehensible as it would have diminished a much-celebrated American exceptionalism and nationalism.

At the time of the American Revolution, thousands of Irish soldiers took considerable pride in their distinctive culture and heritage. Across the thirteen colonies, many recent immigrants still spoke their native Gaelic or with thick Irish brogues (including the Scotch-Irish from Northern Ireland) barely understandable to their non-Irish peers. These transplanted Irish still viewed the Emerald Isle as their true homeland and motherland, especially in cultural and social terms, rather than America. Because hundreds of thousands of these immigrants were far more Irish than American by 1775, it was precisely these distinctive qualities and legacies that created the most ideal, natural, and die-hard revolutionaries in America.

The significant contributions and influences of the "mob" (or the common people who shaped the revolution's course) have been minimized by traditional scholars, especially historians of the New England, "republican," and "ideological" schools. Besides ethnic and cultural biases, an almost exclusive focus on Anglo-Saxon revolutionary contributions developed because American historians, themselves mostly Anglo-Saxon, were naturally motivated to promote not only a stronger national identity, based upon the Anglo-Saxon model, but also to rationalize expansion and imperialism, defined as Manifest Destiny by the 1840s. In this way, they transformed these historical developments into a righteous, moral crusade of God's chosen people, who were not Irish and definitely not Irish Catholics, in America's Protestant eyes to conform with self-serving racial, cultural, religious, and national priorities.

After having migrated thousands of miles to remain still largely marginalized outside the bounds of colonial society, especially the aristocratic world of the elites, the majority of Irish soldiers, especially recent immigrants, were most often without land, education, prospects, or titled property. Instead of a free society of yeoman farmers, as Thomas Jefferson envisioned for the ideal America, large numbers of Emerald Islanders had labored as indentured servants on American soil for wealthy landowners like peasants of their oppressive feudal society back in Ireland. Unlike the colonist of British descent, the typical Celtic-Gaelic soldier in Washington's ranks possessed relatively little, if any, land or political, social, and financial means by 1775.

Generations of Americans never understood a fundamental reality that without the important contributions of the Irish and the Scotch-Irish throughout the American Revolution's tortured course, a new nation conceived in liberty would have almost certainly succumbed to an early death. For the first time and for this fundamental reason, this work will present a more accurate and fresh look at the American Revolution without the romantic myths, legends, or stereotypes: how the Irish and Scotch-Irish, the most independent and rebellious settlers in America, made significant contributions to America's victory on a scale not fully appreciated by historians.

The overall purpose of this work is not only to expose the core fallacies and romantic stereotypes of the mythical American Revolution but also to present a new understanding about a central forgotten truth of America's creation story while giving fuller recognition and credit where it is long overdue. The Irish and Scotch-Irish were the very heart and soul of America's resistance effort from beginning to end, making the greatest dream of the Founding Fathers come true by what they accomplished both on and off the battlefield. With the untold story of the Celtic-Gaelic people in America's struggle for independence, therefore, this work is not a traditional campaign history and conventional analysis. After all, generations of American historians have long focused on the most famous military and political leaders instead of the lowly common soldiers, especially the Irish and Scotch-Irish, who fought and died for American independence.

Unfortunately, the stereotypical view of the Irish soldier has been that of the mercenary because so many Irish served in foreign armies, especially in the British Army and during the Napoleonic Wars. England's early conquest of Ireland ensured that impoverished Irishmen eventually fought in British military service as the only means to support families: essentially, cannon fodder made available by severe economic conditions and political frustration. But the Irish and Scotch-Irish role in the American Revolution was the antithesis of the stereotypical Irish mercenary. In overall percentage terms, the average Irishman, the most ordinary common man and the lowest-class member of white colonial society, was in fact America's patriot second to none.

The disproportionate Irish contributions during the American Revolution shattered the popular mercenary stereotype because for the first time tens of thousands of Emerald Islanders did not battle under a foreign flag of the eighteenth-century major European powers (especially France, Spain, and then England) as mercenaries. Instead, they fought as free men for egalitarian, social, and political ideals with the loftiest of republican goals in mind: a new republic conceived in liberty. Throughout the Revolution's course, therefore, these forgotten Irish soldiers no longer fought and died under the flag of another nation, for another people, or in a foreign army, but under the Stars and Stripes of a new nation.

This invaluable Irish contribution to America's salvation has been forgotten today because the American Revolution's story has been so thoroughly reinvented, romanticized, and mythologized. Consequently, this work has been dedicated to providing a more honest view, a corrective analysis, and a truer perspective of America's difficult birth while exploring in detail the most overlooked reason explaining how and why America ultimately won its struggle for liberty. It is not a strictly chronological history of the American Revolution, but an analytical history of the forgotten Irish Revolutionary War experience. An additional purpose of this book is to tell the long-overlooked story of the common Irish soldier, who sacrificed so much for the great dream of America, as much as possible: a new approach in looking at America's struggle for life from below and from a more personal perspective. Consequently, this book will present a forgotten, unexplored dimension of America's struggle to illuminate one of the best remaining untold chapters of the hidden history of the American Revolution: how the Irish and Scotch-Irish played not only a leading but also a decisive role in winning the American Revolution to change the course of history.

Chapter I

"You Have Lost America by the Irish:"
America's Forgotten Revolutionaries

America lost its first general officer when a British cannon unleashed a blast of canister at point-blank range into Major General Richard Montgomery, who was inspiring his troops onward in America's most desperate offensive effort to date. Montgomery was cut down while encouraging his ill-clad men through a driving snowstorm in a determined attempt to capture the mighty fortress-city of Quebec, the key to Canada, against the odds. He led the way against a well-prepared British and Canadian opponent in the time-honored tradition of generations of Irish revolutionaries, who had fought in vain to free the Emerald Isle from British rule.

Montgomery, who was born as a member of the Irish Protestant gentry near Swords, County Dublin, Ireland and had attended prestigious Trinity College in Dublin, died along with America's ambitious dream of making Canada the fourteenth colony and conquering an empire. When the Irishman fell into the snow on a cold, windswept Quebec street far from his beloved Emerald Isle on the last day of December 1775, he became America's first authentic war hero and martyr to the cause of liberty.[1] Upon receiving the sad news, a shocked General George Washington lamented how "America has sustained a heavy Loss" in the fall of the gifted Montgomery, whom the Virginian described in a letter as "the Gallant Chief" of America's first invading army on foreign soil.[2]

However, in the subsequent glorification of America's first general to fall in battle, something significant was lost, shrouded in a romantic cloak of nationalism. In late January 1776, the Continental Congress appointed a committee, which included Benjamin Franklin, to take the necessary steps to preserve the memory of one of America's first martyrs to the cause of liberty. The committee determined that a stone marker, made by only the finest artists in Paris, France, should be erected in General Montgomery's honor. Therefore, while Montgomery's body remained on Canadian soil, the first monument ever dedicated to a United States war hero was erected at St. Paul's Church on Broadway in New York City in 1787. But nothing was revealed about Montgomery's birth in Ireland in the stone's inscription: a lasting testament of how an Ireland-born major general became thoroughly Americanized for posterity by the erasing of his Irish antecedents.[3]

Worst of all, however, not only were Montgomery's Irish roots (his father was disinherited because he married an English woman) lost, but also his historical memory. Despite his noble sacrifice and lofty rank, Montgomery became just another one of the forgotten Irishmen of the American Revolution. This development was even more surprising because his death in leading America's first invasion of foreign soil inspired an entire generation of revolutionaries across America to embark upon the perilous road to independence against the world's most powerful nation.[4]

Montgomery's contributions and sacrifice at Quebec was only the first of countless examples of the important, but forgotten, Irish heroics and sacrifices throughout the American Revolution. Historian Jay P. Dolan, in his excellent work entitled *The Irish Americans: A History*, correctly called the first section of his book, which included the American Revolution, "A Forgotten Era" in regard to Irish contributions to the making of America.[5]

John Sullivan was another forgotten major general of Irish immigrant parents. On Washington's orders to reverse the dismal situation in Canada, he led the next offensive effort in still another attempt to capture Quebec in June 1776. Although unsuccessful in Canada for reasons not of his making, Sullivan's leadership abilities later explained why Washington appointed him a leading role in the attack on Trenton, New Jersey. Sullivan commanded the First Division, the southern arm of Washington's brilliant pincer movement, in the surprise December 26, 1776, attack on Trenton. Without Sullivan's timely arrival from the northern army to reinforce Washington, the Virginian's audacious strike upon Trenton might well have proved unsuccessful.[6] Clearly, Sullivan (one of five Sullivan brothers who fought for America's liberty) was one of Washington's top lieutenants at an early date. In fact, from the beginning, Washington's well-placed confidence in Sullivan was rewarded. He wrote how Sullivan was an ideal revolutionary leader like Montgomery: "active, spirited, and zealously attach'd to the cause" of America's liberty.[7]

Sullivan was the son of two Irish "redemptionaries" (indentured servants), John and Margery Browne, who settled on the banks of the Salmon Falls River, just below the Maine border. The general's father hailed from a "long line of Irish warriors" who fought and died for Irish liberty. His grandfather, Major Philip Sullivan, battled the English all the way to the surrender of the Limerick garrison in 1690 that led to the fateful Treaty of Limerick. The major then fled to France with many other Irish Jacobite exiles, becoming one of the famous "Wild Geese" who served France with distinction.[8]

Unfortunately, even some of the most important aspects of the American Revolution still remain riddles and enigmas to this day, however. Not long after the American Revolution ended, even Washington himself was mystified as to how it had all come about in America's favor. Other than the blessings of "Providence" that he often invoked, Washington was not fully able to explain how the revolution had succeeded, defying the odds and top military experts on both sides of the Atlantic.

Consequently, a prophetic Washington correctly understood that historians of future generations would never quite be able to explain exactly how and why America's rustic revolutionaries had succeeded against the odds. In a rather remarkable letter written not long after the new nation's independence was won, Washington emphasized how in the future, "it will not be believed that such a force as Great Britain has employed for eight years in Country could be baffled [and] by numbers infinitely less, composed of Men oftentimes half starved; always in Rags, without pay, and experiencing, at times, every species of distress which human nature is capable of undergoing."[9] However, Washington later gave a strong hint in regard to the actual answer. He fully understood and appreciated the importance of the Irish and Scotch-Irish contributions to the winning of America's independence because "Ireland [was] thou friend of my country in my country's most friendless day" during the desperate struggle for liberty.[10]

George Washington Parke Custis, Washington's adopted son and a careful student of the American Revolution, said it better:

When our friendless standard was first unfurled for resistance, who were the strangers that first mustered 'round its staff, and when it reeled in the fight, who more bravely sustained it than Erin's generous sons? Who led the assault on Quebec [Ireland-born General Richard Montgomery] and shed early luster on our arms, in the dawn of our revolution? Who led the right wing of Liberty's forlorn hope [General John Sullivan played a leading role in Washington's victory at Trenton] at the passage of the Delaware? Who felt the privations of the camp, the fate of battle, or the horrors of the prison ship more keenly than the Irish? Washington loved them, for they were the companions of his toils, his perils, his glories, in the deliverance of his country.[11]

This long-overlooked analysis was accurate. In regard to Washington's surprise attack on Trenton that was made possible partly by supplies from Ireland-born merchants such as William

Patterson, Sullivan commanded one of the two divisions that struck simultaneously in a closing of two pincer arms, performing magnificently to cement his lofty place as "perhaps Washington's best field commander."[12] Likewise, Washington's enlisted ranks were heavily dominated by Irish and Scotch-Irish soldiers who followed so many Celtic-Gaelic commanders throughout the war. When thousands of Americans were captured in the Long Island fiasco on August 27, 1776, Ambrose Serle, Admiral Richard Howe's personal secretary, was shocked by the sight of the "vast numbers of Irish" in Washington's ranks while closely inspecting the lengthy lines of sullen American prisoners who had surrendered.[13] And in the South when Charleston, South Carolina, was captured four years later, one British officer was likewise astounded how the "Prisoners [who] have fallen into [our] hands being many of the . . . Irish" soldiers of the primary American army in the Southern theater.[14]

Privates Patrick McFarthom and William McCarthy, a Maryland Continental, were among Washington's forgotten Irishmen of the enlisted ranks. Patrick was "a middle sized well looking Irishman, about 26 years of age, red complexion, dark, curled and short hair." McCarthy hardly fit the romantic image of the Continental soldier. William was described by a comrade as "an Irishman, about forty years old [with] a blanket over-coat, round hat, and his shoes were tied with strings, his feet had been frost-bitten [from service during the Trenton-Princeton Campaign and] he has something of the [Irish] brogue in his language."[15]

However, in regard to later-day historians, as opposed to Washington and his contemporaries, even the most fundamental explanations of America's ultimate success that shocked the world have been proven false because Revolutionary War historiography has been dominated by romance and misconceptions. A natural development in the self-serving formulation of a distinguished national history (as seen in all nations), America's creation story has been narrowly interpreted and romantically portrayed as fundamentally having been won primarily by a single group of colonists—native-born Americans of English stock of the Protestant faith, which led to the yeoman farmer-soldier myth. This one-dimensional and even racially based perspective has led to the popular conception in the American mind and iconic imaginary of the mythical homogenous Anglo-Saxon soldiery, without a hint of ethnicity, especially in regard to Ireland and the Irish people.

Of course, these central myths of America's creation story have been a natural if not inevitable development in the historiography of the United States' birth because the infant nation needed to invent its past into a heroic saga—America's *Iliad*. However, this development resulted in a sanitization and homogenization of not only the American Revolution's story but also the very image of the revolutionaries themselves.

The extensive whitewashing of the overall image of America's revolutionaries was faithfully continued by generations of American historians and scholars (almost always Protestant), who have presented the most nationalistic and racially pristine of interpretations that left no room for the contributions of a distinct ethnic and racial group that was considered "foreign." However, nothing could have been further from the truth. In fact, eight signers of the Declaration of Independence were foreign born, more in Ireland than in any other country. Only one signer was Irish Catholic: Charles Carroll from Carrollton, Maryland, who traced his roots to the O'Carroll family of County Kings in Ireland's fertile midlands of Leinster Province. He was one of Washington's relatively few die-hard supporters who helped to save the commander in chief's position when criticism for the often-defeated Virginian reached its greatest height.

More than any other ethnic group in America, the Celtic-Gaelic people, America's greatest pioneering race, were precisely the right kind of individuals to wage revolution, thanks to the legacies of the searing Irish experience. They first answered the call to arms and continued to faithfully serve year after year in part because as lower-class members they were the most attracted to military service, especially when cash inducements and land bounties were part of the enlistment bargain. In consequence, the poor, disadvantaged, and uneducated people (mostly Irish and Scotch-Irish in America) were the most likely soldiers to serve for extended periods—an absolutely necessary requirement in what was a lengthy war of attrition—as regulars to sustain the resistance effort, especially in Washington's Army. Patriotism combined with Protestant zeal and a Calvinist work ethic that forbade failure to create a moral and determined Irish soldiery. Therefore, the typical Irish soldier was far from the stereotypical mercenary type. In overall terms, these Celtic-Gaelic soldiers were highly motivated not only because of America's struggle for liberty but also because of the overall Irish experience, especially in regard to the centuries-long quest for independence on Irish soil and the fact that England was the ancient enemy of the Irish people.[16]

Besides the lower class and immigrant status of the Irish, one fundamental reason why the revolutionary generation and future historians failed to fully acknowledge the disproportionate Irish contributions to America's amazing victory was because they were considered un-American "foreigners" by colonists and revolutionary leaders of English descent. At this time, the native Irish, or Catholics, who were known as Gaels and Celts, were considered by colonists of English descent as members of a distinct race instead of a nationality because Ireland had been subjugated by England.

The long-elusive answer that explains why the infant republic ultimately won its lengthy struggle for existence actually lies in the key demographic equation; a larger percentage of American colonial society consisted of Ireland-born Irish Catholics (who hailed from most of Ireland) and a far larger number of Scotch-Irish Presbyterians (mostly from Northern Ireland) than at any other time in American history. No American army in United States history ever contained a larger percentage of soldiers, both among leadership (including general officers) and the enlisted ranks, from foreign soil than Washington's Continental

Army.[17] So many Irish filled the ranks of the disproportionately large Pennsylvania Continental Line that it was known as the Line of Ireland.[18] Most importantly, the largely Celtic-Gaelic Pennsylvania regiments "provided the backbone of the American army."[19]

In a letter to his brother John Augustine, whom he affectionately referred to as Jack, Washington understood the difference between so many colonists of British descent who remained either neutral or Loyalist and more worldly but less realistic compared to the lowly Irish: the only realistic choice was to "conquer, or submit to unconditional terms . . . such as confiscations, hanging, etc."[20] For all practical purposes, Washington might as well have been referring specifically to the bitter lessons of Irish history and those Emerald Island colonists who most intimately understood these harsh realities of British imperialism and nationalism far better than any other people in America.

However, in an all-too-common omission, even respected Irish historians, such as Myles Dugan in a popular work, failed to include any mention of Irish participation in the American Revolution. But to be fair, Dugan has only continued the tradition of generations of American historians in ignoring American Revolutionary War contributions, despite the supreme importance of the Irish contribution.[21]

As mentioned, contemporaries of the time of the American Revolution were actually more on target in regard to the importance of the Irish contribution. An observant French nobleman who was a high-ranking member of France's expeditionary army, thanks to the signing of the French Alliance in 1778, Major General Francois Jean le Beauvoir, Chevalier de Chastellux (often simply referred to as the Marquis de Chastellux) provided insightful views about America's revolutionary experience that were decidedly as astute as those made by Alexis de Tocqueville, another French aristocrat of a monarchical regime. The Marquis de Chastellux, an "enlightened philosophe," and Washington, the former Virginia farmer whose military reputation had been first won in battling against the French and Indians in the previous war, became friends.

Henry Grieve, the translator of the Marquis de Chastellux's memoir, knew intimately of the significant Irish contribution to America's resistance effort from personal experience. He explained this singular phenomenon of such disproportionate, widespread patriotism among the Irish (to an extent not seen among colonists of British descent who were badly divided in terms of loyalty to the Crown and whose patriotism had significantly flagged by December 1776 after a series of stunning defeats) who played such a key role in ensuring that America's resistance effort never died and that Washington's Army survived a lengthy war of attrition:

> An Irishman, the instant he set foot on American ground becomes, ipso facto, an American; this was uniformly the case during the whole of [the American Revolution]. Whilst Englishmen and Scotsmen were regarded with jealousy and distrust, even with the best recommendation [by revolutionary Americans in regard to their] zeal and attachment to their cause, a native of Ireland stood in need of no other certificate than his dialect [brogue]; his sincerity was never called in question, he was supposed to have a sympathy of suffering, and every voice decided as it were intuitively, in his favour. Indeed their conduct in the late revolution amply justified this favourable opinion; for whilst the Irish emigrant was fighting the battles of America by sea and land, the Irish merchants, particularly in Charleston, Baltimore, and Philadelphia, laboured with indefatigable zeal, and at all hazards, to promote the spirit of enterprise, to increase the wealth, and maintain the credit of the country; their purses were always open, and their persons devoted to the common cause. On more than one imminent occasion, Congress and their existence, and America possibly her preservation to the fidelity and firmness of the Irish.[22]

Economic contributions of the Irish were as vital to success as sacrifices on the battlefield. Indeed, a heavy volume of trade between Ireland and East Coast ports, especially Philadelphia, had long been robust, leading to the rise of a dynamic and resourceful Irish merchant class of die-hard patriots. The influential Irish merchant class of Philadelphia, America's capital, provided revolutionary leaders on not only the military but also the economic front.[23]

The Marquis de Chastellux never acknowledged Philadelphia's Irish merchants who supplied Washington's Army with invaluable war munitions. However, what was most significant about Grieve's analysis of patriot Irishmen was its candidness and accuracy in bestowing proper recognition upon the importance of the overall Irish contribution to decisive victory. After all, few Americans, either at the time or after the Revolution, were able to entirely put aside their own provincial attitudes, homegrown prejudices, cultural biases, and growing sense of nationalism to bestow such comparable well-deserved recognition on the Irish contribution, especially at the expense of the contributions of patriots of British descent.

For the Irish of the American Revolutionary War generation, no experience was more traumatic or searing than the brutal lessons and ugly realities of Irish history. In the name of God and country, slaughtering Irish, including women and children, without mercy early became the winning formula to not only fame and fortune but also to royal favor in the highest places for ambitious Englishmen. One of Elizabeth I's favorites, a most aggressive Protestant holy warrior and "the queen's man," Sir Humphrey Gilbert won even greater favor from the Queen by closely emulating the brutalities of Genghis Khan. He won well-deserved renown as the "scourge of Ireland" for slaughtering so many Irish Catholics, regardless of sex or age, to secure the richest of south Ireland's lands in Munster Province.

Sent to Northern Ireland from England by the queen in 1566 when the Irish people were rising up in revolt by following the inspirational lead of Shane O'Neill, whose rebellion in Ulster Province spread to other portions of Ireland, Gilbert crushed the rebels of Munster Province during four bloody years, a campaign of terrorism and genocide. As he explained in his boasting report to London, Gilbert's success was based on "putting also all those . . . to the swords that did belong, feed, accompany, or maintain any outlaws or traitors," or Irish Catholics, patriots all.[24] If an Irish castle, fort, or town refused to immediately surrender, he then put every "man, woman, and child of them to the sword," in his own words.[25] During his bloody terrorism campaign, a good many Irish heads were cut off and then carried to the English army's encampment. Here, these grim trophies were arranged in a neat, but grisly, fashion, as ordered by Gilbert, and "laid on the ground by each side of the way leading into [Gilbert's] own tent, so that none could come into his tent but commonly he must pass through the line of heads" to invoke fear among the Irish people.[26] However, there is no comparison between Gilbert and the terrible wrath unleashed on the Irish people by Oliver Cromwell. At the time of the American Revolution, the Irish of the Emerald Isle were "still full of the Catholics' terror of [Cromwell's] name."[27]

Such examples only illustrate why the Irish and Scotch-Irish role in the American Revolution was so disproportionate and important. Ample early evidence of significant Irish martial contributions (that went entirely unheeded by King George III in regard to his initial decision to subjugate the thirteen colonies—based partly on the fear that Ireland would rise up and follow America's example) already existed in the annals of American military history to explain the phenomenon of Irish prowess on America's behalf. Distinguished Irish military contributions were evident as early as the Cartagena (located on today's northern coast of Colombia, South America) expedition of 1741. This expedition was led by British Vice Admiral Edward Vernon, for whom Washington's Mount Vernon was named. The "American Regiment" of colonials, including a good many Irish soldiers, was not trusted by their British allies because the colonials were viewed as "Papists" like the Spanish Catholics, or "Dons," whom they fought against. Washington's half-brother and mentor Lawrence Washington, whose martial exploits against the Spanish kindled his early military interests, led one Virginia company of the "American Regiment" that possessed a decidedly Celtic-Gaelic flavor.[28]

In addition, Irish soldiers filled the ranks of Washington's own First Virginia Regiment during the French and Indian War. Dennis McCarthy Jr., a Protestant-hating Jacobite warrior exiled after the crushing of the last great Jacobite rebellion and the infamous Treaty of Limerick in 1691, fled to Virginia and then served as an ensign in Washington's Regiment. McCarthy was Washington's cousin and hailed from the watershed of Accotink Creek, a slow-moving tributary of the Potomac River, located in southeast Fairfax County, Virginia. But Washington encountered trouble with his free-spirited Irish cousin, writing with a gift of understatement how McCarthy's behavior "was not so becoming and genteel as it ought" to have been.[29] However, during the American Revolution, Washington warmly welcomed just such troublesome Irish, who deserted the British Army, into the ranks of the Continental Army because of their experience and fighting spirit. Outside the army's ranks, Irish contributions were as notable as they were extensive. Northern Ireland-born Hercules Mulligan, a former leader of New York City's Sons of Liberty, became one of Washington's most effective spies. He twice saved Washington's life after acquiring timely intelligence to thwart dual plots on the general's life.[30]

America's most famous frontier fighters, Rogers's Rangers (the forerunners of America's elite Special Forces) of the French and Indian War contained mostly Irish and Scotch-Irish, with the latter the most dominant. These were Presbyterian and Irish Catholic immigrants who had been originally forced by the religious intolerance of Boston, Massachusetts, to migrate to the fringes of the harsh northern New England frontier. Here, amid a pristine wilderness, these Sons of Erin had evolved into savvy frontiersmen, adopting new ways of fighting learned from Native Americans. These legendary rangers were led by their inspirational Scotch-Irish leader, Major Robert Rogers. Known for his hard-hitting tactical ways and his "cantankerous Scots-Irish temperament," Rogers relied upon a good many capable Scotch-Irish rangers of note such as hard-fighting Captain John Stark (his top lieutenant), the son of an immigrant from Londonderry, Northern Ireland, who emerged as a tactically astute major general under Washington during the struggle for liberty; Lieutenant Sam Kennedy; and Lieutenant Andrew McMullen. Like other Scotch-Irish, these capable officers hailed from Ulster Province, Northern Ireland. While creating an unique American way of waging war on the frontier, Rogers and his hardy rangers, who wore uniforms of green as if to represent their Green Isle homeland, became national heroes on both sides of the Atlantic for their stirring exploits against the French, Canadians, and Indians while battling New England's dark forests.[31]

So many Irish and Scotch-Irish (and fellow Celts, the Welsh, but to a lesser degree) settled along the western frontier, stretching for more than one thousand miles from New England to South Carolina and Georgia, that America possessed in essence what was a sprawling Irish frontier where the Celtic-Gaelic people experienced an unprecedented level of freedom from arbitrary and tight governmental control. As early as 1768, the first Scotch-Irish pushed over the Appalachian Mountains and settled in the Watauga, Nolichucky, and Holston River valleys on the west side in today's east Tennessee. The Celtic-Gaelic people were the primary settlers who conquered and tamed America's western frontier and the backcountry (which included the Piedmont) during the colonial period. The martial skills and resourcefulness of the Irish frontiersman, experienced in hunting for daily survival and Indian fighting in a successful process of acclimation to a harsh wilderness, were well utilized in America's struggle for liberty by 1775.

The British waged a two-front war in the South during the summer of 1776, sending a powerful invasion force to Charleston and unleashing the Cherokee, armed with English weapons and powder, to rampage the settlements from Virginia in the north to Georgia in the south. The well-organized response and uniting of the largely Scotch-Irish (who eagerly accepted bounties for enlistment in South Carolina service) of the Carolina and Virginia frontiers and the Piedmont resulted in penetrating expeditions deep into the mountains. The frontiersmen destroyed a large number of Indian villages, storehouses, and fields during the summer and fall of 1776. These strikes that ravaged the Cherokee homeland of western South and North Carolina and Georgia left the formidable Cherokee nation without food or shelter after these mostly Celtic-Gaelic frontier soldiers destroyed their sanctuaries and logistical support systems for launching future raids. The devastation among the once formidable Cherokee was so complete that they sued for peace and signed a treaty in Charleston in early 1777.

At an early date, many of these early Celtic-Gaelic settlers were lowly indentured servants who had escaped their employers or Irish who had ended their terms of indenture and headed west to bask in the absolute freedom of the pristine western frontier. But this freedom came at a high price. Indian raiders emerged out of the dark forests to destroy log cabins, fields of corn, and wives and children. But the Scotch-Irish settlers were determined to never relinquish this new land of pristine beauty and amazing fertility, especially along the rivers and creeks. Therefore, familiar with hardship and suffering, they stubbornly persevered, returning to burned-down cabins and fields to start all over again in making new lives for themselves.

The vast majority of the Ulster Irish, the largest Irish immigrant population that flooded America's shores, populated the western frontier: a region that stretched from New England to western Maryland (including Frederick County), central and western Pennsylvania and Virginia, especially the fertile lands of the picturesque Shenandoah Valley, and then extended south into North Carolina, South Carolina, and Georgia. Here, hardened and tempered by the forge of adversity, the Irish immigrant of the lower class was transformed into an exceptionally resilient frontiersman and yeoman (small) farmer who hacked farms out of the seemingly endless forests. Here, in a pristine environment, they basked in a pure sense of freedom from society's burdensome restrictions, prejudices, and abuses.[32]

This rather remarkable development was as much a product of not only the Irish experience on both sides of the Atlantic but also America's most militant, egalitarian, and revolutionary religion of the Scotch-Irish, Presbyterianism. Ireland-born William "Billy" Hill, a long-haired Son of Erin who hailed from Ulster Province in Northern Ireland, fought as a South Carolina partisan to free his adopted homeland of British domination. For Hill, whose family migrated south from Pennsylvania to South Carolina in 1762 only to have their home burned down by raiding Tories, and so many other Scotch-Irish, this struggle was a holy war fueled by a combustible mixture of religion (Presbyterianism), vengeance, and longings for liberty.

In Hill's words that described a holy war, the "ill behavior of the enemy made an impression on the minds of the most serious men in this little band [of South Carolina patriots] and raised their courage under the belief that they would be made instruments in the hand of Heaven to punish this enemy for his wickedness . . ."[33] Even the fervent Presbyterian faith had originally pushed the Scotch-Irish deeper into the uncharted American wilderness on a righteous, holy-like mission because of their firm spiritual conviction that "it was against the laws of God and nature, that so much land should be idle while so many Christians wanted it to labor on, and raise their bread."[34]

Like no other transplanted people in America, the "Scotch-Irish from Ulster [were especially] tough folk well suited to their dangerous new surroundings" of the western frontier and the severe challenges of the revolutionary struggle.[35] The rough-hewn Scotch-Irish became the most "ideal frontier people because they knew how to suffer. Some would fall by the wayside, others would turn away from the contest . . . but most of them [stayed and] would persevere."[36]

Adam Meek was one such adventuresome pioneer from Ireland who bravely followed the setting sun through the wilderness to make his American dream come true in a new land. A veteran of the October 1780 victory at Kings Mountain, South Carolina, where he served as an inspirational officer in leading his frontiersmen in repeated assaults up the timbered slopes, this Irish signer of the Mecklenburg Declaration of Independence on May 20, 1775, departed North Carolina and crossed the towering Appalachians. Intoxicated by a breathtaking land that seemed to have no end, Meek journeyed so far west that "His was the first [log] cabin in Jefferson County, Tennessee [and] No neighbor [other than Indians] was west of him. . . ."[37] Even the Native Americans marveled at the resourcefulness and determination of these stubborn, tenacious settlers from Ireland because they possessed such a "restless disposition," in the words of an amazed Creek Indian.[38]

Here, in thousands of isolated cabins and small frontier settlements, the seeds of American independence took deep root long before the American Revolution's beginning. Once hostilities erupted, the Scotch-Irish and Irish joined the struggle for American independence en masse in an instinctive and collective response. Following his older brother's example, teenage James Collins, of Scotch-Irish descent, was one who came forth early to serve first as a scout before becoming a South Carolina partisan along with his father, who was a hardened French and Indian War veteran. He wrote with pride of the kind of Celtic-Gaelic rebels who led the way, including the Collins family: "The first class of Whigs [rebels in South Carolina who were largely Scotch-Irish] were those who [were] determined to fight it out to the last."[39] The teenager's Scotch-Irish father perhaps best explained the never-say-die motivation of the average Celtic-Gaelic fighting man: "I have . . . determined to take my gun and when I lay it down, I lay down my life with it . . . We must submit and become slaves, or fight [and] For my part, I am determined" to fight.[40]

But besides the remote frontier regions, a good many enterprising Irishmen also created new lives for themselves in communities all along the East Coast. After retiring from British military service and migrating to America just before the American Revolution, Ireland-born Richard Montgomery wrote in a letter how "I have cast my eye on America, where my pride and poverty will be much more at their ease."[41] Montgomery settled on a small farm at King's Bridge just north of New York City. After his marriage to Janet Livingston, from one of New York's leading families, on July 3, 1773, he purchased additional acres. Here, Montgomery made his American dream come true: owning his own land, plowing his own acres, building fences around luxurious pasture land, and erecting a mill on his own stream. In fact, Montgomery's sense of happiness was so complete on American soil that he worried how "This cannot last; it cannot last."[42] A hero's death as a dynamic major general in the snows of Quebec verified the Irishman's nagging concern because America's blessings seemed endless and almost too good to be true.[43]

Ulster Irish, such as John Haslet, who became one of Washington's finest combat generals and was killed at the battle of Princeton, New Jersey, on January 3, 1777, settled in the east in Kent County, Delaware. Hailing from the little town of Dungiven, County Londonderry, in Northern Ireland, Haslet departed the port of Londonderry and headed for Philadelphia in 1757. Almost immediately, he enlisted in a volunteer company of mostly Scotch-Irish and became a Pennsylvania captain. He served on Scotland-born General John Forbes's expedition into the Ohio Country in 1758 during the French and Indian War. Possessing a prestigious University of Glasgow, Scotland, degree, Haslet provided an excellent example of the Scotch-Irish holy warrior. He was also an ordained minister of the Presbyterian Church. Before migrating to America, Haslet had served for five years as the minister of Ballykelly, County Derry, Ulster Province.[44]

Likewise, not far from the East Coast in New Hampshire, General John Sullivan, Washington's right-hand man in the desperate attack on Trenton, made his dreams come true in this land of seemingly limitless opportunities. The son of the exiled Irish Jacobite rebel,

Major Philip Sullivan, John Sullivan Sr. (the father of General John Sullivan) had his freedom from indentured servitude purchased by a physician, who then established the educated Ireland-born immigrant in a teaching position in 1738. Then Sullivan purchased the freedom of Margery Browne, his soon-to-be wife who had journeyed to America with him as a child on the same vessel. Born of this union at Somersworth, New Hampshire, in mid-February 1740, John Sullivan gained an advanced education from his father. Sullivan was such a competent lawyer in Durham, New Hampshire, that he became wealthy (thanks also to aggressively purchasing land and operating six mills) before the American Revolution's beginning.[45]

Also from New England, the MacFarline family of Massachusetts provided a good example of the representative Scotch-Irish contribution in the enlisted ranks by including a feisty father-son fighting team that was so common among the Irish. Elijah MacFarline Sr., a farmer and father of eight, and his two sons, including Elijah MacFarline Jr., enlisted in 1775 at the war's beginning. After the father was killed in combat on November 29, 1777, his sons continued to fight in Washington's Army. Son David MacFarline died of disease in 1777, and Elijah Jr. was killed in battle in 1778. Born in 1749, he had married a Scotch-Irish woman (Sarah Marshall) in May 1773 and was a lucky survivor of the hard-hit Scotch-Irish clan. No longer able to serve beside his father, Elijah continued to serve in the ranks and at the side of his father-in-law, Josiah Marshall, despite having suffered a wound at the Battle of White Plains.[46]

Hundreds of thousands of Sons of Erin in America, from the western frontier to the East Coast, still retained their distinctive Irishness with a tight grip in a bountiful land that caused one Scotch-Irishman to conclude, "America is a honey of a place."[47] Here, gaining opportunities not found in Ireland, the Emerald Islanders kept their distinctive Celtic-Gaelic traditions, culture, and values alive and well in the new land, including even in the most isolated wilderness areas. Especially in distinctive ethnic communities nicknamed "Little Ulster," "New Munster," and "New Ireland," the Irish and Scotch-Irish reestablished "the religion, customs, and habits of their ancestors, and the Irish wedding was always the occasion of great hilarity, jollity, and mirth."[48]

Similar to other regions across America, the Irish on Virginia's western frontier celebrated "regularly the national festival of Ireland" and honored their patron saint, St. Patrick.[49] Long before the United States was born, the Celtic-Gaelic settlers and soldiers of America spoke in thick Irish brogues and carried distinctive cultural values and folkways with them whenever they settled. They also took an ancient Celtic-Gaelic warrior ethos with them when they went into battle, including taking the fight to native peoples across the western frontier with vigor to repay deadly attacks on their isolated cabins and settlements carved out the wilderness.

Therefore, the overconfident King George III and his highly educated advisers, who thought that only a slight example of military force would be sufficient to quell unrest in America, should have heeded other impressive examples of Irish and Scotch-Irish military achievements during the French and Indian War. Ireland-born Colonel John Armstrong, who hailed from the agricultural community of Brookeborough, County Fermanagh, Ulster Province in Northern Ireland, led one of the boldest preemptive strikes in the annals of frontier history. At the head of Pennsylvania troops during his long-distance raid through the wilderness and across the Appalachians, he caught the hostile Shawnee and Delaware (allied with France) village of Kittanning by surprise. Here, on the east bank of the Allegheny River, Armstrong struck at dawn on a hot August day in 1756. Washington's friend since the dark days of the French and Indian War, Armstrong rose to the rank of major general during the American Revolution. Most importantly, when feeling against Washington was growing strong after the disastrous summer and fall 1776 campaign that included New York City's loss, he remained one of the Virginian's most firm supporters to the end. Meanwhile, his son John

Jr. played key roles as a staff officer for Scotland-born Generals Hugh Mercer, who was a member of the Kittanning raid and a hard-hitting Celtic leader killed in Washington's attack at Princeton, New Jersey, and England-born Horatio Gates.[50]

During the frontier clash of arms in the remote wilderness of western Virginia called Dunmore's War (named after the Royal Governor of Virginia) in 1774, popular Irish frontier leaders led the military expedition that pushed over the Appalachians (in violation of official British policy) in a preemptive strike against the Shawnee and their allies to lay claim to the rich lands of the Ohio Valley. The inevitable showdown was the October 10, 1774, Battle of Point Pleasant at the intersection of the Ohio and Kanawha Rivers. Colonel Andrew Lewis, born in County Donegal, Ulster Province, Northern Ireland in 1720, led more than one thousand of his Virginians, consisting mostly of Scotch-Irish, primarily from the Shenandoah Valley of Virginia, "upland" militiamen from Botetourt, Augusta, and Fincastle Counties, to a decisive victory in the balmy weather of early autumn. With ample experience from when he commanded a heavily Scotch-Irish company that represented Augusta County, Virginia, during the French and Indian War, the savvy Irish commander ordered a flank maneuver that won the day. Andrew's younger brother, Colonel Charles Lewis, also born in Ireland, fell mortally wounded in the vicious fight that raged through the dense woodlands.

Many Celtic-Gaelic veterans of the Point Pleasant victory were destined to play distinguished roles, including those top officers, in the American Revolution. Long before the American Revolution, the Celtic-Gaelic solders on the frontier—from New England to South Carolina—demonstrated the Scotch-Irish martial tradition of early meeting threats head-on by way of bold preemptive strikes before the threat grew stronger and more menacing. And they knew the importance of waging a logistical war, burning down Indian fields and storehouses to reduce the war-waging capabilities of their merciless opponents in the future.[51]

Isaac Shelby was one such respected frontier warrior. He was of Celtic heritage (Wales) on his father's side and Scotch-Irish (Cox) on his maternal side. Shelby had settled down west of the Appalachians on the Holston River near present-day Bristol, Tennessee. He was one of the principal leaders of the western frontiersmen who attacked a sizeable Loyalist force at Kings Mountain to win a remarkable victory on October 7, 1780. He had served in the volunteer company of his father, Evan Shelby Jr., in the victory at Point Pleasant, where Isaac gained invaluable experience for the all-important confrontation at Kings Mountain. Indeed, Shelby's leadership and tactical "contributions proved critical to the survival of Col. Andrew Lewis's army" at Point Pleasant.[52]

Clearly, the Battle of Point Pleasant prepared Isaac Shelby and other Celtic and Celtic-Gaelic (or Irish) warriors for their ultimate challenge at Kings Mountain on October 7, 1780. Ireland-born Lewis certainly appreciated Shelby's significant contributions to victory at Point Pleasant. Born in County Derry, Northern Ireland, in 1738 and migrating to Pennsylvania (and then to North Carolina) around 1763, John Brown, a part-time schoolteacher who married a pretty Scotch-Irish woman named Jane McDowell, was one of the Kings Mountain victors. Other Scotch-Irish men at Kings Mountain were brothers Lieutenant David Witherspoon and Private John Witherspoon: collateral relatives of Scotch-Irish signer of the Declaration of Independence, John Witherspoon. Sizeable Celtic-Gaelic familial clans of Scotch-Irish father-son and brother teams, such as young Captain Isaac White and brother Lieutenant Thomas White, fought side-by-side on October 7. A full dozen members of the Campbell clan of Virginia fought with distinction at Kings Mountain. Around sixty men who overwhelmed the stubborn Loyalist defenders of Kings Mountain possessed common Celtic-Gaelic last names that began with "Mc," such as McKee, McCulloch, McElwee, McHenry, McNabb, McConnell, McCafferty, McQueen, McSpedden, McMillen, McFarland, McKissick, McCutchen, etc.

A typical tough western frontiersman was an Irishman by the name of Captain Thomas Kennedy, who was known for his fighting spirit and deadly aim with the flintlock musket. On that October day of decision in northwest South Carolina, this resourceful Son of Erin commanded a company of rugged volunteers in a battalion commanded by Scotch-Irish Colonel Joseph McDowell, the son of an Irish immigrant. A masterful preemptive strike launched by hundreds of western frontiersmen armed with Pennsylvania Long Rifles and the Dickert rifles (first made by Jacob Dickert of Lancaster, Pennsylvania, and eventually known as the Kentucky Rifle) that unleashed their "terrible firepower" on the large Tory force won the one-sided victory at Kings Mountain.

The lengthy expedition to the east side of the Appalachians that led to the sparkling success at Kings Mountain was funded by John Adair, the entry man for Sullivan County. He had migrated from County Antrim, Northern Ireland, bringing his family to America in 1772. Adair settled in the Holston River country nestled between the Clinch and Watauga Rivers that flowed west. These rough-hewn frontiersmen, including Adair and his son who fought side-by-side, "all had recent immigrant roots," primarily from Ireland. Most importantly, the remarkable success at Kings Mountain was a major turning point of the American Revolution, leading the way to the final showdown at Yorktown.

These citizen-soldiers in buckskin, homespun cotton, and Indian moccasins, including Major William Candler who had been born in Belfast, Northern Ireland, were partly inspired to do the impossible against the Loyalists by the righteous words of Reverend Samuel Doak. Known as the "pioneer clergyman of the Watauga," Doak's parents were married on the crowded ship that sailed from Northern Ireland to America. Reading the words from the Holy Bible (Book of Judges) before the bowed frontiersmen, who wore tomahawks in leather belts and with Long Rifles by their side, Doak emphasized the urgent need for his devoted followers to wage a holy war with the "Sword of the Lord and of Gideon." In an ancient conflict in the Holy

Land, Gideon had led the ancient Israelites to victory over the hordes of Midianites, thanks to God's blessings. A fiery Scotch-Irish Presbyterianism bestowed an emotional, righteous appeal that even inspired the most seemingly godless of men, who looked like they had never stepped into a church or said a prayer in their lives.

Unleashed by their popular commander Colonel William Campbell, certainly the toughest Scotch-Irish leader among the equally hardened western frontiersmen, with the inspiring command of "my brave boys, shout like hell and fight like devils," mostly Scotch-Irish warriors sought to eliminate this potential threat to their frontier settlements west of the mountains. Closing on their opponent, these large-sized Celtic-Gaelic men "with long, matted hair" surged up the heavily wooded slopes of Kings Mountain. They dodged from tree to tree and fired from behind good cover in the traditional manner of Indian fighting while unleashing war cries that began to unnerve the surrounded Loyalists trapped on the crest.

After having been surrounded by a howling tide of frontiersmen, the Loyalists were cut to pieces by the accurate fire of the blazing Long Rifles, including one in the hands of Joseph Dickson of Scotch-Irish stock. And once Loyalist commander Major Patrick Ferguson was toppled off his horse by a hail of bullets and killed, all lingering resistance quickly crumbled. Hundreds of stunned Loyalists surrendered to escape certain destruction. Against all expectations, these experienced westerners vanquished the highly touted Major Ferguson and "a proud little Loyalist army" in record time. In the revealing words of British General Henry Clinton, "Kings Mountain was the first link in a chain of evil events that followed each other in regular succession until they at last ended in the total loss of America."[53]

As a member of a hard-fighting Celtic clan, Scotch-Irishman John McCulloch, a veteran Indian fighter, lost his father, Lieutenant Thomas McCulloch, who was killed in the sweeping attack up the mountain's timbered slope. The son described the triumphant moment when the surging frontiersmen "had driven the enemy, and had got on the top of the mountain [and] the enemy [then] surrendered" to the men who looked more like Indians than white men.[54]

Without pity, another Scotch-Irish soldier named John McQueen viewed the bloodstained body of Major Ferguson. He wrote of the deadly work of the Long Rifles, admiring that "there was 6 or 7 bullet holes through him. . . ."[55] Once the Tories surrendered, the Irish and Scotch-Irish frontiersmen unleashed victory cheers in a great "hurrah for freedom" that echoed over Kings Mountain. They also danced Irish jigs around Ferguson's body in celebration of one of the most remarkable victories in the annals of American military history.[56] As revealed in a rare letter written when he had less than twenty-four hours to live, Major Ferguson should have known better than to tempt fate when he had the audacity to mock his fellow Celts, especially those frontiersmen of the mountain's west side, as nothing but "barbarians:" an insulting threat that stirred up a hornet's nest of enraged Irish and Scotch-Irish frontier warriors, who were determined to eliminate any threat that neared their western settlements and families.[57]

For the Irish people, however, the Irish-hating English, like Sir Humphrey Gilbert, had long been the true barbarians, and their viciousness toward Celtic-Gaelic people continued unabated on American soil throughout the American Revolution.[58] For Gilbert and other English conquers of Ireland, the "native Irish [were] viewed as nothing more than beasts." And Ferguson had brought the same contempt of Emerald Islanders to the western frontier, where he paid a high price for his arrogance.[59] A British major described the Scotch-Irish of the South Carolina backcountry as "more savage than the Indians, and possess *every* one of their vices, but *not one* of their virtues."[60]

As throughout the American Revolution's course, such Irish heroes "were sneered at by the rich merchants of the lowlands [and] was held in contempt by the Continental army's high command, and he was considered less than human by the British [and] Major Patrick Ferguson called him a bandit, a barbarian, a mongrel."[61] The Irish and the Scotch-Irish were winning key victories even while they were still "demonized" by members of the upper crust elite, who "were comfortable members of the establishment living safely east of the mountains."[62] These words of one of America's enemies only mirrored the attitude of so many New Englanders of British descent as soon as the Irish immigrant stepped off the boat upon gaining Boston harbor, where they were long greeted with derisive calls and taunts of "St. Patrick's Vermin."[63]

By this time, the Irish were the world's most natural revolutionaries, forged by a toxic (for England and Indians) mix of tragedy, history, and fate, who rejoiced in the name of rebel, which was a distinguished legacy and badge of honor in Ireland. Knowing as much about the realities of the Irish experience, Charles James Fox, the revered British Whig statesman, said it best: "The great asserters of liberty, the saviors of their country, the benefactors of mankind in all ages, have all been called rebels."[64] Likewise, one of Ferguson's men vanquished at Kings Mountain grew to grudgingly admire the mostly Scotch-Irish victors without relinquishing the same contempt of Englishman Gilbert and other English conquers of Ireland: "This distinguished race of men are more savage than the Indians."[65] Of course, the "race" that he emphasized was the Irish. Upper-class colonials along the Eastern Seaboard viewed the Irish and Scotch-Irish on the frontier was nothing more than "white savages" because they lived on the wilderness edge of the known world.[66]

A lowly Scotch-Irish soldier, Alexander McMillian, who had been born in County Derry, Ulster Province, Northern Ireland, was one such forgotten Celtic-Gaelic "asserters of liberty." Inspired by the memory of his beloved General Montgomery, a fellow Irishman, and his tragic loss in the lower town of Quebec, where he had followed his Ireland-born commander and suffered frostbite on one of his hands, McMillian obtained a measure of revenge on October 7, 1780. Private Alexander McMillian, who had migrated to America that same year as the doomed assault on Quebec (1775) and married his first cousin (Mary McMillian) in 1778, played his part in the remarkable success at Kings Mountain. Here, the Irishman's barking Long Rifle, which was later heard again cutting down British regulars at the Battle of New Orleans when he served under Scotch-Irish Andy Jackson more than a quarter-century later at age sixty-three, claimed a number of unlucky Tory victims.[67]

Described as "a little dry Irishman," Samuel Clowney, who was born in Ireland, was a representative example of the typical Son of Erin soldier: "though he belonged to the Presbyterian Church, like all of his Celtic race of that day, without being intemperate, he could not refrain from getting *dry once* in a while, and dearly loved 'a wee bit of the crathure' occasionally. He possessed a remarkable talent for sarcasm and invective; but he was, nevertheless, a most kind-hearted, benevolent man, greatly beloved by all who knew him. His [Irish] brogue was quite rich, and this, combined with a fund of genial Irish wit, made him a fascinating companion."[68]

But most of all, Clowney was a resourceful fighter. He had migrated from Ireland and eventually built (after moving south from the Catawba River country of North Carolina) a log cabin at the South Carolina "settlement on the waters of Fair Forest, known as Ireland or the Irish Settlement, on account of the large number of settlers from the Emerald Isle."[69] Clowney was known for single-handedly capturing five Loyalist soldiers by acting as if he commanded a detail of patriots who were about to open fire if they did not immediately surrender. He escorted his captives back to camp, where the surprised colonel greeted him with the question, "Why Paddy [the popular name for an Irishman for the non-Irish], how did you take all these men?" He answered with a smile, "May it plase yer honor by me faith, I *surrounded* them."[70]

When America's struggle for liberty reached a new low in December 1776 after Washington's Army had withdrawn through New Jersey and all the way to eastern Pennsylvania after suffering a series of disasters around New York City, the Continental Congress departed Philadelphia on December 12 to escape General William Howe's fast-approaching British-Hessian Army and the almost certain fall of America's capital that would be a death stroke to the sagging resistance effort. Displaying a lack of confidence in General Washington now that their lives were in peril if captured, which seemed likely, the Congressmen fled southeast to Baltimore, Maryland, abandoning their own capital.[71]

But why Baltimore? Historians have long overlooked the major reason why the panicked Congressional members took flight to that city. For the most part, this answer can be found in a rare letter, "Extract of a Letter from Baltimore to a Gentleman in New-York." In this January 27, 1775, letter, months before the opening guns of Lexington and Concord erupted on a warm April morning, the writer described the rebellious state of Baltimore. More importantly, he also gave the exact reason why: "This Town is chiefly settled by Scotch-Irish . . . and it is melancholy truth, that such are, to a man, violently bent on supporting the good old cause, (that is the cause of fanaticism and sedition,) by taking Arms against" England.[72]

In the next war with England, Baltimore became famous for the staunch defense of Fort McHenry, where the national anthem was born. The masonry fort guarding Baltimore harbor was named in honor of one of Washington's finest staff officers, James McHenry. He was born in Ballymen, Country Antrim, Ulster Province, on November 16, 1753. McHenry received a classical education in Dublin.[73] Besides his medical skills, McHenry was noted for his Irish sense of humor, jovial nature, and cheerfulness that enlivened Washington's staff during dreary hours of overwork at headquarters. When fellow staff member Alexander Hamilton, an exceptionally witty young man of Scottish antecedents on his father's side and who had been inspired to full-blown revolutionary aspirations by Irishman Hercules Mulligan, imbued too much wine one night as a social event, McHenry provided a medical remedy that not only cured the young West Indian of his problem, but was calculated to "have a tendency also to correct your wit."[74]

Enduring Mystery

American historians have generally ignored not only the distinguished early pre-Revolutionary War legacy of the Irish in arms for America, but also their 1775–1783 contributions to the winning of independence in what has been a twin silencing of the historical record in regard to significant Celtic-Gaelic contributions on every level. How could the overall image of such sterling patriots who made such important contributions from 1775 to 1783 in winning America's independence have been almost entirely ignored in the historical record?

Long before the American Revolution's beginning, the fear of the Irish posing a serious threat to British descent-based American civilization was a common feature of American life. The situation existed because of not only continued mass immigration from Ireland but also because the Irish, both Catholics and Scotch-Irish, stubbornly retained their Celtic-Gaelic ways on American soil: a development that involved pride in heritage and culture, resulting in a preservation of ancient folkways and value systems rather than relinquishing these qualities for quicker acclimation into the mainstream of American life.

This obsessive fear, if not paranoia, was then heightened into hysteria during the 1840s by the exodus of Irish, mostly Catholics, into America from Ireland's Great Famine with the failure of the potato crop: a social development that profoundly influenced future generations of American historians, who wrote primarily for an upper-class audience. Like the upper-class contemporaries who "demonized" the Celtic-Gaelic people who fought in the American Revolution, they also viewed the Irish, especially lower-class immigrants, in negative terms that mirrored the historical xenophobia of the American public in general. Unfortunately for the Irish who fought and died from 1775 to 1783, these upper-class elites had a disproportionate influence on the writing of American history during the nineteenth and twentieth centuries.

The Celtic-Gaelic settler was widely seen as a degenerate and corrupting influence that threatened British-based American society and culture by colonial officials and non-Irish (almost anyone of British descent) before the American Revolution. Because this prejudiced view of the Irish became the pervasive stereotype, it is hardly surprising that the importance of the Irish role in the American Revolution was consistently long overlooked or minimized by the upper-class elites and the nationalists (themselves of mostly British descent).

One of the earliest concerns (rooted in part of America's historic obsessive fears of racial intermixing) was that the Irish readily adapted to Indian ways on the western frontier because they were poor and largely on their own (without protection from the military or the East Coast-based elites and government). However, this necessary adaptation to their harsh western environment by the Celtic-Gaelic people was viewed by the non-Irish elites, clergymen, and settlers of British descent farther removed from the frontier as a form of debauchery and debasement. Without such a thorough adoption of the wilderness environment and Indian ways by the Celtic-Gaelic people, there would have been no victories by the mostly Irish and Scotch-Irish frontiersmen during the Indian conflicts (both before and during the war) and then at Kings Mountain. It took precisely such thoroughly acclimated soldiers, the "over mountain" men from west of the Appalachians, to achieve the expertise necessary to win such a remarkable victory at Kings Mountain and other pivotal battles of the American Revolution.[75] "Paddy" (the common nickname for an Irishman) Carr was one such Son of Erin, who had acclimated to Indian ways, having been an Indian trader before the war. To the enemy, he was "quite as reckless and brutal as the worst specimens among the Red Men," and took the war to the Loyalists of Georgia with a frontier band of patriots.[76] By the time of the American Revolution, Henry Gillespie, living in a log cabin near the remote Turkey Cove community, was "a hardy Irishman" who "had perhaps been a dozen years in the country, and from whom the neighboring Gap [in the mountains] took its name. . . ."[77]

In fact, such assimilation was necessary for success long before the American Revolution and transformed Rogers's Rangers into such an effective fighting force during the French and Indian War.

Indians, especially warriors from the Stockbridge tribe, early imparted some of the tricks (along with the garb) of fighting Indian-style to a good many Scotch-Irish and Irish fighting men of Rogers's Rangers. Along with Mohawk warriors, the Stockbridge Mohegan served as part of Rogers's Rangers, enhancing war-waging capabilities.[78] These Stockbridge Mohegan were also brilliantly used by Daniel Morgan, of Scotch-Irish descent, in harassing the invading British-Hessian Army of "Gentleman Johnny" Burgoyne, wearing it down week after week, stripping away its initiative, and helping to pave the way for that army's October 17, 1777, surrender at Saratoga, New York.[79]

Although exaggerated, the popular concept of the "Celtic Indian" was not entirely a myth. Irishman Charles Murphy was a mixed-blood (his mother was Indian) interpreter for the Creek people during the American Revolution. He was nearly hanged by patriot militia in consequence.[80] One Irishman who deserted the British Army before the war lived for nearly two decades with the Cherokee in absolute contentment.[81] And during the French and Indian War, some of Rogers's Rangers thoroughly acclimated, including Irishman Quinton Kennedy, who married a Mohawk woman.[82] Pennsylvania-born John Connolly, the son of Irish immigrants, early knew the remote Ohio Valley and Illinois Country, along the Mississippi River, like few others. He also possessed extensive knowledge of Indian tribes and their languages. Major Ferguson was laid low by the Long Rifles at Kings Mountain in part because he had openly taunted these "Backwater men" as the "dregs of mankind" in part because they were "mongrels."[83] Ferguson's words echoed those of the colonial elite, who viewed the Celtic-Gaelic people of the frontier as nothing more than a lowly "pack of beggars."[84]

But the Irish and Scotch-Irish victors of Kings Mountain were certainly not savages. In truth, they were some of America's most die-hard patriots, including a good many immigrants from the Emerald Isle. Instead of turning into Indians as feared by easterners, they most of all retained their distinctive Irishness to a degree that made such a thorough transformation impossible. Ireland-born John Copeland, who had settled in South Carolina, was one of Kings Mountain's victors. He wrote with considerable understatement how in his key battle that finally began to turn the war's tide in the South, he "did his part upon the occasion as far as he was able."[85] Most importantly, the Scotch-Irish and Irish mountaineers who overran Kings Mountain and Ferguson's command achieved "the most decisive, the most glorious fought [and] was of the greatest importance of any one battle that [was] ever fought in America," in the words of a captain who fought there on a glorious October day for America.[86]

But doing their part in reaping an amazing victory at Kings Mountain came at a high price for a good many Celtic-Gaelic settlers. The Ireland-born father (John Crockett) of David Crockett, the former Tennessee Congressman known for his Irish sense of humor and who was killed in the defense of the Alamo on March 6, 1836, learned of the horrors of Indian warfare. While John was serving his country, John's parents David and Elizabeth Crockett were killed by Indians in their isolated log cabin near today's Rogersville, east Tennessee. In total, four Crockett boys fought at Kings Mountain, continuing the Scotch-Irish martial traditional of their Crockett ancestors who defended the walls of Derry, Northern Ireland with other Scotch-Irish in 1688–1689.[87]

Born in County Armagh, Ireland, in 1750, James Hawthorne also lost a great deal to make his American dream come true. In 1762, while living on the South Carolina frontier, he lost his wife and two daughters who were killed by Indians while a surviving son was carried away into captivity. But Hawthorne battled as a patriot during the American Revolution, rising to the rank of lieutenant colonel.[88]

In addition, other Irish victors of Kings Mountain suffered lesser tragedies when their homes were destroyed, such as an Ireland-born soldier named Gallaher. The Gallaher family's log cabin on the Holston River, located in a remote area on the Appalachian's west side, was burned to the ground in an Indian raid.[89] Thomas Brandon was more fortunate. He, his parents, and the rest of the family migrated from

Pennsylvania "with a colony of Irish Presbyterians," who were forced "to fort against" rampaging Cherokees around a decade before the American Revolution.[90] Carrying closely the injustices and tragedies from both sides of the Atlantic, the typical Irish soldier of America's struggle for independence was highly motivated to even old scores. Teenager Thomas Young, of Scotch-Irish descent, evolved into a resourceful partisan in the vicious warfare that raged through South Carolina's backwoods. In his own words, "my brother, John Young, was murdered [by Loyalists and] I shall never forget my feelings when told of his death . . . and swore that I would never rest till I had avenged his death. Subsequently a hundred Tories" were laid low by Thomas Young.[91]

But except for a precious few, like Young, who wrote memoirs, the stories of the common Irishmen who fought and sacrificed so much for their country have been forgotten, lost in the mists of time. The deliberate minimizing of Irish military achievements can be understandable from the purely nationalist point of view from which American history was early written, especially from the New England school at a time when even the Protestant Irish of the middle and upper classes in America wished to separate themselves from the lower-class immigrant Irish Catholics by embracing the designation of "Scotch-Irish," while the Irish Catholics were designated as simply Irish. However, the story of the Irish and Scotch-Irish people, regardless of changing definitions, that reflected complex class and economic issues and conflicts between Irish Catholics and Protestants on both sides of the Atlantic, has far transcended simply their disproportionate military contributions. For example, historians have most often overlooked the significant political contributions of the Irish, including the Irish and Scotch-Irish signers of the Declaration of Independence.

The hidden story of the evolution of open revolt in the most populous colony of the thirteen, thanks to an exodus of Irish and Scotch-Irish (the vast majority of the population) who flooded Virginia between 1740 and 1770, has provided a notable example of the crucial importance of the revolution from below. While the gentry of Virginia, the upper-class elite that included Thomas Jefferson, Washington, and other Founding Fathers, have been long praised for solely persuading and leading common Virginians to support the drive for independence, the reality of the situation was in truth very much the opposite.

No people more forcefully applied greater political, religious-based, and social pressure by way of mounting social unrest and open agitation for radical change in regard to electing pro-independence and voting non-independence men out of office than the Scotch-Irish and Irish. Virginia's common people, in debt and burdened by taxes, were behind this effort that hurled Virginia down the path of revolution. And most importantly, none of these angry "insurgent" (initially aligned against the American—not British—colonial aristocratic elite who looked upon the lower class and Irish as mere "peasants") people were more common than the Celtic-Gaelic people.

The disgruntled Scotch-Irish also pushed for a permanent break from the Anglican Church to ensure freedom of worship. And this long-coveted religious freedom for their dissenter religion of Presbyterianism would be only permanently guaranteed with independence and creation of a new people's republic that would disestablish the hated Anglican Church, which was the church of most of the ruling elite and government officials. At this time, Jefferson estimated that two-thirds of all white Virginians were dissenters of the established church of the mother country, and the Irish Presbyterians (and Irish Catholics to a lesser degree) saw the establishment of a new nation as a guarantee of freedom of worship.

The social unrest in Virginia reached a zenith shortly before the American Revolution, with the common people demanding greater religious freedom—especially for dissenters to be freed from payments of the inflated salaries of Anglican clergymen in economic hard times—and political inclusion. Ironically, during this period, Virginia had been transformed into the most inequitable of situations, analogous to Ireland. Wealthy landowners had turned their farmlands into rental properties and then raised rents and demanded that they be paid in scarce cash, including hard money—gold and silver—that was impossible to pay, which resulted in mass evictions that caused rental strikes and social unrest for already hard-pressed tenant farmers of the lower orders.

The rising tide of social unrest, anti-elitism, and the very real threat of an "agrarian insurgency" among the lower orders against the established elite proved decisive in turning the revolutionary tide. This unrest forced the refined gentleman leaders of Virginia to consider that an entirely new government was now needed to address the common people's increasingly radical demands. The conservative, wealthy, and privileged members of the gentry class were "monarchy-men"— versus the pro-independence men—who believed in the concept of "Royalty" and lived in the eastern Tidewater cities or nearby countryside in lavish comfort with everything to lose by an agrarian social revolt. Lower-class anger toward the privileged upper-class elite was about to erupt into the horrors of class warfare in a revolution that might well include violence. It was both the political demands (from pro-independence delegates for the May 1776 Virginia Convention that the lower orders had elected) and the growing social threat posed by the lower class that pushed the ruling elite of Virginia to embrace the patriot cause.[92]

For good reason in April 1776, a desperate member of the Virginia elite, John Page, revealed what was truly at stake when he implored Thomas Jefferson, "For God's sake declare the Colonies independent at once, and save us from ruin."[93] As the most populous colony, Virginia led the way down the road to independence, serving as the vanguard for the drive among the colonies to declare independence. Virginia's wealthy elite won their desperate gamble that preserved the existing social order and power base of the upper class because they created a conservative revolution that largely kept the upper class's traditional leadership roles.[94]

However, the role of the lower classes in paving the way to open revolt and independence has been lost in the romanticized annals of the mythical revolution. Only a few scattered hints of the significant contributions of the Irish and the Scotch-Irish throughout the revolutionary struggle surfaced in a pervasive climate of anti-Irish, anti-immigrant, and anti-Catholic sentiment that was exacerbated by the arrival of tens of thousands of Irish Catholics, who fled Ireland and the Great Famine's horrors. For instance, a journalist of the *New York Daily Times,* commenting on the exodus flooding into America during the early 1850s, offered a grim warning (that applied to the colonial period as well) to Great Britain by explaining how the Irish were

> driven from [their] home by English misrule [therefore] the Irish in this country will always cherish towards England feelings of intense hatred—feelings rooted in those sufferings which drove them from their homes, and threw them upon foreign shores[.] If the day of England's adversity should ever come—if, especially, events should ever plunge her into a war with the United States— her fiercest foes would be those of [Ireland and] Foremost in every blazing line arrayed against her, would stand the Irish troops. Fiercest in every fight would be those who had been crushed and starved, and finally driven across three thousand miles of sea. Ireland will one day be the Nemesis of Great Britain.[95]

The Irish and the Scotch-Irish have become the forgotten patriots of the American Revolution in part because their ethnic and cultural distinctions and Celtic-Gaelic identities faded away so thoroughly from the popular imagination and memory after the conflict. In addition, the overall process of Americanization, even among American historians with deep Irish roots, has guaranteed the overlooking of the Celtic-Gaelic contribution.[96]

While the revolutionary patriot of Anglo-Saxon descent has been mythologized, the Irish and Scotch-Irish soldier have become the forgotten fighting man, seldom recognized. Even "the son of an Irish-American World War I hero" Thomas J. Fleming failed to devote his considerable literary talents as a leading American historian and writer to telling the full story of the Irish and Scotch-Irish contributions to America's greatest victory. In his own words that revealed still another Americanization-first focus, "I never wanted to be an Irish-American writer, my whole idea was to get across that bridge and be an American writer."[97] In contrast to the negligence of modern historians, Thomas Paine, who rose to the fore in America's darkest hour during the fall of 1776, was the foremost of America's most patriotic writers and employed the death of Ireland-born Major General Richard Montgomery to rally and inspire greater resistance among Americans.[98]

The primary reason how and why Great Britain lost a vast overseas New World empire to "turn the world upside down" can be understood in a simple answer: this distinctive Celtic-Gaelic people, the largest ethnic group of colonists in America, played crucial roles because they (unlike colonists of British descent who yet possessed pride in their English roots and heritage) were already estranged from England and fiercely antagonistic toward the king long before the American Revolution's beginning. Most significantly, the Irish and Scotch-Irish, especially recent immigrants of course, were largely influenced and inspired less by the American experience than the Irish experience. After all, the Irish retained their distinctive cultural values on American soil as much as England remained the historic foe to the Irish people, contradicting the long-accepted myth that the American Revolution was simply a fratricidal cousin's war between two primary Anglo-Saxon families in terms of race.

Forgotten Genesis of the American Revolution
A host of ancient historical legacies had already laid the foundation for irreconcilable differences in the political thinking, psychology, and

attitudes between the people of Ireland and Great Britain. In 1172, the first English troops set foot on Irish soil and, after quickly seizing Dublin and Waterford, never left. Wealthy English barons followed this initial conquest and began to create huge estates from the most fertile lands of Ireland. But when King Henry VIII broke with Rome and Catholicism in 1534, the English became die-hard Protestants and determined foes of all things Catholic. Ireland's curse was England's close proximity, religious zeal, and imperialism.

England's strategic concerns that Catholic France and Spain might take possession of Ireland and use the island as a staging area to invade Protestant England led to the conquest of all Ireland over an extended period due to fierce resistance. To make sure that the Irish Catholics never again rose up against their masters, the Penal Laws (forbidding education, landownership, teaching, practicing law, political careers, free worship of Catholicism, and weapons for Irish Catholics) were enacted by the English to keep the common people of Ireland suppressed and impoverished for easier domination. Ireland became England's first colony of a future empire that spanned the globe.

While England, which continued hereditary rule by kingship, was largely shaped by four centuries of Roman rule and evolved into an imperialistic and expansionist nation, the Irish people, who had never lived under the single centralized political system of imperial Rome, had evolved into a distinctive civilization and far different culture with unique Celtic-Gaelic qualities, including egalitarian characteristics, centuries before the Age of Enlightenment. Celtic-Gaelic culture in Ireland was distinguished by a passionate appreciation of individualism, a vibrant democratic tradition based upon individual merit, revered Brehon Law, and especially a deep-seated distrust of centralized authority and hatred of a ruling aristocracy that was first anti-Anglo-Saxon and then anti-English and anti-Anglo-Irish.

By the time England attempted to impose tighter control over its thirteen colonies, which had enjoyed salutary neglect after the French and Indian War, it revealed itself to be the inheritor of not only Greco-Roman culture but also the old Roman imperialism. Unfortunately for the Irish people, England had also inherited a righteous "divine mission" of spreading "civilization" (always a good excuse for stealing the homelands of other people, especially a beautiful, fertile land like Ireland) that proved fatal to an agrarian Celtic-Gaelic people rooted in traditional ways. A sense of cultural and moral superiority had fueled worldwide conquest by Rome's sword and mercantile system, with a small aristocratic elite class—another political legacy inherited by England—ruling large numbers of conquered people with "divine" authority supposedly sanctioned by all-knowing gods.

Ireland's egalitarian and democratic traditions were a little-known political legacy bestowed upon America by the time of the Revolution. While an elitist, upper-class hierarchical rule was accepted for centuries in England, vastly dissimilar cultural and political foundations, based upon a distinctive Celtic-Gaelic egalitarian tradition, flourished on American soil. Then, after the American Revolution, the core of these same distinctive Irish and Scotch-Irish qualities served as a central foundation for American working-class values and military values, especially in the United States heartland, while even "shap[ing] the emotional fabric of the nation [and] defin[ing] America's unique form of populist democracy."[99]

But what has been most forgotten was that these influential Irish democratic traditions and egalitarian legacies, along with a deep-seated militancy and longtime revolutionary (including Jacobite) influences, were so vitally important from the very beginning of America's story. According to the traditional Americanized view of the nation's creation story, this homegrown democracy emerged on its own exclusively out of the New World experience and wilderness without significant Old World influences, especially from Ireland: basically the theory of American exceptionalism.

In truth, what was far more decisive in America's creation story was the fact that Celtic-Gaelic cultural, egalitarian, and martial traditions were seamlessly transferred from Ireland to America to lay a solid revolutionary and democratic foundation (based on experience versus abstract ideology) for the creation of a people's democracy in America. This development was especially the case far beyond the East Coast, where the most lofty egalitarian dreams (unlike in Ireland) were finally transformed into reality by Irish and Scotch-Irish settlers on the western frontier, including on the Appalachians' west side. Consequently, the dominance of this distinctive Celtic-Gaelic culture, heritage, and egalitarianism from the faraway Emerald Isle were as important, if not more, in providing a sturdy foundation for America's political development both *before* and *during* the American Revolution itself.

The Irish and Scotch-Irish were able to play such leading political, economic, and military roles throughout the American Revolution because they represented the largest ethnic group in America at the time. In his book *Liberty!*, Thomas J. Fleming, although underestimating the total number of Irish by a sizeable margin but yet correctly emphasizing the totality of Irish and Scotch-Irish patriotism, briefly mentioned that "They responded en masse to the call for resistance to England [and] With more than 300,000 [Irish] in the colonies, they had a major impact on the war."[100] Unfortunately for England, the crucial factor of timing could not have been better for America's fortunes because the height of Irish migration to America of these natural, ideal revolutionaries occurred in the period from 1770 to 1776.[101]

Most of all, because of the omnipresent egalitarian and revolutionary legacies of the Irish past, this great gathering of the Celtic-Gaelic clans in support of revolution and independence was a spontaneous and almost instinctive response for the Irish and Scotch-Irish. This was primarily due to the vast majority being

> sensitive to the waves of political and agrarian excitement [that was revolutionary in nature] which had swept separate parts of Ireland since around 1760 [but most] came from

Belfast [Northern Ireland's largest port], Dublin and Cork, regions predisposed to a rhetoric of confrontation, and carried frustrations which for many may have been intensified by the experience of [indentured] servitude in America[.] For the majority who underwent unpaid subjection in these years in America itself, the slogan of Liberty had a real connotation [and most of all the] Irish and American experience combined to make the immigrants respond at once to the idea that Britain was once again about to enchain them in their new home, and deprive them of the homely contents of an untithed farm, of usually rent-free acres.[102]

In this sense, the synthesis of Ireland's past and America's future was complete. And the most important example of this remarkable phenomenon and symbiotic relationship between Ireland and America came be seen in regard to the disproportionate military, political, and economic contributions of the Irish and Scotch-Irish people throughout the American Revolution.[103] The American Revolution cannot be adequately understood without first thoroughly appreciating the significance of Irish history in the early shaping of America in almost every way. First and foremost, a legacy of conquest was the decisive catalyst that forced so many Irish, both Catholics and Protestants, to migrate to America. To ensure a permanent presence on the Emerald Isle, England created a Protestant Northern Ireland (the Plantation of Ulster after the Irish Catholics were pushed off their land) by early populating fertile Ulster Province with English Army veterans and Scottish Protestant settlers (eventually the Scotch-Irish) from Scotland's southern lowlands. These interlopers became the proud owners of the confiscated properties of the native Irish Catholics, who thereafter became dispossessed menial laborers to work the land as lowly tenant farmers. Greed later fueled an ever-rising of rents of the tenant farmers by the already wealthy landlords (lairds), impoverishing the Catholics and forcing them off the land.

At first immune to such crass exploitation because of their Protestantism, the Scotch-Irish were also eventually utilized as cheap labor as exploited as the Irish Catholics. Both groups were forced to pay tithes to the Anglican Church, although they were not members, and became second-class citizens in an ancient land ruled with a heavy hand by the Anglican religious, social, and government elite based in London.[104]

Therefore, America's golden promise beckoned as never before because this was a place where "there are no Rents, no Tithes" to ensure poverty and shame.[105] For almost an entire generation of Irish and Scotch-Irish who fled to America immediately before the American Revolution, the Emerald Isle was viewed by the long-suffering Irish as "A Land of Slavery," while America stood like a shining beacon, "A Land of Liberty and freedom," in one Irishman's 1773 words.[106]

John Sullivan, before he became one of Washington's best generals, caught the representative thinking among the Celtic-Gaelic people in America. Almost as if talking about Ireland's tragic fate, this defiant son of Irish immigrants took up arms against England because it was a deplorable situation in which "Tyrants [were] Endeavouring to Enslave them [because of a well-calculated] plan for Enslaving America. . . ."[107] Consequently, Sullivan served as a New Hampshire delegate to the First Continental Congress of 1774, advocating independence at this early date.[108]

After so many Irish Catholics and Scotch-Irish had been forced off their native lands and were forced to migrate to America by the time that Sullivan wore a general's uniform, tens of thousands of fertile Irish acres across the Emerald Isle supplied provisions and foodstuffs from busy Irish ports like Kinsale, County Cork in south Ireland, not only for England but also for the British Army in America from 1775 to 1783.[109] The first British invasion fleet that planned a swift conquest of the South sailed out of the port of Cork, Ireland, in the spring of 1776 with great expectations. But the invasion force was thwarted by a gritty defensive effort, including from Irishmen like Privates John Ryan and

John Fleming, who were killed just outside of Charleston on June 28, 1776, at Fort Sullivan, which held firm against the odds.[110]

Of course, demographics remain the key to demonstrating the widespread impact of the Celtic-Gaelic people on the overall course of the American Revolution. Fleming's estimation of three hundred thousand Irish living in America by the time of the American Revolution was in fact a significant understatement. For ample good reason, King George III emphasized the major source of rebellion in America: "Those pestiferous Presbyterians are always in unrest and will be until they are wiped out."[111] Although not mentioning numbers, historian Stephen Brumwell, winner of the George Washington Book Prize in 2013, came closer to the truth by emphasizing how "the backcountry of Virginia, North Carolina, and Pennsylvania was also attracting the so-called Scotch-Irish from Ulster, tough folk well suited to their dangerous new surroundings [and their arrival was] slowly changing the ethnic balance of the hitherto overwhelming 'English' colonies."[112] And most importantly, "these mobile people seemed to thrive among the wilds of the frontier" like few other people in America, representing an entirely new "breed of people filling the valleys and invading the lands beyond the mountains."[113,114]

America's Largest Number of Patriots

More attuned to the Irish experience and its supreme importance, in part because he himself was the son of Northern Ireland immigrants, early American historian David Ramsay got it right in understanding the totality of this Celtic-Gaelic contribution: "The Irish in America, with a few exceptions, were attached to independence," and multitudes of "common soldiers in [Pennsylvania] were for the most part natives of Ireland [who were] inferior to none in discipline, courage or attachment to the cause."[115] These Irishmen served for years as the dependable "shock troops of Independence fired with hereditary anti-British feeling."[116] In a most revealing 1775 letter to the aristocratic Earl of Dartmouth, the Anglican Bishop of Londonderry, Ireland, wrote how the most important and central "rebellious source" across the middle colonies stemmed primarily from "nearly three hundred thousand fanatical & hungry republicans [from Northern Ireland who had migrated to Pennsylvania, Maryland, and Virginia only] in the course of a few years."[117] This astute conclusion (although excluding the large population of Irish Catholics, including on the frontier) was fully supported by the realities and demographics of the Irish diaspora.[118]

The bishop's analysis in describing only the Scotch-Irish contribution in the middle colonies and only for a three-year period of Irish migration (numbers that failed to include women and children) was most significant, revealing not only a far higher number of migrants than Fleming's estimation of three hundred thousand for the *entire* colonial period, but also the fact that these freedom-loving Celtic-Gaelic men and women were already America's most fervent anti-monarchical "republicans." The bishop also emphasized how the Emerald Islanders were motivated by the deep-seated concepts of self-determination, anti-aristocracy, and egalitarianism long before reaching America's shores: the central foundation for the most rebellious colonists in America.

Even more significant, this revered Northern Ireland bishop presented a total number of Irish immigrants from only one province (Ulster) without mentioning the flood of migrants from the other three-fourths of Ireland (Munster, Connacht, and Leinster Provinces), where most Catholics resided. In the estimation of Irish historian David Noel Doyle, who lamented the seemingly always too-low estimates by historians of Irish and Scotch-Irish numbers, especially during the revolutionary period, then the overall total might have been as high as four hundred fifty thousand or five hundred thousand Irish and Scotch-Irish: basically a one-quarter percentage of the estimated two million colonial population in America at the time of the American Revolution. During the colonial period, the "great majority" of Irish migrants who settled in what became the two primary revolutionary bastions of resistance (Virginia and Maryland) to Great Britain hailed from southern Ireland after having migrated from ports like Cork, in south Ireland, and Waterford, in southeast Ireland.[119]

Long before the American Revolution, the overwhelming majority of Irish and Scotch-Irish were already hardened, determined, and "fanatical . . . republicans," Irish rebels, and "Irish Tories," who had long been England's greatest enemies. Most importantly, therefore, what cannot be denied was the fact that the Scotch-Irish and Irish in every colony served as the vital "revolutionary vanguard" of the resistance effort throughout the American Revolution's course and to a degree unlike any other ethnic group in America.[120]

Indeed, after the initial mass uprising of New Englanders in the minuteman tradition at the war's beginning and by late 1776, Washington could count relatively little upon new troops from New England to bolster his thin ranks because so many New Englanders no longer served on land but on a vast fleet of privateer ships. And large numbers of New Englanders in Washington's Army eagerly awaited for their 1776 enlistments to expire in order to enlist in privateer service, where a percentage of the lucrative spoils (unlike on land) could be obtained by the average seaman. Indeed, perhaps as many as "10,000 New Englanders were manning privateers, men who by rights should be enlisting in the army destined to decide the fate of America:" a significant manpower gap eventually filled by the Irish and Scotch-Irish landlubbers who were consumed by no comparable passion for going to sea because Ireland lacked a vibrant seafaring tradition, especially compared to England.[121] Paying dividends for Washington's Army, "the Irish are not a seafaring people."[122]

In the end, all of the lofty Age of Enlightenment revolutionary rhetoric spewing from the privileged East Coast elites and upper-class leaders in smoky taverns, revolutionary committees in the major cities like Philadelphia and New York, and stylish plantation mansions were not sufficient to vanquish a formidable opponent and a professional army on the battlefield. These large numbers of determined Irish and

Scotch-Irish soldiers of the lower class were exactly the kind of highly motivated fighting men needed against the British, Tories, Hessians, and Indian allies. While the vast majority of American colonists—especially those of English descent—had initially believed that only the king's ministers (and not King George III) actually lay at the root of the difficulties between England and her thirteen colonies and, hence, either refused or were hesitant to completely sever ties with the mother country, almost all of the more cynical, world-wise Irish and Scotch-Irish knew and thought very differently.

Lord George Germain, the British Secretary of War for the American colonies, sought to subdue America with Ireland's brutal lessons of subjugation foremost in mind. After all, he had grown up in Ireland, where the spirited resistance of the Irish people had been crushed. Germain had even played his part in cutting down attacking Celtic rebels at Culloden to deal a death stroke to the Jacobite cause in 1745. Along with British General Thomas Gage, who held high command in America, Germain was a graduate of the bloody Culloden "school of counterinsurgency." He knew how to smash people's rebellions with businesslike, ruthless efficiency. Picking up a musket and fighting an ancient foe was a natural, knee-jerk act for America's Irish and Scotch-Irish, including Celts (the Welsh), who had fought these same British on the Scottish moor of Culloden in mid-April 1746.

Thomas Paine's *Common Sense*, published in January 1776, finally convinced many hesitant, neutral-thinking colonial Americans that the king was not divine after all and complete independence from Great Britain was America's only solution under the circumstances. Unlike non-Irish Americans who believed that England yet played an enlightened maternal role and that a permanent separation from the mother country was the worst of all evils, the harsh reality of an imperialistic London government that crassly exploited its colonial peoples for a growing empire's benefit had been an omnipresent part of life in Ireland for centuries. As the Celtic-Gaelic people of the thirteen colonies fully realized, Ireland's tragic fate only revealed what America would ultimately become—a thoroughly subjugated, exploited land—if Great Britain gained domination.[123]

Agitating Boston attorney Josiah Quincy had no reason to harangue the Irish and Scotch-Irish people in demanding "a very different spirit necessary for our salvation [because] we must be equally ignorant of the power of those who have combined against us [and] we must be blind to the malice, inveteracy and insatiable revenge which actuate our enemies. . . ."[124] Even before this time, ever-militant John Sullivan warned in December 1774 how England possessed arbitrary and sought abusive "powers [like those that already] have spread Tyranny and Oppression over three quarters of the Globe: & if we Tamely submit to their authority, will soon Accomplish that slavery which they have long been Endeavoring to bring upon America."[125]

Once the war erupted, British military leaders, including General Gage who helped to ruthlessly crush the Jacobite revolt in Scotland during 1746, attempted to suppress the American resistance effort in a far less harsh manner than in Ireland.[126] However, Irish people across America feared the worst. No English name was more bloodstained and unforgettable in Irish history than Oliver Cromwell. During his ruthless invasion of Ireland, he turned his righteous wrath on Irish Catholics, especially priests who were killed out-of-hand in a Protestant crusade to conquer the Green Isle in the most brutal way. After landing in Dublin with war banners flying at the head of an immense invasion force, Cromwell viewed his systematic massacres of Irish peoples, especially in the murderous sack of Drogheda (north of Dublin in east Ireland) and Wexford (south of Dublin in east Ireland), in 1641 as "a righteous judgment of God." In his own words, Cromwell's holy mission was "to extirpate the idolatrous" Irish Catholics without mercy. Thousands of Irish Catholics, including civilians and women, were killed on Cromwell's orders.[127]

Ireland-born Thomas Francis Meagher was one die-hard Irish revolutionary and nationalist leader of the nineteenth century. He was sentenced to be drawn and quartered (punishment reserved for Irish Catholic religious leaders who inspired their oppressed flocks to revolt) by British authorities for his revolutionary leadership role in the "Young Ireland" movement of 1848 to free Ireland from despotic British rule. After escaping imprisonment on the island of Tasmania and fleeing to America, he described the importance of the Irish experience upon the typical thinking, psychology, and motivations of the average Irish soldier, including during the American Revolution: "Whether in the camp or the field, or in the loud thunders of the battle, with death or victory staring him in the face, he sees not death, he sees not victory—he sees only his beloved Ireland [because] Ireland inspires him to deeds of valor, which beckons him to heroism in the cause of liberty. . . ."[128]

Another "Young Irelander," Thomas Davis, penned the poem entitled "Fontenoy," the famous battle in which the Irish exiles fighting for France played the leading role in winning victory over the hated English with a sweeping bayonet charge: "How fierce the look the exiles wear . . . The treasured wrongs of fifty years are in their hearts today" on May 11, 1745.[129] For the Irish exiles, these wrongs were simply too many to count. The exodus of Irish Catholics began with the crushing Jacobite defeat at the battle of the Boyne, which was fought two miles west of Drogheda, a port on the Irish Sea north of Dublin. This "most famous of all Irish battles" on July 1, 1690, along the River Boyne determined who permanently ruled Ireland: Protestants or Catholics. This defeat led to the famed "Wild Geese" of Irish Catholic exiles, who fought in Catholic armies, especially Spain and France, around the world while initiating the mass exodus to America when the Jacobite cause crumbled not long thereafter.[130] The Irish ancestor, Thomas Carroll, of the only Irish Catholic signer of the Declaration of Independence (Charles Carroll), died fighting at the battle of the Boyne.[131]

The Ireland-born parents of General John Sullivan, who was an early advocate for independence as an outspoken New Hampshire delegate in the Continental Congress, have provided a good example of the significant impact of the Irish revolutionary past and longing for liberty. Descending from legendary "Irish chieftains," his grandfather on his paternal side was one such determined revolutionary who fought until the surrender of Limerick and the subsequent treaty that led to his exile to France and "Wild Geese" role. The general's mother, Margery Browne, was quite formidable in her own right and well known for her "force of character." She likewise brought a legacy of spirited defiance to authority that her promising son inherited in full.[132]

Another revealing example of this deep-seated cultural phenomenon of the transplanted Irish in America occurred during a campaign of Washington's troops in the New York wilderness in 1779. This grueling campaign, led by two Irishmen, Generals John Sullivan and James Clinton, devastated the Iroquois Confederacy, England's most powerful Indian ally since the French and Indian War. Far from supply bases and the home front, thousands of veteran American troops, who had been dispatched by Washington himself, achieved a sparkling success of eliminating an opponent in the rear. General Edward Hand was one of the leading commanders of the arduous expedition into the uncharted depths of western New York wilderness. He hailed from the central midlands of the Emerald Isle and still thought a good deal about the vibrant beauty and people of his native homeland.

Appropriately, Hand presided over the victory celebration of his veteran brigade, which consisted of a large percentage of Irish and Scotch-Irish soldiers. On November 25, Lieutenant Erkuries Beatty, a proud member of the Fourth Pennsylvania Continental Regiment and the son of a Presbyterian reverend who had migrated from Northern Ireland to America in 1729, was one young officer who celebrated with other members of Hand's brigade. A festive dinner was held on the ground under a sprawling pine bower illuminated by the bright glow of blazing torches. The feast was dominated by the consumption of thick steaks of oxen, freshly killed for this special occasion, and bouts of heavy drinking. The Irish immigrant's son penned in his journal how General Hand, in his Irish brogue, made a rousing toast that appealed to so many of his Celtic-Gaelic men, which bestowed recognition on the extensive contributions of the Irish in liberty's struggle: "May the Kingdom of Ireland merit a Stripe in our Standard."[133]

Disciplined Irish soldiers of Washington's Army marching west were most symbolic. Besides combating Indians for survival, Irishmen on the frontier also became radicalized early by imperial policies, adding to the long list of Old World abuses. When the British government established the Proclamation Line of 1763, which was to have been enforced by large numbers of British troops to restrict the westward push of small farmers of little means (mostly Irish and Scotch-Irish) into the lush wilderness lands of the Ohio Valley, the Celtic-Gaelic people had simply pushed over the line and settled where they pleased. Clearly, this arbitrary proclamation "certainly did not please the Irish and Scots of the backcountry, who had their own contentious definition of liberty—born of the strife-ridden worlds [especially Ireland] from which they had emigrated."[134]

Although an understatement, one modern historian penned quite correctly how the "ordinary people [especially the Irish and Scotch-Irish] seemed more inclined to prepare for war while their leaders talked peace."[135] Ireland-born Edmund Burke knew more intimately of the temper of his hardy Celtic-Gaelic countrymen in America than modern armchair historians, warning the House of Commons as early as May 1774, "If you govern America at all [then] it must be by an army [because] they never will consent without force being used . . . a great many red coats will never be able to govern it."[136] Because the Irish were still looked at as savages without intelligence or reasoning ability, British officials ignored Burke's wise words. In regard to first Ireland's subjugation and then pertaining to America by 1775, "For Britain, the Irish [were] the Indians to the far west, circling the wagons for imperial civilization," in the words of historian Fintan O'Toole.[137]

Continuing this theme that applied to an entire generation of Celtic-Gaelic people in America, historian Michael Rose correctly ascertained how "The War of Independence had never been about 'taxation without representation' [because] It had been about the freedom of Americans to develop their own society in the way that they wished." This situation most of all applied to the anti-government and self-autonomy-oriented Celtic-Gaelic people, who already possessed a distinctive Irish identity, culture, and egalitarianism that they nurtured and preserved almost as things that were considered sacred.[138]

As early as December 1774, John Sullivan was already emphasizing to the people of America of the absolute necessity of "Defend[ing] the Liberties which God and Nature have given to us."[139] Perhaps historian Jay P. Dolan said it best when he summarized the overall Irish experience in America and an undeniable cultural reality (fortunately for America) that guaranteed an entire generation of die-hard patriots fought to the bitter end: "One of the most remarkable achievements of the Irish in America is that they have stayed Irish."[140]

This sprawling frontier society—stretching around 1,500 miles from New England to Georgia and where Irish culture, festivals, and customs were celebrated—was more ethnic than at any other time in American history because of the overwhelming numbers of Irish and Scotch-Irish. In contrast, colonial society, especially along the East Coast, consisted primarily of people of British descent, who were hardly distinguishable from millions of citizens of England and the British Empire. But what was not only entirely different but also diametrically opposed to the mother country was the entirely dissimilar society and culture, including religion (fervent Presbyterianism and Catholicism) and a more lengthy tradition of rebelliousness of the most already radicalized immigrants on American soil. All in all, this was the most potent and combustible mix in America by 1775.

Chapter II

Enduring Irish Legacies, Myths, and Popular Modern Memory

Unfortunately, before the publication of this present work, the thesis of the decisive impact of the Irish and the Scotch-Irish in early fueling, sustaining, and ultimately winning independence had not been seriously entertained by either American or Irish historians because that fact has seemed so improbable at first glance and contrary to the romantic, traditional concepts of the mythical revolution. However, one leading modern Southern historian, Grady McWhiney, PhD, vaguely hinted at the distinct possibility of such a viable Celtic-Gaelic thesis in explaining the American Revolution's ultimate outcome in his 1988 work, *Cracker Culture: Celtic Ways in the Old South*. In this book that explored the deep Celtic roots of the South's settlement that had been long ignored and even denied in some cases by American historians, especially New England scholars, McWhiney explained the overall importance of the Celtic role in determining the course of American history: "This cultural conflict between English and Celts [that had been ongoing for centuries in Ireland] not only continued in British North America, it shaped the history of the United States."[1]

Although McWhiney broke new ground in regard to his thesis about how the South, because of the dominance of demographic and cultural influences, was essentially another distinctive Celtic region (like Ireland, Wales, and Scotland), he only focused primarily upon Irish and Scotch-Irish settlement on a one-dimensional regional basis of the South, not in regard to the overall Celtic-Gaelic role in the American

Revolution. However, for whatever reason, McWhiney decided not to make the logical next step by exploring the pivotal Irish and Scotch-Irish roles in America's independence struggle that would have more forcefully verified his thesis to deflect the inevitable criticism.

This glaring negligence has been especially ironic. After all, the most effective way to have fully demonstrated the supreme importance of Celtic and Gaelic contributions in America was not by just analyzing the South as a separate Celtic region or by presenting demographic statistics. In this respect, McWhiney's central focus, like so many other American historians, has been much too narrow and one-dimensional, neglecting to appreciate the overall importance of the Irish and Scotch-Irish contribution in virtually every aspect of the revolutionary struggle.

American historians' love affair with the Civil War period has long obscured the supreme importance of the Irish and the Scotch-Irish role during the American Revolution, which has been much more difficult to research because of the scarcity of eighteenth-century records and primary documentation, especially in regard to the Irish because such a large percentage were illiterate. In contrast to the negligence demonstrated by historians in regard to Irish and Scotch-Irish revolutionary contributions, the story of the Irish, especially that of the famed Irish Brigade, Army of the Potomac, has been widely emphasized for generations in part to demonstrate that the Irishman was a super-patriot. However, that much-embellished story was largely a romantic myth not only because such a small percentage of the Irish population wore the blue, but also was far less important in terms of overall decisiveness compared to the vital Irish and Scotch-Irish Revolutionary War contributions.

This intense fascination of American historians with the Civil War and a corresponding over-exaggeration of the Irish contributions to Union victory have been the very antithesis of the Irish and Scotch-Irish during the American Revolution. Even the number of Irish (in percentage terms to the overall population) who served in

Union armies during the Civil War was extensively dwarfed by the overall percentage and numbers of Irish who served in the American Revolution. As James M. McPherson emphasized, "Despite the fighting reputation of the Irish Brigade [which was led by General Thomas Francis Meagher, a Jesuit-educated Catholic and the popular leader who organized the Irish Brigade in 1861 but was hesitant about going to war against his fellow Catholics of the Confederacy, for the war's first half], the Irish were the most underrepresented group in proportion to population" in the North.[2]

Irish-American filmmaker John Ford, the son of an Irish immigrant, who was christened Sean Aloysius O'Fienne in a Catholic church, emphasized the post-Civil War military role of the Irish fighting man in his famous film trilogy—*Fort Apache, Rio Grande,* and *She Wore A Yellow Ribbon*—about the United States cavalry on the western frontier. This was no myth because even George Armstrong Custer's Seventh Cavalry Regiment was heavily Irish by the time of Custer's last stand on June 25, 1876. Combining the western frontier with the Irish experience like no other film artist, Ford's popular post-Second World War films brought long-deserved recognition to the post-Civil War cavalry in the west and Irish contributions in the nasty campaigns of pacification in the name of Manifest Destiny.

When the director died in the summer of 1973, Ford had finally expanded his horizons beyond the post-Civil War Old West and his much-filmed Monument Valley on the Arizona-Nevada border. To his great credit, he had planned to make two feature films devoted to the American Revolution, *Valley Forge* and *April Morning*. If these Ford films had been made and resembled his films that featured Irish cavalrymen in blue, then they would have almost certainly emphasized Irish contributions to bring a belated measure of long-overdue recognition to the forgotten Irish revolutionary role to the America public for the first time.[3]

Today, one can only imagine how the famed Irish-American director would have masterfully told such a dramatic Celtic-Gaelic moment as when two Ireland-born Maguire brothers from opposing sides met in dramatic fashion (after a long separation) at the surrender of an entire British-Hessian Army under "Gentleman Johnny" Burgoyne, who thereafter became commander in chief of British forces in Ireland, at Saratoga, New York, on October 17, 1777. Dublin-born Sergeant Roger Lamb was the poor son of Protestant parents, the youngest of eleven children who grew up playing along the banks of the Liffey River that meandered through the tree-lined streets of Dublin. During the American Revolution, he served as a steadfast soldier of the Ninth Regiment of Foot, which was a hard-fighting Irish regiment that he had joined as a teenager. Immediately after one of the war's most decisive battles at Saratoga, Sergeant Lamb wrote:

> the time of the cessation of arms, while the articles of capitulation were preparing, the soldiers of the two armies often saluted, and discoursed with each other from the opposite banks of the river . . . a soldier in the 9th regiment [of Foote], named Maguire, came down to the bank of the [Fishkill River, which entered the Hudson River a short distance to the east, that separated American forces on the south side and the British army on the north side], with a number of his companions, who engaged in conversation with a party of Americans on the opposite shore [on the Fishkill River's south side]. In a short time something was observed very forcibly to strike the mind of Maguire. He suddenly darted like lightning from his companions, and resolutely plunged into the stream. At the very same moment, one of the American soldiers, seized with a similar impulse, resolutely dashed into the water, from the opposite [or south] shore. The wondering soldiers on both sides, beheld them eagerly swim towards the middle of the river, where they met; they hung on each others['] necks and wept; and the loud cries of "my brother! My dear brother" which accompanied the transaction,

soon cleared up the mystery, to the astonished spectators. They were both brothers, the first had emigrated from this country, and the other had entered the army; one was in the British and the other in the American service, totally ignorant until that hour that they were engaged in hostile combat against each other's life.[4]

Sergeant Lamb's vivid description revealed the most forgotten realities of the American Revolution: a brothers' war between the Irish people, including relatives, on American soil. For good reason, therefore, an indignant Ireland-born Henry Grattan, educated at prestigious Trinity College and a distinguished member of the Irish House of Commons, angrily denounced London's plans to dispatch British regiments, consisting of a good many Irish soldiers, from Ireland to America because so many Celtic-Gaelic troops were being expressly "sent to butcher our brethren in America."[5]

Young Sergeant William Jasper became one of South Carolina's legendary folk heroes when the British launched their first attempt to garner Loyalist support and conquer the South in the summer of 1776. British strategists first targeted the richest city in all America, the port of Charleston, for capture. Born in Northern Ireland, Jasper played an inspirational role in bolstering the defender's resolve during the Fort Sullivan defense on Sullivan's Island (the key to the city formerly known as "Charles Town") outside Charleston to protect the vulnerable port. Charleston, the most important city south of Philadelphia, was distinguished by Caribbean-inspired architecture and a large multi-ethnic population. Fort Sullivan's mission was to deny the entry of a mighty invasive British fleet into expansive Charleston harbor.

When the fort's colorful silk banner was cut down by a screeching British cannonball during the heavy naval bombardment on June 28, 1776, the Irish sergeant dashed atop the parapet and risked his life to retrieve it amid the falling shells. Ignoring the danger, the daring Son of Erin then "leisurely fixed" the flag to an artillery sponge staff and raised the colorful banner for all to see. Along with the spirited actions of another Scotch-Irish sergeant of the Second South Carolina Infantry Regiment (Jasper's unit) named James McDaniel (often mistakenly thought to be McDonald) who fell mortally wounded, Jasper's courage inspired the garrison during the battle of Sullivan's Island (appropriately named after an Irishman), which helped to ensure that the earthen and palmetto log fort successfully held off the British invasion armada.

When the Irish soldier was offered a lieutenant's rank for his heroics the day after the fort's successful defense, the humble Jasper politely declined. He used his lack of education as an excuse, emphasizing with pride "I am but a sergeant" and that he wanted to remain one. However, in leading the Second South Carolina Continental Regiment as a revered member of the prestigious Grenadier Guard (a company of elite soldiers) in the bloody assault on the powerful British defenses of Savannah, Georgia, Sergeant Jasper's luck finally ran out. Among the attackers on Savannah was the largest unit of French regulars in the assault, the legendary Dillon Regiment. This famed command was led by Ireland-born Count Arthur Dillon, whose name was derived from a Viking word. The Dillon Regiment was part of the "Irish Brigade," which had been formed in 1691 from Irish Jacobite exiles from French service after the Treaty of Limerick. It consisted of mostly Irishmen, including the descendants of the original exiles. Consequently, the soldiers of the Dillon Regiment continued the revered martial tradition of the Irish "Wild Geese," who served with distinction in the Spanish and French Armies. During the doomed allied attack on the strong British fortifications protecting Savannah, the self-sacrificing Sergeant Jasper was mortally wounded on bloody October 9, 1770.[6]

But in the dramatic raising of the blue banner with the white crescent (that emulated the silver crescents worn with pride on the common soldiers' hats) that was the "Colonies' first independent flag" designed in 1775, Sergeant Jasper has been best remembered for inspiring the outgunned defenders of Fort Sullivan (later renamed Fort Moultrie for the commander William Moultrie) of South Carolinians. This defiant garrison consisted of "a significant number of Ireland-born troops" who helped to save the strategic port of Charleston.[7] Sergeant Jasper was a well-known Irish hero who inspired the 1860s generation of Confederate Irish from Savannah from New Orleans, Louisiana. These Irish Rebels later named their respective volunteer companies (Savannah's Jasper Greens was the most famous unit) in his honor. However, this widespread recognition for Irish heroics in the American Revolution was quickly forgotten after the Civil War.[8] In an 1876 memorial written to honor Jasper, the sergeant's Irish roots were entirely expunged from the historical record. He was merely described as "of humble origin and slender means, without the advantages of education [and] Of his antecedents . . . we are not definitely informed."[9]

Or perhaps master filmmaker Ford also might have told the unforgettable story of the trials of one rather remarkable Scotch-Irish family of lower-class origins who migrated as part of a mass exodus from Northern Ireland. Ten boys of the George Alexander family fought and sacrificed on behalf of North Carolina and their new nation during America's struggle for survival.[10] Likewise the dramatic gathering (without authority, advice, or even the assistance of any Continental Army leaders or government officials) of the Celtic-Gaelic clans of western frontiersmen, who "all had recent immigrant roots," to launch the daring preemptive strike and reap one of the revolution's most amazing victories at Kings Mountain would have provided a great story in the hands of any modern filmmaker.[11] Additionally, Ford could have brought the spirited Irish tunes sung by the Celtic-Gaelic frontiersmen of Kings Mountain to the big screen for an American audience, such as: "Rise you up, my dearest dear/ And present to me your hand/And we'll take a social walk/To a far and distant land/Where the Hawk shot the Buzzard/And the Buzzard shot the Crow/We'll rally in the cane brake/And shoot the Buffalo."[12]

Who were these unknown Irish and Scotch-Irish members of the enlisted ranks who rose so splendidly to the challenge in reaping the amazing success at Kings Mountain, the pivotal turning point of not only the war in the South but also of the American Revolution? While the Celtic-Gaelic commanders, like Joseph McDowell and William Campbell, of patriot forces at Kings Mountain are well known, the average enlisted man from Ireland has been forgotten. However, the story of the common Irishman at Kings Mountain has revealed those finest qualities of the Irish soldier of the Revolutionary War.

Among Kings Mountain's victors, Private John Allison left Ireland and first settled in Pennsylvania before continuing west to settle in Sullivan County, east Tennessee. His two sons, Finly and John, followed their father, putting down roots in the remote western frontier region. John Allison was wounded in the attack at Kings Mountain, leaving ugly scars and a bad limp for the rest of his life.[13] Not as fortunate as John Allison, Private Michael Mahoney was killed at Kings Mountain. He was born "in the south of Ireland" in Munster Province. To start anew, his parents brought him to America when he was young. Mahoney trekked across the mountains to settle along the clear waters of the Nolichucky (a Cherokee word and one of the Tennessee River's headwaters) River that flowed west, not east like the nearby rivers on the mountain's opposite side.[14]

Another hard-fighting enlisted man, Private Patrick Murphy was born in County Kerry on the southwestern coast of Munster Province and north and west of County Cork. Like so many of his fellow countrymen, he served with distinction in the remarkable success at Kings Mountain. Like Private Mahoney, Murphy fell to a Tory bullet that cut his windpipe and splattered blood over his chest. When his comrades attended to him, the feisty Irishman retained his Celtic-Gaelic spirit and sense of humor. While his wound was washed with rum, very likely by North Carolina surgeon William McLain, whose father, Alexander who also served at Kings Mountain, Murphy took the opportunity to drink "a portion" of the liquor, quipping in his thick Irish brogue how the rum "was as good in as it was out."[15]

Like their Celtic-Gaelic neighbors, the Patterson clan from Northern Ireland also saw distinguished service at Kings Mountain. Arthur Patterson had been born in Ulster Province. With the call to arms to meet Ferguson's Tory threat, Patterson and his three sons, Arthur Jr., William, and Thomas, all blasted away with their Long Rifles at Kings Mountain.[16] The Ireland-born Beattie clan also fought side-by-side in the assault up the bullet-swept slope of Kings Mountain. Lieutenant John Beattie, born on the Emerald Isle, was killed by Ferguson's well-trained Loyalists. However, John's three brothers, Francis, William, and David, who held a captain's rank, survived the tenacious contest for possession of an obscure South Carolina mountaintop in the Piedmont.[17]

Quite a few Irish father-son teams fought with distinction at Kings Mountain, including Ireland-born Alexander Carswell and his son John.[18] Age fourteen but big enough to handle a Long Rifle with consummate skill in rapidly loading and firing, Irishman Private Thomas Gillespie Jr. was one of the youngest attackers who fought his way up the heavily wooded slope of Kings Mountain.[19] Yet another fourteen-year-old Irish soldier, Silas McBee from Thicketty Ford, South Carolina, played his part in the overwhelming of the Loyalist task force on the barren mountaintop on October 7, 1780.[20]

In an example of how the American Revolution was also a civil war among the Irish in America, these teenagers had no idea that they were facing one of Ferguson's top lieutenants in Ireland-born Captain Alexander Chesney. He migrated to South Carolina in 1772 and put on an officer's Loyalist uniform in 1780. Chesney somehow survived the hail of bullets from the blazing Long Rifles and surrendered to the long-haired frontiersmen in homespun and buckskin after Major Ferguson was shot off his horse. He returned to Ireland after the war, a rare occurrence.[21]

The Disappearance of Irish Contributions

Perhaps the crucial battle of Kings Mountain has provided the best example of this pervasive phenomenon of the obscuring of notable Irish contributions to the war because the western frontiersmen victors were members of what was essentially a "ghost army." This frontier army quickly vanished into the virgin wilderness mostly on the Appalachian's west side (the Holston and Watauga River country of today's east Tennessee) from where it had come just as suddenly and unexpectedly after the one-sided victory was secured at Kings Mountain.

In a tribute to the mostly Scotch-Irish army of western frontier volunteers, one rather mystified modern historian summarized how, "In a strange fashion, the over-the-mountain army, so swiftly assembled [then] abruptly vanished from American legend. But it was not a myth. It was a fighting force of hardy, physical men that, though lacking in training and discipline [won a remarkable victory at Kings Mountain and] then disappeared into the backwoods from which it had come."[22] However, the Irish and the Scotch-Irish soldiery were the ones who fought, sacrificed, and died for America's liberty in more disproportionate numbers and for a longer period than any other members of American society.

The biased New England perspective, based upon an Anglo-Saxon-centric explanation that especially magnified the overall decisiveness of the contributions of New England where relatively few Irish and Scotch-Irish were located (especially in the cities) compared to the Middle Colonies (especially Pennsylvania) and along the western frontier's extensive length, has prevailed to become conventional wisdom. In this way, the New England school created the myth of the embattled Anglo-Saxon farmer-soldier of middle-class status, especially the heroic minuteman, as primarily sustaining the Revolution rather than the lowest orders of society, especially the Celtic-Gaelic people, in every colony. However, as mentioned, thousands of New Englanders decided not to serve in Washington's Army during the most crucial moment of the revolutionary struggle in late 1776 and early 1777, preferring privateer service on the high seas.

Generations of mostly upper-class historians across the United States have faithfully embraced the Anglo-Saxon interpretation. One famed American historian, Hubert Howe Bancroft, articulated anti-Irish and anti-Catholic opinions that included the assassination of General Thomas Francis Meagher's character after his death, when in fact the Irishman's honesty—not to mention heroism in leading the Irish Brigade during some of the Civil War's greatest battles in the Eastern theater—was well beyond reproach. Unfortunately, this prevailing New England and northeastern bias has played a large role in dooming the legacies of the Irish and Scotch-Irish people to dark obscurity. In the words of historian Thomas H. O'Connor, "Successions of Harvard-trained, New England-bred historians had assured their readers quite categorically that no Irish were to be found in North America before 1830."[23]

In his 1898 book, *The Story of the Revolution*, Harvard-educated Henry Cabot Lodge, born in Massachusetts and a revered member of the northeast's cultured elite, emphasized that those colonists who ultimately won America's independence after eight years of fighting were "almost of pure English blood. . . ."[24] The vibrant Celtic-Gaelic tradition of oral history by way of ancient folktales and family history, especially in regard to the Revolutionary War period, has vanished. Dr. John Rice Lewis reflected on this peculiar phenomenon of a lost Irish history in East Tennessee, which was settled largely by Scotch-Irish pioneers who crossed the Appalachians before the American Revolution: "I wondered why the old folks . . . never talked about their European origins [and] never got beyond Virginia, North Carolina or possibly Pennsylvania [because] the continuing flow of lore and stories of ancestry was almost totally broken down."[25]

In a sad lament, Dr. Ian Adamson, of Belfast, Ireland, correctly concluded how "English ascendancy and Irish chauvinism have combined to suppress knowledge of Ulster and Ulster-American history, to deny the very concept of the Ulster nation [and the Ulster diaspora] at home or overseas and to deprive Ulstermen [today] of legitimate pride in their heritage and national identity."[26] The majority of modern writers of Irish history, both in America and Ireland, have been mostly journalists and popular writers instead of professionally trained historians and scholars. This development has also ensured a lamentable lack of the necessary high-level scholarship, leading to an even greater obscuring of Irish contributions in the American Revolution.[27]

This unfortunate development was also ensured by the fact that the Irish and the Scotch-Irish people eventually lost their ethnic distinctiveness and traditional Celtic-Gaelic ways when they gradually merged into the mainstream of white Anglo-Saxon Protestant (WASP) culture. This acclimation process (or ethnic and cultural disappearing act) actually began relatively early for many single Scotch-Irish and Catholic male immigrants. After all, they far outnumbered Irish women, especially among the former indentured servant class, on the western frontier and married Protestant American women. In consequence, the largest percentage of the Celtic-Gaelic people simply vanished "under the rubric of 'British' ancestry" in the decades after the American Revolution's conclusion.[28]

This acclimation process was so thorough that one Irish soldier, from County Fermanagh near the town of Enniskillen, Ireland, who fought in the American Revolution, became known to his American-born children of an American mother (his common-law wife) as "Old Britannia."[29] When a later-day historian naturally assumed that Captain Levi Preston, an aging veteran of Lexington and Concord, had been inspired to fight against the British after reading the most popular Enlightenment writers and philosophers such as John Locke and Tom Paine, he was stunned to receive the answer that the old soldier had "never heard of these men" now famous. The mythical revolution has long fostered the grossly distorted stereotype that the alleged unwashed, unthinking masses had to be inspired by intellectually superior others (or led by the nose because they were unable to reason for themselves as so confidently assumed by the elites).[30]

In part because of its prolific writers and influential publishing houses, Boston has been portrayed as the rebellion's heart and soul from beginning to end. However, an Ireland-born prisoner, William Crawford, of the Twentieth Regiment of Foot, was shocked by the personal realization that a myth existed about the citizens of Massachusetts as the most zealous revolutionaries in America. When near Boston in 1777, he "found the inhabitants, or at [least] many of the principle people among them, not so friendly to the rebel cause, but favorable to the success of his majesty's arms. . . ."[31] Indeed, thousands of New England's patriots, who were now badly needed in Washington's Army during crucial campaigns, were out to sea, sailing the waves aboard wide-ranging privateers.[32]

Faithful service from the Irish was guaranteed because of powerful egalitarian longings that were deeply rooted in the overall Irish experience and that thrived among the lowest orders of society, especially the recent immigrants. Time-honored religious motivations were also extremely strong among the Scotch-Irish, whose egalitarian-minded and anti-king Presbyterian ministers preached equality, moral duty, and revolution as one and the same. From the harsh world of Northern Ireland, these revered religious leaders advocated that God's word was the highest authority (not King George III) while preaching the core radical, republican, and revolutionary tenets of the true meaning of democracy. Presbyterian ministers also emphasized the moral right for an oppressed people to rise up in revolution as a sacred duty against abusive government and a despotic king, who had usurped God's "divine" right. And this was at a time when most American colonists, especially those from England and members of the Anglican Church, still firmly believed that obedience to a benevolent king was a great sacred moral obligation. Therefore, the Scotch-Irish were the most fervently religious (hence militant) colonists in America.

All in all, such religion-based egalitarian factors served as the central foundations of the political and moral revolution from below by way of the Celtic-Gaelic people.[33] Reverend Charles Inglis explained in no uncertain terms how "the Principles of Republicanism had kept pace" with the spread of Presbyterianism across America until religious faith and political aspirations were fused.[34] The full depth of Presbyterianism's powerful influence was perhaps best personified by a rather remarkable incident at the battle of Kings Mountain where a young soldier of "Irish descent" cursed the enemy in the heat of combat. An older comrade, who had heard the curse words, planned to inform the young man's father about the blasphemy of Robert Edmondson: an act that would get the boy, a wounded hero of the amazing victory, in serious trouble because his stern father was a "strong Presbyterian."[35]

Compared to New England's literate Captain Levi Preston, the majority of Irish and Scotch-Irish who migrated to America stayed together both on the western frontier and in urban areas, especially in small communities: along with a high level of illiteracy, a situation that minimized the overall influence of revolutionary propaganda and pamphlets, including Paine's works, on them. To suppose that these uneducated Celtic-Gaelic colonists, including many Emerald Islanders who still spoke only Gaelic, had been inspired primarily by Locke's treatises and other revolutionary ideology, or even by the Declaration of Independence's words, would be wrong.

Unlike colonists of British descent, the common people early learned egalitarian ways from their Celtic-Gaelic matriarchal societal legacies and value systems, which still rested upon an ancient Brehon law (known as the traditional "ways of the Irish people") that laid the solid foundation for religious, cultural, and personal experiences based upon egalitarianism, especially those of a political and revolutionary nature. Such fundamental concepts were long part of the very fabric of the Celtic-Gaelic family, kinship group, and social, religious, and political life, and left their lasting imprint on the thinking of the common people.

Because the Celtic-Gaelic people were cultural products not only of Ireland but also of the lowest social and economic rungs of colonial society primarily beyond the cities in the Piedmont and especially on the western frontier, they were an extremely religious and egalitarian people with the deepest-seated ethno-cultural animosity toward England in America. At an earlier date than the non-Irish in general, they readily embraced the most radical forms of political and social activism, especially revolutionary, as a natural right and as part of their religious faith, accurately "described as a democracy run riot." Especially on the frontier, they were far more "hyper-politicised" by the liberating faiths of a "radical Whiggery," egalitarian and revolutionary legacies from Ireland, and a vibrant dissenter religion, especially the ultra-individualistic faith of Presbyterianism, than their America's non-Irish colonists: a natural and effortless transference of cultural values, folkways, egalitarianism and political and revolutionary thought from Ireland to America.[36]

No wonder that an experienced Hessian, Captain Johann Heinrichs, who served in the elite German Jaegers, green-uniformed riflemen of the British Army, and who knew intimately of the men he fought against on American soil, wrote to a friend in a letter: "call it not an American Rebellion [because] it is nothing more nor less than an Irish-Scotch Presbyterian Rebellion."[37] The "Ulster American commitment to independence," the sheer power of a radical Whiggery, the grassroots political activism, and the strong revolutionary tendencies transferred from Ireland to the New World significantly shaped America's struggle for life and institutions. An early example of this remarkable phenomenon of Scotch-Irish ultra-democratic values and egalitarian traditions that came to fruition politically in America long before the Declaration of Independence's signing can be seen in the independence declarations of the Scotch-Irish frontier settlers at Pine Creek, Pennsylvania, the May 20, 1775, Westmoreland Declaration at Hanna's Town, Pennsylvania, and in Mecklenburg County, North Carolina.

The Mecklenburg Declaration of Independence has often been dismissed by many historians precisely because these highly educated scholars from America's leading academic institutions in the northeast believed that it was incomprehensible that uneducated, backwoods Scotch-Irish (the chairman was Abraham Alexander and John McKnitt Alexander served as secretary) were capable of issuing such a truly revolutionary declaration more than a year before Thomas Jefferson and the other Founding Fathers in Philadelphia did. The Mecklenburg Declaration of Independence that was issued from Charlotte, Mecklenburg County, in southwest North Carolina was so politically ahead of its time that the document was officially silenced by the Continental Congress because of existing hopes of possible reconciliation with England. For the Irish and Scotch-Irish people, there was no interest or hope in reconciliation or compromise with their ancient foe. The seeds of independence were first planted and blossomed in these remote areas principally because these western frontier regions were primarily the domain of the Scotch-Irish, who early led the way to independence.

But the most notable example of this Celtic-Gaelic-based egalitarian development was in the establishment of America's first truly independent, self-governing, and free community, the Watauga Association, created by mostly Scotch-Irish pioneers. These settlers established themselves in what were then the remote western reaches of North Carolina, now east Tennessee, an untamed wilderness region along the westward-flowing Holston and Nolichucky Rivers in the pristine Watauga and Nolichucky Valleys. Here, they created their own homes, government, and democracy. For the ever-anti-authoritarian Celtic-Gaelic settlers, even moving across the mountains was an act in direct violation of the British Government's arbitrary dictates to protect its imperial economic interests and official regulations about not settling west of the mountains and across the Proclamation Line.

Most of these hardy Wataugan settlers who thought for themselves and defended themselves against native people were Irish and Scotch-Irish. These incredibly tough Celtic-Gaelic borderers had migrated from primarily Virginia and North Carolina. In 1772, these mostly Celtic-Gaelic settlers not only established America's first free government, but also created their own militia of experienced riflemen for self-protection. For survival in a harsh land, they waged their own personal war against the Indians, including at the October 10, 1774, battle of Point Pleasant in the coveted Ohio country under Ireland-born commander Colonel Andrew Lewis.

And in the same way after Lexington and Concord, mostly Scotch-Irish and Irish frontiersmen from the western settlements beyond the mountains were members of the quickly formed "ghost army" that unleashed the brilliant preemptive strike that wiped out the strong Loyalist force at Kings Mountain. These hardy Celtic-Gaelic "mountain men" fought under another Scotch-Irish commander, Ireland-born William Campbell, and his top Scotch-Irish lieutenants like Charles McDowell to preserve not only their largely Celtic-Gaelic communities west of the mountains, but also their own unique democratic experiment and egalitarian way of life that they had created in the wilderness. An old Celtic saying is that "War begins when hell opens," which was evident in the combat prowess of the Celtic-Gaelic clans on battlefields across the Carolinas.

Before the revolution, the Wataugan's novel republican experiment caused shock waves on both sides of the Atlantic. As revealed in a May 10, 1774, letter, a stunned John Murray, Lord Dunmore, royal governor of Virginia, condemned this most "dangerous example" of the audacious republican establishment of a largely Celtic-Gaelic people's democracy (not to mention the potential lethality of so many Irish and Scotch-Irish rebels) for the rest of the thirteen colonies. He warned the British government of this ominous ultra-republican development: "It is an encouragement to the people of America of forming government distinct from and independent of His Majesty's authority."[38] To the British who ruled a world empire, this was a dangerous example not only for the rest of America but also Ireland.[39]

This analysis by the astute royal governor was no exaggeration. The widespread and disproportionate roles played by the Celtic-Gaelic people, including the so-called "wild Irish Roman Catholicks" (a derogatory term certainly not appreciated by Declaration of Independence signer Charles Carroll because it was part of the long-existing anti-Irish stereotype among the British) and Scotch-Irish, can be seen in the most basic and fundamental terms. The dream of independence and the struggle for liberty by 1775 was viewed by the lower Celtic-Gaelic people, especially indentured servants and others who occupied society's lowest rungs, as a means for a significant personal transformation (never possible or obtainable in Ireland) because they had nothing to lose and everything to gain by a revolutionary upheaval, unlike so many colonists of British descent from the gentry class who became Loyalists to preserve their preexisting gains.[40]

After all, by the 1770s, an estimated two-thirds of the Irish who migrated from Ulster Province at Ireland's northern end consisted of lowly indentured servants who occupied the lowest rungs of society. As mentioned, and fortunately for America, they were precisely the kind of individuals who had the most to gain by rising up in revolution and in overturning the existing inequitable social order based on the Great Britain model.[41] And the number of indentured servants was even higher among the Irish Catholics who migrated from the other three-fourths of Ireland (the other three provinces outside, or south of, Ulster Province). These immigrants, who treated their crosses and rosaries as sacred relics, embarked for America primarily from the bustling port of Dublin (the government's nerve center) and mostly southern Ireland from ports like Cork and Wexford and then journeyed primarily to Virginia and Maryland.[42]

Unfortunately, the traditional focus upon New England as the American Revolution's heart and soul has come at the expense of more decisive theaters of operations with regard to military, political, and demographic factors: the middle and upper South colonies, especially Pennsylvania, Maryland, and Virginia. These three colonies produced a disproportionate number of Celtic-Gaelic soldiers in coarse homespun and hunting coats who served with distinction in Washington's Army, including the elite rifle regiments. The expansive length of the western frontier of Virginia, Maryland, and Pennsylvania contained the largest Irish and Scotch-Irish populations. These three regions, not New England, supplied the most lasting and important source of manpower for Washington's Army. Knowledgeable contemporary American and British opinions, as expressed from 1775 to 1783, have echoed this proper historical perspective.

A good deal of emerging evidence has revealed that such earlier contemporary viewpoints of leading military and political men on both sides were in fact actually far more accurate barometers of the true situation at the time. Even the Founding Fathers, who were also strongly influenced by the radical Presbyterianism and Whiggery of Ireland, basically only articulated the intellectual and philosophical concepts of revolution long after the Irish and Scotch-Irish of America's lowest orders had already understood and even defined its meaning on both sides of the Atlantic. The Celtic-Gaelic people spoke loudly by way of their own personal anti-authoritarian and anti-crown activities and inclinations, egalitarianism, and even the course of their lives.[43]

Jefferson's earliest draft versions of the Declaration of Independence were much more radical. But such fundamental Celtic-Gaelic sentiments were unacceptable to Jefferson's more conservative Founding Father peers precisely because these concepts were too democratic in so thoroughly reflecting the more extreme influences of an ultra-democratic Irish Presbyterianism, heightened egalitarianism, and an activist radical Whiggery.[44]

In terms of grassroots origins (more Ireland than America), this same situation developed in regard to the Mecklenburg Declaration of Independence, signed in May 1775, which was not chaired or even considered by the Continental Congress in Philadelphia more than a year before Congress issued its own declaration on July 4, 1776. Later, Thomas Jefferson downplayed the significance of the Mecklenburg

Declaration of Independence, ensuring that the spotlight remained on his own words and efforts in Philadelphia in regard to his own declaration.[45]

Dr. Whitfield J. Bell Jr. correctly placed the invaluable revolutionary contributions of America's lowest orders in a proper historical perspective: "The Franklins and the Jeffersons on the one hand, the scoundrels and the killers on the others, are all well known; they crowd history's galleries. But [the people] who keep alive the ideas other men conceived and hold together the institutions other men create . . . They are the ideal trustees, the perfect friends [and] They are the useful ones."[46] The most useful ones and most ideal egalitarian trustees of the American Revolution were the highly radicalized, ever-independent, and highly politicized Irish and Scotch-Irish.[47]

In a February 2003 editorial in the *Philadelphia Enquirer*, Revolutionary War historian Thomas Fleming correctly emphasized the widespread, disproportionate contributions of these "useful ones" in military terms throughout the long years of struggle. However, Fleming only grudgingly and belatedly emphasized how "some historians have estimated that a third of Washington's army was Irish born or of Irish descent."[48]

Newly discovered primary evidence has now revealed that this overall percentage of the Celtic-Gaelic contribution was actually higher than Fleming's 2003 estimation.[49] Such a sizeable military contribution was possible in part because the total number of Irish who migrated to America during the eighteenth century was in fact much higher than has been previously recognized or acknowledged by historians. Two recent leading historians on the Irish experience in America estimated that "perhaps as many as a half-million" Irish migrated to America during the eighteenth century.[50] These numbers are closer to the actual truth. Consequently, the figure of around five hundred thousand Irish and Scotch-Irish (and this is not counting the large number of fellow Celts, like those who fought at Kings Mountain, such as Micajah Lewis, James Williams, and William

Meredith) among a colonial population of around two million can illuminate the disproportionate Celtic-Gaelic contribution of the winning of America's independence.[51]

Counting only the Scotch-Irish and not the Irish Catholics of colonial America, historian James Webb emphasized in 2004 how "Estimates vary, but it is undeniable that the Scots-Irish comprised at least one-third and as many as one-half of the 'rebel' soldiers during the Revolutionary War."[52] This conviction was entirely in agreement with the insightful views of England-born Thomas Paine, America's greatest inspirational voice in promoting independence to America's common people, that "Europe [Ireland is in the westernmost part of Europe], not England, is the parent country of America."[53]

However, with a greater appreciation of the Irish and Scotch-Irish wartime contributions—in part because Americans of the time were much closer to the struggle than today—around the turn of the century, many estimates of the overall percentage of Irish soldiers in Washington's Continental Army were higher than from historians today and even beyond the one-half number. Indeed, "50 percent of the soldiers of the army of Washington were Irish by blood or birth," wrote one historian in 1898, who combined the numbers of both Irish Catholics and Irish Protestants to conform closely to wartime estimations. However, these early Irish and Irish-American historians, especially Michael J. O'Brien of the American Irish Historical Institute, and their insightful conclusions about the full extent of Celtic-Gaelic contributions have been dismissed and ignored by the modern academic community.

This more thorough appreciation of the extensive Irish role in the American Revolution came at a time when the confident American nation was flushed with a new sense of military and moral superiority after achieving victory in Cuba at the expense of a decaying Spanish Empire during the Spanish-American War. Therefore, to a surprising degree, some of America's traditional ethnic divisions were temporarily diminished by the growing sense of national unity (with the North and South overcoming longstanding sectional divisions lingering from the Civil War). Amid America's euphoria of victory, even some traditional anti-Irish feelings and anti-Irish stereotypes briefly faded away when patriotism ran especially high.[54] But in time and as mentioned, this greater acceptance of the Irish and renewed appreciation for their widespread military, political, and economic contributions to American victory in 1775–1783 were forgotten.

In the modern introduction to the popular Revolutionary War memoir, *A Young Patriot in the American Revolution, 1775–1783*, about Joseph Plum Martin (released in 2001, just a hundred years after the Spanish-American War), the editor noted that this teenage Connecticut militiaman recalled the large numbers of Irish soldiers who served faithfully in Washington's Army: "Martin tells us other things about the War of Independence that most people have forgotten. One is the prevalence of 'old countrymen,' as Martin [and other New Englanders] calls them, in the Revolutionary army's ranks [and] Most of these were recent immigrants were Irish—they constituted about thirty percent of the Continental Army."[55]

Despite the disappearance of so much colonial and Revolutionary War period source material by thief, fire, moth damage, and other destructive elements during the more than 230 years since the American Revolution's conclusion, considerable new primary documentation has recently revealed that the Irish and Scotch-Irish contribution was not only extensive but also more important to the winning of independence than previously realized. This new evidence has verified that a disproportionate percentage of Irish and Scotch-Irish served among those relatively small number of Americans (an estimated one-third and perhaps far less) who actively supported and fought throughout the Revolution, including in Washington's Army. This total number and overall percentage were much higher than has been previously recognized by historians even well past the twenty-first century's beginning.[56]

For longer periods of time and during the revolution's darkest days, including the 1777–1778 winter at Valley Forge, a larger percentage of

Irish soldiers remained in the ranks than their non-Irish peers, whose numbers in British Loyalist units eventually grew to exceed those of Washington's Army: perhaps still another factor explaining why traditional and nationalistic American historians have failed to disclose this contradictory, if not somewhat disturbing, myth-shattering truth about the American experience, especially during the nation's initial struggle for existence. Of course, the exposure of these unpleasant truths has openly challenged a host of comfortable self-congratulatory stereotypes and traditional views of America's highly romanticized creation story of the mythical revolution.[57]

Although focusing only on a limited region but explaining the situation that also applied to other areas like the South, Irish historian David Noel Doyle correctly emphasized how "the Irish of the middle colonies, particularly the Presbyterians, [played a leading] role in the revolution very disproportionate to their numbers [because] In New Jersey, Delaware and Pennsylvania, (and somewhat less so in New York and Maryland), they were at the heart of the revolution."[58] And in regard to New Jersey's Irish contributions that reflected the demographic of other states as well, New Jersey historian Joseph G. Bilby concluded in 2011 how "over half of General George Washington's New Jersey Continentals were Scotch-Irish Presbyterians. . . ."[59] In addition, around 40 percent of one Maryland Continental Regiment consisted of foreign-born soldiers, mostly from Ireland, including indentured servants.[60]

But most of Washington's Scotch-Irish soldiers hailed not from New Jersey but from Pennsylvania. One of the first rifle units that reached Washington's Army at Cambridge, Massachusetts, from Pennsylvania was Ireland-born Colonel William Thompson's Pennsylvania Rifle Battalion (First Pennsylvania Rifle Regiment). The command was distinguished by "new imported Irish," in Washington's September 1776 words, from the Emerald Isle.[61] In fact, so many lower-class Irish and recent immigrants filled Washington's ranks that this demographic caused a spread of consternation and even disgust among some of the highest ranking, non-Irish officers, of the upper class, of Washington's Army. By legal definition, Washington's officers were proper gentlemen: the antithesis of the lowly immigrant Irish, including former indentured servants. Therefore, the Irish and Scotch-Irish were ideal cannon fodder because they were the most expendable fighting men in America. For long-term service, Washington's recruiters (like their British counterparts) targeted the lowest class, landless, illiterate, and impoverished, which was the very definition of overwhelming numbers of Celtic-Gaelic males. Most importantly, these individuals were more likely to sign up for prolonged service as regulars, which was required in a lengthy war.

William Tudor, a wealthy aristocrat from Boston and Harvard College graduate and the army's judge advocate general, was shocked by the unsavory (in his view) sight of so many lower-class Sons of Erin of Washington's Army, including the rifle companies: "Many of them are Irish & foreigners & are thus wid[e]ly suspected of being transported convicts."[62] To partly explain Tudor's obvious anti-Irish prejudice, the overall percentage of convicted criminals was far greater in the British Army than in Washington's Army, especially in regard to men convicted on American soil.[63]

Tudor's elitist fears were not entirely unwarranted because convicts did serve in Washington's Army. The vast majority of these (an estimated from ten to twenty thousand migrated to America from Ireland before the American Revolution), sent to America by anti-Irish English judges, had been convicted of minor crimes. The offenses (today's minor misdemeanors) included petty theft (for taking as little as two shillings or a few articles of clothing, including even blankets in winter) and so-called "vagabondage" that reflected their impoverished and homeless condition because they had nowhere to go in a land of gross social inequities. Multitudes of Irish people in dire straits fled to America because of exorbitant rents that forced them off the land, grain (especially wheat and corn) and potato crop failures, a collapsing economy in the rural countryside, depression of the weaving and linen industry, etc.[64]

The overall image of the average American rebel, especially because so many were Irish and Scotch-Irish, could not have been more disparaging or lower from the viewpoint of the British people, especially the leaders of Parliament: a stereotype that portrayed those individuals in rebellion as almost subhuman beings worthy only of extermination. Of course, this was a common view that fueled a dangerous overconfidence and hubris of an already arrogant superpower. In an attempt to overturn this popular stereotype and to offer a warning to his overconfident peers, British Whig statesmen, who were against this unpopular war, emphasized the sterling character of Ireland-born General Richard Montgomery "to refute the ministerial argument that American rebels were nothing more than uncouth, renegade provincials."[65]

Reflecting his elevated background in society and the prevalent views of the elite planter class, even Washington also felt some concern for his army's ethnic composition that clashed with his own views of the ideal revolutionary and proper gentleman. A wealthy aristocrat who possessed Irish servants at his beloved Mount Vernon, raised the rents on his tenants, and demanded payment in cash (versus produce) during the war years, Washington possessed a measure of the typical upper-class anti-Irish sentiment of the gentry class. Like other officers who considered themselves proper gentlemen in the British tradition, he also felt a comparable contempt in regard not only to the enlisted ranks but also to some lower-class officers of Celtic-Gaelic heritage. Washington was appalled by "an unaccountable kind of stupidity in the lower class of the people."[66]

However, even if that were the case in regard to intelligence (rather than lack of education among the lower class), these common soldiers of the lowest rank actually made for some of America's best and most durable fighting men, who took orders without question and fought like the devil. In the hard-fought campaigns in the Middle Colonies, especially New York, New Jersey, and Pennsylvania, where Washington's Army served in this most important theater of operations, all of the patriot "armies were disproportionately composed of Irish Presbyterians."[67]

General John Sullivan, the aspiring son of a Scotch-Irish immigrant, worked closely with the army's Presbyterian chaplains, encouraging, if not ordering, them "to remind soldiers they fought for a righteous cause blessed by God." In this way, Sullivan bolstered the morale, fighting spirit, and *esprit de corps* among the common soldiery from the Green Isle.[68] Even General Winfield Scott, America's War of 1812 hero who commanded the small American army composed of a large percentage of Irish immigrants during the arduous campaign that resulted in Mexico City's capture in September 1847, emphasized the key factor that also applied to the American Revolution's Celtic-Gaelic soldiers, who were the ancestors of those men who raised the "Stars and Stripes" over Mexico City: the "strong peculiarity of the Irish character" that had long made "the Irishmen . . . among the best soldiers in the world—they fought valiantly [and] he never knew an Irishman . . . to desert—they were always among the first and foremost in the fight, and among the very last to leave the field [and] never knew an Irishman to turn his back on his friend or foe."[69]

This knowledgeable, respectful opinion about the sterling qualities of the Irish fighting man, expressed by the republic's leading general, was repeatedly verified by both American and British military leaders throughout the American Revolution. General Henry Clinton, who commanded British forces in America longer than any other Briton, ascertained to his consternation how during the war years "the rebels themselves drew most of their best soldiers [from] the Irish and other Europeans [especially Celtic fighting men from Scotland and Wales] who had [recently] settled in America."[70] Among a good many others, one veteran British captain agreed completely with General Clinton in this regard. He wrote how the Irish "are in general much better able to go through the fatigues of a campaign . . . than the Americans [and] They certainly have more spirit," especially in terms of combativeness.[71] Such examples that have fully verified these fact-based opinions (not stereotypes) about the superior qualities of the Irish soldier were numerous and well deserved.

What has been most overlooked by modern historians was the fact that this widespread Irish contribution to America's bid for liberty was more fully appreciated and far better understood by those individuals—American, British, and Hessian military and politician leaders—who actually lived through those turbulent days, especially those fighting men who faced the patriots on the battlefield. These knowledgeable contemporaries, on both sides and from the military, political, and civilian realms, knew the facts and realities of the true composition of America's revolutionaries more intimately and thoroughly than modern armchair historians, who wrote their studies in their ivory towers generations later.

Washington's step-grandson, George Washington Parke Curtis, who devoted much of his adult life to studying the American Revolution, including in-depth research in order to paint accurate battle scenes, was firmly convinced that during the war, "Ireland furnished one hundred men to any single man furnished by any other foreign nation."[72] Other leading Americans emphasized—sometimes with an odd mixture of dismay and admiration—the extensive Irish participation in the struggle for liberty. John Randolph, who hailed from one of Virginia's most distinguished planter elite families, was a proper gentleman proud of his English aristocratic antecedents. He wrote of the widespread Irish participation and significant contributions by employing an appropriate metaphor that indicated a widely accepted realization among the revolutionary generation: "I have seen a white crow [albino] and heard of black swans, but an Irish opponent of American liberty I never either saw or heard of."[73] Likewise, another knowledgeable observer, a respected member of the Episcopalian faith in Philadelphia, emphasized the importance in the revolutionary struggle of the most radical, anti-king religious faith in all America, which fueled the motivations of vast multitudes of rebellious Scotch-Irish from Pennsylvania: "a Presbyterian loyalist was a thing unheard of."[74]

Washington early realized as much. Feeling thankful for the hard-fighting, steadfast Celtic-Gaelic soldier, he basked in his most

solid and always forthcoming support. In fact, the Celtic-Gaelic people so wholeheartedly supported the cause that long-forgotten Irish
civilians made important military-related contributions to American
victory. Therefore, Washington formulated his most risky strategy of the
war in planning to cross the Delaware River on the night of December
25, 1776, partly with a patriotic Irishman in mind, Sam McConkey.
At this time, Washington was well supported by one of his best staff
officers, Colonel John Fitzgerald, a Catholic from County Wicklow,
Ireland, who had migrated to America in 1769 and became a thriving
merchant in Alexandria, Virginia, on the Potomac. In a region swarming with Loyalists and traitors, Washington knew that any betrayal of
his secret river crossing from the shoreline of eastern Pennsylvania to
western New Jersey and audacious plan to march upon Trenton from
the north to attack the Hessian-held town just before dawn on December 26 would certainly doom his most desperate enterprise. He chose
to cross the Delaware at a place where he knew beyond all doubt that
his brilliant master plan would never be betrayed precisely due to a true
blue Irishman, Sam McConkey, who operated McConkey's Ferry.[75]

Other Irish civilians played key roles. Born in County Antrim,
Ireland, in 1740, Hercules Mulligan, a New York City tailor who lived
on Queen Street and was a proud graduate of King's College (today's
Columbia College), could "sling [Irish] blarney as well as anyone."
Having migrated to New York City with his family around 1746 at
age six, he gained renown for a "roiling rebelliousness." After his
capture by Tory militiamen and then exchange, Mulligan became an
effective spy in New York City, where he owned his own tailor shop,
for Washington. Because of his forgotten important contributions to
America's independence, he is one patriot Irishman whose "name every
schoolchild should know."[76]

Likewise, "Irish merchant" William McCafferty, born on the
Green Isle, made a stealthy key contribution to a remarkable battlefield
success when he directed Major Ferguson's task force down the wrong
Carolina road, ensuring that the pursuing patriots were able to catch up

to the Loyalists, who had no choice but to make their ill-fated defensive stand on Kings Mountain. McCafferty also fought at Kings Mountain, reaping his revenge on the redcoat enemies of his old country and his adopted homeland.[77] Captured at Kings Mountain and when still in custody, Loyalist surgeon Uzal Johnson was shocked by the effectiveness of one especially resourceful Irish intelligence agent, penning in his journal on November 16, 1780: "one Smith, an Irishman [who] gave a very good description of our Works [in South Carolina] at Camden, Ninety Six, Augusta & even Chs. Town [Charleston], he said that he had been at each place as a Spy" for America.[78]

Thanks to endless reports from his commanders reaching cosmopolitan London on the Thames River, even King George III declared with some astonishment how the conflict being waged across America's breadth was in fact nothing more than another holy war. The king came to this astute conclusion because of the stream of military reports that told of the overwhelming numbers of Scotch-Irish revolutionaries, who were in the political, economic, and military forefront of the contest for America's independence.[79] He became so frustrated at one point that he angrily denounced the conflict in America as that "Damned Presbyterian War."[80] Countless numbers of Scotch-Irish were fueled by their fiery Presbyterian faith that motivated so many Ulstermen "to punish this enemy for his wickedness," in one Ireland-born soldier's words.[81]

With a thorough understanding of the nature of this increasingly brutal war in America, especially in the Southern theater after 1780, one of the King's faithful officers, like so many other soldiers who attempted to crush a common people's rebellion that was largely Celtic-Gaelic, echoed the identical view. He emphasized the fundamental centrality of the Scotch-Irish role in the overall resistance effort at multiple levels, penning without any doubt in 1778 how this was a "Scots Irish Presbyterian rebellion" of the first magnitude.[82] Writing from New York City in November 1776, a frustrated representative of Lord Dartmouth revealed his detailed knowledge of the endless source of the rebellion that had been raging like a wildfire across America when he described in a letter of the all-important Scotch-Irish contribution in resisting the mother country from the beginning: "Presbyterianism is really at the Bottom of the whole Conspiracy, has supplied it with Vigour [sic], and will never rest . . . . "[83]

And in the hallowed halls of the British Parliament, where the social and political elite of the island nation loudly voiced their educated opinions with a mixture of intelligence and wit, Horace Walpole explained, with a fatalistic sense of humor and in an appropriate analogy, not only the initial development but also the very heart of America's resistance effort in simple terms. To enlighten his fellow English politicians, Walpole emphasized the disproportionate role played in the resistance effort by the independent-minded common people, mostly former tenant farmers, from Northern Ireland: "There is no use crying about it [as] Cousin America has run off with a Presbyterian parson, and that is the end of it."[84]

This insightful evaluation of the American Revolution's true core, central foundation, and most persistent source of resistance from 1775 to 1783 was also supported by a young Irishman named Thomas Sullivan from Dublin. After enlisting in British service in Cork to fulfill his youthful wanderlust, he found an early principal source of revolutionary sentiment in Boston. This young soldier of the Forty-Ninth Regiment of Foot presented a striking contradiction to the Anglo-Saxon myth constructed by romantic-minded, elitist New England historians of the upper class.

With a keen eye on his fellow countrymen, Thomas Sullivan described Boston in 1775 with considerable insight: "The inhabitants were chiefly Presbyterians [members of the mercantile class who remained after the British occupation of the port city consisted] of English, Irish, and Scotch Merchants with their adherents." The leading rebels of Boston were "chiefly Presbyterians" rather than leaders of British descent, according to the traditional stereotype of the Anglo-Saxon-based uprising, especially in the revolution's early days.

Unable to tolerate English occupation, these influential Scotch-Irish of Boston then "left the town" out of necessity to escape the oppression, fled to interior areas that had been earlier settled by the Scotch-Irish, and joined Washington's Army to continue their holy war against the longtime oppressors of Ireland and now America.[85]

Dublin-born Sullivan described the central reason for making the boldest decision of his life by deserting the British Army in 1778 and joining the patriot cause, an act which guaranteed execution (especially for an Irishman) by hanging if captured. He drew the appropriate symbolic analogy between the struggle of the subjugated Irish homeland and that of America, which he saw as one and the same. Viewing this war as a fight for a people's self-determination and great dream of liberty long denied on the Green Isle, Sullivan wrote how, "My seeing America under Arms . . . and upon my examining the reason, finding they were striving to throw off the Yoke, under which my native Country—sunk for many years; induced me upon a serious Consideration to share the same freedom, that America strove for."[86] However, to be sure, a good many other Irish remained in the British Army's ranks, ensuring a forgotten civil war among the Celtic-Gaelic people.[87]

Also possessing considerable insight into what was really happening in America in regard to the true source of rebellion, Englishman Ambrose Serle, Admiral Richard Howe's personal secretary, declared that the passionate faith of Presbyterianism that fueled fanatical Scotch-Irish resistance by December 1776 "was really at the bottom of this whole Conspiracy" that was the American Revolution.[88] Like Serle's and so many other people's (including King George III) well-informed opinions on both sides of the Atlantic, one revolutionary of the Quaker faith concluded in 1776 how the Loyalists were firmly convinced that "the Presbyterians are the cause of all this bloodshed."[89] Seale's opinion that the colonists of British descent were less revolutionary than the Scotch-Irish coincided with not only with the facts but also the revealing words of a knowledgeable Hessian,

Captain Johann Heinrichs, who penned in a 1776 letter to a friend that this was "not an American rebellion [because] it is nothing more than an Irish-Scotch Presbyterian Rebellion."[90]

In fact, so many determined Irish and Scotch-Irish soldiers served in Washington's Continental Army and other people's armies of America that George Washington Parke Custis, Martha Washington's grandson and father of the wife of Robert Edward Lee of Civil War fame, who became an authority on Washington's Army, later emphasized without exaggeration that this vital Irish contribution to the final victory was entitled to be officially recognized by all America: "Let the shamrock [of Ireland] be entwined with the laurels of the Revolution. . . ."[91]

Knowing well of the extensive Celtic-Gaelic contributions and sacrifices in the name of liberty, Custis also emphasized in no uncertain terms how "The grass has grown green over the grave of many a poor Irishman who died for American [as] Ireland furnished one hundred men to any single man furnished by another other nation."[92] As mentioned, this disproportionate Irish contribution in important situations came before the American Revolution to bestow an early legacy to America. True holy warriors, the Scotch-Irish Virginians who were led to their key western victory at Point Pleasant by their Ireland-born commander, Colonel Andrew Lewis, who died at the battle in October 1774, were paid an Old Testament-inspired tribute: "As Israel mourned and her daughters did weep for Saul and his hosts on the mount of Gilbo, Virginia will mourn for her heroes who sleep in tombs on the bank of the O-hi-O."[93]

As late as 1777, General James Murray, a senior British commander who was well informed, was firmly convinced that "Washington's only reliable men were recent immigrants" from Ireland. And a respected physician, who traveled through the lines, reported to the British government that "the Continental army consisted chiefly of transported Irishmen [and among British generals and troops in America] The idea that Washington's Continentals were mainly Irishmen and other recent immigrants [especially fellows Celts from Scotland and Wales] was widely held" by people on both sides of the Atlantic.[94] Like other experienced British military leaders, Murray possessed great respect for the overall quality of the Irish fighting man as superior to Washington's non-Irish soldiers, whom he considered "very unfit and impatient of war."[95]

Raised in Dublin and serving in the Royal Welch Fusiliers, Captain Frederick Mackenzie, as revealed in his diary, knew from hard-earned experience in the field that "the only sure, reliable strength of the rebels army [under Washington] consisted . . . particularly [of] Irishmen," who "made up a preponderance of many regiments" of the Continental Army.[96] Battling the rustic revolutionaries as a member of the Twenty-Third Regiment of Foot (Royal Welch Fusiliers), Captain Mackenzie concluded that Washington's hardest-fighting and most determined soldiers were Irishmen. In fact, he was convinced that the Celtic-Gaelic warriors were "much better able to go through the fatigues of a Campaign, and live in the manner they at present do, than the Americans."[97]

This often-repeated evaluation of the Irish soldier's physicality and durability based on firsthand experience was no exaggeration or stereotype, but educated opinions and accurate evaluations based upon what had been long demonstrated by Irish soldiers on both sides of the Atlantic. The fighting prowess of the Irish reached such lofty heights that one Irish historian (but a non-military scholar) has even challenged this pervasive view (despite all the ample evidence that says otherwise) because "the concept of the 'Fighting Irishman' carries with it an implicit element of condescension." However, in truth, this historian has basically confused the military prowess of the Irish fighting man with the negative stereotype of excessive pugnacity, which has been long incorrectly applied to Irish civilians in general and partly based on the anti-Irish stereotype of drunkenness, as a people. While the concept of the "Fighting Irish" soldier was entirely true in regard to the American Revolution and other conflicts on both sides of the Atlantic, the negative stereotype of the drunken, brawling Irish civilian was a dark stain on the Irish character.[98] Indeed, "the Irish had more spirit than the Native American, Mackenzie believed, plus a desire to rise above their traditional state of poverty" to gain acceptance in American society and to create a better life for themselves and their families: powerful motivations that caused disproportionate numbers of Irish to fill Washington's ranks.[99] And after acquiring all available information based on reliable intelligence, Dr. John Berkenhout wrote to Lord George Germain, Secretary of State for America, and concluded how "the Continental army consisted chiefly of transported Irishmen" whose patriotic zeal was unbounded.[100]

Only recently, one modern historian, Arthur Herman, emphasized in his 2001 book *How the Scots Invented the Modern World* how the Scotch-Irish "suppl[ied] the backbone of George Washington's Continental Army [and perhaps] half the army at Valley Forge were Ulster Scots [.] Certainly they brought military experience, leadership, and a fighting spirit to a revolution that badly needed all three."[101]

Herman was not guilty of exaggeration. When combined with the number of Irish Catholics, the vast majority of Ireland's residents, from the other three-quarters (the other three provinces) of Ireland outside Northern Ireland's Ulster Province, then the high percentage was much closer to the truth of the actual Irish participation, however. Like no other American leader, Washington well understood the most reliable and steadfast principal source of sustaining the rebellion (one of America's longest wars) and the true heart and soul of the resistance effort across America. And most importantly, this source of support and resistance was something that he could count upon year after year. As Washington explained with ample justification, "If defeated everywhere else, I will make my [final] stand for liberty among the Scots-Irish of my native state," Virginia.[102]

During the lowest ebb of American fortunes in the ill-fated autumn of 1776, Washington planned to cross west over the heavily forested Allegheny Mountains with what little remained of his Continental Army to gain not only safety but also the guaranteed support from the largely Scotch-Irish and Irish frontiersmen on the western Virginia frontier, which is today's eastern Kentucky and Tennessee. Washington had early conceived this desperate plan based upon the reassuring comfort of Celtic-Gaelic demographics of the western frontier. As he penned in a most revealing early 1776 letter to his brother-in-law, Washington maintained that "in the worst event," this sprawling Scotch-Irish western frontier would provide "an asylum" for his beaten rebel army, when the revolution was at its nadir.[103]

Indeed, during November 1776 after the loss of New York City and Fort Washington at Manhattan Island's northern end, Washington revealed his well-thought-out strategic formula of eventually securing a safe western refuge populated mostly by Scotch-Irish if necessary when he told his aide-de-camp Colonel Joseph Reed how he might well have to withdraw his reeling army first to the heavily Scotch-Irish Shenandoah Valley, then farther west beyond the Allegheny Mountains to keep the "flames of revolution" alive.[104] Virginia's Shenandoah Valley was the homeland of John Lewis, who was the enemy of "the Irish lord" on the Green Isle, and had encouraged five sons off to war to fight the British and Hessians.[105] Scotch-Irish blacksmith Andrew Kincannon was a native of the Shenandoah Valley before moving west of the mountains, where he "made the first horse-shoe in Kentucky" around 1775. He led a company with distinction at Kings Mountain and was destined to marry a Scotch-Irish woman, Catherine McDonald.[106]

Even more, the commander in chief carefully chose his army's winter quarters at the most opportune places, including Valley Forge (located between Philadelphia to the east and the Western frontier), Pennsylvania, and Morristown, New Jersey, where large nearby Scotch-Irish and Irish populations could be relied upon for ample timely support and intelligence. Here, in the heart of these largely transplanted Scotch-Irish regions that were in essence "little Ulsters" and "New Irelands," Washington safety situated his army with complete confidence, resting with the reassurance of the availability of immediate assistance in case of a serious emergency.[107]

During the revolution's darkest days toward the end of 1776 and with only a relative handful of men remaining faithfully in the army's depleted ranks, a desperate Washington relied heavily upon the most dependable resource and always most anti-British colonists when he descended upon the unprepared Hessian brigade and captured Trenton on snowy December 26. To gain additional troops to bolster this newfound aggressiveness, Washington had early targeted the manpower-rich Irish and Scotch-Irish communities in the rural Pennsylvania countryside and far beyond Philadelphia to the east.

Therefore, he dispatched Ireland-born Colonel John Armstrong, a popular frontier leader, on a special mission of extreme importance. Wiping out a hostile Indian sanctuary along the Allegheny River in September 1756 that had long posed a threat to the vulnerable western settlements, this hard-hitting Irishman was the revered leader of the Kittanning expedition. During that surprise attack, Armstrong had counted upon mostly Celtic-Gaelic soldiers, including Ireland-born Colonel William Thompson, who survived disaster in Canada and then took command of Washington's Pennsylvania rifle regiment, and Scotland-born Hugh Mercer, who had emerged as one of Washington's top lieutenants by 1776.

At a time when he was never more short on manpower and desperately needed to bolster ranks at the nadir of America's resistance effort after New York City's fall, Washington sent Armstrong into Cumberland County west of Philadelphia and along the western frontier, where Irish and Scotch-Irish were most heavily concentrated. During his vital mission, Armstrong secured hundreds of Celtic-Gaelic revolutionaries in time for Washington to reverse the revolution's course in his Cannae-like success at Trenton (named for its Scotland-born founder, William Trent) on an early December morning along the Delaware.[108]

Consequently, an appreciative Washington paid a sincere tribute to the invaluable service of the Irish and Scotch-Irish fighting men when almost everyone believed that the rebellion had already failed because they refused to desert and forsake the struggle for liberty: "Ireland [was the dearest] friend of my country in my country's most friendless days" and no days were more desperate for America than mid-December 1776.[109] Washington also emphasized how he hoped that America would never "forget the patriotic part which the Irish took in the accomplishment of our rebellion and the establishment of our government."[110]

In much the same way, the realities of Irish and Scotch-Irish demographics and the steadfastness of the Celtic-Gaelic people to the cause dictated the course of strategy in the Deep South as well as in the Middle Colonies and Upper South. After the main theater of operations shifted to the south after his victory in October 1777 at Saratoga and after Charleston's fall in May 1780 (America's greatest military disaster to date), the ambitious General Horatio Gates, upon whose staff John Armstrong Jr. (the son of the Ireland-born leader who led the daring strike on Kittanning) capably served, made his first strategic move in the new theater of operations. After taking command in the South in July 1780, Gates pushed south from the barren pine forests of North Carolina to exploit the friendly Celtic-Gaelic demographics of South Carolina.

To gain reinforcements, Gates advanced upon the Piedmont town of Camden, South Carolina, where he sought to utilize the extensive support of the mostly Irish and Scotch-Irish populace in the region. Gates's top lieutenants had wisely proposed a movement, rejected by Gates, through Charlotte, Mecklenburg County, and Salisbury, Rowan County, North Carolina, in order to gain supplies and manpower from supportive populations expressly because this region was so heavily dominated by Scotch-Irish settlers primarily from Ulster Province.[111] The top British cavalry commander in the Southern theater of operations, Oxford-educated Colonel Banastre Tarleton, complained with astonishment how the Celtic-Gaelic people in this section of the North Carolina Piedmont, especially Mecklenburg and Rowan Counties in southwest North Carolina, "were more hostile to England than any other in America."[112]

Battling elusive partisans, Tarleton was infuriated by the effective guerrilla tactics that steadily sapped the army's strength. In the North Carolina Piedmont of Mecklenburg and Rowan Counties, he described how British "foraging parties were every day harassed by the inhabitants, who did not remain at home . . . but generally fired from covert places to annoy British detachments [and] they continued their hostilities with unwearied perseverance" that was typically Celtic-Gaelic in nature.[113] A disgusted Lord Charles Cornwallis, utterly befuddled by the stiff challenges of guerilla conflict stemming mostly from hit-and-run Celtic-Gaelic patriots, also concluded how Mecklenburg County was in fact "a damned hornet's nest of rebellion."[114]

Much of the same situation also existed in North Carolina's sister state of South Carolina. After a series of disasters in the South— starting with Charleston's fall in mid-May 1780, the rout of Gates's Army (the primary American army in the South) at Camden in mid-August 1780, and other sharp military setbacks—South Carolina was lost and left undefended, so never-say-die Celtic-Gaelic leaders and fighting men rose to the fore.

Thomas Sumter, of Welsh heritage and known as "the Gamecock," was the first South Carolina leader to organize guerrilla activities to challenge the victors. And naturally the first place where Sumter went to rally fighting men for his guerrilla activities was the most heavily Scotch-Irish populated region of South Carolina, the Waxhaws. To arm his followers, Sumter even procured lethal Long Rifles from the Scotch-Irish Gillespie brothers, legendary rifle makers, who lived near North Carolina's Blue Ridge. Meanwhile, the guerrilla effort in South Carolina was destined to grow to extensive proportions to harass the occupiers, who were not prepared for the challenges of asymmetrical warfare.[115]

During the darkest days of America's resistance effort in South Carolina, the long-haired Sumter took command of "the only corps of Whigs still organized and fighting in South Carolina [but most importantly] he knew the mettle of his Scotch-Irish troops [because more than any others] these immigrants would fight to protect their fields, cabins, and barns."[116] The significant Celtic-Gaelic influences of this last-ditch resistance effort in South Carolina were best represented by these ethnic die-hards who proclaimed how their "arms was never to be laid down until the British troops was drove from the State of South Carolina and the independence of the United States acknowledged."[117]

But, of course, the contributions of the Celtic-Gaelic people in South Carolina rose to the fore in the very beginning of America's struggle for liberty. Providing a good representative example of an inspiring Celtic-Gaelic leader, Lieutenant Colonel Alexander McIntosh, a future general of St. David's Parish and eventually a follower of the "Swamp Fox" Francis Marion, led the "expert Rifle-men" of the Fifth South Carolina Regiment, which was authorized by Congress in February 1776 and consisted of Low Country marksmen.[118] Another inspirational Celtic warrior of the same last name, Colonel Lachlan McIntosh, born in Scotland and from a Scottish Highlands family who had migrated to Georgia in 1736, defiantly refused to surrender the surrounded Fort Morris at Sunbury, in southeast Georgia, on November 25, 1778. He declared, "As to surrendering the fort, receive this laconic answer: Come and take it!"[119]

Major James McCall, a veteran commander from the Ninety-Sixth District, South Carolina, led a battalion of South Carolina state cavalrymen. During the most important battle of their lives, McCall and his horsemen "exceeded all expectations" in fighting beside Lieutenant Colonel William Washington's Continental Light Dragoons and vanquishing the much-feared cavalry of "Ban" Tarleton's Legion at the battle of Cowpens on January 17, 1781.[120]

In the lands between South Carolina's "Up Country" and "Low Country," the Scotch-Irish people dominated. Here, in the fertile lands along the Santee River, some Irish who had migrated long before the American Revolution had obtained their share of the American dream, clearing the land and raising cash crops on plantations of hundreds of acres. Tiege Cantey was one of these Celtic-Gaelic settlers, having come to this fertile land of the Santee River country as "a penniless immigrant from Ireland." His descendant Charles Cantey continued the Irish revolutionary tradition on American soil, battling for America.[121] The Cantey clan thrived in the Santee River country like other enterprising Irish immigrants, such as William Jameson who carved out a magnificent plantation of ten thousand acres.[122] To defend the lands of the Palmetto State that they loved, so many South Carolina Irish immigrants served in Colonel William Thompson South Carolina Rangers at the war's beginning that they outnumbered the men in the ranks who were South Carolina-born.[123]

Across South Carolina, other fiery Irish leaders early rose to the fore, such as Thomas Brandon. Born of Ireland-born parents, Brandon served with distinction as a regimental commander under Sumter and fought at Kings Mountain and Cowpens. Leading "his Irishmen" against the British occupiers of his homeland, Brandon was described as "a burley rough-and-tumble fighter from the Irish settlement along Fair Forest" Creek near Newberry, South Carolina.[124] At the battle of Cowpens, Brandon killed three of Tarlton's dragoons with his trusty saber, which he welded like his ancient Irish ancestors who fought against the Vikings and English in defending Green Isle soil.[125]

In the end, the uprising against the British who had conquered South Carolina after Charleston's fall and defeat of Gates's Army at Camden was only possible because of so many distinct Irish settlements, colonies, and enclaves across the state. Beginning in 1737, so many Irish settled in the Piedmont (around today's Newberry) along the Wateree River that it became known as Ireland, or the Irish Settlement. Other Irish settlements sprang up nearby in subsequent years. A father-son patriot team by the name of O'Neall, William and Hugh, hailed from this area. Tarleton's cavalry burned down the William O'Neall farm, turning the woman and children out into the forest while Hugh served in the patriot army.

Francis Marion, the "Swamp Fox," drew his first volunteers from South Carolina's Irish settlements, where "the bitter heritage of hate to the English" had long flourished, along the Pee Dee and Black Rivers.

Symbolically, with the formation of "Marion's Brigade," three of the first four captains (elected by their mostly Celtic-Gaelic men) were Scotch-Irish. Then, after Gates's defeat at Camden, Sumter's defeat, and other reversals, Marion was left with the only patriot force in South Carolina—one that was largely Scotch-Irish. Teenage William Dobein James, one of Marion's men, described how the last remaining resistance in South Carolina came from the lands stretching "from the Santee to the Pedee [because the] inhabitants of it were generally of Irish extraction; a people, who at all times during the war, abhorred either submission or vassalage."

Quite a few Irish brothers fought side-by-side to repel the British and Loyalists, including William and Matthew Maybin, who hailed from a small market and linen industry town on the River Braid, Ballymena, County Antrim, Ulster Province. As bright-eyed immigrants, they landed in Charleston in 1771 and were then part of the expedition launched against the Cherokee in 1776. The brothers then served under Sumter's partisan band. William Maybin was captured at the Battle of Hanging Rock and died in a British ship-prison in Charleston harbor. Likewise, the Ireland-born Boyce brothers, John and Alexander, paid a high price for their patriotism after migrating from Northern Ireland in 1765 and locating in an Irish settlement christened with the familiar name of Mollohon. While Alexander fell in the assault on Savannah, John fought on in the battles of Kings Mountain and Cowpens.[126]

From the Revolution's beginning to end and in every major theater of operations, an undeniable fact was widely acknowledged just before the Mexican-American War's beginning in 1846. At that time, Americans were generally aware how "the best blood of Ireland, has been freely shed to serve the good cause of 'The Land of the Free and the Home of the Brave'."[127] In early May 1777, General Nathanael Greene, Washington's longtime top lieutenant, emphasized the importance of perpetuating the memory of the lamented Ireland-born Richard Montgomery, who was killed leading a late

December 1775 attack on Quebec, and Scotland-born High Mercer, who was killed before his men at Princeton, all "great heroes," which "will be a pleasing circumstance to the army in general."[128] From General Montgomery to the final showdown at Yorktown more than a half decade later, the best and brightest of an entire generation of Irishmen served their adopted country with distinction in disproportionate numbers during the Revolution's most crucial moments.[129]

Although belatedly, the novel concept of the widespread Irish role has been only recently embraced by the traditional New York City historian Fleming. In Fleming's impressive 2001 *Washington's Secret War*, the author explained his most lasting original contribution to the field, writing how he "looked forward to reporting on recent research that exploded the myths about . . . the ethnic composition of Washington's army."[130] Drawing upon new primary research and documentation, Fleming at long last emphasized the importance of the high percentage of Irish soldiers who served faithfully in Washington's ranks for so long. However, this recent research of the respected historian, a longtime journalist, in fact corresponded almost exactly with the identical views of Washington's step-grandson and so many other knowledgeable observers, generals, and officials on both sides during the American Revolution to solidly reconfirm that Ireland's shamrock, an enduring cultural and nationalistic symbol of Irishness, indeed should have "been entwined with the laurels of the Revolution," because of the widespread Irish and Scotch-Irish contributions to America's independence.[131]

The latest primary evidence and documentation have revealed that these earlier estimations of the widespread Irish participation by members of the revolutionary generation (on both sides) were actually much closer to the actual truth and far more than has been previously recognized or appreciated by later-day scholars and modern historians. Although only recently and although not entirely, Fleming has been one of the few modern American historians to begin to belatedly appreciate the crucial role played by the Irish in Washington's Army. In 2005, Fleming concluded that the Irish "constituted two-fifths of the Continental Army by the time [Washington] reached Valley Forge in 1778."[132] Fleming's numbers are higher than those of historian Jay P. Dolan, who wrote in 2008 that "In fact, as many as one-third of the Continental Army was Irish."[133]

Such lofty percentages are far beyond what has been generally believed by the vast majority of other historians and the American public for generations. Most importantly, this large percentage of Irish soldiers in Washington's Continental Army existed at the most crucial periods of the struggle, including Washington's surprise attack on Trenton and at Valley Forge. Unlike so many non-Irish troops, especially of English descent, who had deserted in droves throughout the tragic year of 1776 (in which Washington did not win a battle until Trenton at nearly the year's end), a large percentage of Irish soldiers generally remained in the Continental Army's thinned ranks. This phenomenon was also seen at Valley Forge during the miserable winter of 1777–1778 and later at the Morristown winter encampment, when Washington's ill-clothed men starved, went barefoot, and died of disease by the hundreds. An Irish officer serving in Lieutenant General William Howe's Army that contained many Celtic-Gaelic soldiers, Dubliner Captain Frederick MacKenzie, Welch Fusiliers, fully understood (in no small part from his experiences in viewing first-hand so many Irish soldiers in the British Army) how the Irish and Scotch-Irish in Washington's Army "are in general much better able to go through the fatigues of a campaign, and live in the manner they at present do, than the Americans [soldiers of British descent and] They certainly have much more spirit" on the march and especially during the fury of combat.[134]

Therefore, fortunately for America, Washington's Army evolved into a surrogate Celtic-Gaelic enclave, as best exemplified by enthusiastic celebrations of St. Patrick's Day (including at Valley Forge) and the splendid service of elite Irish troops of the so-called Line of Ireland, or the Pennsylvania Continental Line, which was one of the largest and best combat units under Washington's command. This distinctive societal and cultural factor explained partly why Washington's Irish and Scotch-Irish troops endured and remained faithfully for so long in the ranks from one campaign (especially disastrous ones) to another, even when the war effort reached its all-time lows and so many other non-Irish soldiers deserted. A larger percentage of the determined Irish and Scotch-Irish warrior stayed faithfully in Washington's ill-clothed ranks year after year and campaign after campaign, because "he feels instinctively that the honor of his native land, and the military traditions of his race" were at stake, and could not be betrayed.[135]

One never-say-die Irishman of patriot sentiments was encountered by the Marquis de Chastellux during his travels in America. He described an average Irish rebel soldier of high spirits and considerable resilience who fought for America with unbridled enthusiasm, as if he was defending his Celtic-Gaelic homeland so far away: "He was an Irishman, who though but lately arrived in America, had made several campaigns, and received a considerable wound in his thigh by a musket ball; which, though it could never be extracted, had not in the least affected either his health or gaiety. He related his military exploits [and had originally] settled in North Carolina. . . ."[136] This North Carolina Irishman was much like James Johnson, who was the "son of Henry of Ireland." He served at Kings Mountain where his ample Indian fighting experience paid dividends during the hard-fought battle.[137] Johnson was a member of the extensive span of Scotch-Irish communities of the Piedmont, and also along the western frontier just beyond the Piedmont. Susan Smart Alexander, known as "Aunt Susie," summarized how in regard to the most Scotch-Irish settlers around Charlotte, North Carolina, the "People were not anxious about money [which was but] a small matter [since] Nothing attracted their attention but liberty. That was their whole object."[138]

Historian John Sly came close to the mark in regard to the hidden truth of the American Revolution beyond the thick shroud of romantic mythology when he correctly concluded that "The men who shouldered the heaviest military burden were something *less* than average colonial Americans [and] As a group, they were poorer, more marginal, less well anchored in society."[139] And no ethnic group in America better fit this accurate description than the Irish and the Scotch-Irish, especially recent immigrants to America's shores.[140]

The first colonial army of New Englanders that Washington inherited outside Boston at Cambridge, Massachusetts, in early summer 1775 indeed resembled the romantic myth of a military volunteer force consisting primarily of members of the middle classes of New England society, mostly yeoman farmers who served mostly short term in the militia tradition. However, what was most needed for victory was a solid foundation of the lower-class Irish and Scotch-Irish soldiers fighting for the war's duration as Continentals (long-term regular troops). This early dominant demographic of a largely New England army soon proved to be a fleeting reality, to Washington's shock, by early December 1776, having all but faded away because of short-term enlistments.

Not long afterward, as the initial enlistments expired, the first excitement of the great adventure of going to war in 1775 inevitably wore off, and humiliating American defeats and casualties increased, America's military effort was soon "shouldered almost exclusively by the poorest segments of American society"—the Irish and Scotch-Irish—in time to reap success during the war's major turning points, first Trenton in late December 1776, Princeton in early January 1777, Saratoga in October 1777 in the northern theater, and in the South at Kings Mountain in October 1780 and Cowpens in January 1781.[141]

Throughout the revolutionary's tortured course, American leaders, especially the mostly wealthy, property-owning aristocrats in the Continental Congress, became disturbed by the overwhelmingly ethnic and lower-class composition of Washington's Continental

Army. Beyond the traditional fear of a standing army, this unsettling, if not shocking, realization fueled a widespread distrust among the privileged elite for America's first national army that was much too democratic (and hence too radical and potentially threatening). Contrary to the myth, the winter of 1777–1778 was relatively mild and Washington's soldiers suffered more from the selfishness and the lack of assistance from disloyal Americans, especially large numbers of non-Irish in nearby Philadelphia (the opposite situation throughout rural Pennsylvania, especially along the western frontier), and from a contemptuous Congress.

This distrust of well-educated, upper-crust Congressmen stemmed in no small part from the fact that Washington's Army was so heavily dominated by lower-class Irish and Scotch-Irish: former indentured servants, lowly common laborers, and landless "peasants" who were seen as "foreigners" or Europeans. After all, these Sons of Erin closely resembled Ireland's peasant class of a backward feudal society. This unsettling demographic reality for America's first national army was considered nothing less than a national disgrace to many members of the privileged and aristocratic elite.

Most shocking to America's aristocrats, the most recently arrived Gaelic-speaking Catholic immigrants could barely, if at all, speak English, made the sign of the cross before entering battle, and remained far more Irish in outlook and attitude than American. Fresh from the Green Isle, these Irish peasants, mostly from the rural countryside, naturally shunned the alien environment of the intolerant East Coast cities, as in Ireland where the elite and the English language dominated, unlike in the rural areas where Gaelic was widely spoken. These lowly Irish were viewed by colonists of British descent as "not Natives" of America or England. Nevertheless, active army recruiters specifically targeted Irish indentured servants (the lowest and poorest class), who filled Washington's ranks. And the enticing promise of one hundred acres of land was too much to resist: all in all, a dream come true for the still-impoverished, landless Irish, especially Catholics who had been long outlawed from owning land in Ireland. For moneyless Irish immigrants without land, education, or prospects and Celtic-Gaelic indentured servants whose lives were not their own, service in the newly created United States military represented a dramatic leap up the social ladder. Hence, Washington's Army was early "something of an embarrassment to many Americans [and t]he decrepit state of this particular assemblage of lower-class men and boys was particularly shameful," especially to the aristocratic eastern elites from Boston to Charleston.[142]

Like so many other non-Irish in the revolution's darkest period during the autumn and early winter of 1776, a patriot of English heritage, Elkanah Watson of Plymouth, Massachusetts, lost his faith in this fledgling revolutionary movement, which seemed bound to lose against a vastly superior professional army. This discouraged New Englander lamented how already, "We considered ourselves a vanquished people."[143] Most Celtic-Gaelic soldiers were not nearly as pessimistic as this disillusioned Massachusetts soldier and so many other Americans. Based upon a mixture of irony and bitterness as a means of coping with life's harshest offerings, a lively wit, satire, dark humor, sense of parody, and ribaldry early developed among the Irish people as a survival mechanism. Sons of Erin in patriot ranks found humor even in the midst of their bungling amateur army and its inexperienced leaders (including Washington), who lost more battles than they ever won. Even physically, the Irish soldier possessed another key advantage over his fellow non-Irish patriots by having a greater immunity and stronger resistance to smallpox—the greatest disease threat faced by American troops—because it had long existed on the Emerald Isle and Europe.

But most of all, the tragic course of Irish history had presented a good many comparable no-win situations, severe adversity, and stunning defeats (like Washington experienced during the late summer and autumn of 1776) against the same professional, well-equipped opponent. Such widely acknowledged exemplary characteristics of an exceptionally durable and reliable soldiery were also shared by Irish troops serving with the British Army: an obvious testament to the Celtic-Gaelic soldier's renown (a true fact rather than a romantic stereotype) and widely demonstrated abilities as a highly dependable fighting man par excellence.

Most of all, a distinctive cultural trait of stoicism and perseverance emerged from the suffering, tragedies, and losses of the Celtic-Gaelic people that spanned generations. These qualities that fortified a hardy endurance and perseverance rose to new heights among the Irish soldiery during even the greatest defeats of the revolutionary struggle. Such well-known Irish characteristics played a key role in keeping such large and disproportionate numbers of these hardy Green Isle fighting men steadfast in Washington's ranks year after year and during its most severe trials: the same resilient characteristics and cultural glue that had long kept the Celtic-Gaelic people together and persevering as a distinctive culture, despite all manner of severe adversity and difficulties, including English conquest and oppression.

Consequently, the seemingly irrepressible spirits among these lowly Irish soldiers remained surprisingly high, thanks partly to a distinctive Gaelic sense of humor, a powerful faith in God, a well-honed cultural resiliency, a sense of determination, and an optimistic faith that all obstacles could be overcome in the end. In fact, the greater the hardship, then the greater the humor and determination among the Irish soldiers to persevere and succeed in the end: part of the well-honed art of simple survival for generations in Ireland and then transferred to America. Such distinctive Celtic-Gaelic qualities helped the common Irish soldier in the Continental ranks to serve year after year and keep the faith in a better day in the future, despite so many sharp reversals and cruel twists of fate.[144]

In New England, the ever-analytical French officer and nobleman, the observant Marquis de Chastellux, understood this forgotten secret of Irish success (both in regard to settlement and to serving in Washington's Army) on American soil. He observed upon getting to know the "Irishman [was] translated to America [and how] he is more gay than the Americans [of British descent], and even to irony," which was a principal ingredient of an especially sharp Irish humor.[145]

The vast majority of non-Irish American soldiers had deserted Washington's Army by the fall of 1776, before his surprise attack on Trenton, because it appeared that the British and their Hessian allies had already won the war. This was an unpleasant reality for generations of American historians because this "foreigner" demographic so sharply contradicted the comfortable myth that heroic Anglo-Saxon soldier of British descent were the ones who primarily sustained America's resistance effort, including in Washington's Army.

The resistance effort among the Anglo-Saxon populace across the colonies, including the Continental Army, was all but over by the early winter of 1776. Not only Washington's Army but also the Revolution seemingly had been all but crushed just before Christmas 1776, after strategic New York City's capture, Forts Washington and Lee's captures, and the Continental Army's long withdrawal across New Jersey all the way to the Delaware River—the last natural obstacle lying before the panicked capital (Philadelphia) of America—to eastern Pennsylvania. As revealed in the diary of Captain Thomas Rodney, who was the brother of Declaration of Independence signer Caesar Rodney and whose Delaware Continental Regiment, commanded by Ireland-born Colonel John Haslet, contained a good many reliable Irish officers and noncommissioned officers, the defeatist Continental Congress prepared to not only evacuate Philadelphia, but also to authorize Washington to ask the British for surrender terms by mid-December 1776.[146] But determined men like Colonel John Fitzgerald, born in County Wexford, Ireland, described by one woman as "an agreeable, broad-shouldered Irishman," who greatly assisted Washington as a staff member, were determined never to cease fighting against the invaders of America.[147]

Unlike so many non-Irish soldiers (in part because their lives had faced much less adversity and hardship, especially as a people subjugated by a powerful neighbor), large numbers of Irish remained steadfast in the revolution's darkest days. And reflecting the multitudes of Celt-ic-Gaelic soldiers who early filled the Continental Army's enlisted ranks, Washington's regimental and brigade commanders likewise contained a disproportionate number of Irish and Scotch-Irish officers of outstand-ing leadership abilities. Like no other ethnic group in America, these Celtic-Gaelic fighting men, both officers and enlisted men, remained generally more resilient, in higher spirits, and stood more steadfastly in the depleted ranks of both armies and partisan bands.[148] No wonder that Ambrose Serle was astounded by the sight of the "vast numbers of Irish" in Washington's ranks when the prisoners were herded together after Fort Washington's surrender in mid-November 1776.[149]

Thanks to the rise of a new patriotism, many young revolutionary soldiers, mostly sons and grandsons of Irish immigrant parents, naturally looked proudly upon their newly acquired status as Americans by 1775, when they enlisted. Pride in a new republic caused some image-conscious soldiers who enlisted in America's armies to write down their nativity as "America" or the United States, and not Ireland. Therefore, a large number of these "new" Americans have been long considered non-Irish by histo-rians who were naturally unable to decipher this widespread subterfuge. Additionally, as if to enhance chances for promotion and upward social mobility, many Irish were determined to distance themselves from lowly roots as tenant farmers (especially the derogatory European term of "peas-ants") from the Atlantic's other side, a "foreign" Celtic-Gaelic identity, and even the older generation of their immigrant parents and grandparents. But in the case of the majority of Revolutionary War records, especially army muster rolls and rosters, no places of origin, birthplace, or nativity were ever included, which also fostered the erroneous perception among so many historians of a much lower level of Irish participation.

In addition, many Irish immigrants, including the family of Robert Treat Paine (O'Neill), who was a Declaration of Independence signer, had already changed their Gaelic last names to Anglo-Saxon ones: a smart tactic to avoid discrimination and to enhance their future prospects in a British-dominated world in Ireland and in America. The distinctive Celtic prefixes of "O" and "Mac" were early eliminated. Such was the case of Irish Catholic Declaration of Independence signer Charles Carroll (O'Carroll) of Maryland. This same process of eliminating distinctive Irish names and Celtic-Gaelic identities occurred when so many indentured Irish Catholics and Scotch-Irish fled their masters. They hoped to escape capture by wiping out their former Celtic-Gaelic identities and any traces of their Irishness, which meant changing their names and losing their Irish brogues as much as possible.

The Robert McChesney family, from the Scotch-Irish community of Dunclug, Northern Ireland, consisted of ten members who migrated from the town of Larne (a former Viking settlement and a port that competed with Belfast), County Antrim, Ulster Province, to Charleston, South Carolina, in 1772. The McChesney family lost an eight-month-old baby to smallpox on the sailing ship during the fifty-two-day journey across the turbulent Atlantic. When they landed at Charleston harbor, this Ulster family immediately changed its name to Chesney, dropping the "Mc."[150] Of course, this situation was not the case of the nearly sixty Irish and Scotch-Irish patriots by the name of "Mc" who fought at Kings Mountain.[151]

This deliberate, widespread obscuring of Irish roots began long ago in Ireland in order to force assimilation into a harsh anti-Catholic society of conquerors. "With a politic cruelty, the English of the Pale passed an Act compelling every Irishman within English jurisdiction [around the seat of British power in Dublin] 'shall take to him an English sir name of one town, as Sutton, Chester, Trym, Skyrne, Corke, Kinsale; or colour, as White, Blacke, Browne; or art of science, as Smith, or Carpenter; or office, as Cook, Butler'."[152]

With understandable bitterness about losing even ancestral Celtic-Gaelic family names (like their ancestral lands) to autocratic English dictates, Irishman Douglas Hyde described how "all our Irish names of places and people turned into English names; the Irish language [Gaelic] completely extinct; the O's and the Macs dropped."[153]

Like the Irish, Scottish immigrants migrating to America's shores also changed their names for the same reasons as the Irish: to enhance prospects of success in a new land. Scotland-born Daniel Forbush transformed his last name to Forbes to disguise his Celtic roots. A die-hard American patriot from beginning to end like so many Irish and Scotch-Irish across the thirteen colonies, this resourceful Celtic patriot served on a revolutionary committee of correspondence in Westborough, Massachusetts, an agrarian community established in 1717 amid the pastoral, rolling countryside just west of Boston.[154]

But the vast majority of Celtic-Gaelic people proudly kept their names, refusing to relinquish any of their distinctive Irishness. A McPherson patriot in the South Carolina Low Country was one such individual. In the words of a Tory officer, Anthony Allaire, while marching with an invasion force through a hostile country-side: "Remained at McPherson's plantation . . . the Mr. McPherson being a great Rebel and a man of vast property [now] at present in Charleston."[155] And when the young Loyalist officer entered a small Scotch-Irish (and naturally very hostile) community, where members of the fierce McDowell clan resided, he penned with utter amaze-ment: "This settlement is composed of the most violent Rebels I ever saw, particularly the young ladies."[156] Clearly, among the Scotch-Irish, patriotism was hardly the domain of the male gender because Irish women also made contributions and sacrifices to the cause of liberty.

However, because of their "rush to become Americans," large numbers of Irish themselves thereby contributed to their own lost Celtic-Gaelic revolutionary legacy and later-day obscurity by relin-quishing their distinctive ethnic identifiers not only before and during the revolution but also after the war. Irish people across Amer-ica continued to perpetuate the rich oral Celtic-Gaelic traditions of old Ireland so far away, ensuring that they "have not always provided either a written or an accurate record of their long and fascinating role in American history," and especially in regard to their 1775–1783 wartime contributions.[157] Storytelling about the past, including ancient and Irish revolutionary history, was a deeply ingrained part of a vibrant Celtic-Gaelic culture that was transferred from Ireland to America, where it continued to thrive for generations.[158]

Historian Thomas H. O'Connor, with his insightful understanding of Irish culture and folkways, explained this unique development among the Irish people, whose vibrant Celtic-Gaelic culture was dominated by a lively oral tradition that had thrived for centuries:

> Nor did the Irish [in America] adopt the custom of confiding their innermost thoughts, their personal experiences, the stories of their families, or the events of their neighborhoods to the pages of a diary or a memoir[.] They seldom encouraged their children to adopt the practice of record keeping so that family histories could be traced from one generation to another[.] Then, too, there seems to have been a strong element of humility or self-abnegation in the typical Irish-Catholic [and Irish Protestant] upbringing that discouraged individuals from feeling that they were important enough to record their own stories [and as members mostly of the lower class]. They harbored the conviction that they were not good enough, important enough, deserving enough, influential enough to be considered part of real history.[159]

Chapter III

Complexities of Ethnicity and
Forgotten History

In overall historical terms, and besides the discovery of new documentation, the recent emergence of a slightly greater appreciation for Irish contributions has partly developed because modern historians recently have begun to more thoughtfully examine the role of ethnic and racial minorities in American history. The stories of the Buffalo Soldiers of the post-Civil War period and the Tuskegee Airmen of the Second World War have provided the most recent examples of the belated recognition of contributions of African-Americans that first began in the 1960s and 1970s. This recent focus has revealed greater black participation in the American Revolution—more than five thousand who served the patriot cause—especially in the Continental Army than previously recognized by historians. But, of course, the Celtic-Gaelic participation greatly dwarfed this black contribution by an excessively wide margin.[1] It was most of all "[General Henry] Knox's artillery, [General Anthony] Wayne's bayonets, and [Colonel Daniel] Morgan's rifles, all Irish, [who] wrote the history of the battle of Monmouth," during the longest-fought and last important engagement in Washington's theater of operations.[2]

Known for his hard-hitting ways that garnered a general's rank for him in early 1777, Anthony Wayne, the son of an Irish immigrant and only in his early thirties, commanded the mostly Scotch-Irish and Irish soldiers of these three above-mentioned commands. He led two crack Continental Pennsylvania infantry brigades (of the Continental

Line) with distinction—the famed Line of Ireland. The men of Wayne's Pennsylvania brigade consisted largely of "Scots-Irish Pennsylvanians who spoke with the brogue and burr of Northern Ireland."[3] However, these elite Celtic-Gaelic soldiers looked nothing like the best fighting troops of Washington's Army. As Wayne lamented in a report to the Pennsylvania Board of War about the ragged condition of the tried veterans of the First Pennsylvania Continental Infantry on June 3, 1777, "they never Rec'd any Uniform except hunting Shirts which are worn out—and Altho a body of fine men—yet from being in rags and badly armed—they are viewed with Contempt by the Other Troops," who displayed a measure of anti-Irish sentiment.[4]

Because they represented the lowest rung in colonial society, just below the Irish, African-American soldiers faced greater contempt from their white comrades-in-arms. At Valley Forge, even a relatively small number of soldiers of African descent in the ranks was rather significant because of Washington's Army's overall diminutive size at this time. By the time the Continental Army departed Valley Forge with the end of the winter of 1777–1778, a full 10 percent of Washington's total manpower was African-American.[5]

By comparison, the Irish and Scotch-Irish contribution was at least several times greater in overall percentage terms at the time of the Battle of Trenton and at Valley Forge during these crucial periods. Most importantly by comparative reasons, the Irish and Scotch-Irish commanders were among General Washington's top lieutenants, unlike the African-Americans who served exclusively as common soldiers with ranks no higher than private.[6]

In the opening lines of his introduction of *Washington's Secret War*, Fleming candidly made a rather startling admission: "After forty years of reading and writing about the American past . . . I already knew more than a little about Valley Forge [and in writing the book] I looked forward on reporting on recent research [about] the ethnic composition of Washington's army."[7] Clearly, even for one of America's leading Revolutionary War historians, only in the twenty-first century's first decade has the "ethnic composition" of Washington's Army become a revelation. James Webb concluded, "Estimates vary, but it is undeniable that the Scots-Irish comprised at least one-third and as many as one-half of the 'rebel' soldiers during the Revolutionary War."[8] And another historian gave a measure of belated recognition to the disproportionate Irish contribution from the middle colonies, or states, especially Pennsylvania. He wrote how the "middle states contributed nearly half of the total force of the main Continental army [under Washington] in 1777 and 1778 [and] The Irish presence [was] around 45 percent of their entire strength."[9]

Most importantly, these realities were fully realized by British military and government leaders (like their American counterparts at the time) throughout the American Revolution. A shocked Ambrose Serle, Admiral Richard Howe's secretary, revealed in a September 25, 1776 report to the Earl of Dartmouth, Secretary of State: "Great Numbers of Emigrants, particularly Irish, are in the Rebel Army."[10] The timing of Serle's report was most revealing: written less than a month after Washington's ragtag army suffered their most grievous loss to date at the disastrous Battle of Long Island on August 27, 1776, which was the largest engagement in North American history up to that time. Thereafter, America's military fortunes continued to plummet to their lowest point in the early winter of 1776 before Washington's victory at Trenton. An epidemic of mass desertions had dramatically reduced Washington's Army to little more than a skeleton force, but large numbers of Irish and Scotch-Irish (an estimated 40 percent) remained in the ranks, despite what many less staunch Americans believed was the revolution's end.[11]

Naturally the vital contributions made by the Irish were more widely understood by those men who were much closer in time to the struggle for liberty than later-day Americans, partly because of pervasive anti-Irish, anti-immigrant, and anti-Catholic sentiment that only increased in the nineteenth century, due to the antebellum period's Nativist Movement, and even well into the early twentieth century. Popular acceptance (thanks partly to the popular press and journalists of Irish descent) of the Irish revolutionary role was often expressed in America's major newspapers, such as the *Washington Post* and the *New York Times* toward the nineteenth century's end and at the twentieth century's dawn. A *Chicago Tribute* article, reprinted in the *Washington Post*, from a respected historian emphasized how "the Irish formed sixth or seventh of the whole population, and one-fourth of all the commissioned officers in the army and navy were of Irish descent [and] The first general officer [Major General Richard Montgomery] killed in battle, the first officer of artillery [Colonel Henry Knox] appointed, the first commodore [John Barry] commissioned, the first victor to whom the British flag was struck at sea, and the first officer who surprised a fort by land were Irishmen."[12]

During the Civil War of 1861–1865, the heroic example of the Ireland-born Major General Richard Montgomery, who died in the storming of Quebec, was embraced by a new generation of Irish in America. The memory of the martyred Montgomery inspired large numbers of blue-clad Irish soldiers, who answered the call of "Come, my country, in the name of Richard Montgomery, who died to assert the liberty, and in the name of Andrew Jackson [a South Carolina partisan of Scotch-Irish immigrant parents]" to fight for the Union.[13] Mystified journalists of America's major newspapers, especially writers in the nation's capital, theorized as to why such an important Irish story of the American Revolution had been long overlooked and forgotten. In an August 31, 1902, article from the pages of the prestigious *Washington Post*, one history-minded editor mused about this vital missing chapter in America's creation story that seemed to defy all explanation: "It may be partly owing to the fact that Ireland does not figure on the list of independent nations that there appears a tendency to forget or ignore the aid given by men of Irish birth or Irish parentage in the War of the Revolution."[14]

While the young Marquis de Lafayette, a well-educated French nobleman inspired by the republican faith, early journeyed from

France to assist America's struggle for liberty and worked closely beside Washington to make the great dream of America come true, the Catholic nation of Poland looked with great pride upon Polish patriot Thaddeus Kosciuszko, who served with distinction in America's struggle. Meanwhile, on American soil, Prussia and its rich military traditions of Frederick the Great were represented in splendid fashion by Prussian Lieutenant General Baron Friedrich Wilhelm von Stuben. He established a formalized system of drill for the American army, improving the capabilities of Washington's Continental Army by the opening of the 1778 Campaign. Ireland dispatched no such comparable high-ranking representative of high visibility to America because none existed among a conquered people at the time.[15]

A somewhat perplexed James Webb wrestled with this vexing problem of why the Irish role in America's struggle for existence had been forgotten for so long, especially after he concluded that these Celtic-Gaelic warriors made up 40 percent of Washington's Army: the percentage earlier ascertained by historian Owen B. Hunt in regard to the vital Irish contribution at the all-important Battle of Trenton that brought new life to America's struggle. Explaining the glaring absence of the Scotch-Irish role, this graduate of the United States Naval Academy at Annapolis, Maryland, lamented the striking paradox of how the Scotch-Irish contributions were all-important, "yet the story has been lost under the weight of more recent immigrations, revisionist historians, and common ignorance."[16]

Even one of the most astute nineteenth-century observers of the American experience, French aristocrat Alexis De Tocqueville, in his 1835 classic *Democracy in America*, was guilty of completely overlooking the importance of the Irish contribution. He incorrectly concluded in regard to pre-revolutionary America that "All the immigrants spoke the same language and were children of the same people."[17] Like America's upper-class elites living on the East Coast, the Paris-born De Tocqueville, a sophisticated and highly educated member of the aristocratic Norman upper class, was thoroughly out of touch with the personal experiences of the lowest classes in America, especially on the western frontier. For such reasons, De Tocqueville, whose family hailed from a sprawling estate near the English Channel, revealed his lack of understanding of the complexities of the overall Irish experience by writing, "But all the immigrants who came to settle on the shores of New England belonged to the well-to-do classes at home."[18]

Instead of the traditional middle-class stereotype of the Anglo-Saxon yeoman revolutionary, the vast majority of common soldiers of Washington's Continental Army, and other American armies, were members of the poorest classes of colonial society, including large numbers of landless immigrants, especially as the war lengthened. This sizeable contingent of fighting men was dominated by tenant farmers, indentured servants, common laborers, and western frontiersmen, who were mostly of Celtic-Gaelic origin. No group of Americans of this lowly stratum more thoroughly filled Washington's Army than the Irish and the Scotch-Irish, especially recent immigrants. The keen focus of recruiting and relying heavily upon lower-class soldiers continued not only a British Army practice but also that of Virginia and Washington, in regard to his own Virginia Regiment during the French and Indian War.

Such was especially the case in regard to volunteers from the western frontier, which was dominated by Irish and Scotch-Irish settlers who had been forced to push farther west to carve out a new life for themselves far away from those of British descent, who discriminated against them. On the western Maryland frontier of more than one hundred recruits raised for the Continental Army, none were landowners. For the vast majority of the Irish and Scotch-Irish, the revolutionary struggle was very much a rich man's war and a poor man's fight.

While most of the Founding Fathers, especially those from the aristocratic upper crust of Virginia, came from a highly structured hierarchical colonial society that looked most unfavorably on the Celtic-Gaelic people, most Irish and Scotch-Irish inhabited an entirely different world. They hailed from the untamed western frontier and, of course, rural Ireland, and were of a lowly social and economic status, and a distinctive ethnic background: a situation that represented an extensive gulf of differences, wide cultural disparity, and an inequitable situation on American soil not unlike in Ireland. Indeed, across the breadth of colonial America, most Irish Catholics (discriminated against for religious reasons in a Protestant-dominated America) were members of the servant, or indentured, class.

During the seventeenth and eighteenth centuries, the vast majority of Irish Catholics had migrated across the Atlantic as indentured servants, like a large percentage of Scotch-Irish. For them, life in America began in this binding form of semi-slavery, an ugly cross between apprenticeship and the world's harshest labor system. Indentured servitude was fueled by a lucrative trade that included English slave dealers, who even dealt in stolen Irish children for profit. Coming to America as an indentured servant meant working for seven years without pay to reimburse the conveniently inflated costs of transportation across the Atlantic. Ireland had long served as the greatest indentured servant market in the world. Two typical Irish indentured servants (or redemptioners) of the colonial period were John Sullivan, of Limerick, and feisty Margery Browne. Known for her defiant ways, Margery hailed from Cork, the largest port in southern Ireland. After his term of indenture ended, John purchased Margery's freedom. Along with four brothers who fought in the Revolutionary War, Sullivan was destined to become one of Washington's hard-fighting generals regardless of the odds, seemingly always rising to the challenge.

For the same reasons that explained why they had first departed their native Green Isle to escape mind-numbing poverty and abusive English and Anglo-Irish landlords who supervised a feudal land of misery, thousands of Irish and Scotch-Irish likewise fled from the "ugly, class-based system" of the large Tidewater plantations along the East Coast. Here, these lowly common laborers were subjugated to the dictatorial whims of "masters" and colonial government leaders of the Eastern Seaboard, a lengthy belt of oppression stretching from Maryland to Georgia. Large numbers of white indentured servants became runaway fugitives from the expansive Virginia and Maryland tobacco plantations and South Carolina rice plantations of the Tidewater. After escaping their tormentors, the Celtic-Gaelic people then headed west to live as free men and women in the wilds beyond civilization and far from the East Coast.

Lowly immigrant Irishmen, especially the Catholics who were generally less better off than the Scotch-Irish, were naturally as staunchly (to say the least) anti-aristocracy and egalitarian-minded in America as in Ireland, as if not separated by the Atlantic's waters. After all, they occupied the lowest rungs of society, laboring as either indentured servants, or tenant farmers of large landowners as back in Ireland, or common laborers in the sun-baked tobacco and rice fields beside gangs of black slaves on the large landholdings of the Southern aristocratic elite. Of course, this oppressive situation as redemptioners was a contrarian experience for the Scotch-Irish, who had enjoyed a relative measure of autonomy compared to Irish Catholics in Northern Ireland as small tenant farmers. In keeping with their disadvantageous circumstances, some lowly Irish indentures were given nothing to wear but "Negro" clothing, including during winter.

After attempting to escape a dismal feudal existence as peasants in Ireland, many Irish found themselves little more than white slaves in America. To protect their hefty investments in black slaves, wealthy landowners across the South possessed a self-serving tendency to severely overwork Irish and Scotch-Irish indentured servants. Because these indentured servants would be free after their term of indentured had expired, wealthy landowners often exploited this advantage to the fullest and gave black slaves lighter workloads. As in Ireland, therefore, the worst abuse of indentured servants involved the exploitation by Protestant landowners of Irish Catholics, who suffered the same inequitable situation as in Ireland. While the upper-class elites, including the Founding Fathers, were conservative, moderate revolutionaries who possessed a vested interest in maintaining entrenched institutions such as slavery, the system of indentured servitude, and upper-class status and rule, and were less inclined to embrace the most sweeping egalitarian concepts, the lowly Irish and Scotch-Irish were exactly the opposite in sentiment even before they reached America's shores.

Before the American Revolution, the aristocratic ruling elite of Virginia's revolutionary generation, including Washington and Jefferson, hailed from distinguished families solidly entrenched in the European, or British, aristocratic tradition of the ruling class, which was the very antithesis of the Irish experience. The colonial ruling class was fundamentally royalist in politics, conservative by instinct and inclination, Anglican in religion, and passionate believers in the natural God-given right of the upper crust to rule the land and the lower-class masses of less educated common laborers, tenants, indentured servants, immigrants, small farmers, and the landless. During the colonial period, Virginia's leaders created their own idealized hierarchical world of an elitist "Cavalier Utopia" on the British aristocratic model. This modern utopia was based not on the concept of equality but primarily on the premise of large numbers of lowly Irish indentured servants (former peasants) working the vast lands of the wealthy like slaves.

Inspired by a sense of righteousness bolstered by their respective Presbyterian and Catholic faiths that had convinced them that God was on their side (a belief only confirmed when vengeful British and Loyalist officers burned down Presbyterian Churches of the Scotch-Irish, especially in South Carolina) were America's most common lowest-ranked people, who fought for a far more radical change in colonial society than the higher-class peers of English ancestry. Also explaining the continued course of egalitarian developments before and during the American Revolution, the mostly Ulster Irish, but also many Irish Catholics, served as the most radical and revolutionary members of American society for generations.

These freedom-loving Celtic-Gaelic people from Northern Ireland were described as "God-provoking Democrats" second to none in all America. Significantly for the American Republic, the Scotch-Irish and Irish of the revolutionary generation continued to perpetuate their egalitarian feelings, sentiments, and utopian visions long after the Revolution's end.[19]

John Randolph, a privileged member of the Virginia planter elite, expressed the common views of most Founding Fathers that sharply contradicted with the deeply entrenched, natural radicalism of the Irish and Scotch-Irish, especially among the lowest classes: "I am an aristocrat, I love liberty, I hate equality." Randolph's elitist views made him a natural lifelong enemy of Celtic-Gaelic people in America and Ireland. After all, these same upper-class, aristocratic types had denied the Irish equality and freedom on the Emerald Isle for hundreds of years. And in much the same way, even middle-class members across America also continued to look down upon with contempt upon the lowly Irish, especially immigrants and indentured servants, on American soil.[20] As written in an April 1776 letter to Joseph Reed barely three months before the Declaration of Independence's signing in the "City of Brotherly Love," Washington was correct in his disgust about the Virginia elite's conservatism. Like the lowly Irish and Scotch-Irish people across America, he deplored Virginia's conservative and wealthy elites because of their "steady Attachment heretofore to Royalty, will come reluctantly into the Idea of Independency."[21]

More than any other people in the thirteen colonies, consequently, the transplanted Irish became the most natural, instinctive opponents of either the ruling British in London or the colonial elite, such as Virginians Randolph and Jefferson, long before they ever saw America's seemingly endless bounty. During their lengthy passages across the Atlantic, some Irish indentured servants plotted in an exquisitely spoken traditional Gaelic to overthrow the ship and kill all the English onboard, continuing the anti-British agitation of the Green Isle. In attempting to overturn the abusive social order, revolutionary Irish workers united with slaves in a daring attempt to burn down Savannah, Georgia, in 1738. And during the Stono Rebellion in coastal South Carolina just outside Charleston the following year, exploited Irish indentured servants joined the black rebels because of their comparable lower-class grievances against the ruling class and the aristocratic elite.

Clearly, the upper-class colonial elite possessed good reason to keep the lowest orders of the Irish repressed because they represented a serious potential threat to the existing social order. When Royal Governor Lord John Murray Dunmore issued his November 1775 proclamation for martial law and for Virginia's slaves to rise up against their masters, he also appealed for support from the colony's "indentured Servants," who were mostly Irish and Scotch-Irish, to exploit their abused plights. Joseph Wilson, of Irish heritage, escaped indenture at Washington's Mount Vernon and joined Dunmore. Fortunately for America's fortunes, the Celtic-Gaelic people, including indentured servants, were wholeheartedly patriots by this time when Americans were badly divided. Therefore, Dunmore's ambitions were thwarted and he was soon forced from Virginia.

But such longtime Irish radicalism that played a key role in paving the way to open revolution and independence have been obscured because of the intense focus on the Founding Fathers. America's most ordinary people, especially the Irish and Scotch-Irish of the Mecklenburg Declaration of Independence (with signers by the name of McClure, Alexander, Polk, Barry, and Kennan) of May 1775, were destined to see their wealthy, more conservative non-Irish aristocratic leaders (such as Jefferson, whose final, edited version of the Declaration of Independence was less radically Presbyterian and Irish-influenced than originally intended, Benjamin Franklin, and John Adams) hijack a common people's revolution (fundamentally Celtic-Gaelic) by making it less radical. Many of Jefferson's egalitarian and republican sentiments had been earlier articulated by Scotch-Irish Enlightenment thinker Francis Hutchenson.

In the end, the Founding Fathers and the powerful elite along the East Coast not only preserved but also strengthened the institution of slavery and maintained a traditional upper-class rule over their alleged inferiors. The Founding Fathers' personal views about the natural right of upper-class rule and class-based superiority were eerily comparable to the traditional conservative views held by the British and the Loyalist elites. Even Benjamin Franklin was horrified by the news of the people's uprising known as the Boston Tea Party, condemning it as "an act of violent injustice on our part."[22] By the time of the Revolution, Franklin, who demonstrated elitist proclivities that were entirely in keeping with his lofty station in life, was shocked by the undeniable "fact that the Irish emigrants and their children are now in possession of the [revolutionary] government of Pennsylvania by their majority in the Assembly, as well as of the great part of the territory" of Pennsylvania.[23] And the same situation developed in Virginia, where the small landowners and yeomen farmers had all but propelled the elite and conservative upper-class gentry, who always feared the so-called "mob" and feared what might happen with the bestowing of greater freedoms to the common people, to ultimately embrace the urgent necessity of declaring for independence as the only solution.[24]

John Adair was just the kind of average young and lowly Irish immigrant who was feared by the ruling elite in part because he was among society's rootless and liberty-loving rovers who simply kept moving westward in search of greater opportunity and more fertile lands. Adair was born in County Antrim on the northeastern corner of Ulster Province, Northern Ireland, in 1754. John's father brought the family to the port of Baltimore when he was only a teenager. Spending less than a year on Maryland soil, the Adair family then moved farther west to Pennsylvania. They then journeyed over the mountains and settled in what eventually became Sullivan County in east Tennessee. The movements of the Adair family provide an excellent example of how a good many Irish immigrants on America soil remained very much rootless individuals without long-term stability for extended periods of time. Father and son joined the local militia to protect their frontier community in the Holston River area, embarking on preemptive strikes against the troublesome Cherokee—British allies who opened a dangerous second front in the west in the summer of 1776. Therefore, by the time that John Adair joined his fellow frontiersmen on yet another preemptive strike against another growing threat, which resulted in the October 1780 victory at Kings Mountain, he was well aware of the wisdom of the frontier axiom that the best defense was an aggressive offensive[25]

Silencing of a Distinguished Past and Frontier Survival

In 1908, a decade after the Spanish-American War's conclusion, historian John Haltigan was concerned about how thoroughly the significant Irish revolutionary role had been forgotten by America. He lamented how although "We are assured on the authority of General [Charles] Lee that fully half the Continental army was derived from Ireland, yet we find no mention of that and other equally important facts in our school histories of the United States."[26] By the 1920s, the much-maligned Irish in America attempted to counter dominant anti-Irish prejudices (both regional and national) of America's leading historians, who mirrored society's prevalent views by overlooking Irish revolutionary contributions with monotonous regularity. Mostly Protestant northeasterners of the privileged Ivy League establishment that was decidedly anti-Irish as part of their upper-class birthright, some respected historians even went so far as to make repeated "statements derogatory to the part played by the Irish race in Ireland and America during the War of the Revolution" to additionally distort the historical record beyond simple omission.[27]

As if continuing the same xenophobic, anti-Irish biases of the Nativist Americans (the Know-Nothings) during the intolerant nineteenth century, leading American historians throughout the early twentieth century exhibited in their writings varying levels (mostly high) of anti-Catholic, anti-immigrant, and anti-Irish sentiment. And this development manifested itself most thoroughly by completely overlooking or minimizing Irish and Scotch-Irish contributions in the American Revolution to continue a great silencing to ensure a legacy of general obscurity in the historical record.[28]

By denying the Irish well-deserved recognition for their widespread contributions in the republic's birth and struggle for life, consequently, the Irish seemed to generations of Americans of British descent as entirely undeserving of true equality based upon the false premise that they had not fought and sacrificed for their adopted country like non-Irish Americans. Such gross distortions were made entirely plausible by a thorough silencing of Irish past contributions to America's creation, especially during the American Revolution, allowing an opportunity for the rise of even greater anti-Irish prejudice and discrimination well into the twentieth century.

Unfortunately, the greatest omissions and distortions in America's historical record have long obscured the contributions of minorities, especially African-Americans. Colonel Teddy Roosevelt and his mostly blue-blood Rough Riders—amateurs at war and overly publicized "heroes" created largely by the influential northeastern press—won everlasting fame for capturing San Juan Hill, just outside Santiago de Cuba, in early July 1898. This alleged achievement was largely due to falsehoods generated by the influential eastern press. In truth, black regular infantry troops (hardened veterans from the West) actually accomplished this much-heralded tactical feat. Roosevelt and his white troopers had in fact only captured the more lightly defended Kettle Hill, not the main Spanish defensive position at San Juan Hill. While Roosevelt's rise to the presidency stemmed from the gross inflation of his military record in Cuba, "most of the battlefield accounts published in the weeks after the action ignored the deeds of the black troops in Cuba, and generally cast them in a support role."[29]

Of course, the greatest distortions of the historical record have been fostered by the modern media, especially Hollywood, in regard to the American Indian. In the 1965 words of novelist John Oliver Killens, who denounced American historians' excessive distortions of history, "Thanks particularly to Hollywood, it has already blamed the American Indians and made heroes of the men who practiced genocide against them."[30] The Puritans, early English colonists who were members of a theocracy, of New England were the first to unleash no less than genocide against the native peoples by wiping out the Pequot tribe, not only warriors but also women and children. Irish historian Fintan O'Toole correctly concluded that the "native Irish [Catholics] were treated much as the original settlers of New England treated the Indians."[31]

Another fundamental reason why the Revolutionary War roles of the Irish and Scotch-Irish were forgotten was because the majority of the Celtic-Gaelic people, especially the Scotch-Irish, lived in general obscurity on the remote western frontier. Of course, the taking of Indian lands led to open warfare long before the revolution, providing valuable military experience, training, and preparation for Revolutionary War challenges. Punitive expeditions led by daring Irish and Scotch-Irish frontier commanders, who adapted to a prevailing war of extermination patterns to ensure the survival of their isolated frontier communities, struck back with a vengeance. During a brutal war of survival of the fittest amid the pristine wilderness, they often embraced a no-quarter policy like the English (in Ireland) and the Indians. Native Americans had long struck their isolated homes and vulnerable frontier communities after the Celtic-Gaelic men marched off to fight as early as the French and Indian War or departed on lengthy hunting expeditions far from home. Before defeating Major Ferguson's Tories at Kings Mountain, the "over mountain men" had taken the war to the Cherokee in 1776, paying them back for the bloody raids from southern Virginia to northern Georgia (the sprawling Scotch-Irish and Irish borderland and frontier), thanks to tons of British powder delivered into the Indians' hands by the Crown.

Likewise, to the north, the powerful Iroquois Confederacy was similarly smashed by the July–September 1779 expedition led by Ireland-born General John Sullivan. The British were relying more on the Iroquois to play a larger role in the war (which had shifted to the Southern theater) in the north, and they devastated the western frontier of Pennsylvania in 1778 in consequence. Dispatched by Washington, who promised the "total destruction" of Indian villages, Sullivan followed his commander's orders to the letter. Known for his meticulousness and strict adherence to orders, Sullivan demonstrated that Washington had picked the right man for the job. Unfortunately, driving the Indians off their ancestral land by any means possible out of necessity has bestowed a dark historical legacy upon the frontier Celtic-Gaelic people in today's politically correct era, staining their overall image and making them evil incarnate.[32]

In his controversial book *A Little Matter of Genocide*, Ward Churchill described how in 1763 young "Scotch-Irish immigrants called the 'Paxton Boys' vented their rage over" a band of Conestoga Indians, who were under Quaker protection, resulting in the murder of an allegedly peaceful group of Indians. Unfortunately, he omitted the fact that a good many Scotch-Irish families had been wiped out by Indian raiders during the French and Indian War and Pontiac's uprising, which ravished the western frontier.

These angry Celtic-Gaelic frontiersmen suspected or possessed direct evidence that the Conestoga Indians had played a supportive role in the hard-hitting Indian attacks. They also felt quite correctly that the Pennsylvania Assembly, which was dominated by eastern, upper-class elites and was the Quaker-based government of Philadelphia (where a large community of Irish Quaker merchants had first settled before the Irish mercantile class grew to dominate the city's commerce), was more concerned about protecting these Christian Indians than the Scotch-Irish and Irish settlers on the distant western frontier.[33] Therefore, these mostly Scotch-Irish western frontiersmen, with tomahawks in belts, wearing moccasins, and carrying Long Rifles, marched on Philadelphia to redress the wrongs. Clearly, the wealthy upper class of Philadelphia was fully content to have the Celtic-Gaelic people slaughtered on the western frontier to keep the Indians far from Philadelphia's streets. A last-minute negotiation prevented the descent of the enraged Irishmen into Philadelphia, where "the burghers had remained within an insulating urban cocoon, out of harm's way—indentured servants [largely Irish and Scotch-Irish] and others recruited [in the Philadelphia militia] to fight were notable exceptions."[34]

What has been most overlooked was the fact that the so-called "Paxton Boys" (as we know them today) were actually then known as the "Hickory Boys," which revealed distinct revolutionary and political Irish antecedents from the Atlantic's east side. Before the American Revolution, the "Oak Boys" were among the foremost groups of Irish peasants who unleashed a wave of revolutionary agitation and open violence in Ireland against the excessive taxes and ever-rising rents of the wealthy landlords before the Irish migrated to America.[35] Historian Ray Raphael correctly concluded that "By instilling fear and threatening the established order, the Paxton Boys foreshadowed the Revolutionary protest movements of the following decades [and] There is another significant parallel between the march of the Paxton Boys and the American Revolution: control of the American interior was at issue in both instances."[36]

However, instead of the "Paxton Boys" being viewed in the context of Irish revolutionary agitation that played a role in leading the way to revolution and independence, a long-existing negative stereotype of the Celtic-Gaelic people on the frontier was reinforced. Indeed, in the popular imagination, "What matters is that the Irishman, in his slaughter of the Indians, has become himself a savage," in Fintan O'Toole's analysis.[37] Therefore, the Irishman on the western frontier has been long seen as the greatest Indian hater who was bent on genocide for little more than the love of killing. During his campaign against the Iroquois Confederacy, General John Sullivan shattered these simplistic stereotypes. He destroyed Indian villages but not Indian people, especially women and children, who were spared, maintaining "the moral high ground" in this regard.[38]

These long-suffering Irish of the backcountry (generally the region beginning around fifty miles from the East Coast and stretching to the Appalachians and beyond in the case of the Holston River country settlers in today's east Tennessee) feared that the Quakers were "acting in collusion" with the Indians, leading to massacres of the vulnerable Celtic-Gaelic people on the remote frontier.[39] But in truth, the Irish and Scotch-Irish of the western frontier were not waging war on strictly racial terms as long generally assumed. Showing no mercy to the Cherokee was duplicated in often showing no mercy to Tories, especially in the South, because what the Celtic-Gaelic warrior on America's untamed frontier waged so fiercely was most of all a war against America's enemies. If they failed to kill their enemy, then they themselves and their families would be killed; color and race made relatively little difference in such brutal struggles for survival. During the American Revolution, the only difference was that leading Loyalists were hanged while Indians were killed with tomahawks, knives, musket butts, and Long Rifles.[40]

If the Irish fighting man deserved to be denounced as a savage, as so often emphasized by the British, then it was in regard to superior combativeness and fighting prowess once unleashed, especially if driven by desires for vengeance. Irishman Thomas Brandon, who joined in the victory cheers that echoed over the top of Kings Mountain, was part of the "Scotch-Irish colony in Union county, South Carolina." Here, he lived with his Scotch-Irish wife, Elizabeth McCool, before the war's horrors descended upon South Carolina to create a civil war long before the brothers' conflict of 1861–1865. Even with a colonel's rank, he continued to prove especially proficient at killing. In the savage civil war that raged across South Carolina, Brandon was "a bitter enemy of the [T]ories, who received little mercy from him."[41]

Another fierce Celtic-Gaelic warrior was Patrick Carr, a veteran of Kings Mountain. He migrated to America from Ireland before the American Revolution. The Irishman claimed "that he killed one hundred [T]ories" during the war years.[42] Likewise, with old scores to settle because of so many family tragedies, including his brother's death at Loyalist hands, another Scotch-Irish killing machine in the civil war that raged through the Carolinas was Thomas Young. He was extremely proud of the fact that "a hundred Tories felt the weight of my arm" and bit the dust in consequence.[43]

Unfortunately, however, even the stories of other ethnic groups in America have helped to diminish Irish and Scotch-Irish wartime contributions, usurping their more significant roles. Ireland-born Mary McCauley, a survivor of the miserable winter at Valley Forge in 1777–1778, won fame as "Molly Pitcher," when she bravely manned a cannon of her husband's artillery unit at the Battle of Monmouth, New Jersey, on June 28, 1778. She had been carrying water to the sweat-drenched Pennsylvania artillerymen on this scorching day, but gamely took her husband's place in the gun crew when he fell wounded.

Mary had faithfully followed her husband, William Hays, during the campaigns of Washington's Continental Army for an extended period, learning all the duties of firing a field piece. However, German-American historians and writers have hijacked McCauley's heroine image, claiming her as their own. In consequence, the courageous Irish woman has become known as Mary Ludwig, a Teutonic woman. Earlier "accounts that Mary McCauley was clearly Irish were ignored" to obscure yet another, and most unique, Irish contribution.[44]

But, of course, the patriotic activities of Irish women have been even more ignored than those of their husbands, fathers, and sons. A frontiersman and scout from the mountains of North Carolina, John Weir, born in Ireland in 1743, was another Celtic-Gaelic warrior who also served during the Kings Mountain Campaign. Later in the war, his Irish wife, a "Miss McKelvey," fell into the hands of revenge-seeking Loyalists. She was "beaten" by the Tories "because she would not tell where he was" hiding in the bitter guerrilla war that consumed the Carolinas.[45] Patriotic Scotch-Irish women especially suffered in South Carolina, where guerrilla conflict between Americans reached new depths of depravity. When Tarleton's men raided the Captain John McClure plantation on July 11, 1780, they captured the officer's son, James McClure, and his brother-in-law molding bullets. The two boys were immediately ordered to be hung at sunrise. When Mrs. McClure pleaded for her young son's life in desperation, the commanding officer Captain Christian (of all names!) Huck "slapped her with the flat of his sword."[46]

Obscure Revolutionary Roots

Today, Americans know all about Boston's Founding Fathers, especially Samuel and John Adams of the privileged colonial elite, but not the contributions of the lower-class Irish of Boston at an early date. What has been conveniently forgotten is the fact that these wealthy Boston aristocrats, who lived in fine brick mansions and basked in luxury, never would have become effective revolutionary leaders to spark any revolution at all without the widespread support of Boston's lowest class, consisting of mostly sailors, indentured servants, and common laborers. Likewise on the distant frontier, lower-class Sons of Erin had long protected the port of Boston and the Massachusetts Colony, whose intolerant, self-righteous leaders and people had forced them to settle on the northern and western frontiers because of open hostility.

By 1771, nearly 30 percent of Boston's adult males were members of society's lowest order, consisting of a "propertyless proletariat" of potential urban revolutionaries, who were eager to change their inequitable world by any means. Especially in major urban areas stretching along the East Coast from New England to Georgia, this heavily Celtic-Gaelic group represented the unruly, lower-class "mob" or unpredictable "rabble" to the stuffy aristocratic members of genteel colonial society, including the Founding Fathers. Most of this disgruntled class of angry individuals who resided in New England's largest port city consisted of cantankerous Irish and Scotch-Irish, who had been long marginalized in their English-based stratified society and hence radicalized on both sides of the Atlantic.[47] It made no difference that this bustling port had grown rich and had been long protected by the settlers of Ireland from the frontier, including Rogers's Rangers, who consisted not only of Scotch-Irish but also Irish Catholics. In regard to these famed frontier rangers, Governor William Shirley wrote in 1756 how the "best of their men [not personally recruited by Rogers were] Irish Roman Catholicks," who fought to protect the Massachusetts Colony, including Boston, from external threats.[48]

Sadly, the full record of Irish contributions has been lost forever, partly because so much civil and military documentation simply no longer exists. However, United States census records, begun only in 1790, revealed that a quarter of the white population of both South Carolina and Georgia was Celtic-Gaelic. Before that time, no systematic census records were taken in the colonies, leaving a giant void to additionally obscure Irish origins and sizeable numbers, especially on the western frontier. And as mentioned, military records of Revolutionary War service were relatively few, sketchy at best, and wholly incomplete, diminishing additional knowledge of Irish and Scotch-Irish contributions from 1775 to 1783.

Yet another fundamental reason for the general obscurity of the Celtic-Gaelic contributions in America's desperate struggle for existence was deeply rooted in the internal dynamics of the Irish experience that had existed for centuries. In order to keep the Irish, especially Catholics, in their subordinate places, British policy (thanks to the anti-Catholic Penal Laws that were created after the final Jacobite defeat in 1691) officially denied educational opportunities: a tragic legacy of cultural imperialism and a cynical manipulation that even included a 1695 act that Irish children could not be sent overseas for an education. Of course, such repressive measures by British leadership were calculated to eliminate the rise of educated Irish free-thinkers, intellectuals, and leaders—all potential revolutionaries in the future. The vast majority of Celtic-Gaelic people who migrated to America remained illiterate, ensuring impoverished status and menial roles as indentured servants, menial workers, domestics, and common laborers. Therefore, relatively few Irish and Scotch-Irish patriots ever wrote Revolutionary War diaries, memoirs, or reminiscences to illuminate their dramatic stories in America's struggle for liberty.

In addition, a good many fighting men of English descent and Protestants were decidedly anti-Irish because of historic anti-Irish and anti-Catholic prejudices carried over from England, which had long waged war against Catholic France, England's oldest enemy, and Spain. The recent French and Indian War, the conflict for possession of the North American continent, was only the continuation of this ancient struggle. Alexander Graydon, an aristocratic, well-educated young officer who was well known "for the elegance of his person" when strutting down Philadelphia's cobblestone streets beside rows of stately brick townhouses, has provided a most revealing example. He sought to disassociate himself entirely—like so many colonists of English descent during the revolutionary period—from the lowly Irish by 1846, when thousands of potato famine (a number of pre-Revolutionary War potato famines, such as in 1765, fueled exoduses to America to set the stage for a people's revolt in timely fashion) Irish poured into the United States, including his own hometown of Philadelphia, to raise the level of anti-Irish feeling to fever pitch, when he published his memoirs.

This period, despite including the Mexican-American War when national unity was needed, was an intolerant time in America, especially for the unfortunate Irish. Anti-Catholic, anti-Irish, and anti-immigrant feeling ran so high among Protestant officers of General Zachary Taylor's army on the Rio Grande River and opposite the city of Matamoros, Mexico, that scores of Irish Catholic soldiers deserted, including men who had been severely flogged for minor infractions. After swimming across the Rio Grande to gain the comforting haven of Matamoros and a welcoming, friendly Catholic people, they then formed their own combat unit to serve in the Republic of Mexico's defense, the St. Patrick's Battalion, or San Patricio Battalion. Named in honor of Ireland's patron saint, this largely Celtic-Gaelic command became one of Mexico's finest combat units, battling in major engagements across Mexico on behalf of their adopted Catholic homeland.[49]

As if in conflict with his own ethnic roots because his own father had migrated from Ireland in 1730, in a classic case of projection, Graydon deliberately minimized the Revolutionary War contributions of the Pennsylvania Irish and Scotch-Irish in his writings. Evidently, he felt considerable resentment toward the recent immigrants, who were mostly impoverished, uneducated Irish Catholics of the lower class. Graydon even attempted to rewrite history in 1846. He audaciously refuted the popular view of so many wartime leaders, including General Henry "Light-Horse" Lee (Robert E. Lee's tactically astute father) and one of Washington's finest young cavalry commanders, who lavishly praised the Line of Ireland: "It has been supposed that the Pennsylvania line consisted chiefly of Irish, but this would by no means appear from my company [and] Out of seventy-three men, I find there were twenty from Ireland, four from England, two from Scotland, two from Germany, and the remaining forty-five were Americans. To these, adding four American officers, the proportion of Irish is but little more than a fourth."[50]

Surprisingly, modern historian Charles J. Stille also diminished the overall numbers and contributions of the Irish Catholics, reflecting in part the prevalent anti-Catholic and anti-immigrant attitudes of 1893 (when the book was published) of the Pennsylvania Line. This Protestant author emphasized:

> A curious error has been fallen into by many historians [...] in speaking of the Pennsylvania line, that 'it was composed in a large degree of new-comers from Ireland,' and this has been said not only to account for the alleged lawlessness and disaffection of the men . . . but also (by General Harry Lee)

to explain the extraordinary brilliancy of their courage on the battle-field. These writers are evidently thinking of the characteristic qualities of the Celtic Irishman in war; but there were not, it is said on good authority, more than three hundred persons of Irish birth (Roman Catholic and Celtic) in the Pennsylvania line. Two-thirds of the force were Scotch-Irish, a race with whose fighting qualities we are all familiar, but which are quite opposite to those that characterize the true Irish Celt. Most of them were descendants of the Scotch-Irish emigrants of 1717-1739, and very few of them were 'new-comers.'[51]

Stille, the Historical Society of Pennsylvania's respected president, took perhaps the most extreme measure in not only denying the widespread Irish Catholic participation, but also denigrating their fighting qualities for good measure! Contrary to Stille's conclusions, Irish Catholics from Connacht, Munster, and Leinster Provinces possessed a far more lengthy revolutionary tradition against the abuses of centralized authority and injustice not only than colonists of English descent but also the Scotch-Irish. After all, their Celtic-Gaelic ancestors fought for hundreds of years as revolutionaries against the English invaders and most recently as political and social agitators, whose "peasant violence" had been unleashed against the wealthy landlords, unlike the Scotch-Irish, who were relative "new-comers" to Northern Ireland.[52]

Both the Stille and Graydon examples have revealed the extent of the persistent ethnic resentment and prejudice that has long existed toward recent immigrant Irish Catholics, resulting in deliberate, widespread distortions of the historical record. Not surprisingly, therefore, when non-Irish soldiers (especially those men of British descent) wrote letters, memoirs, or reminiscences of their revolutionary experiences, they seldom, if ever, bestowed proper recognition upon the Irish soldier, both Catholic and Scotch-Irish, with the written word, because of considerable personal bias that denied the bestowing proper recognition upon those Irish whom they still viewed as detested "foreigners."

Like so many other high-ranking officers and leaders and reflecting his own anti-Irish English heritage and upper-class views, the aristocratic General Charles Lee held a lifelong contempt and hatred of the Irish, even toward those many Irish and Scotch-Irish soldiers who served faithfully under him in his ranks, fighting and dying for America. In a 1776 letter to Washington and echoing long-existing ethnic stereotypes that were seldom, if ever, questioned, although he was second in command of the Continental Army 1776–1777, the well-educated Lee denounced the Celtic-Gaelic soldiers serving in the Continental Army as little more than "Irish rascals."[53] The class-conscious Englishman described with disgust how the rawboned frontiersmen of the Virginia's Shenandoah Valley, which had been early settled by Scotch-Irish and Irish settlers who had migrated south from Pennsylvania after initially landing in the port of Philadelphia, consisted of "a Banditti of Scotch-Irish [indentured] Servants or their immediate descendants."[54]

General Lee, who had narrowly survived General Edward Braddock's disastrous defeat in the Battle of the Monongahela in July 1755, especially despised the Irish partly because they served in such large numbers in Washington's Army. In his mind, the fact that Lee commanded so many lowly Irish troops reflected badly upon him and stained his lofty self-image, his elevated social and leadership status, and even the struggle for independence in his non-egalitarian world of rigid class lines and hierarchical social order.

What was also reflected in the Englishman's discriminatory words was the fact that so many Irish and Scotch-Irish in Washington's Army were rawboned western frontiersmen who wore hunting shirts and carried Long Rifles. Making especially durable, resilient fighting men, these rough-and-tumble westerners brought a stream of coarse talk, including the flow of a melodic Gaelic and the distinct accents of Ulster Province, a unique mix of Irish and frontier mannerisms, ancient folkways, and an especially belligerent Celtic-Gaelic sense of individuality and extreme egalitarian notions with them into the army's encampment. Reflecting a host of free-spirited personal characteristics that had made British merchants of major port cities like Philadelphia (the center of the Irish American trade to the Emerald Isle) initially reluctant to work with hard-driving Scotch-Irish and Irish merchants who were considered too "rancorous and disagreeable," these transplanted Celtic-Gaelic fighting men of the New World shocked Lee, a traditional Old World man.

He felt threatened by the fact that so many Celtic-Gaelic lower-class members, especially indentured servants and common laborers, had suddenly risen in overall esteem, gaining an elevated status as proud American soldiers. Most of all, aristocratic officers were intimidated by these feisty Sons of Erin who thought for themselves, spoke their minds to their so-called superiors, and rejected elitist concepts about the God-given superiority of finely attired gentlemen of the hated upper class.[55] These ultimate survivors of searing experiences on both sides of the Atlantic were especially hardened and just plain tough at a time when a popular joke and axiom was that "an Irishman's coat of arms [was] two black eyes and a bloody nose," in the words of one Irishman who served in the British Army.[56]

As demonstrated by General Lee, deep-rooted prejudices toward Irish Catholics and Scotch-Irish Protestants thrived throughout the war years, including within the army's upper echelons. Colonel Daniel Morgan, of Scotch-Irish antecedents, contributed more to the decisive victory at Saratoga in October 1777, which garnered important French intervention in the following year, than any other American officer after the hard-fighting General Benedict Arnold. However, the gifted Irishman was contemptuously snubbed and ignored in the reports to Congress by army commander England-born General Horatio Gates, who allowed himself undeserved credit for the crucial success. When Gates gave a traditionally fine dinner for the captured General Burgoyne and his top officers in the glow of Saratoga's victory, Morgan was not even invited to the table by his commander. To the thinking of this haughty Englishman, Morgan was not considered a proper gentleman worthy of equality on any level: a rough-hewn, independent-minded, and outspoken Ireland-born general, who had risen to high command (unlike so many other leaders) by way of his own abilities, tactical skills, and battlefield accomplishments.[57]

The numbers of Irish separated more widely (one, two, and sometimes even three generations) from the immigrant experience considerably elevated the total number of Irish and their descendants who served in revolutionary armies, either close to or perhaps very likely surpassing the one-half percentage figure of all men who served in Washington's Army at crucial moments. This higher percentage of Celtic-Gaelic warriors was especially the case when the number of soldiers in Washington's Army fell to their lowest levels in 1776 just before the battle of Trenton and also in 1777 and from 1781–1783, when totals were 13,292, 14,256, and 13,476, respectively. Even when they tried, second- or third-generation Irish in America were unable to completely distance themselves from their background. Enduring Irish qualities and characteristics still served as the basic fabric of their lives and ensured that the Irish were still as much, if not more, Gaelic and Celtic than American, even by 1775.[58]

Even the second- and third-generation Irish in America were equally indoctrinated with not only a distinguished and lengthy revolutionary heritage from the Green Isle but also distinctive Celtic-Gaelic faiths, value systems, and cultural beliefs that were extremely anti-British and anti-aristocratic. For the Irish people, anti-centralized government ideology was a fervent faith as sacred as their religion, both Catholicism and Presbyterianism. Traditional Irish ballads, including the hauntingly beautiful "Barbara Allen" and "Johnny Doyle," and the revered Irish tradition of lively storytelling thrived from the western frontier to the urban ghettos, such as Irish Town in north Philadelphia, keeping memories of Ireland alive.[59]

Even in the relatively few times when America belatedly recognized a courageous Irish soldier, his immigrant status was often deliberately left out of the biographical sketch, including from official sources. Such was the case of a hero of the Battle of Princeton: Captain Daniel Neil of Essex County, New Jersey. Refusing to run even while his own artillerymen fled around him, Neil commanded his New Jersey battery, the Eastern Company of Artillery, to the bitter end. The young Irish captain was killed when his guns were overrun by seasoned British regulars at Princeton on January 3, 1777. Washington described him as "a brave Officer [who] was killed at [P]rinceton [as] a great Loss" to his army. In the twentieth century, a bronze memorial plaque that recognized Captain Neil and his valor at Princeton was dedicated by the city of Passaic, New Jersey, where he had been an enterprising merchant. Significant details about Neil's life were included, except the fact that he was an Irish immigrant.[60]

However, the appropriate data about Neil's background was readily available. Information possessed by the Daughters of the American Revolution described Captain Neil's Irish roots as early as 1897. In the *Daughters of the American Revolution Magazine*, it was finally revealed that Neil hailed from the O'Neil clan of Shane Castle, built in 1345 on the shore of Lough Neagh, County Antrim, Ulster Province in Northern Ireland, and that he had migrated from Ireland to New York City.[61]

But the thousands of patriotic Irish soldiers were not the only significant contributors. The major seaport of Philadelphia became the crown economic jewel of America and its bustling capital in part because of the large Irish community of not only skilled artisans and tradesmen (often connected with the shipping industry) but also a large number of Irish and Scotch-Irish merchants who possessed strong commercial ties to Ireland. All manner of goods had been long imported from Ireland in a vibrant Irish-American trade while strengthening economic, political, and cultural ties between the Irish on both sides of the Atlantic.

The wealthy Irish merchant class of America's infant capital contrasted sharply with the lower-class Irish families who lived mostly on Philadelphia's north side, the appropriately named Irish Town. These Irishmen worked on the docks and wharves and even engaged in other kinds of menial labor. Significantly, the primary leaders of the Irish community, including entrepreneurs who were proud members of the prestigious Irish Club and then the Friendly Sons of St. Patrick founded in 1771, hailed from the thriving merchant class. They early became influential leaders of the vigorous drive toward independence.[62]

Chapter IV

Half of Washington's
Continental Army Was Celtic-Gaelic?

The sizeable number of Irish, both Protestant and Catholic, across America naturally revealed the significant role of the Celtic-Gaelic people, who were almost all patriots, in the winning of America's independence. But most importantly, these numbers also revealed something not seen in the colonial population of British descent long before the first disagreements erupted between the thirteen colonies and the mother country. What has been overlooked by traditional historians has been the undeniable fact that no people who migrated to America were more radicalized and politicized than the oppressed Irish and Scotch-Irish because of the preexisting and widespread agrarian, revolutionary, and social unrest of the lower agrarian classes, organized in revolutionary groups like the radical "Oak Boys" and "Steel Boys," and even open violence that was transferred to America, especially Virginia, from Ireland since around 1760.

The leading roles played by the Celtic-Gaelic people from 1775–1783 were entirely predictable, if not inevitable, on multiple levels. Just before the American Revolution, social unrest reached new heights in the most populous colony of Virginia, where the ruling elite feared an open agrarian revolt of the lower-class masses, especially among the Irish and Scotch-Irish. That mighty explosion finally swept across America with full force with the American Revolution's opening shots. Clearly, America was most fortunate in having thoroughly benefited from the arrival of such large numbers of its lowest and, hence, most revolutionary and rebellious underclass of Irish, who already had been indoctrinated and pushed to the edge of open rebellion by Ireland's ugly realities and tragic legacies not long before the revolution.[1]

Unlike any other of America's wars, the exact number of Irish and Scotch-Irish soldiers who fought for America from 1775 to 1783 cannot accurately determined because of the incompleteness of military records, as mentioned. These developments led to a dramatic underestimation of the actual number of both Ulster Irish and Irish Catholics in America, especially in regard to the number of Celtic-Gaelic people who fought for independence. A recent scholarly work estimated that a total of one hundred fifty thousand Irish migrated from Northern Ireland and another fifty thousand came to the thirteen colonies from southern Ireland before the revolution.[2]

However, this estimation has once again represented nothing more than yet another dramatic underestimation, which has been only too prevalent. Historian Thomas Fleming estimated that at least three hundred thousand Irish were living in America by the Revolution's beginning out of a total population of around two million.[3] But again, Fleming's estimation was also far too low. In fact, the actual figure of around one-half million Irish (at least one-fourth of America's total population of two million) who came to prewar America was much closer to the true demographic situation.[4] The estimated total of nearly 20 percent (versus around 25 percent) of all Americans who were Irish and Scotch-Irish by the time of the American Revolution was too low. They actually represented a far larger percentage compared to the remainder of the colonial population in regard to more active and longer participation in the American Revolution, especially in Washington's Army and during the darkest days. Along with other collaborating evidence, these realities have partly substantiated the fact that the Irish represented an impressive total of 40 percent of Washington's Army at Valley Forge.[5]

The crucial role played by the Irish can be perhaps best understood by the fact that if only around one-third of colonists across America were patriots, as generally accepted, then a large percentage, perhaps even the majority, of this estimated one-third consisted mostly of Irish and Scotch-Irish soldiers.[6] Of this estimate, a larger percentage of patriots existed among those colonists who had the most to gain from a radical change of the old social order. Naturally, colonists with a lofty or even a middle-class (mostly of British descent) stake in the existing social order were less inclined to embark on a high-risk radical revolutionary course than those disgruntled members of society's lowliest ranks. Although American colonists enjoyed a relatively high standard of living, an estimated 40 percent of the total white population consisted of members of the poor, laboring class. And by far the largest percentage of America's lower order consisted of Irish and Scotch-Irish.[7]

From the beginning, and especially as the war progressed when serving in the army became less popular, Washington's Army "was highly dependent on poor non-American immigrants, mostly Scotch Irish" from Ulster Province until the final showdown at Yorktown. At that time, Washington commanded an army that was more multi-ethnic than has been generally realized by historians.[8] One French officer was shocked by the sight of the obviously lower-class qualities of Washington's Army just before the decisive showdown at Yorktown, writing, "There were some fine looking men; also many who were small and thin, and even some children twelve or thirteen years old. They have no uniforms and in general are badly clad."[9]

In their hierarchical society of deep social and class divisions not significantly changed by egalitarian thought because this was a conservative revolution, Washington and his officers, of middle- and upper-class status, felt that they possessed the natural right as proper "gentlemen," because they believed themselves vastly superior, to command lower-class Irish. Indeed, the very foundation of the army—even more traditional and conservative than the revolution itself—rested on the premise of upper-class gentleman officers leading uneducated, lower-class individuals who failed to meet the cultural, racial, social, and educational requirements of proper gentlemen. After all, it has always been the poor who have fought and died in America's wars. Savvy army recruiters focused primarily on gaining recruits from the lowest and poorest elements of American society, especially the landless, propertyless, and indentured servants, who hoped to improve their lot by faithfully serving their adopted country.[10]

Private James Reed, age twenty-one and a member of the Tenth Pennsylvania Continental Infantry, Anthony Wayne's Brigade, and the Line of Ireland, was one such lowly immigrant. Born in County Antrim, Northern Ireland, Reed migrated to Chester County, Pennsylvania, in 1774. He was captured at Fort Washington on November 15, 1776, and then thrown into a hellish prison ship in New York harbor. Fortunately, he survived the nightmarish experience, thanks to a timely parole that might well have saved his life. A "true Revolutionary" of the deepest dye, Reed then promptly enlisted for three years in the Continental service and proudly served under a fellow countryman, General "Mad" Anthony Wayne.[11] Like other Celtic-Gaelic members of the hard-fighting Line of Ireland, Private Reed might have been one of the so-called "Black Irish" or "Black Celts." Dark complexions and black hair were often features of many Irish soldiers who hailed from the west and south of Ireland, while in general more fair-complexioned men (the so-called "White Celts" with blue eyes and light hair) hailed from the north and east of the Emerald Isle.[12]

Not surprisingly, alarmed aristocratic members of colonial society, who never wore a uniform, often not only looked down upon faithful soldiers like Private Reed but also denounced the fact that so many of Washington's men were "taken from the lowest of the people," especially Irishmen. Such widespread contempt expressed openly toward the Irish and Scotch-Irish soldiers, including officers, was so great that they were considered by the colonial elite as "unfit for a seat at his excellency's [George Washington] table."[13]

Even one common Irish fighting man who held respect for his upper-class British officers felt a measure of disgust about the fact that among America's officers, including so many Irish and Scotch-Irish of all ranks, "there is but very few of them that appear gentleman, consequently cannot have a proper sense of honor."[14] Indeed, the overall high percentage of Irish and Scotch-Irish soldiers in Washington's Army considerably galled a good many high-ranking non-Irish leaders. Washington's top lieutenant after the Battle of Bunker Hill, General Charles Lee, maintained an undisguised contempt because he was convinced that a full half of the Continental Army was composed of Irish soldiers. In sworn testimony, Major General James Robertson also stated before an investigative committee of the House of Commons in London in 1779: "I remember General Lee telling me that he believed half the rebel army were from Ireland."[15]

But because Robertson's testimony, under oath and based upon certain knowledge, to this parliamentary committee was considered unreliable second-hand information, this most revealing statement from the second highest-ranking American commander has been dismissed by modern historians as simply too high. However, Major General Robertson's sworn testimony has been fully collaborated in regard to an even higher percentage, thanks to new evidence and numerous other well-placed opinions of knowledgeable officials and leaders, including the revealing words written in a July 18, 1775, letter to Basil Fielding, Earl of Denbigh, from British Army Lieutenant William Fielding. In describing the composition of Washington's feisty army that refused to quit fighting year after year despite the seemingly endless setbacks and hardships, the seasoned lieutenant wrote, "it is said to be above half Irish & Scotch, but far more of the former than the latter."[16]

These most revealing words have corresponded roughly with the analysis of a relative handful of modern scholars, usually Irish and Irish-American themselves. These scholars were either not influenced by or simply relinquished the romance of the yeoman farmer-soldier of British descent mythology in regard to the twentieth century's early years' estimation that 40 percent (10 percent above the standard one-third—or 33 percent—figure as emphasized by historians like Jay P. Dolan) of patriots were either Irish or Scotch-Irish. Michael J. O'Brien was the earliest of these historians. After scrutinizing O'Brien's extensive research, the president of the American Irish Historical Society (although he still supported a too low percentage) emphasized how O'Brien "establishes unequivocally that thirty-eight per cent of the Revolutionary army that won American independence was Irish."[17]

However, O'Brien's 1920 book was discredited because he was a historian of the so-called Irish-American School. Dismissed by traditional and Anglo-Saxon-first historians, O'Brien's conclusions (although grounded in available primary research) emphasized how the Irish, especially Catholics, as opposed to the Scotch-Irish, played an all-important role in the American Revolution. With his primary thesis of demonstrating that the Scotch-Irish "were not the backbone of Irish" contributions to the struggle for liberty, O'Brien's work has been ignored because critics felt that it was too politically influenced and too pro-Catholic since his views corresponded with the rising of nationalist and independence sentiment among Catholics across Ireland. The author's name alone resulted in an automatic dismissal of almost everything that O'Brien emphasized, more for political than historical reasons.

James H. Smylie concluded in 1990 that O'Brien "expressed the feeling that the term Scotch-Irish was used by Irishmen who were ashamed of being Irish [and] He maintained that the contributions of the Scotch-Irish claimed to have made to America were really made by the Irish."[18] But while O'Brien has been dismissed for having seemingly overestimated the overall Irish revolutionary role, an increasing amount of recent primary research and documentary evidence has proved that General Lee's seemingly too-high and widely ignored estimation of 50 percent was actually much closer to the truth. In May

1778, Lee returned to Washington's Army's winter quarters at Valley Forge after a year and a half as a British prisoner of war. On December 13, 1776, at Basking Ridge, New Jersey, he had been captured by British dragoons that included Oxford-educated Banastre Tarleton, the privileged son of a wealthy mayor of Liverpool, merchant, and prosperous slave trader. Therefore, by the time he made his estimation about such a widespread Irish contribution in the ranks, because he was such an exacting commander, General Lee possessed an intimate knowledge of the exact composition of Washington's Army from an ample number of detailed muster rolls, inspection reports, and other army records at Valley Forge.

The expert opinions of Lee, who has been long viewed as a villain in the eyes of American historians largely because of his well-known animosity toward Washington and his summer 1778 court-martial for his controversial performance at the Battle of Monmouth, should be bestowed with new credibility today. However, the truthfulness of Lee's knowledgeable words about the widespread extent of the Irish and Scotch-Irish composition of Washington's Army after Valley Forge were right on target: "the Irish . . . constituted two-fifths of the Continental Army by the time that [General Lee] reached Valley Forge."[19]

The distinct possibility exists that in the less than one-year period between when Lee reported to Washington's Army in May 1778 and June 1779 and when Major General James Robertson, the New York governor who became "chummy" with Lee during his captivity, presented his Parliamentary testimony, which included an emphasis on the truth of General Lee's conviction that half of Washington's Continental Army was Irish, additional Celtic-Gaelic soldiers had continued to join the army in large numbers by this time to increase Fleming's "two-fifths" to perhaps close to one-half.[20] Even more, Lee's estimation of the high percentage of Irish and Scotch-Irish in Washington's Army was fully collaborated by Joseph Galloway, another parliamentary committee member like Major General Robertson, and other respected leaders in high places. Meticulous by nature as an experienced lawyer and one of the leading politicians of the Quaker-dominated Pennsylvania government, Galloway was well known for his intimate knowledge about the exact makeup of Washington's Army that even the commander in chief might not have possessed at the time. As a highly placed, conservative Pennsylvania Congressman, he had advocated moderation rather than revolution. Galloway later became a Loyalist official who provided vital intelligence for the British Army, which he then accompanied. He had ascertained through his detailed research, intelligence-gathering, and "careful records" that precisely 1,134 men of Washington's Army had deserted from the Valley Forge winter encampment as of March 25, 1778.

The cerebral Maryland-born Galloway was the former Speaker of Pennsylvania's House of Assembly and Benjamin Franklin's friend. A fellow Pennsylvanian, Franklin had attempted to transform him into a patriot. But this former First Continental Congress member found safety and a high-level position with the British in December 1775. Long enjoying the lavish comforts of his estate, known as Trevose, located just outside Philadelphia, Galloway had been stunned by the sudden rise of Pennsylvania's lowly Irish Presbyterians, or the Irish "mob." This emerging grassroots dominance of Pennsylvania's Irish and Scotch-Irish helped to push Galloway out of government. Galloway then headed an appointed group of governing officials in charge of affairs, established by General William Howe, in Philadelphia, after America's capital city was captured in late September 1777.

Along with other high-ranking personnel, both military and civilian, Galloway's sworn testimony before an investigative committee on the British conduct of the war in the House of Commons revealed detailed, firsthand knowledge about the widespread participation of the Irish and Scotch-Irish in Washington's Army. With more accurate knowledge of colonial affairs than British officials in London by this time, Galloway was thoroughly quizzed by parliamentary investigators about a central mystery that had perplexed British military leaders and politicians since the rebellion's outbreak: "of the rebel army that enlisted in the service of the Congress, were they chiefly composed of natives of America, or were the greatest part of them, English, Scotch, and Irish?"[21]

Since the highly respected Galloway was a prominent intellectual politician who had departed Pennsylvania's Quaker-dominated government for exile in England in October 1778 before General Lee rejoined Washington's Army, he answered this key question in regard to the exact nature and makeup of America's resistance effort and the precise composition of Washington's people's army during this crucial period. "The names and places of their nativity being taken down, I can answer the question with precision [and] There were scarcely one-fourth natives of America; about one-half Irish; the other fourth were English and Scotch," or Scottish. Therefore, according to Galloway's analysis based upon sound evidence, firsthand knowledge, and available intelligence, including even from American deserters who had exchanged uniforms, more than half of the Continental Army was Celtic in composition: Irish, Scotch-Irish, and Scottish.[22] In no uncertain terms, Galloway emphasized that "the majority of the men who fought against England in America were of Irish extraction. Earlier [in the war], this expression seemed to many people absolutely absurd [and] It may seem the same to many today but investigation of officially recorded facts and historical documents shows it to be the well-ground impression of a contemporary who was in close contact with the actual events" in America's war, wrote historian Charles Murphy in 1976.[23]

Galloway's tabulation corresponded exactly with the opinion of an equally knowledgeable Lieutenant William Fielding in a July 18, 1775, letter, where he emphasized that "above half [the American army consisted of] Irish and Scotch" soldiers.[24] What has been primarily overlooked by today's historians was the fact that British officials and commanders knew how Washington's Army was reinforced by large numbers of professional soldiers, who were already disciplined and well trained from years of service in the British Army, to enhance its overall combat capabilities long before the arrival of Baron Frederick Wilhelm Von Steuben, a former Prussian Army officer. The experienced Prussian did not reach Washington's Army until late February 1778, long after Washington's men had demonstrated considerable tactical skill and discipline on numerous battlefields. Frustrated British military leaders, unable to suppress the most persistent of people's rebellions, were alarmed because so many sympathetic Irish (including drill sergeants) were taking off their scarlet uniforms, deserting the British Army, and joining the American revolutionaries by August 1776, even before the first major showdown at the Battle of Long Island, New York, in late August 1776.[25]

Private William McCarty, a Maryland Continental of Washington's Army, was one experienced common soldier who had been trained in the British Army. This seasoned Irishman "was an old soldier in the British Service [and] he has something of the [Irish] brogue in his language," wrote one non-Irish American.[26] One of Howe's veteran officers who possessed a special interest in his fellow countrymen of Washington's Army, Captain Frederick MacKenzie, of Dublin and the Royal Welch Fusiliers, revealed what he knew from firsthand experience. As penned in his diary in October 1776, "The chief strength of the Rebel Army at present consists of Natives of Europe, particularly Irishmen:—many of their Regiments are composed principally of these men" from the captain's own homeland.[27]

Such a disturbing ethnic and class reality, especially one that cast a perceived negative shadow on America's cause to the aristocratic English and American eighteenth-century mentality (as seen by General Lee) was especially vivid in Galloway's class-conscious mind. After all, Galloway had lost his considerable privilege and prestige from the dramatic rising of a grassroots democratic movement that he viewed as essentially the most radical of all social revolutions stemming primarily from the lowly Irish and Scotch-Irish in

Pennsylvania. Galloway had been driven from his beloved Pennsylvania homeland by the democratic rising of society's lowest orders, or the much-derided "rabble," which consisted of so many Celtic-Gaelic people who believed that they now possessed a God-given right to be equal to their alleged superiors regardless of official rank, wealth, or social position.

Such a broad, sweeping social upheaval by the lowest white ranks in colonial society presented the ultimate social nightmare for the Crown's ruling aristocracy, both the British and American-born elite, on both sides of the Atlantic. Feeling threatened that an authentic democratic social revolution might evolve to overturn upper-class rule immediately before the revolution, wealthy Virginia planters feared the prospect of losing the Celtic-Gaelic common laborers, who worked in the fields of their vast plantations, to the revolutionary winds of change. In Pennsylvania, Galloway's worst social nightmares and political fears were realized, precisely because so many Irish and Scotch-Irish rose up politically and took up arms against the mother country. To high-ranking officials like Galloway, the rising of the Irish and Scotch-Irish people across America was comparable to the Jacobite and Presbyterian rebellions, respectively, of old: something that had to be crushed at all costs in order to save the social order, society, and civilization itself.

But of course what made America's uprising seem most of all like another grassroots rebellion in Ireland to British and Loyalist officials (and soldiers) like Galloway was precisely that such a large percentage of revolutionaries were Irish and Scotch-Irish. All of these corroborated facts and testimonies from these knowledgeable political and military men to high-ranking British officials in the halls of power in London verified that the one-half percentage figure of Irish soldiers composing Washington's Army was most likely entirely true during the period before the Continental Army went into winter quarters at Valley Forge for the winter of 1777–1778, before dropping by May 1778 to "two-fifths," or 40 percent.[28]

Whatever the exact numbers and percentages, this disproportionate contribution was an impressive large overall percentage of Irish and Scotch-Irish participation in America's first national army, especially considering how Valley Forge witnessed one of the revolution's bleakest periods for Washington after his twin 1777 defeats at Germantown and Brandywine outside Philadelphia. While General Lee's 50 percent estimation and comparable estimates of Irish American historians in fact might well be too high, a 45 percent figure would very likely be closer to the actual percentage of the Irish and Scotch-Irish participation in Washington's Army in December 1776 by the time of the Battle of Trenton, however.

A handful of modern historians have at least acknowledged the high percentage of Irish in Pennsylvania units, if not Washington's Army as a whole. In a masterful 2003 work, *Irish Immigrants in the Land of Canaan*, four respected historians—Kerby A. Miller, Arnold Schrier, Bruce D. Boling, and David N. Doyle—estimated that "Nearly half the Revolutionary War soldiers who fought in the Continental Army and state militia units raised in Pennsylvania were of Irish birth or descent, and in some companies (as the seventh regiment) the proportion was as high as 75 percent."[29]

Indeed, of 1,068 recruits destined for service in the hard-fighting Pennsylvania Line, "75 percent said they were not American-born," with the vast majority of soldiers from Ireland.[30] But exact figures of the number of Irish who fought in revolutionary armies cannot be fully verified with a degree of certitude, and therefore past estimates have been almost always too low. But perhaps a possible glimpse of the potential of the actual number of Irish and Scotch-Irish who served from a single colony (Pennsylvania, where the majority of the Scotch-Irish lived on the Revolution's eve) can be partly revealed by a little-known secret intelligence report by Baron Johann von Robais de Kalb for the French government. Born in 1721, de Kalb hailed from a humble background of Bavarian peasant antecedents from the south in today's Germany before rising to high rank in French military service on European battlefields and in America during the French and Indian War.

After the end of this global conflict, the capable de Kalb embarked upon a secret mission to ascertain anti-British sentiment in the American colonies. He hoped to decipher the extent of support in the thirteen colonies to "withdraw from the British government" to regain what had been lost (Canada) by France to Great Britain during the French and Indian War: a first early hint of a possible future alliance between France and the American colonists against England. Such an international alliance (of course eventually established between France and America in 1778, thanks to victory at Saratoga) could provide a winning strategy.

As a Continental major general, de Kalb suffered eleven bullet and bayonet wounds at the disastrous battle in the sweltering pine forests just north of Camden, where enterprising Scotch-Irish merchants had early set up shop in the South Carolina Piedmont, on the morning of August 16, 1780. Ignoring a strong premonition of impending death, in part because he decided that he would not run if the army's militiamen broke in the face of the inevitable British bayonet charge as he anticipated, General de Kalb was mortally wounded when bravely standing before the charging opponent beside his elite Continental troops of the Maryland Line while Gates (the army's commander) fled the field. The army's rout by the experienced forces under Lord Charles Cornwallis in the so-called "battle" of Camden doomed de Kalb, who was badly wounded. He died three days later, far from home, in his early fifties.

In 1767, long before de Kalb was dispatched by the French to bestow his considerable military expertise on American forces, he wrote of his findings in a secret report to the French government. In his estimation, the fact-finding German reported that the "Pennsylvania Dutch alone" could provide sixty thousand fighting men if war suddenly erupted between the colonies and Great Britain.[31] But this anticipated exodus of Germans (the Teutonic population was not sufficiently large enough to support such a high number) into the patriot ranks never developed as so optimistically envisioned by either de Kalb or so many hopeful Americans. In fact, only one Continental Army infantry regiment possessed a distinctive German character, at least on paper: the "German Regiment" of Washington's Army, which fought exceptionally well at Trenton (despite the regiment's baptismal fire) and played a key role in that victory. This German Regiment contained not only Pennsylvania and Maryland Germans but also a good many Irish soldiers in its ranks. These Irish revolutionaries added a decidedly Celtic-Gaelic flavor to what the Continental Congress had originally envisioned as a regiment composed entirely of Germans or men of Teutonic extraction.[32]

Compared to the Scotch-Irish, however, the German response to the call to arms was less enthusiastic. During the summer of 1775, the Provincial Congress dispatched a team, which included an Irish Presbyterian minister named William Tennent, to the South Carolina Piedmont—the "back country"—to rally support for the patriot cause. Tennent was the son of an Irish immigrant father who brought his family, including young William, from Northern Ireland to Philadelphia in 1718. On August 7, 1775, they reported with great disappointment to Congress how in regard to the Germans, they "were so much adverse to take up arms, as they imaged, against the king, least they should lose their lands."[33]

However, thousands of Germans had in fact settled on Pennsylvania's frontier, but more in the towns rather than in isolated cabins in the wilderness. And the total number of Teutonic settlers represented as much of one-third of Pennsylvania's population by 1776, only behind the Scotch-Irish and Irish in overall numbers. In his journal, Major John Burrowes, Fifth New Jersey Regiment and a member of the Sullivan-Clinton expedition (in which the German Regiment served) that trekked into the depths of the New York wilderness to strike at the homeland sanctuaries of the Iroquois Confederacy, wrote that the two mostly log cabin communities, separated only by the

Susquehanna River, of Northumberland and Sunbury, Pennsylvania, consisted of "Irish and Germans."[34] The far larger number of Irish to Germans in Pennsylvania was verified by the Marquis de Chastellux during the war years. He emphasized how the "Irish and Germans form the most numerous part of the inhabitants of Pennsylvania [and] The latter . . . constitutes a fifth, if not a fourth, of the whole number. . . ."[35]

But de Kalb's estimation failed to correspond with the known facts because the Irish and Scotch-Irish presence was far larger than that of Germans in Pennsylvania, especially along the western frontier. Based on this ratio established by de Kalb, therefore, it was the Irish and not the Germans who actually could have come closer to providing the estimated sixty thousand fighting men from Pennsylvania, where more Celtic-Gaelic people could be counted than any other ethnic group, from 1775 to 1783. His calculations were not only inaccurate and imprecise, but far too high.

During his hasty fact-finding mission that might have precluded his visitations to Pennsylvania's western frontier, because of obvious language barriers, de Kalb may have mistakenly believed that the vast majority of immigrants in Pennsylvania were Germans because his sixty thousand estimation would have been far closer to the overall impact of Irish and Scotch-Irish numerical contributions to the resistance effort from 1775 to 1783 rather than German. After all, the Irish and Scotch-Irish possessed a far greater hatred toward England than the Protestant "Dutch," as the Germans were erroneously called in America. And, of course, tens of thousands of Germans (Hessians) fought not for liberty but to conquer America. Some German settlers wished not to fight their own countrymen, including relatives, for obvious reasons.

Even Pennsylvania's German regiment was noted for the large number of Irish who served in its ranks because not enough Germans could be secured for military service: another indication of the lack of German patriots, as early ascertained by Scotch-Irish Reverend Tennent in regard to his South Carolina tour during the summer of

1775, at a time when every man was needed in the ranks, especially in Washington's Army. Although it is not known, perhaps de Kalb's total number was a combined estimation of all Irish and Scotch-Irish and Germans together in Pennsylvania. Or perhaps de Kalb might have meant the middle colonies (where most of the Irish and Scotch Irish lived), including the western frontier, in his estimation of sixty thousand whom he believed would fight against England. And, of course, the most significant fact of all was that far more Irish and Scotch-Irish had settled in the middle colonies than anywhere else in America.

However, modern scholars have only ascertained that in total 25,678 men from Pennsylvania served in the Continental Army. The vast majority of these Pennsylvania soldiers were certainly either Irish or of Irish extraction, especially the Scotch-Irish. Therefore, with an estimated Irish and Scotch-Irish population of around five hundred thousand at the American Revolution's beginning, when the total colonial population was around two million but with "no more than 100,000" colonists in total serving in America's military, Pennsylvania alone easily could have provided from fifteen to eighteen thousand Irish or Scotch-Irish fighting men to the Continental Army. But even this estimate might be too low. All in all, de Kalb's total was not unreasonable, especially when considering the large numbers and high percentages of Ireland-born soldiers in various Pennsylvania regiments, especially Pennsylvania's Continental Line of Washington's Army. By way of comparison, the estimated total of Irish who served from a much smaller, less populated Maryland was around six thousand men, but most likely even more soldiers were part of the total.

Of the 582 soldiers of the Pennsylvania Line who designated their place of birth, only 195 listed themselves as native-born Americans. But caught up in the heady idealism and euphoria of becoming an "American" in a revolutionary struggle, many Irish and Scotch-Irish were eager to distance themselves from their Old World past and an older generation of Ireland-born immigrants. These were mostly the sons and grandsons of Irish immigrants. Two-thirds of these 582 men were foreign born, with Ireland topping the list and Germany second. Of the 387 foreign-born of the Pennsylvania Line, a total of 56 percent—or 217 men—were born in Ireland, as revealed from existing information and documentation.[36]

Clearly, the number of Irish and Scotch-Irish who served in America's struggle for liberty was certainly much higher than modern historians have previously imagined. Appropriately, America's first capital of Philadelphia consisted mostly of Presbyterian congregations of lower-, middle-, and upper-class Irish, with the Quakers only a distinct minority. Symbolically, Philadelphia was not only the capital of America but also America's Irish capital. Benjamin Franklin "was of the opinion that about one-third of the Pennsylvania population of 350,000 was of Irish background as the American Revolution approached," or around one hundred thousand.[37] This number has given some credence to de Kalb's high estimation if he actually meant the Celtic-Gaelic people instead of the Germans. In addition, a Quaker lamented in a letter that "the Presbyterians . . . are the most numerous, I imagine, of any denomination in the province" of Pennsylvania.[38]

The exact total of Celtic-Gaelic men who served in America's armies from 1775 to 1783 will never be accurately determined, but the number of Irish and Scotch-Irish of military age and capable of bearing arms and thus provided by Pennsylvania was higher than in any other colony in America. Giving an early hint about what was to come, Charles Smith had warned British officials in 1773 of the overwhelming "disposition which savours too much of rebellion," especially along the western Pennsylvania frontier, where "eight–ten thousand people were imported from Ireland in one year."[39]

"Testifying before Parliament in 1779, Galloway emphasized that half of Washington's army was Irish [and this estimate in fact] was only a mild exaggeration," wrote Fleming, who was certainly accurate in his evaluation.[40] And in a letter regarding the crucial period of 1773–

1774, England-born Captain Charles Lee, the future Continental general who coveted Washington's leadership position with ambitious eyes, described with some astonishment how "Twelve thousand fresh colonists, half German, half Irish, were imported this year into Philadelphia alone, and not a much less number in the Colonies of Virginia and New York."[41]

Lee's written statement indicated that in a single year just before the American Revolution's beginning, some six thousand Irish and Scotch-Irish settlers had poured into Philadelphia, and about the same number to Virginia and New York, for an overall total of at least fifteen thousand. Therefore, the possible figure of sixty thousand, based on de Kalb's estimation if the Celtic-Gaelic people were considered and not the Germans, might not seem like a gross exaggeration at first glance because it would have in part reflected the massive influx of nearly one hundred thousand Irish to America in the early 1770s just before the Revolution. Combined with the earlier Irish and Scotch-Irish migrations, such a massive exodus of liberty-seeking Irish to America just before the Revolution's outbreak meant that it was far more likely that the numbers of Celtic-Gaelic soldiers in the Continental Army's ranks were far higher than has been generally recognized by historians. Indeed, from 1717 to 1775, more than fifty thousand immigrants entered Pennsylvania from Ulster Province alone.[42]

As mentioned, Benjamin Franklin estimated that the Scotch-Irish and Irish made up one-third of the three hundred fifty thousand colonists in Pennsylvania in 1774, or around one hundred fifteen thousand Scotch-Irish and Irish.[43] Therefore, in Pennsylvania alone, if only one in three of the Scotch-Irish settlers was a male of military age from his teenage years to a man in his forties, then Pennsylvania alone perhaps potentially could have provided as many as forty thousand fighting men, at the very most, in a war in which "no more than 100,000 different men actually bore arms" for America, in one modern historian's educated estimation. But how many of this total consisted of Irish and

Scotch-Irish soldiers cannot be accurately determined because of the lack of records and documentation.

Nevertheless, such impressively high figures are significant not only in terms of determining actual manpower contributions of the Irish and Scotch-Irish, but also because of the importance of Pennsylvania's overall wartime role and its key geographical position sandwiched between North and South, which gave it considerable political and strategic importance. In overall percentage and strategic terms, "The middle states contributed nearly half of the total force of the main Continental army in 1777 and 1778 [and] The Irish presence [was] around 45 percent of their entire strength."[44] No wonder that near the revolution's end, Luke Gardiner emphasized to the members of the Irish House of Commons: "I am assured, on the best authority . . . that the Irish [Gaelic] language was as commonly spoken in the American ranks as English," indicating widespread Irish Catholic participation.[45]

But traditional modern historians have also especially overlooked the distinct possibility of these high figures in terms of drawing an appropriate correlation between these massive numbers and what they meant in terms of providing the crucial manpower over an extended period. With a population of 3.7 million, nearly double that of the thirteen colonies, Ireland served as America's most vital manpower resource pool both before and during the American Revolution. After all, at this time, America possessed a population of 2.4 million, including slaves, according to one estimation that was almost certainly too high. Dublin in 1775 was more than seven times larger than New York City, with twenty-five thousand people, more than ten times larger than Boston, with a population of sixteen thousand, and more than four times larger than America's largest city, Philadelphia, one hundred eighty thousand (Dublin) versus forty thousand (America's capital) people. Even the southern Ireland port of Cork, with eighty thousand people, was twice as large as the first capital of the United States.

A large number of contemporary British primary sources at the time have thoroughly verified the overwhelming numbers of Irish and Scotch-Irish in America's armies, especially Washington's Continental Army. One refined upper-class British Loyalist officer from Westchester County, New York, located just north of New York City, Captain Joshua Pell, estimated on June 1, 1776, in regard to the composition of Washington's Continental Army stationed in and around New York City that "The Rebels consist chiefly of Irish Redemptioners and convicts [including political prisoners, who had been exiled for their resistance to the British government], the most audacious rascals existing" on this earth.[46]

But Pell was aware of the large number of Irish indentured servants who filled the patriot ranks. The always manpower-short Continental Army only continued a tradition of a systematic recruitment of the large population of Irish servants first begun by the colonial militias during the French and Indian War. Tapping into a reliable manpower pool, even Washington recruited servants for his Virginia War in the struggle against the French, Indians, and Canadians.[47] However, Pell's insightful words were in fact gained from intimate knowledge, verifying a good many other high estimations of the disproportionate Irish and Scotch-Irish role as repeatedly voiced in the halls of Parliament. Clearly, the Celtic-Gaelic advocates of liberty were indeed the "most audacious rascals existing," ensuring that they became Washington's finest soldiers in terms of combat prowess, durability, and resiliency.

For decades before the American Revolution, America's vast expanse had served as England's largest dumping ground for generations of angry, revenge-seeking Irish rebels, convicts, "Irish Tories," political prisoners, fiery radicals, die-hard revolutionaries, and the most "audacious rascals": the most rebellious men in America. These natural rebels included recent participants in social unrest, political agitation, and militant activities against the wealthy English and Anglo-Irish landlords and British occupying troops in Ireland, especially in the always-troublesome Catholic south, such as Counties Cork and Wexford.

Large numbers of independent-minded, nationalistic, and British-hating Irish had "run afoul" with British law "only because they thought Catholic Irishmen should be free," a radical revolutionary stance that laid the solid groundwork and set the stage for a common people's uprising. Likewise, the Ulster Irish had long believed that they should live freely in a Presbyterian Northern Ireland without British governmental and economic control or the Anglican Church's interference, tithes, and domination. And all of these anti-authoritarian sentiments were transferred across the Atlantic, creating a highly combustible environment on America's soil.[48]

By 1775, these much-derided renegades and "misfits" were just other names for die-hard Irish and Scotch-Irish revolutionaries, who possessed so many long-term grievances against injustices that extended back as long as they could remember. Quite unintentionally, the observant Pell bestowed the ultimate compliment that well defined the rebellious nature, democratic spirit, and egalitarianism of both Irish Catholics and Scotch-Irish. From a cultured, landed upperclass family of Westchester County, New York, Captain Pell saw the Irish and Scotch-Irish as little more than savages compared to the more refined colonists of the New York City area.

The fact that the exact numbers of the Irish and Scotch-Irish and their first- and second-generation descendants who served in the Continental Army's ranks were much higher than has been generally recognized by historians was perhaps not even the most important point in terms of these Emerald Islanders playing a leading role in winning America's independence. Perhaps most significant of all was the simple fact that this multitude of young men and boys from the Green Isle were no ordinary soldiers in any sense. For the most part, and as was widely known on both sides of the Atlantic and even stemming back to ancient times, the Celtic-Gaelic warrior was an exceptional fighting man. Equally as impressive as the high numbers of Irish and Scotch-Irish patriots who served throughout the struggle was the fact that these Celtic-Gaelic soldiers became Washington's most dependable and hardest fighting troops year after year.

In a compliment from a leading British officer about the combat prowess of the average Celtic-Gaelic fighting man, General Henry Clinton, who was still deeply affected by the death of his young wife, concluded correctly that the principal source of Washington's finest combat troops were Irish soldiers. Therefore, hoping to exploit this invaluable resource (long utilized to fight Great Britain's wars around the globe) to secure the best fighting men, Clinton explained that he desired to gather equally hard-fighting men for British service from "those sources from whence the rebels themselves drew most of their best soldiers—I mean the Irish . . . who had [recently] set-tled in America."[49] Learning how suddenly America's fortunes in the South could be turned while he remained in overall command at New York City, Clinton knew well of the combat prowess of the Irish fight-ing man when a western frontier army, which was almost exclusively Scotch-Irish, won one of the war's most dramatic victories at Kings Mountain on October 7, 1780.[50]

The son of an Irish immigrant who had migrated to Pennsylvania and one of Washington's Celtic-Gaelic soldiers from that heavily Irish-populated state, Alexander Graydon paid a rare compliment when he described an undeniable truth in regard to what made the Sons of Erin such die-hard patriots: "As to the genuine sons of Hibernia, it is enough for them to know that England was the antag-onist [and in] the contest with Englishmen, Irishmen [who] only require reining in" of their enthusiasm to fight the British.[51]

Not surprisingly from an early date, therefore, "the interior North Carolina [and South Carolina] militias were almost wholly Presbyterian," consisting of mostly Ulster Irish, or "commoners," who had long naturally opposed the aristocratic elite of the East Coast. This demographic reflected the heavy flood of migration of Irish immigrants primarily to Charleston (then known as "Charles Town") as early as 1669 from the port of Kinsale, County Cork, in southern Ireland. From Charleston, the Irish then headed north and west to set up homes in the wilderness. One Irish family established the Lymerick Plantation (named after Limerick, Ireland) that was situated along the sluggish Cooper River. Explaining the early exodus to South Carolina, this was the same year (1669) that the constitutions of the Carolinas offered a warm welcome for people of any religious persuasion. Consisting of many veterans of the Cherokee Wars, these Carolina patriots, including men who had fought guerrilla-style as in Ireland against their oppressors, bravely risked all in resisting the victorious British during the dark days after Charleston's fall in May 1780 and the surrender of the sizeable Continental garrison: the largest surrender of American troops until the surrender of Corregidor in the Philippines in 1942.

Known as the "Gamecock" (a name bestowed by Scotch-Irish patriot brothers-in-arms) for his never-say-die resolve, Thomas Sumter was the first South Carolina guerrilla leader to rise up at the struggle's nadir in the South. Sumter was a fiery Celtic commander whose father of little means had migrated from Wales. Sumter led mostly Scotch-Irish soldiers, who were the first to offer resistance after a series of sharp setbacks, beginning with Charleston's surrender.

Hundreds of never-say-die Celtic-Gaelic rebels served in hard-riding guerrilla bands that fought under other resourceful Scotch-Irish leaders of South Carolina. These dynamic guerrilla commanders included Andrew Pickens, a "dour Presbyterian" who waged a holy war against his homeland's invaders, and William Campbell, who rose to the fore at Kings Mountain and other clashes against the British and Loyalists. Pickens was the son of Scotch-Irish immigrants from Ulster Province. In the early 1750s, the Pickens family settled in the largely Scotch-Irish community of the Waxhaws. The family's favorite black mare was bestowed with the Irish name of Bonney.

Hailing from the Santee River country, Francis Marion commanded the most famous group of partisans who often struck the British out of the swampy darkness of the low-lying Pee Dee River (known as the Catawba River in North Carolina from where it descended from the Appalachians) country. Consisting mostly of Scotch-Irish, these resourceful guerrillas served with distinction under the famed "Swamp Fox." Thanks to experience gained in battling the Cherokee as far back as the 1760s, Marion evolved into a brilliant tactician of small-unit action. He defied the stereotype of a traditional guerrilla leader known for an outsized ego, outlandish bluster, and over-aggressiveness that bordered on recklessness. Instead, Marion was quiet, unassuming, and modest: a thinking man's commander. And unlike most of South Carolina's resourceful guerrilla leaders who played key roles in keeping the large Loyalist population (upon whom British strategy for conquering the South was based) from rising up en masse, Marion was a commissioned Continental officer who wore a regulation uniform of blue.

With audacity and boldness, in stealthy partisan fashion he led Irish and Scotch-Irish, who carried trusty Long Rifles, shotguns loaded with buckshot, and newly captured "Brown Bess" muskets, in strikes that emerged from the dark, swampy environs of the Santee, Pee Dee, and Black Rivers of the Low Country. With Celtic-Gaelic demographics in mind as part of his strategic formula to harass the victors of Charleston, the Pearl of the South, Marion proved so successful in part because he centered his area of operations exactly where the most Irish and Scotch-Irish lived: an ideal and reliable support system that enhanced his quick-strike capabilities and chances of survival. Along with his brothers, Gavin Witherspoon, a Scotch-Irish warrior from South Carolina, was one such volunteer. He became Marion's finest marksman, earning a reputation for dropping redcoat, Hessian, and Loyalist soldiers.

But more importantly for Marion and other partisan leaders, larger numbers of Scotch-Irish, mostly second generation, had migrated to South Carolina via the port of Charleston than any other Southern colony. Many of these Irish had gained invaluable experience in Indian warfare both before and during the American Revolution, protecting their communities from British-inspired and supplied raids. This was especially the case during the Cherokee War of 1776, when the Cherokee were devastated by slashing raids by mostly Celtic-Gaelic frontiersmen who took the war to the enemy. New partisan leaders emerged from the Cherokee War experience (extending back as far as the French and Indian War) with invaluable tactical insights and skills, including Marion, Pickens, and Sumter, and just in time to meet the Revolutionary War's challenges.[52]

Guaranteeing a severe backlash from the Ulster Irish settlers, Lieutenant Colonel Banastre "Ban" Tarleton's men turned their wrath on Irish Presbyterian churches, including the house of worship of "rebel" Scotch-Irish minister John Simpson. He was a holy warrior who relied on the Bible as much as the flintlock musket. With his usual ruthlessness, Loyalist Captain Christian Huck burned down Simpson's Fishing Creek Church, South Carolina, on June 11, 1780, leaving the largely Scotch-Irish community without a church and the wife and children of the New Jersey-born Princeton College graduate (Simpson graduated in 1768) homeless.

For ample good reason, as in John Simpson's case, Tarleton called these Scotch-Irish houses of worship "sedition shops." Lord Charles Cornwallis's most aggressive top lieutenant was entirely correct. A synthesis of fiery republicanism and revolutionary zeal had early blossomed among the Scotch-Irish from the deeply planted seeds of Presbyterianism on a scale not seen among South Carolina's German settlers or any others. After learning some hard lessons about attempting to subdue them, Tarleton declared that the Irish were "the most adverse of all other settlers to the British government in America."[53]

One historian correctly concluded that the very "backbone of Irish participation [of the struggle was] in the middle colonies and to a less degree in the Carolinas."[54] But even this tribute was an underestimation of the overall contributions of the Irish and Scotch-Irish patriots of both North and South Carolina, where the resistance effort could not be stamped out despite Cornwallis's best efforts after Charleston's fall. Bringing their distinctive cultural traditions with them, the Celtic-Gaelic people had flooded into North Carolina singing a popular song entitled "Going to Seek a Fortune in North Carolina." Indeed, even more than the influence of Age of Enlightenment ideals and writings (including England's John Locke), the enduring legacy of the tragic course of Irish history and the overall Irish experiences were decisive catalysts: dual influences—one personal, one historical—that fueled powerful motivations of the Irish in the Carolinas to continue to wage war against an ancient foe.[55]

The timing of the mass Irish migrations to America's shores was vital in explaining the disproportionate Irish and Scotch-Irish participation in the revolutionary struggle, providing thousands of ready-made revolutionaries and the most radical political and military leaders, from the enlisted ranks to regimental commanders, in America. Indeed, "the total number of Irish immigrants to America during the years 1771, 1772 and 1773 was not far short of one hundred thousand. And [because] so many of these people left their native land [due to] the harsh treatment which they received from government and landlords it [is no] wonder that large numbers of Irishmen are found fighting under the standard of Washington" throughout the American Revolution's course.[56] Much more intimately than the non-Irish and especially those colonists of English or German descent, the highly motivated Irish and Scotch-Irish intimately "understood that failure to come together would mean that colonial Americans would find themselves in a situation much like the eighteen-century Irish, a subjugated people within the British Empire."[57] More than twenty Irishmen or sons of Irish immigrants became generals either in the Continental Army or in the state militias during the eight years of struggle. A total of twenty-two generals or their fathers or grandfathers were born in Ireland.[58]

The overall high percentage of leading Irish and Scotch-Irish players (in the enlisted, officers', and general officers' ranks) resulted in many notable achievements on the battlefield. This development was especially the case because America's struggle was only an overall minimal resistance effort, since the vast majority of the American people remained either neutral or Loyalist during the conflict. In terms of overall demographics, the greatest numbers of Celtic-Gaelic patriots hailed from the more than one thousand-mile length of the western frontier, especially in Pennsylvania, where most Irish and Scotch-Irish people lived by 1775, while Loyalist sentiment was primarily an East Coast phenomenon: the continuation of the historic east-west divide resulting from wide class and economic disparities.

In a May 1776 letter to a Virginia congressman, General Charles Lee early realized, "I do not believe that many of the native Virginians [non-Irish] will offer themselves [to serve in the Continental Army, while] The Irish, I am persuaded, will enlist in crowds."[59] Known for his intelligence and insight, Lee accurately predicted the overwhelming participation of the Irish and Scotch-Irish, especially in Washington's Army, but also in every American army in every theater of operations.[60]

The large percentage of Irish and Scotch-Irish who served America was also mirrored by British Army demographics, both in the enlisted and officer ranks, during the eighteenth and early nineteenth centuries. Large numbers of British officers were either Irish or Scots by the time of the American Revolution; 31 percent of the England's officer corps was Irish and another 27 percent was Scottish. Additionally, the Irish dominated the ranks of England's royal artillery regiments, with the vast majority of Sons of Erin manning field artillery pieces against many of their fellow Celtic-Gaelic countrymen on American soil.

After the opening muskets were fired at Lexington and Concord on April 19, 1775, five of the British Army's "Irish regiments," whose battle flags were decorated with the Irish harp that had symbolized the Emerald Isle since the medieval period, were dispatched from Irish ports, including Cork, to America. The Eighteenth Regiment of Foot (the Royal Irish) was one such well-trained British unit, which arrived in America in 1767. Detachments of the Royal Irish, who wore buttons distinguished by the letters "R.I.," fought at Lexington and Concord. During the Battle of Bunker Hill, Irishman Lieutenant William Richardson was the first "British" soldier to gain the parapet at Breed's Hill just before he was seriously wounded.

Another reliable Irish regiment of the British Army was the appropriately named Volunteers of Ireland, or the Second American Regiment. Organized in 1778 and known as the King's Irish Regiment, this fine command served with distinction in both the northern and southern theaters. However, many Irishmen in red uniforms were reluctant soldiers, having been impressed into British service as cannon fodder. Many Irish deserted the British Army because they were unwilling to meet fellow countrymen, including even relatives, in deadly strife on America's battlefields.[61] As before the struggle, this longtime Irish tradition and legacy of British military service continued after the American Revolution. During the Napoleonic Wars of the late eighteenth and early nineteenth centuries, the Irish made up an estimated 40 percent of the British Army.[62]

Worst of all, these Irish were at the mercy of abusive English officers and court martial officials while serving on American soil. Irish Private Thomas MacMahan took one thousand lashes for the crime of receiving stolen goods while his Irish wife, Isabella MacMahan, a camp follower, was given one hundred lashes for the same offense since they evidently worked as a team.[63] Likewise, American commanders, most likely non-Irish themselves, also were quite harsh (in an age known for brutality) to Irish women, who were caught between a sense of responsibility to spouses or relatives in uniform and rigid military regulations known for intolerance. Major Alexander Spotswood, Second Virginia Regiment, which had been authorized in mid-July 1775 to defend Virginia, tried Florence Mahoney, a high-spirited Irish camp follower who might have been addicted to drink like so many men (both Irish and non-Irish) in the ranks, before a court martial "for Rioting after sun set."[64]

Spotswood had his hands full with this tempestuous Virginia Irish lady. And, of course, the Irish soldier of both sides hardly relished taking orders from autocratic officers any more than they had when being ordered around in a high-handed way by England landlords in the old country. An Irish soldier named Bernard Clary was court-martialed for his impassioned activities in "Spreading and Incouraging [sic] Mutiny" in the Second Virginia Regiment's ranks.[65]

Nevertheless, despite the cruel discipline and battles in a strange land, these Irishmen fought bravely for Great Britain, including against their fellow Irish in every major battle. The Volunteers of Ireland, British Army, passed the time in singing their own lively regimental song, emphasizing their well-known combat prowess, especially in the South: "Success to the Shamrock . . . So Yankee keep off, or you'll soon learn your error, For Paddy shall prostrate lay every foe."[66]

Of course given the Irish people's distinctive brand of humor and wit, comparable Irish bravado was seen on the other side, especially in Washington's Army, as in a spirited ditty entitled "An Irishman's Epistle to the Troops in Boston." This song was sung when the British garrison was besieged by Washington's Army until Howe's evacuation of the strategic port city and departure for Canada on St. Patrick's Day 1776: "With your brains in your breeches, your ____ in your skulls . . . You see now, my honeys, how much you're mistaken, For Concord by discord can never be beaten . . . And what have you got now with all your designing, But a town without victuals to sit down and dine in . . . I am sure if you're wise you'll make peace by dinner, For fighting and fasting will soon make ye thinner."[67] Because of the shortage of uniforms among the ragtag revolutionaries, some of Washington's Irish soldiers wore British regimental buttons captured from English supply ships made by Irish firms, such as Cox and Mair, in Dublin.[68]

Many modern historians, American and English, have maintained low opinions of the Irish and Scotch fighting man compared to the yeoman farmer-soldier of British descent from New England. After all, the Celtic-Gaelic people of America were often severely denounced by the British, especially the aristocracy, who considered the Irish "second-class human beings" in the traditionally distorted racist view that legitimized England's conquest over those "dam[n] Irish," while expressing a common sentiment throughout among the English people throughout British history: "Damb [sic] the Scotch and Irish."[69] In pre-revolutionary Virginia, some aristocratic members of the ruling gentry held the transplanted Scottish and Scotch-Irish revolutionaries of America in such open contempt that the greatest possible insult was to denounce them as nothing more than a "Scotch rebel."[70]

However, President William Jefferson Clinton, himself of Irish heritage and a former Rhodes Scholar, correctly emphasized the importance of the Irish contribution. In a 1995 speech, he stated, "In the fight for our independence . . . there were Irishmen from both traditions [Catholic and Protestant] serving side by side in all-Irish units [and] they were among the most feared warriors. They put freedom over faction, and they helped to build our Nation."[71] These much detested and unfairly maligned Irish served faithfully so that America never suffered Ireland's tragic fate: "If Washington and his men failed, America would never again be permitted to pursue a separate destiny [as] She would be as mercilessly a part of England and Europe as Ireland—and with perhaps as many sorrows to tell."[72]

Although unappreciated by traditional historians, a unique phenomenon developed on America soil and rose to a level of dominance during the American Revolution: "Of the natives in the army most were of Irish, Scotch, Welch, and French descent, mostly Celts, and a large proportion of the so-called 'English' were of Cornish, Welch, Manx, and other Celtic Calvanist extraction, enemies of the English Church and state, so that the American Revolution was almost exclusively Celtic."[73] In truth, America's revolution was very much a Celtic-Gaelic one.

Chapter V

A New Generation of the Most Radical Revolutionaries in America

Not only militarily but also politically, the Celtic-Gaelic people led the way as the most radical revolutionaries in all America. Around 1700, the alarmed Virginia House of Burgesses in Williamsburg, the capital of the Virginia Colony, described the growing threat posed to autocracy and upper-class rule from the unruly byproducts of the Irish experience: "The Christian Servants [especially Irish Catholics] in this country for the most part consist of the Worse Sort of the people of Europe [and] such numbers of Irish and other Nations have been brought in of which a great many have been soldiers in the late wars that [now] we can hardly governe [sic] them [and] they may rise upon us."[1]

Such omnipresent fears of a bloody uprising among the "rabble," especially those Irishmen with military experience and revolutionary backgrounds in Ireland and Scotland, among America's landed colonel elite and the transplanted British aristocracy were well founded long before the American Revolution. Much more radical as revolutionaries in every way than the fundamentally conservative Founding Fathers who feared the "mob," the Virginia rebels of Nathaniel Bacon's 1676 revolution rose up against the abusive royal governor and his corrupt administration of cronies centered at that "little sodom" of Jamestown, then Virginia's capital.

These radical revolutionaries rallied behind young "General" Bacon. They had earlier gathered under arms to save themselves and their families by vanquishing the Susquehanna Iroquois, who raided the frontiers, before turning their sights to the abuses of autocratic government. Bacon and his mostly lower-class followers then turned upon their other privileged upper-class tormentors who ruled like wealthy feudal lords at Jamestown. These commoners, mostly frontiersmen but also black slaves and Irish indentured servants, served as the liberty-minded members of the self-styled "Army of Virginia." These divergent individuals were united as one with the idealistic goal of overturning an exploitative colonial society. They waged a righteous war against the ruling elite and their abuses—including unfair land policies, non-protection from Indian attack (like the "Paxton Boys" of the Pennsylvania frontier), and arbitrary heavy taxation—in a social upheaval that swept away the flimsy foundations of the Virginia's troubled Chesapeake society based on elite rule.

As in other American colonies, the powerful ruling aristocracy had long crassly exploited lower-class settlers on the western frontier as an expendable commodity and buffer to protect Williamsburg, Jamestown, and the genteel world of Virginia's upper-class elites from Indian attack. With the lower-class, poor colonists rising up as one, this miniature social revolution (incorrectly known as Bacon's insurrection) was an authentic grassroots movement that led to America's first establishment of independence by the common people after they forced the dictatorial governor, Sir William Berkeley, to flee for his life. In the end, however, Bacon's revolution and his infant republican government were smashed, and royal control was then reestablished in Virginia.

But a radical tradition was destined to be resurrected in the Virginia Tidewater, and a much more successful revolution—although not in social terms like the attempted goal of Bacon's radical one—to break away from British imperial domination and establish political independence erupted one hundred years later. Once again the people of Virginia, this time mostly Irish and Scotch-Irish people instead of mostly British settlers, played leading roles on military, economic, and political levels from 1775–1783: one of the principal differences and forgotten reasons to explain why true political independence was achieved in 1776 and not in 1676.[2]

Thanks to the synchronization of cherished democratic traditions of Ireland and Northern Ireland's political activism with its anti-authoritarian and egalitarian Presbyterianism, the Irish and Scotch-Irish played prominent revolutionary political roles from the beginning. While the majority of American colonists, including the Founding Fathers, remained conservative, initially hesitant about breaking completely with England, and only loudly debated the day's complex issues in refined formal circles unheard by the lower-class masses, the Celtic-Gaelic people had evolved in revolutionary terms far beyond simple debate and compromise to outright action. Consequently, they led the way by agitating and advocating the absolute wisdom of separation from Great Britain earlier and more forcefully than the vast majority of America's non-Irish, who remained either neutral or Loyalist.

This direct correlation between the extent of the social and political radicalization of the Irish and Scotch-Irish, both in Ireland and America, and consequently the leading roles that they played in serving as the revolution's vanguard, was best represented in Pennsylvania. Here, their significant egalitarian influence resulted in America's most extreme revolutionary radicalism and militancy of the period. The presence of so many lower-class Irish and Scotch-Irish in Pennsylvania, both in the cities and western frontier areas of this large middle colony, translated directly to the birth of an unsurpassed egalitarian ideology in its most radical, or purest, form on American soil and a determined drive for greater equality in Pennsylvania that was more energized than in any other colony, and later state, in America.

At the army's first encampment at Cambridge, Washington was initially horrified that the egalitarian officers of New England's citizen-soldier army consisted of the much-despised "lower class." Under the circumstances, Washington's reaction was a perfectly natural response. This cultural and political tradition of elitism brought over by the upper class from England (after which the Virginia upper crust modeled themselves), to create an inequitable situation in which power rested with a relatively few autocratic members of the British elite and then wealthy colonial Americans, ensured that the Irish and Scotch-Irish became the most radical, militant, and extremist people in the thirteen colonies by 1775.

Situated along the expansive length of the frontier lands nestled between rampaging Indians, who emerged from the Ohio Valley's depths, and the wealthy ruling elite along the East Coast, including Tidewater Virginia (Washington's home), the Irish and Scotch-Irish detested this ruling autocracy that was comparable to Ireland's landlords. Therefore, upper class non-Irish of Pennsylvania had long feared the threat of a "Mac-ocracy." Demanding more equality and fair representation, disgruntled frontier Pennsylvanians, especially the Scotch-Irish who were already heavily armed to protect themselves against Indian attack, marched upon Philadelphia. Here, more than a decade before the American Revolution, these homespun revolutionaries (later known as the "Paxton Boys") had boldly presented a "Declaration and Remonstrance" of their grievances in early 1764.

More of an egalitarian legacy stemming from the old Ireland than the New World experience in the wilderness, according to the overly generalized Frederick Jackson Turner frontier thesis, a pristine demonstration of democracy on America's frontier also made an early dramatic impact. Mostly Irish and Scotch-Irish squatters in the West Branch Susquehanna River valley of Pennsylvania, part of the fertile lands of central Pennsylvania and the heart of Ulster America that stretched from Lancaster west to Barton County, created their own system of enlightened self-rule, known as the Fair Play System, in 1773. These "Fair Men" of humble origins were overwhelmingly anti-British and central-government-hating Scotch-Irish. They declared their own independence from Great Britain in the Pine Creek Declaration of Independence in the early summer of 1776, following the example of the "Westmoreland [County] Declaration" at Hanna's Town in Westmoreland County, Pennsylvania, during May 1775 and the

Mecklenburg Declaration of Independence at Charlotte in May 1775: bold moves that all predated the Continental Congress's Declaration of Independence of July 4, 1776.

With so many Irish and Scotch-Irish located in Pennsylvania, both in Philadelphia and along the western frontier, historian Gordon S. Wood explained that "nowhere else was there more social antagonism expressed during the Revolution [and] of all the states in the Revolution [Pennsylvania] saw the most abrupt and complete shift in political power [and caused] a revolutionary transference of authority that was nowhere in 1776 so sudden and stark."[3] The same could be said before the American Revolution in regard to early agitators in Pennsylvania, including the "Paxton Boys," who were predominantly disgruntled Scotch-Irish settlers and frontiersmen.[4] Even before the first shots were fired in anger on Lexington Green to shock the world, Pennsylvania witnessed the dramatic rising of the Scotch-Irish in urban areas like Philadelphia. Here, influential political leaders, like Dubliner George Bryan and Charles Thomson, who hailed from the town of Maghera in County Derry, Ulster Province, Northern Ireland, simply detached themselves from government and boldly bypassed the Quaker-controlled assembly. These radicalized Irishmen represented the common people of both the western frontier and city's interests of the greatest mass of Scotch-Irish, now of the "Presbyterian Party." For the first time, the lower-class Scotch-Irish now possessed a true voice in representative government. These defiant Scotch-Irish declarations of independence on the western frontier, especially in Pennsylvania, were genuine grassroots movements of self-determination stemming from the most sizeable concentration of Scotch-Irish in America.

In contrast, the Founding Fathers' official declaration of independence on the Fourth of July, 1776, was actually a case of the aristocratic elite following behind the defiant egalitarianism already acted upon by the mostly lower-class Scotch-Irish people of Pennsylvania's western frontier and in Philadelphia. However, the enduring power of the mythical revolution—a highly romanticized creation that evolved afterward—designated the revered "Signers" as those inspirational leaders who galvanized and led the common people forward (as if they had no common sense or intelligence of their own) to embrace independence and revolution. In 1774, fearful of the "mob," Sam and John Adams even slowed down the drive toward independence, contrary to the egalitarian longings of their lowly constituents, consisting of many Irish and Scotch-Irish, who were already way ahead of these two revered Founding Fathers from Boston.[5]

Like no other single catalyst, the overall Irish experience had set the stage for the rise of republican government and shaped the dramatic push toward independence, but this time in America. The Irish and Scotch-Irish across the colonies fully realized that it was "the aristocrats who were running England and Ireland [and] Bereft of all leadership since the exile of the Catholic nobility after the battle of the Boyne in 1690, Ireland was a perfect example of how aggressive governments such as England could fire crush and then exploit another nation:" a lesson never forgotten by the tens of thousands of transplanted Irish of humble origins in America.[6]

Clearly, what had evolved was very much a massive grassroots uprising and nationalistic "Ulster Revolution" on American soil before it went through an extraordinary evolutionary process and was properly renamed the American Revolution. In this fashion, the Scotch-Irish had laid the earliest and most solid central foundation for the shaping of a "nascent American [sense of] nationalism [built upon the foundation of a sturdy anti-British Irish nationalism, which essentially] became heavily Presbyterian in tone" and thorough egalitarian sentiment, which primarily pitted the common man of humble origins (especially farmers, laborers, indentured servants, and western frontiersmen) against the privileged upper class—not only in Pennsylvania but also elsewhere in the thirteen colonies, including New York and Virginia. But the most thorough transformation first occurred in Pennsylvania, where the Irish "Presbyterian Triumvirate" of fiery leaders rose up to take power.[7]

A keen, analytical foreign observer, the Marquis de Chastellux described the powerful appeal of the shining dream of America that had already come true for the average Irish of the western frontier long before the Declaration of Independence. This highly educated French aristocrat explained how, when traveling in the "western mountains" (the Blue Ridge) of western Virginia, he and his small party "stopped at a little lonely house, a Mr. MacDonnell's, an Irishman [and although] in the centre of the woods, and wholly occupied in rustic business, a Virginian never resembles an European peasant; he is always a freeman, participates in the government [and] resembles the bulk of individuals who formed what was called the people in the ancient republics," especially ancient Greece and Rome.[8]

While the Founding Fathers have become the immortalized leaders of the much-romanticized revolution of legend and fable, modern historians have continued to treat the lower-class Irish and Scotch-Irish, including key revolutionary political leaders, almost as if they were nonentities, while also ignoring the decisive impact of the Irish experience on both sides (especially Ireland) of the Atlantic. What has been especially overlooked is that a generation of militant Ulster revolutionaries, who had already been radicalized and politicized by the Irish experience and knew intimately how the British had subjugated Ireland and the ugly consequences upon generations of the Irish people, directly and significantly influenced the Founding Fathers by word, action, and deed, not the other way around.

For instance, Charles Thomson, born in County Derry, Ireland, in 1729 and formerly an indentured servant, played the key role in turning Benjamin Franklin against the Quaker moderates of Philadelphia and toward a more defiant revolutionary stance, which eventually transformed him into America's most effective diplomat in France, especially in orchestrating the eventual French Alliance. The Scotch-Irish and Irish, who were experienced in the Machiavellian wiles of faraway centralized government, located at the same distant seat of power (London), were among the very first to sound the prophetic warning when the British government attempted to impose tighter government controls and imperial authority. Irish leaders like Bryan, Thomson, and James Smith in Pennsylvania and Thomas McKean and George Read in Delaware continued to sound the wise warning that America was bound to suffer Ireland's tragic fate at British hands, playing leading roles in creating revolutionary committees of correspondence. This dramatic rise of the Irish resulted in McKean and Thomson's winning control of the Pennsylvania government in what was essentially a Scotch-Irish political coup in a peaceful, but decisive, takeover.[9]

The misrepresentation of Irish and Scotch-Irish roles and their seemingly endless contributions to the winning of independence have continued unabated to this day. Robert Leckie in *General Washington's War* demeaned the hard-fighting Scotch-Irish frontiersmen, who reaped one of the war's most important successes at Kings Mountain, South Carolina, in early October 1780: "The phase Declaration of Independence meant about as much to them as it did to their livestock." In this way, Leckie sounded much like British and Hessian leaders, including Major Patrick Ferguson, the Loyalist leader who was killed at Kings Mountain, whose contempt for the Scotch-Irish frontiersmen west of the mountains (the "Overmountain Men") could not have been greater, denouncing them in his official October 1, 1780 proclamation as "barbarians." Ray Raphael rightly criticized Leckie, who was born in Philadelphia, Pennsylvania, the Irish capital of Revolutionary War America, for reducing the Irish to "animals, not Americans, [so that] their deeds need not reflect poorly on the cause."[10]

Leckie's opinion of the lowly Scotch-Irish frontiersmen, who reaped one of the most dramatic and important patriotic victories at Kings Mountain, was comparable to that of Ferguson, who labeled some of America's most fierce patriots as nothing more than "banditti."[11] It was true that these rugged men, who knew nothing of proper manners, etiquette, or protocol, were in fact "America's first hillbillies," in the words of historian Ed Southern, but they were not barbarians, except when unleashed against their opponent as at Kings Mountain and on other battlefields across America.[12]

But the most significant political contributions of the Celtic-Gaelic were evident in the Declaration of Independence. Jefferson's "earlier drafts showed influences of the 'Presbyterian document of the Pennsylvanians, and this latter document . . . was probably closer to the revolutionary reasoning of a largely Protestant and Calvinist American [that was] Rooted in radical Whiggery [such as Scotch-Irishman Francis Hutchenson], honed in Dublin, fused with Presbyterianism [and therefore] the depth of the Protestant [or Presbyterian] colouring of the Revolution cannot be underestimated," correctly analyzed David Noel Doyle.[13]

Clearly, from beginning to end, dynamic pro-independence leaders from far outside the pre-revolutionary establishment and the wealthy upper-class elite rose up in Pennsylvania and elsewhere to significantly influence the ultimate Declaration of Independence. This emerging generation of dynamic Celtic-Gaelic leaders of Pennsylvania included the successful Dublin-born Philadelphia merchant, George Bryan, and of course Charles Thomson. An egalitarian-minded Presbyterian educated in Dublin, Bryan had first migrated to America as a middle-class Irish immigrant. Other vocal radical leaders of revolutionary Pennsylvania included Scotland-born James Cannon, Robert Whitehill, born in Pennsylvania with Scotch-Irish roots, and Timothy Matlack, who was a close associate of Ireland-born McKean. These influential leaders of the common people eagerly embraced the mantle of a grassroots rising to gain political power in Pennsylvania after engineering their political coup over the colony's wealthy ruling elites who operated the Quaker-dominated assembly, which failed to represent Scotch-Irish or Irish lower class interests, especially on the western frontier, for generations.

A natural Celtic-Gaelic "brawler" from Ireland's Catholic south (warmed by the Gulf Stream's mild temperatures and rains) who not only opposed British domination but also all things upper-class, elitist, and aristocratic like so many other down-to-earth Irish of common antecedents, Bryan was almost as well known for his hot Irish temper as his considerable political skills devoted to revolution and the egalitarian and republican faiths. Quite unexpectedly, this remarkable Irishman, who never lost sight of his roots, rose to the very top in the rough-and-tumble world of Pennsylvania revolutionary politics. In this new land of so much promise (the "New Canaan" to the Irish Presbyterians), he was an idealist like so many Irish and Scotch-Irish immigrants who fully embraced America's egalitarian dream. In 1752, he had migrated to Philadelphia to operate a branch of his family's mercantile business (the firm of Wallace and Bryan) in the bustling port city.

But most of all, Bryan represented the common sentiments of Pennsylvania's Irish and Scotch-Irish people, opposing "whatever was British." These radicalized, aggressive "new" leaders of Pennsylvania were proud of their distinctive Celtic-Gaelic political and vibrant revolutionary traditions. Most of all, they possessed an uncompromising egalitarianism carried across the Atlantic from Ireland as part of their cultural and historical baggage. Such fiery Scotch-Irish leaders represented the Celtic-Gaelic people on the western frontier and Philadelphia's influential Irish Presbyterian community while "clothed with the most extreme Whig rhetoric" that was more radical (or essentially Irish in all respects) than American in the most purely revolutionary and democratic terms.[14]

A highly respected leader of the First Presbyterian Church in Philadelphia and the main spokesman of his distinctive ethno-religious Scotch-Irish community on the banks of the Delaware River, Bryan was an ideal revolutionary leader. He reflected the dissenter radicalism and egalitarianism of southern Ireland, a longtime revolutionary hotbed for anti-British sentiment and agitation. He was militantly outspoken, defiant toward established authority of almost any kind, and strongly against entrenched privilege and power, either British or colonial. And this was especially the case in regard to Bryan and his Celtic-Gaelic people after the Pennsylvania government had long failed to protect the Irish and Scotch-Irish settlers on Pennsylvania's western frontier from Indian raids during and after the French and Indian War. Outraged Scotch-Irish were united by their ever-mounting grievances against the autocratic governor and the pacifist Quaker-dominated government. One smug Quaker assemblyman dismissed the destructive Indian raids that brought widespread death to the largely Scotch-Irish western frontier settlements because "only some Scotch-Irish [were] killed, who could well enough be spared."[15]

Realizing that the pacifist Pennsylvania government was almost as much an obstacle to the Celtic-Gaelic people's survival on the isolated western frontier as rampaging Native American warriors in search of scalps and other war trophies, Irish Presbyterian leaders of Philadelphia had long advocated the launching of an aggressive war against the Indians, and Bryan loudly called for "a spirited attack on their villages" in retaliation. A savvy Quaker was correct in doubting that any Irish Presbyterian was loyal to Crown authority because "ancient or present, Presbyterianism and Rebellion were twin-sisters, sprung from faction, and their affection for each other, has been ever so strong."[16]

Most of all, the Scotch-Irish and Irish leaders of Pennsylvania such as Thomson and Bryan, who had been taught by the ultra-republican Presbyterian minister Dr. Francis Alison, were motivated by their fervent religious faith. The uncompromising Thomson early advocated breaking away from Great Britain because it was as unjust as the despotic rule from ancient times, especially in regard to the enslaved Israelites in Egypt. Bryan's urging of retaliation invoked revered Biblical moral lessons long held as sacred by generations of Irish Presbyterians.

After the Irish Presbyterians (or radical Whigs) rose to power in Pennsylvania to establish the most radical state constitution in America in 1776, Bryan served as the very vanguard of republican ideals by becoming the vice president and acting president of Pennsylvania.

Like so many other of his fellow countrymen, this republican-minded Irishman represented the day's most radical revolutionary principles and the still-revered egalitarian heritage of Ireland (including ancient Brehon Law) in America. Even more, in what was very much of a social conflict, Bryan was also the leading voice of the poor against the rich. What he emphasized was an especially fiery brand of Scotch-Irish radicalism, based upon an unprecedented and utopian quest for "perfect equality," in Bryan's words, which especially appealed to Pennsylvania's poor, lower-class Irish, who were in the majority.

New England's revolutionary leader John Adams, like Franklin, was shocked upon learning how the lower classes (primarily the Scotch-Irish) had triumphed in Pennsylvania. Adams lamented with some dismay, "Good God! The people of Pennsylvania in two years will be glad to petition the crown of Britain for reconciliation in order to be delivered from the tyranny of the commonwealth," which was dominated by the radical Scotch-Irish revolutionaries. They had finally accomplished on American soil what generations of their forefathers had been unable to achieve on the Green Isle with so much blood and sacrifice.[17]

This unique democratic phenomenon that swept Pennsylvania to overturn the existing hierarchical social order was more radicalized than in any other colony or later state, thanks largely to the strength of Ireland's cultural, historical, religious, and political legacies. Clearly the most enlightened and egalitarian faiths and aspirations originally "framed in Ireland and kept alive by wave after wave of immigrants" had played a decisive role in the birth of a true democracy on American soil long before the Declaration of Independence's signing.[18]

Appalled in watching his tidy hierarchical world of the social elites turned upside down, conservative, pro-British leader Joseph Galloway had feared "a coup of [Irish] Presbyterians and radicals that might seize power" in Pennsylvania as early as 1764. And when anti-British feeling among the people erupted during the Stamp Act crisis in 1766, an angry Galloway "blamed the Presbyterians"

(Scotch-Irish) for the swelling tide of radical revolutionary sentiment. Quite correctly, Galloway viewed the Scotch-Irish as the most zealous and main driving force behind the establishment of the most extreme "republican institutions" in Pennsylvania.[19]

But what most astonished Galloway (and is most revealing in regard to Celtic-Gaelic roots) was that the groundswell of rising hostility against the mother country, which actually ruled quite benignly (especially when compared to Ireland), taxing Americans less than its own citizens in England or the West Indies, was, in his view, "without cause." Like British leaders on the Atlantic's other side, however, Galloway was unable to understand how thoroughly the enduring egalitarian and revolutionary legacies and sheer trauma of the Irish experience had long ago transformed the Irish and Scotch-Irish into passionate haters of aristocracy, centralized government, and authoritarian power. Of course, one of the fundamental concepts of America's mythical revolution was that taxation was the chief catalyst, as if the crucial Irish experience was no factor whatsoever.[20]

Exemplified by its radical 1776 constitution, Pennsylvania's extremist revolutionary ideology articulated the most radical aspects of social revolution, which had been derived largely from the Irish experience and a deep-seated Presbyterianism that burned brightly in hearts and minds of the Scotch-Irish. As historian Wood concluded, "In fact, to judge solely from the literature the Revolution in Pennsylvania had become a class war between the poor and the rich, between the common people and the privileged few [and] It is ironic that both the Revolution and the rhetoric should have been so violently extreme in Pennsylvania. . . ."[21] But there should have been nothing ironic about the dramatic rise of democratic and egalitarian ideology in Pennsylvania that resulted in America's most radical constitution during the American Revolution.

Pennsylvania's heavily Irish and Scotch-Irish demographics, which fueled the rise of the ultra-nationalist "Presbyterian Party," explained this remarkable development. What was recreated in official form by

Pennsylvania's new largely Scotch-Irish leaders—when James Smith, who led the frontier Scotch-Irish, united political forces with Bryan and McKean, who led the urban Scotch-Irish—was the dominant thoughts and sentiments of the colony's lowest order and most common people, who were mostly the sons and daughters from Ulster Province: the highly combustible fuel that propelled this rising tide of revolutionary spirit and a new nationalism.

What these dynamic new leaders of the most extremist Whig leadership in America articulated in Pennsylvania and elsewhere (such as the May 1775 Mecklenburg Declaration of Independence in North Carolina) was only what had already long existed for generations in the hearts and minds of the Irish and Scotch-Irish people on both sides of the Atlantic. Across America, the Irish and the Scotch-Irish, especially the indentured servants, had the most to gain from overturning the existing social order and beginning the world anew. Most importantly, these most radical and ultra-republican developments in Pennsylvania clearly revealed that the earliest and most enlightened egalitarian thought in America existed among the Celtic-Gaelic common people of society's lowest order in Pennsylvania's urban and rural areas.

These unrecognized and unsung common folk from the Emerald Isle were in fact the revolution's true architects of America's great dream of liberty, which was essentially a resurrection of some of the oldest and most cherished of Irish dreams. Imbued by this extreme republican faith, the Celtic-Gaelic revolutionaries were then the ones who fought and died on the battlefield in disproportionate numbers for their extreme egalitarian beliefs (a case of turning idealistic rhetoric into action) unlike America's wealthy political elite, who, if not Loyalist, remained secure in the servant-attended mansions, busy managing their gangs of slaves on plantations and engaging in operating lucrative business enterprises (including trading with the enemy) in major cities far from the front lines throughout the war years. While most Founding Fathers only remotely understood history's harsh lessons stemming primarily from those of ancient Greece and Rome, the common people of Ireland intimately knew the ugly realities of persecution and defeat like no other colonists in America, especially the Germans and those of British descent.

In this Celtic-Gaelic political revolution, what resulted was the systematic rise of the lower classes of Pennsylvania Irish and Scotch-Irish, the rapid upward movement of middle-class Scotch-Irish spokesmen into lofty revolutionary leadership positions, and their application of an especially egalitarian ideology. Instead of merely repeating the lofty words of long-standing Age of Enlightenment ideology as espoused by John Locke and penned by Jefferson in the Declaration of Independence, direct action and confrontation to fulfill the loftiest egalitarian visions in America spoke louder than words for thousands of lower-class Pennsylvania Irish and Scotch-Irish, who led the way in key political and military roles throughout the revolution.

The largely illiterate, uneducated common people of Pennsylvania never needed to attend prestigious universities, learn Latin, or read classical works of history and inflammatory revolutionary pamphlets by either Locke or Thomas Paine to become the most radicalized and militant rebels on American soil. The fundamental basis of the long-existing ultra-egalitarian thought among the Irish and Scotch-Irish people was only a natural, instinctive reaction stemming from the tragic lessons of the Irish past and the personal experiences of severe adversity. What had manifested itself in Pennsylvania to a truly remarkable degree was a natural and authentic grassroots revolution from below, led mostly by Irish and Scotch-Irish revolutionaries.

For the Irish and Scotch-Irish, radical revolutionary sentiment was not only deeply embedded in hearts and minds but also had been spread by the vibrant oral tradition, especially among the illiterate, of the close-knit Irish communities on the western frontier and in distinctive Celtic-Gaelic ethnic enclaves farther east. By this means, a more extreme and militant revolutionary ideology was forged on American soil by 1775, evolving far beyond what was envisioned, or even imagined, by the more conservative Founding Fathers. Like in faraway Ireland and especially on the sprawling western frontier, egalitarian sentiment already not only existed but also thrived, reaching full bloom by the time of the revolutionary upheaval. In contrast to the core tenets of the mythical revolution, the Irish and Scotch-Irish were not manipulated pawns who were directed to embrace radicalism and to take forceful revolutionary action by the heated rhetoric of better educated upper-class leaders. What had developed in America was in essence the timely resurrection of the Celtic-Gaelic grassroots revolutionary and egalitarian traditions (including enlightened legacies of Irish society, including from Ireland's ancient Brehon law) brought across the Atlantic by hundreds of thousands of migrants from Ireland. They attempted to transform a conservative revolution into something much more egalitarian, more truly democratic, and, hence, more meaningful than anything imaged by the conservative Founding Fathers, who looked upon so many of the Celtic-Gaelic people as little more than a mob or "rabble."

While the Founding Fathers employed lofty words not often understood by them, the ordinary Celtic-Gaelic people articulated the authentic and true meaning of the most egalitarian concept of liberty based more upon the radicalism of a true social revolution rather than the Founding Fathers' conservative revolution. In this sense, Pennsylvania's political situation more closely resembled an authentic social revolution and Celtic-Gaelic liberation struggle as in the past, because seemingly countless Irish revolts had sought to completely overturn the existing exploitative social and political order by fiery revolution.

Without having read anything from Age of Enlightenment writers, Andrew Jackson's family represented the plight of the typical Scotch-Irish patriot family. Born in the Scotch-Irish community of the Waxhaws, South Carolina, Andrew Jackson was the son of two impoverished Ulster immigrants, Andrew Sr. and Elizabeth Jackson. After their father had died from overwork, the Jackson brothers, teenage Andrew, Robert, and Hugh, fought against the British who burned down the Waxhaws Presbyterian Church. Only Andy survived.

Elizabeth, a remarkable Ireland-born woman and die-hard patriot, died of disease while nursing American captives in Charleston.

By any measure, Pennsylvania provided the most revealing example of this distinctive Celtic-Gaelic phenomenon of the dramatic rise of the excessively radicalized egalitarianism, because more Irish and Scotch-Irish lived there than any other state. The fiery words of these egalitarian-minded Scotch-Irish revolutionaries expressed a radical, extremist faith not previously heard in America. As back in Ireland, the crown's leaders were widely denounced by the Irish and Scotch-Irish as a "minority of rich men," whose self-serving efforts and private interests had long been directed toward making "the common and middle class of people their beasts of burden." Pennsylvania's Scotch-Irish leadership declared their extremist radical egalitarian faith with commonsense Celtic-Gaelic reasoning, emphasizing that privileged aristocrats in power derived "no right to power from their wealth."[22] For the most part, consequently, this greater extreme radicalism and egalitarianism in Pennsylvania was fundamentally more Irish than American in almost every way. As recently manifested in Ireland, including Ulster Province, this new wave of militancy, open agitation, and political activism was rooted in cultural and political traditions extending back generations. Formed during the summer of 1776, Pennsylvania's new government struck hard at the very core foundations of an existing social order based upon long-established inequalities and injustices that reminded the Celtic-Gaelic people so much of Ireland's tragic legacies.

Raising ancient cries for justice long heard across the Emerald Isle, these ultra-extremist Celtic-Gaelic revolutionaries on the western frontier and in urban areas, especially Philadelphia, angrily denounced aristocratic rule as back in Ireland. As a precaution that indicated an intimate knowledge of centralized authority abuses, a rotating system of political office was established by the Scotch-Irish leadership of Pennsylvania to eliminate any possibility of "the danger of establishing an inconvenient aristocracy" as in Ireland.[23]

Consequently, far "more than in any other colony in 1776 the Revolution in Pennsylvania was viewed as a social conflict and an authentic revolutionary upheaval between people and aristocracy [and] These new radical spokesmen for the people . . . found themselves compelled to stretch the republican conception of equality to lengths few Revolutionary leaders . . . had ever anticipated."[24] In his desire to tear down the unfair aristocratic and inequitable social structure that had ruled for so long, James Cannon, one of the most passionate Celtic radical leaders in Pennsylvania, emphasized the words that were more deeply appreciated by the Celtic-Gaelic people than even those lofty pronouncements of John Locke and Thomas Paine (both England-born) when he denounced the ruling by "great and overgrown rich Men" while simultaneously proclaiming the inherent decency of the "virtuous freeholders" of Pennsylvania.[25]

But the most revealing aspects of the full egalitarian extent of this radical social revolution based upon Presbyterianism and democratic fundamentals that was led by Pennsylvania's Scotch-Irish Presbyterians was perhaps best revealed in the case of slavery. While the Founding Fathers sought to protect slavery for social, political, and economic reasons in order to ensure an united North-South front against the British, the more truly egalitarian Irish and Scotch-Irish revolutionaries viewed slavery quite differently from most non-Irish, especially elitist members of the upper class from the South. Proving himself a true radical revolutionary and advocate of universal rights of all men regardless of color, Ireland-born Bryan was the dynamic leader of a determined abolition effort in Pennsylvania. He denounced the institution of slavery as an incompatible "disgrace" to a new nation conceived in equality, echoing longtime Irish egalitarian sentiments rooted in Celtic-Gaelic culture and traditions. After all, slavery was unknown in Ireland.

During the American Revolution and thanks to Bryan's tireless efforts, the revolutionary, ultra-democratic Pennsylvania government passed a law providing for the eventual abolition of slavery in

Pennsylvania, the first of its kind in America. Unlike the leading Founding Fathers who failed to advocate slavery's abolition in an infant republic battling for equality and freedom while keeping tens of thousands of slaves in bondage, the most cherished Enlightenment concepts of the rights of man was not an abstract idea to this influential Pennsylvania revolutionary leader from Dublin. This no-nonsense Irishman was an authentic Founding Father who advocated a truly forward-looking progressivism based upon universal human rights and not merely revolutionary rhetoric that translated into nothing more than hollow words to the multitudes of his lower-class Scotch-Irish followers and even African-Americans.[26] In the words of author Joseph S. Foster in regard to Bryan's forgotten contributions to the true meaning of equity in America, "Men like [conservative Thomas] Mifflin and Washington, generals of the revolution, were the new heroes, not the revolutionary zealots who had brought about the destruction of the old order and its violent replacement by 'radical' republicanism."[27]

What happened in Pennsylvania in regard to true democratic advances also eventually occurred in other colonies, largely for the same reasons. For instance, the Irish political and revolutionary leaders also led the way in Delaware, which had been separated from Pennsylvania in 1776. Here, popular Celtic-Gaelic political leaders—John Haslet, Thomas McKean, John McKinly, George Read, and William Killen, who had migrated from the Green Isle in 1737 and who was also a religious-political leader like minister-warrior Haslet—rose to the fore to lead the way to independence. These passionate Celtic-Gaelic leaders, two of whom had been schooled by Reverend Alison, were the primary revolutionary visionaries and most militant leaders who served as the hard-driving vanguard of the resistance effort in Delaware, where the Scotch-Irish influences and contributions proved decisive.[28]

This same process of Scotch-Irish radicalization in the middle colonies in paving the way for open revolution also occurred in the South. Some historians have even emphasized that the true father of the country was not Washington, an aristocrat who owned more than three hundred slaves and one of the wealthiest men in Virginia who dressed accordingly, but Patrick Henry, a non-aristocrat who owned no slaves and dressed in coarse homespun of the Virginia Piedmont's common people. With Scottish and Welsh roots, Henry was truly Celtic to the core, a guarantee that he was the first Founding Father to call for independence.

Even more, Henry's dramatic cry of "Give Me Liberty or Give Me Death" inspired an entire generation of revolutionaries across America. Appropriately, this dynamic Presbyterian son of a Scottish immigrant born in Aberdeen and a self-made man of the common people named his Hanover County, located in the rolling hills and hardwood forests of the Virginia Piedmont northwest of Richmond, home "Scotch-town." In the Celtic tradition, Patrick Henry became well known for his fiery defense of the common people while also knowing how to play a fiddle and sing old bawdy Scottish ballads with as much skill as using a rifle in the pursuit of game. Married to a Presbyterian wife of Welsh heritage and a member of a dissenting Presbyterian clan, Henry gained popularity early by condemning the all-powerful Anglican Church for "extracting the last pennies from poverty-stricken farmers," who were largely Celtic-Gaelic. Living modestly like the common people he adored, Henry became the champion of the small yeoman farmer who struggled to survive. He was the first Founding Father to challenge the ruling colonial aristocracy and the British right to tax (beginning with the Stamp Act in 1765) and govern the colonies. Thomas Jefferson admitted that "Henry gave the first impulse to the call of the revolution."[29]

With the ancient clans rising, Celtic-Gaelic leaders led the way across America. While the urbanities of bustling New York City were dominated by a "reluctance to embrace independence" in 1776, William Smith had been one of South Carolina's most radical leaders from the beginning. When he was a boy, he followed his father Ralph from Bucks County, Pennsylvania, where he had been born, as part of the migration south in a Scotch-Irish exodus. The Smith family eventually settled in the Spartanburg district of South Carolina. As the proud grandson of an ambitious Irish immigrant and still dressed in plain, homespun clothes despite his wealth, Smith's "Irish ancestry had prompted him to take the lead in defying the British government since 1765."[30]

Talking as much about the Irish and Scotch-Irish as any other people in colonial America, Dr. Whitfield J. Bell Jr. understood how this common people's revolution was only won by way of the widespread support and actions of the most ordinary people (the Scotch-Irish and Irish) in America: The "Franklins and the Jeffersons on the one hand, the scoundrels and the killers on the other, are all well known; they crowd history's galleries. But (the people) . . . are the ideal trustees, the perfect friends," who transformed words into victory on the battlefield.[31] And in this regard, no common people in America were more thoroughly dedicated to overturning the social order and achieving a new nation's independence than tens of thousands of Irish and Scotch-Irish, who were determined to accomplish what had been so long denied in Ireland.

In the Declaration of Independence, therefore, Jefferson actually only echoed the common, long-held views of the Celtic-Gaelic people and Scotch-Irish leaders in part because he was so thoroughly influenced by the rising tide of new radicalism and egalitarianism fueled by Irish Presbyterianism, especially in Pennsylvania and Virginia. In 1776, "Ulstermen George Bryan, Robert Whitehall, John Smilie and William Findley, a frontier Ulster leader, had such a decisive impact on the writing of the Pennsylvania state constitution that Benjamin Franklin [to his consternation] was of the opinion that the Irish emigrants and their children were now in possession of the government of Pennsylvania."[32]

Most importantly for the overall outcome of the struggle of liberty, "the radicalism of Pennsylvania had served its purpose; it had rallied that state to Independence, bringing with it Delaware and New Jersey [where the Scotch-Irish once again played a disproportionate role in leading their assemblies to a pro-independence stance and] In the process, the Scotch-Irish . . . in all their strengths and narrowness . . . had their finest political hour, and their military services kept pace."[33]

The Most Important Difference

For the Irish, as seen in such significant democratic advances and actions of Pennsylvania's Celtic-Gaelic revolutionary leaders, going to war was a natural, instinctive response deeply rooted in the depths of Ireland's egalitarian traditions, bloody history, and the turbulent course of the Irish experience.[34]

Unlike most American colonists, especially those individuals of English descent, on the American Revolution's eve, the vast majority of Irish and Scotch-Irish had never embraced an English colonist identity or close identification with the mother country. Consequently, from the beginning, the Celtic-Gaelic people took little, if any, pride of being good English citizens of the mighty British Empire, which yet oppressed their Green Isle native homeland and people, including relatives.

While the vast majority of American colonists of British descent took great personal satisfaction and pride in their status as English citizens, felt a deep moral obligation to obey King George III, and thoroughly enjoyed the mother country's relatively enlightened paternalism, the Irish and Scotch-Irish people viewed England in an entirely different light. Long before the troubles developed between England and the thirteen colonies, the Celtic-Gaelic people in America held a deep-seated contrarian experience close to their hearts because it was part of their very being: viewing England as an imperialistic oppressive power from the beginning. The suffering of generations of Emerald Islanders on the subjugated native Green Isle was the very antithesis of the benign experience enjoyed by English settlers and colonists.

Consequently, in many fundamental ways, the American Revolution was most of all only a mere continuation of an ancient conflict against a hereditary foe in a new land. While the American colonists only experienced the relatively brief and extremely light sting (more hypothetical and rhetorical—in potential terms—than real) of imperial British authority, the Irish on the Emerald Isle had suffered under British repression for centuries, beginning in the twelfth century when Pope Adrian IV bestowed upon the king of England the title of the lord of Ireland with the exclusive right to conquer and retain the Green Isle as England's own. In fact, no single element distinguished Ireland's history more thoroughly than the seemingly endless struggle of the Irish people attempting to defend their native land and distinctive Celtic-Gaelic culture and traditions against centuries of invaders: the Vikings, the Normans, and then the British.

Beginning in the late 1300s, lusting to gain Ireland's nearby fertile lands, English kings Richard II and then Henry VIII had conquered parts of Ireland before the mid-1500s. Fueled by a religious zeal to accomplish God's mission in Ireland, England's Protestant forces brought fire and sword to the native Catholic people, bathing this picturesque land in blood. Besides fulfilling its own imperialistic ambitions and righteous sense of national and religious destiny, the desire to conquer Ireland was also part of England's ruthless quest to ensure its security from Catholic France and Spain. A subjugated Ireland ensured a steady flow of wealth, resources, and prestige to the mother country.

The crusading zeal of England, at some points within sight of the Emerald Isle, paved the way for the eventual subjugation of all Catholic Ireland. The "Catholic-hating" Oliver Cromwell and his Puritan forces waged the most brutal of wars against the Irish people. Bold Gaelic chieftains and their warriors, including the Gaelic war society the Fianna, had long fought to preserve their ancient homeland, culture, and way of life against the English interlopers, but to no avail. A ruthless application of the Protestant Reformation by Cromwell's mighty sword guaranteed a lengthy, but futile, struggle across Ireland. In only nine months in the fateful year of 1649, Cromwell's holy warriors slaughtered thousands of Irish Catholics. They cut a bloody swath through southern Ireland, especially the people of ever-defiant County Wexford, located in southeast Ireland below Dublin. British conquest and occupation of the Green Isle thereafter spawned repeated revolts by the native Irish, but always in vain.

Of course, Europe's intense geopolitical rivalries were often played out on Ireland's soil and always at the expense of the Irish people. To keep William of Orange off the European continent and away from Paris, Louis XIV, the king of France, supported a Jacobite invasion of Ireland led by King James II. After centuries of seemingly endless warfare and slaughter across the Emerald Isle, the English conquest of Ireland was all but completed when Catholic forces, under the exiled English monarch King James II, were defeated by the mostly English Protestants of William of Orange at the Battle of the Boyne in County Meath, Ireland, on July 1, 1690. England's victory over the Jacobites along the narrow River Boyne near Drogheda, which was nestled beside the Irish Sea in east Ireland, paved the way for Ireland's complete subjugation.

This sharp Jacobite reversal among the green lowlands of south County Louth, Leinster Province, ensured the rise of the Protestant Ascendancy to rule the Green Isle. Enforced by overpowering English military might, the Ascendancy dominated the Irish Catholic people politically, socially, and economically for generations in what was truly a dark age, fueling mass migrations to America. Most of the best native Irish ancestral lands were confiscated by England and then handed over to around ten thousand Protestant families and the conquering army's leadership as lucrative spoils of war.

After the Jacobites' rout at the River Boyne, the imposition of the draconian penal laws of the late seventeenth century and early eighteenth century were enacted by the victorious Protestants to tighten their permanent grip. These legal discriminatory measures were guaranteed to keep the Irish Catholic people in a permanent position of social, cultural, and political inferiority and economic bondage

The death of Ireland-born Major General Richard Montgomery during a raging snowstorm on December 31, 1775, while leading the desperate assault on the mighty fortress-city of Quebec during his audacious bid to conquer Canada. Montgomery was America's first general to be killed in combat during the American Revolution and became its first martyr. Author's Collection.

BRIG. GEN^t DANIEL MORGAN.
U.S.A.

Proud of his Ulster Province, Northern Ireland heritage, General Daniel Morgan was a tough Virginia frontiersman of exceptional leadership ability. He continued to lead the doomed assault on Quebec after Major General Montgomery's death. Morgan was captured with most of his men in attempting to do the impossible on the last day of 1775. Morgan conceived one of the few tactical masterpieces of the American Revolution when he won a remarkable victory at the battle of Cowpens, South Carolina, on January 17, 1781. Author's Collection.

General Henry Knox was the dynamic son of County Derry immigrants. A talented, self-taught visionary with an abundance of tactical and strategic insights, Knox played early and multiple key roles that bestowed George Washington with a highly efficient artillery arm. The commander in chief and his army benefited immeasurably from Knox's many gifts as a natural leader, organizer, and innovative free thinker. Author's Collection.

General John Stark
1728-1822

General John Stark was a resourceful Indian fighter who had served with distinction as the top lieutenant of Major Robert Rogers's famed Rangers during the French and Indian War. The exploits of this son of Northern Ireland immigrants became the stuff of legend in both the French and Indian War and the American Revolution. Leading mostly Presbyterian Irish soldiers like himself, he orchestrated a masterful victory at Bennington, Vermont, on August 16, 1777, which helped to pave the way for the decisive victory of America's northern army at Saratoga, New York, in October 1777. Author's Collection

General John Sullivan was the pugnacious son of immigrants from Ulster Province, Northern Ireland. He was captured at the disastrous Battle of Long Island, New York, on August 27, 1776. In a solid vote of confidence from Washington, who greatly respected this self-made man and former attorney, Sullivan commanded the First Division of Washington's surprise attack that captured a full Hessian brigade at Trenton, New Jersey, on December 26, 1776. Author's Collection.

Of Scotch-Irish descent, General Anthony Wayne was one of Washington's best lieutenants and he commanded the elite Pennsylvania Continental troops. Wayne's Pennsylvania troops consisted of so many Irish and Scotch-Irish soldiers that the Pennsylvania Line, one of the largest units of Washington's Army, became known as the "Line of Ireland." These troops were among the finest fighting men of Washington's Army. Author's Collection.

General Anthony Wayne's audacious attack overran the formidable British bastion of Stony Point on July 16, 1779. Throughout the war, Wayne was well known for his aggressiveness and hard-hitting style. Wayne's capture of Stony Point was an amazing tactical success that displayed his skill and daring. Author's Collection.

Map of Wayne's brilliant assault on Stony Point, resulting in a remarkable success that astounded leading military men on both sides.

Andrew Jackson was the son of Irish immigrant parents from Northern Ireland who became the seventh president of the United States. Continuing the Scotch-Irish family tradition of fighting against the British, the wiry teenager served as a South Carolina partisan in the nightmarish civil war that consumed South Carolina and destroyed his family after the disastrous fall of Charleston in May 1780. Author's Collection.

Partisan Francis Marion, of part Scotch-Irish descent, won widespread fame as the daring "Swamp Fox" of the American Revolution. During the darkest days of the war in the South, he kept South Carolina's resistance effort alive against the victorious British and Loyalists after the surrender of Charleston. This famous scene depicts Francis Marion offering his meager fare of potatoes to a British officer at the hidden partisan encampment on Snow's Island, South Carolina. Author's Collection.

An early depiction of Colonel Henry Knox's artillery firing from the high ground of Trenton's northern edge, where Washington's Second Division under General Nathanael Greene attacked in conjunction with General John Sullivan's First Division. Originally published in *Life of George Washington* by Washington Irving, 1859. Author's Collection.

A black Irish soldier, an Irish immigrant who was distinguished by dark hair and features, of the second Pennsylvania Continental Regiment. 1778 by Don Troiani. Citation: Don Troiani, www.historicalimagebank. com.

James McHenry

JAMES McHE
* Signer of the

Born in Ballymena, Ulster Province, and formerly a physician, Lieutenant Colonel James McHenry served as one of George Washington's most able staff officers of his headquarters "family." Baltimore's Fort McHenry, birthplace of the national anthem, was named in honor of this capable, gregarious Irishman. Author's Collection.

A Celtic soldier of the British Army, which contained large numbers of Irish and Celtic fighting men who battled for years against the Irish of Washington's Army. 42nd Highland Drummer © Jaime Cooper, 2007

for generations. Catholic bishops and priests were persecuted and banished from the Emerald Isle. The penalty of being hanged, drawn, and quartered was reserved for any bishops who remained behind or dared to preach liberation theology. Calculated to ensure their perpetual "impoverishment and degradation," in Edmund Burke's concise words, the Catholic people were also denied their once-cherished places in the professions and the right to vote and to own and bear arms: all calculated to diminish political and military uprisings by eliminating a potential leadership class.

In true Machiavellian fashion, the discriminatory penal laws dominated every aspect of Irish Catholic life, leaving the Gaelic people powerless and uneducated for future generations. Of course, without the emergence of an educated revolutionary leadership dedicated to Ireland's liberation, the Irish people could be more easily controlled and exploited. Even the ancient language of the native Irish was officially replaced by English.

But of course the permanent subjugation of Ireland was neither easy nor quick, providing a first hint of what the British government should have fully anticipated facing in America in the 1770s. One of the most famous of these ill-fated Irish insurrections was led by Hugh O'Neill, the irrepressible Earl of Tyrone educated in England and the chief of his Celtic clan of Ulster, during the Nine Years' War (1594-1603). In this vicious struggle, he reaped a series of dramatic victories, such as Yellow Ford in 1598, to nearly end English domination until he and his Spanish allies were finally defeated by the English in the green fields just outside the port of Kinsale, County Cork, Munster Province, on Christmas Eve 1600. This ended the power of the old Gaelic order in Ireland forever.

Another bloody Irish revolt was led by Sir Phelim O'Neill in Ulster in 1641 before it was finally crushed by Cromwell. This unmerciful Puritan warrior believed he was only doing God's work by slaughtering hundreds of Catholics while grabbing as much Irish land—initially Ulster Province, which was among Ireland's most fertile regions—as possible. He then expelled the Irish Catholics to the rocky-covered regions west of the Shannon River in infertile Connacht Province: the grim option for the Irish people known in the saying "To Hell or Connacht."

Other Irish revolts followed: the 1642 revolt of Owen Roe O'Neill, former Spanish Army officer and nephew of the legendary Hugh O'Neill, nearly regained all of Ulster Province with dramatic victories won on such hard-fought fields like Benburb in 1646 until Cromwell smashed the uprising; the nationalistic revolt of handsome Patrick Sarsfield, the first earl of Lucan and the most brilliant Irish Catholic cavalry commander during the Irish Wars of Independence, in 1688; King James II's invasion to reclaim Ireland, resulting in the 1688–1689 siege of Derry, one of the few remaining strongholds not yet captured by Catholic forces, by the Jacobites. After the Jacobites' defeat at the battle of the Boyne, Sarsfield continued to rally resistance to fight on against the odds and a cruel fate, becoming one of the last great revolutionary heroes of the Irish Catholic people. After the Treaty of Limerick in 1691, Sarsfield led his Irish Catholic revolutionaries to France. Here, as the famous "Wild Geese," they continued to gamely battle their Protestant foes on European soil in the hope of returning with an invading army to liberate Ireland.

All of these tragic legacies of successive failed bids for freedom from English domination played a large role in preparing and then motivating large numbers of Irish in America, especially the "dissenters," both Catholics and Presbyterians who had been driven from their own lands and exiled Irish rebels, and "Irish Tories." Therefore, driven from their own homeland, the transplanted Irish and Scotch-Irish across the thirteen colonies were ever mindful of Ireland's bloody historical legacies, especially the many defeats and persecutions suffered by themselves and their ancestors: quite unlike the average colonial of English descent who possessed no comparable searing memories of the horrors of such a tragic past that motivated the Celtic-Gaelic people to fight against their ancient foe from 1775 to 1783.[35]

Consequently, when Benjamin Franklin asked, in regard to Great Britain imposing its imperial will on the American colonists, "Why must they be stripped of their property without their consent?" and warned that the thirteen colonies faced "absolute slavery," this central question was anything but emotionally charged rhetoric from still another seemingly endless of stream of revolutionary propaganda to the Celtic-Gaelic people long traumatized.[36]

Unable to allow the memories of past injustices from an ancient adversary or the urge for revenge to fade away, the Irish tenaciously clung to their traditional kinship networks, folkways, religious ways, value systems, cultural beliefs, egalitarian political legacies, and even language while remaining close together in distinctive clannish enclaves in urban and rural areas. Even by the American Revolution's beginning, the Irish and Scotch-Irish across America "remained Irish to the bone" long after they had settled in the thirteen colonies.

Herbert Asbury, a skilled journalist, explained correctly in his 1928 work *The Gangs of New York* about the story of the Irish of New York City, including the infamous Five Points in lower Manhattan, which also applied to the Irish during the colonial period: "Like most of the sons of Erin who have come to this country, they never became so thoroughly Americanized that Ireland did not remain their principal vocal interest."[37] Asbury's insightful analysis emphasized how Ireland and her tortured past long remained a permanent part of the hearts and minds of transplanted Irish in America: an anguished memory and legacy almost as strong and enduring as family and religious faith. This animosity held them closer together as a people, like other distinctive aspects of their vibrant Celtic-Gaelic culture and traditions that refused to diminish.

From the dank boarding houses and brick row houses of New York City, including crowded ethnic ghettos in lower Manhattan (especially the Five Points), and the seedy Delaware waterfront of eastern Philadelphia, to the isolated Celtic-Gaelic communities and enclaves on the Western frontier, the Irish still possessed a burning desire to defy British control and to settle a good many old scores in the name of family, national, and ethnic honor by 1775. Fortunately for America, this revolutionary synthesis resurfaced with renewed strength and vitality just in time to play a most vital role in the struggle for America's destiny.

From the conservative colonial ruling class of the Eastern Seaboard from New England to Georgia, the Irish people had already rebelled against central authority and upper-class rule by moving far west, or "up country," well beyond government control to live freely in their separate ethnic enclaves far from the colonial elite to practice their religion as they pleased in true "dissenter" fashion. In consequence, more than any other colonists in America and long before the American Revolution's beginning, the Irish had never viewed the mother country as anything but the most dangerous potential threat, a symbol of oppression, and the longtime persecutor of free people: a firmly seated revolutionary disposition and inclination born of a Celtic-Gaelic cultural legacy and tragic inheritance that played a large part in setting the stage for the staunch Irish resistance effort throughout the American Revolution's course.

Centuries of defeat, slaughters, confiscations of ancestral lands and family properties, and English domination of the native Celtic-Gaelic homeland played the major role in creating America's most natural and radical revolutionaries by 1775. Therefore, the Irish and the Scotch-Irish were determined by 1775 that the same imperial process of cultural, political, and military domination, that proved so destructive in Ireland for generations, would not be allowed to be repeated in the New World.[38]

Victims of centuries of English domination and persecution, the dispossessed Irish who migrated to America had little choice but to depart their native homeland in the hope of gaining better lives. Systematically, by cynical design, they had been reduced to the lowly status of tenant farmers across Ireland by the wealthy British and Anglo-Irish power structure. By 1775, more than 90 percent of Ireland's land was owned by aristocratic Anglican (British and Anglo-Irish) landlords of seemingly endless wealth. Without hope or prospects for improving their tragic plight in life and through no fault of their own, generations of Irish worked the land in an oppressive feudal-like system after having lost their ancestral lands through conquest long ago.

In July 1736, Alexander Crawford, a lowly tenant farmer in Killymard Parish, County Donegal, wrote in a letter of a dismal existence in Northern Ireland for the Scotch-Irish Protestants, who were "I[m]povrist by [high] rents and tyths." The misery of Irish life for both Protestants and Catholics ensured not only an exodus to America, but also guaranteed that they would become Washington's most faithful soldiers. Clearly, unlike the majority of non-Irish Americans long before the revolution's outbreak, the Irish and Scotch-Irish possessed far more valid personal, emotional, historical, and cultural reasons to not only rise up in revolt in 1775, but also to serve in the army's ranks to the bitter end. Not surprisingly, therefore, the Irish and Scotch-Irish, especially those recent immigrants born in Ireland, early became the leading and most vocal advocates for independence.[39] Indeed, in a historical continuum, the Irish seemingly were always "in an almost perpetual state of rebellion" against English authority.[40]

For such reasons, the sharply contrasting experiences between the Irish colonists and the sons and grandsons of Celtic-Gaelic immigrants and settlers of British descent often spelled the difference between wholehearted commitments to America's struggle versus neutrality or Loyalist sentiments. While an American statesmen of British descent only spewed rhetoric, an Irish leader or the descendant of Irish immigrants was far more likely to advocate an immediate taking up of arms and independence. Such was the case in regard to the early pro-independence-minded New Hampshire politician John Sullivan, who evolved into one of Washington's top lieutenants. Author Karl F. Stephens correctly emphasized how "unlike some, such as the more revered Thomas Jefferson, Sullivan didn't just talk about independence for the colonies, he actually fought for it."[41]

Ireland-born Charles Thomson was one of the foremost early proponents of independence and one of the most radical revolutionaries in Pennsylvania. He fully embodied and perpetuated the radical Presbyterian faith and egalitarian ideal that bordered on utopianism. Along with his fellow Irishman George Bryan and other Presbyterian "dissenters" against the established colonial government dominated by Quakers, Thomson was one of the young radical revolutionaries of a new generation of dynamic, revolutionary leadership. He played an inspirational role in organizing resistance among Philadelphia's thriving merchants and tradesmen, who were heavily Irish and Scotch-Irish and possessed close commercial ties with Ireland, against repressive British policies as early as 1768. Samuel Adams paid the ultimate compliment to Thomson in describing him as the "chief incendiary" in the Irish capital of America, one of the most vibrant Irish urban communities on the North American continent, to Governor Thomas Hutchinson, the Royal Governor of Massachusetts.

As the capable secretary of the Continental Congress that belied his background as a lowly indentured servant, Thomson signed the Declaration of Independence while Ireland-born George Duffield served as the inspirational third chaplain to the Continental Congress. Like Reverend Samuel Doak, the son of Irish immigrants who were married on the ship to America, Duffield fortified the moral resolve of that legislative body with spiritual faith and the righteous conviction that they were doing God's work in destroying the enemy.

Thomson hailed from the small village of Maghera, County Derry, in the heart of Northern Ireland. This rich countryside consisted of level, green lowlands, unspoiled landscapes, and excellent farmlands nestled along the fertile northern coast, with the towering Sperrin Mountains looming on the southern horizon. Thomson's twisting road in life began with considerable difficulty and personal trials. He was orphaned at age ten when his father John Thomson, who had been employed in Ireland's linen industry before it went into a depression thanks to England's mercantile policies to eliminate competition, passed away during the several months' passage to America in 1739. Dying before the sailing ship, where cramped quarters led to the spread of disease, entered the wide expanse of tidal Delaware Harbor, the hard-luck Irishman was buried at sea. This tragic loss only compounded the young man's suffering because Thomson's mother had recently died in Ireland, evidently while giving birth to daughter Mary in 1738.

Upon landing at New Castle, Delaware, without their parents, the six orphaned Thomson children from faraway County Derry were sold to the highest bidder as indentured servants. Instead of laboring as an overworked blacksmith apprentice in New Castle, the young man broke his indenture bonds and fled. Desiring to move up the social ladder, the ambitious Irish youth then struck out on his own with the seemingly improbable vision of becoming a respected scholar.

Thomson's egalitarian zeal first stemmed from a hard-earned education about the perils of living under arbitrary rule in Ireland and then from the teachings of an enlightened Presbyterian minister from Northern Ireland, Dr. Francis Alison, who was decidedly anti-British in the Scottish Presbyterian tradition, at the Thunder Hill Academy. Here, at New London, Chester County, Pennsylvania, located amid the gently rolling hills of the Piedmont just west of Philadelphia, Thomson excelled in preparing to become a lawyer.

Thomson secured a teaching position at the Philadelphia Academy thanks to Benjamin Franklin's friendship and significant influence. The Irishman then became the headmaster of the Latin School. Indicative of his rise in society, Thomson was even involved in Indian affairs by the mid-1750s, a diplomatic role that continued until at least 1758. Like other Irish who felt a distinctly un-English-like empathy for the Indians, Thomson dealt fairly with the Delaware of Pennsylvania. In the process, he earned their trust and rare respect. Thomson even won the Delaware name of "the man who talks the truth." The overachieving Irishman, who was highly skilled with dealing with

Indians, English, and Irish, then embarked upon a successful career as a Philadelphia merchant in 1760.

A natural revolutionary with a burning passion for liberty, Thomson aroused widespread opposition against the royal governor and Joseph Galloway, the speaker of the Pennsylvania Assembly from 1757 to 1774. He gained widespread recognition as "the Sam Adams of Philadelphia" for early galvanizing resistance and leading the opposition in Philadelphia against the hated Stamp Act. He garnered recognition as the respected leader of Philadelphia's heavily Irish merchant and mechanic class, thanks partly to no restrictions having been placed on the economic and social rise of an Irish Catholic or Irish Presbyterian in Pennsylvania.

Naturally, this mostly middle-class and lower upper-class Irish class of Philadelphia aligned early against the British government's attempt to impose tighter economic and commercial control. They were determined to go to war rather than risk losing everything to the arbitrary British dictates that led to tighter control. Bestowing inadvertently the highest compliment on a natural Irish revolutionary, Galloway denounced Thomson, who remained proud of his humble Ulster Province roots, as "one of the most violent Sons of Liberty in [all of] America."[42]

In 1764, when the British government declared its right to impose arbitrary laws and taxation upon the thirteen colonies without either their representation or consent, a distraught Benjamin Franklin lamented in a letter to his friend and Pennsylvania neighbor, Thomson, "The sun of liberty is set [and now] The Americans must light the lamp of industry and economy." The radical Ulsterman responded with a typically Irish answer: "Be assured we shall light torches of quite another sort."[43] Like so many others, John Adams likewise paid a fine tribute to fire-eating Thomson by writing how "This Charles Thomson is the Sam Adams of Philadelphia, the life of the cause of liberty. . . ."[44]

Like his fellow Ireland-born Presbyterian George Bryan, Thomson possessed a feisty Irish temperament that was well known, especially to his enemies who were not friends of America. He even feuded with Joseph Reed, another promising leader of Irish descent whose ancestors hailed from Ulster Province's green hills and meadows. By this time, Reed was the president of Pennsylvania's executive council after having served on General Washington's personal staff, including during the Trenton-Princeton Campaign in late 1776 and until early 1777. He resigned from the army in late January 1777 after the tight personal bond that had once existed between him and Washington was severed after he lost faith in America's savior.[45]

Clearly, as the Secretary to the Continental Congress, Thomson, who hailed from Northern Ireland, was a good example of the powerful influence of the radical revolutionary legacy of America's Scotch-Irish Presbyterians, whose forefathers had been first persecuted because of their dissenter faith by the British in Scotland before they migrated to Northern Ireland. Now the most revolutionary religion in America, this radical Protestantism had been first spread by Scotsman John Knox to spark the sweeping Protestant Reformation in a break from the Catholic Church. The Scotch-Irish people were infused with a religious nationalism, fanaticism, and radicalism that forged generations of righteous revolutionaries on Irish soil while ensuring that the people from Ulster Province were in the very forefront of the American Revolution year after year.

Scotland had been also conquered by the English invaders, who became experts at crushing the nationalist aspirations of indigenous people, especially the Celts, in bloody fashion. To smash the common Scottish people's uprisings, they often gave no quarter against civilian and soldier alike, utilizing scorched-earth tactics. The British systematically crushed each Scottish Jacobite revolt of the ordinary people, who followed their vibrant dreams of Scottish nationalism, especially among the hard-fighting Celtic clans of the Scottish Highlands, in the name of imperialism and preemptive national security.

Like the Irish, the Scots' failure to win freedom during their Wars of Independence led to the tragedy of the Scottish diaspora, especially to America's shores, where Scottish culture, values, and longing for independence were transplanted to a new land. The vanquishing of Scotland's dream of nationhood resulted in a large number of Scottish soldiers serving in the British Army during the American Revolution.

The systematic destruction of the Scottish Highland clans and the Jacobite cause came with the decisive British victory and slaughter of the Highland Clans on the grim killing fields (or moors in this case) of Culloden, in northern Scotland, on April 16, 1746. Here, in the "last grand stand" made by the Scottish Jacobites, the traditional Celtic tactics of spontaneous headlong charges (including unordered attacks among overeager soldiers) proved suicidal in the face of superior English discipline, training, and firepower, including cannon. The repulsing of the relentless Celtic attacks and subsequent rout resulted in the inevitable massacre of hundreds of Scottish rebels. The commander of the Protestant forces, William Augustus, Duke of Cumberland, was known thereafter as the bloody "Butcher of Culloden" after the slaughter of so many Jacobite rebels.

A promising teenage graduate of Aberdeen University, Hugh Mercer was one of the relatively few fortunate survivors of the massacre of seemingly countless Scottish Jacobites on the cold expanse of soggy Culloden Moor. This red-haired Scotsman became one of Washington's top generals by the crucial year of 1776, providing invaluable expertise and tactical skill. Mercer played key roles in the battles of Trenton and Princeton in helping to rescue America's floundering resistance effort, which had reached low ebb.

With a typical Celtic-Gaelic hatred of the British and haunted by the memories of the cries of "No Quarter" from redcoat soldiers at Culloden, Mercer demonstrated an enterprising tactical skill and hard-hitting aggressiveness in leading seasoned Continental troops against the ancient enemy of his Celtic people. Upon sighting the arrival of British forces on the field of Princeton, he not only ordered but also led the sweeping attack up the slope and achieved initial tactical success until veteran English regular troops dispatched to reinforce Cornwallis counterattacked with the bayonet. Attempting to rally his hard-hit troops during the battle's opening phase in early January 1777, Mercer remained in the forefront under heavy fire. Then the general's horse was shot out from under him. With drawn saber, he defiantly refused to flee, standing his ground before the onrushing red tide.

As on Culloden's gory field more than thirty years before, Mercer refused to ask for quarter when surrounded by soldiers in scarlet coats while slashing with his saber to defend himself as best he could. All the while, he ignored calls to surrender. Mercer was well aware of the an all-too-common British practice of no-quarter warfare directed toward rebels in Scotland, Ireland, or America. General Mercer was repeatedly bayoneted by British regulars after refusing to surrender.

Leading by example not far from the mortally wounded General Mercer, who breathed his last on the cold ground under a sprawling oak tree bare of leaves, was another one of Washington's top lieutenants, Ireland-born Colonel John Haslet. He was also fatally cut down on this cold January 3 at Princeton while attempting to rally the foremost American troops, who had broken in the face of the fierce British bayonet attack. Here, amid a shroud of battle noise, he was last seen "rushing to the rescue" in an attempt to assist his surrounded Celtic friend, the fallen General Mercer. Haslet and Mercer were among the first of Washington's generals to be killed in battle: another testament to Celtic fighting spirit.

The tragic legacies of the tortured history of both Ireland and Scotland ensured that thousands of Celtic soldiers, like Scotland-born Mercer and Ireland-born Haslet, fought fiercely against any odds to the end. Haslet and Mercer had served together in the French and Indian War and had been raised in different Celtic regions separated by the Irish Sea, only to die together on Princeton's freezing field in close proximity to each other on another continent to fulfill a dream long coveted by Celtic people: self-determination and freedom.[46]

In honor of their home country and traditions, Irish soldiers across America celebrated St. Patrick's Day (March 17, the anniversary of his death), in honor of Ireland's revered patron saint, with unbridled enthusiasm. This celebration was especially festive in Washington's Line of Ireland of Pennsylvania Continentals. Of Irish heritage, Colonel Francis Johnston, Pennsylvania Line, wrote that "Washington desires that the celebration of the Day should not pass by without having some rum issue to the troops . . . celebrating the bravery of Saint Patrick in innocent mirth and pastime, he hopes they will not forget their worthy friends in the Kingdom of Ireland [because] like us [they also] are determined to die or be free": a close identification between two people's struggle of liberty. After all, this was a national celebration that had been outlawed in Ireland, just like the wearing of green colors on St. Patrick's Day, a cherished tradition extending back to the seventeenth century. In the words of the popular revolutionary song "The Wearing of the Green:" "Oh Paddy dear, and did you hear the news that's going around? The shamrock is forbid by law to grow on Irish ground; St. Patrick's Day no more we'll keep, his colours can't be seen, For there's a bloody law against the wearing of the green."[47] Ironically, St. Patrick's Day was celebrated in both the Continental and British Armies: "observed separately by groups of Irishmen committed to killing each other."[48]

Matching their men in commitment to the patriot cause, countless Irish women (like Andrew Jackson's mother Elizabeth, who lost her life) across America sacrificed for the dream of winning a new nation's independence. The vast majority of these women—their names and contributions—have been long lost to the pages of history. Nancy Jackson, who lived in the so-called "Irish Settlement" in the South Carolina Piedmont, fought not only for America but also "in defence [sic] of her right; for she kicked a Tory down the stairs as he was descending, loaded with plunder. In his rage, he threatened to send the Hessian troops there the next day, which obliged the heroic [Irish] girl to take refuge with an acquaintance several miles distant."[49]

And when another group of Loyalists raided the South Carolina home of Irishman Samuel McJunkin, the elder man's feisty daughter rose up in the home's defense in the absence of the men, who were off at war. When one Tory attempted to steal the family's prized "bed-quilt," Jane McJunkin went on the offensive. "McJunkin's sturdy daughter, Jane, snatched it, and a struggle ensued for the possession. The soldiers amused themselves by exclaiming—'Well done, woman!' . . ."[50]

Only seventeen, Susan Twitty, of Scotch-Irish roots, played an even more distinguished role. She, her nineteen-year-old brother William Twitty, and other patriots made a determined defense of Graham's Fort against a Tory raiding party. Repeated refusals to surrender in the Scotch-Irish tradition (famously exhibited during the 1688–1689 siege of Derry) only infuriated the Tories. She spotted a Loyalist aiming his flintlock through a crack in the fort's logs at close range directly at her brother. Susan dashed forward and jerked William down just before the shot was fired and slammed into the opposite wall of the fort. She then saw one vulnerable opponent and yelled to William, "Brother William, now's your chance—shoot the rascal!"[51]

William Twitty, who later fought at Kings Mountain, then placed a shot through the Loyalist's head. "So eager was Miss Twitty to render the good cause any service in her power, that she at once unbarred the door, darted out, and brought in, amid a shower of Tory bullets, [the dead Loyalist's] gun and ammunition, as trophies of victory. She fortunately escaped unhurt. It was a heroic act for a young girl of seventeen."[52] Certainly Susan Twitty's acts were more heroic than James Quinn's, an "indentured Irish servant," who deserted the army in the autumn of 1776, earning a "Three Pounds Reward" for his apprehension.[53] The Irish were saints and sinners, patriots and deserters, in the struggle to determine America's destiny.

Chapter VI

More of Washington's Invaluable Irish Commanders

Washington depended upon a high-ranking officer corps that was disproportionately Irish. A most promising Son of Erin who had been born in the picturesque Roe Valley, Dungiven County, Ulster Province, John Haslet had migrated with his brother William from the Northern Ireland port of Londonderry (formerly Derry) around 1757. He journeyed to America as a grief-stricken Presbyterian minister who had already seen too much suffering among the seemingly ill-fated Celtic-Gaelic people. Haslet's wife had died in childbirth in 1752, which shattered the Irishman's world forever and led to Haslet's sojourn across the Atlantic to America.

During the French and Indian War, Haslet served with distinction as a capable fighting-preacher captain. He raised a Pennsylvania militia company from the predominantly Scotch-Irish immigrants among his Presbyterian congregation, who fought as well against their "heretical" enemies as they intently memorized verses of the Holy Bible, to serve in the Pennsylvania regiment. Along with other Irish immigrants, including his close Irish friend Captain John McClugan, Haslet settled along the Mispillion River on the border of Kent and Sussex counties in lower Delaware. Here, as a leading revolutionary politician and man of God, he won the esteem of the Three Runs community and represented the people in the assembly, including many Irish and Scotch-Irish settlers, beginning in 1770.

All the while, Haslet remained a close friend of the inspirational man of God, Ireland-born Dr. Francis Alison from Ulster Province. Besides worshipping together in a plain church in the Presbyterian tradition that contrasted dramatically with Catholic cathedrals, the two dynamic men from Northern Ireland also spent time together at a popular inn (long a safe haven for America's revolutionaries plotting against the royal government) named after yet another Emerald Islander who had made his American dream come true: Murphy's Tavern.

Before the American Revolution's outbreak, Haslet evolved into a widely respected politician, enterprising agriculturalist, community leader, physician, and preacher of Dover, Kent County, Delaware, and the western shore of Delaware Bay. Handsome and charismatic, he commanded the Delaware Continental regiment he had raised in Dover before the Declaration of Independence's signing after joining Washington's Army in the summer of 1776. In fact, he was considered the capable "father" of this command of young Delaware soldiers, in neat blue uniforms with red trim, after molding them into a highly disciplined unit. As first demonstrated at the Battle of Long Island on August 27, 1776, Haslet's Delaware Continentals was one of the best combat units of Washington's Army. This widespread reputation of the only continental regiment from America's smallest colony was due largely to Haslet's inspiring leadership style, hard work, and discipline.

With meticulous care, Haslet had trained these men week after week in the grassy meadows near a little general store, owned by an enterprising Irishman named Cullen, in Dover. He relied upon a good many Irish and Scotch-Irish comrades in the ranks, including Reverend Joseph Montgomery, who served as regimental chaplain, and one of his top lieutenants, Major Thomas McDonough. Washington likewise long depended upon the elite qualities of Colonel Haslet and his troops in leading the attack or in serving as the army's trusty rearguard when closely pursued by British and Hessian troops, who especially enjoyed killing as many Delaware Continentals as possible as a ruthless means of ending the war more quickly. One of Washington's most reliable high-ranking officers, Haslet was an excellent example of the typical never-say-die and aggressive Irish commander. A former theology student who had earned a divinity degree at the University of Glasgow, Scotland, before being ordained as a Presbyterian minister in 1752, Haslet was truly a righteous holy warrior.

This versatile Irish colonel and battle-hardened French and Indian War veteran should have been hospitalized instead of commanding his beloved Delaware regiment during an arduous winter campaign. Not long after Washington's dramatic victory over a full Hessian brigade at Trenton on the freezing morning of December 26, 1776, he had lost his balance and fallen into the icy waters of the rain-swollen Delaware. As the tall and robust Haslet penned in a January 1, 1777, letter to Caesar Rodney before his death at Princeton only two days later, he had suffered severely from swollen legs. Most tragic of all, Washington had already granted permission for Haslet to return home to Delaware on a recruiting mission. But the determined Irishman ignored the opportunity to return home on January 3, 1777, and led a daring bayonet attack instead.

With Washington's personal note ordering him home to recruit a new battalion still in his pocket, Haslet was hit in the forehead by a British bullet while encouraging his Delaware Continentals onward. Despite having still to recover from a serious October illness, the Ireland-born Haslet had faithfully stayed beside his men long after he should have departed for the hospital or home. But this gifted Emerald Islander had prudently made out his will on August 6, 1776, as if anticipating his impending death in battle.

Along with the capable Scotland-born General Mercer and a disproportionate share of Irish and Scotch-Irish soldiers who were cut down at Princeton, Colonel Haslet's death caused Washington to weep in despair. But Washington and the army's loss of still another capable Irish officer at Princeton was not in vain. Combined with his recent Trenton victory and again catching the British by surprise on

New Jersey soil, Washington's much-needed Princeton success in early 1777 played a key role in restoring sagging faith in the revolution and bringing thousands of newly emboldened soldiers into the ranks to join the struggle by the spring of 1778.[1] Loyalist Nicholas Cresswell lamented the sudden turn of fortunes in his diary that revealed a major turning point of the revolution had been reached at last: "The minds of the people are much altered [because only] A few days ago they had given up their cause for lost [but Washington's] late successes have turned the scale and they are all liberty mad again."[2]

Sadly, the bloodstained body of Colonel Haslet had been left behind during the rapid withdrawal from Princeton's frozen field. A young Irish lieutenant named McCall from Delaware recognized Haslet's bayonet-riddled body. Determined to perform a solemn duty for a fellow countryman whom he also knew had been a revered Presbyterian minister from not only Delaware but also from Ulster Province, McCall dashed over to Haslet's body and hastily attempted to dig a grave. But the kindhearted comrade of the Irishman was forced to flee from the sudden approach of British soldiers.[3] However, Colonel Haslet's fall was not in vain. He died with the reassuring firm conviction and spiritual faith that "the Supreme Manager . . . makes his sun to shine," in his own words, on all good things in his world.[4]

Haslet had sacrificed himself for the good of his county that he loved as much as his native Ireland. In an emotional December 24, 1775, letter to Caesar Rodney, who lived in Dover and who became Delaware's president by late March 1778, in regard to accepting command of the Delaware troops, the morally minded Haslet wrote, "Were I to consult my private interest or domestic satisfaction, I should be induced to refuse, but, sir, I have for some time past thought it my principal business to support the present virtuous opposition and think every wise and good American must sooner or later second the generous struggle. In this view of the matter, it would be infamy to refuse, rather than virtue to accept."[5]

After the bitter fighting at Princeton, the bodies of Mercer and Haslet were carried by wagon to Philadelphia in a sad final sojourn.

Here, these two revered Celtic warriors were laid side-by-side for public viewing by a grieving citizenry in the manicured yard of the State House, reminding their fellow countrymen of the high cost of freedom. A grief-stricken Caesar Rodney wrote with admiration to William Killen, a Scotch-Irishman who had been born in Northern Ireland in 1722 and migrated to Kent County, Delaware in 1737, that "We know we lost a brave, open, honest, sensible man, one who loved his country's more than his private interest."[6] On October 5, 1776, Haslet had emphasized to Rodney in a letter how absolutely nothing in the world was more important than "serving your country, guarding her rights and privileges" to the very end.[7]

Most importantly, Haslet's inspirational legacy was destined to live on long after his death at Princeton. A new force of Delaware Continentals, the Second Delaware Regiment, known as the "Fighting Delawares," was raised in 1777 after Washington's success at Princeton. This elite command "carried the spirit of the First Delaware Continentals and the soul of John Haslet" with them into future battles, including sparkling victories at Stony Point and Cowpens, and all the way to the decisive victory at Yorktown.[8]

But the story of Mercer and Haslet's heroics was not all that helped to turn the tide on January 3, 1777, allowing Washington to win his second battlefield victory during this brief winter campaign in western New Jersey. A good many common soldiers from Ireland likewise played key roles in reversing America's fortunes during this crucial period. At least sixteen Ireland-born generals served in the patriot cause, and another half dozen general officers were either the sons or grandsons of Irish immigrants as well.

At the field of Princeton, a young Irish Catholic drummer inspired his reeling comrades to rally before the charging British ranks. Young John Mullowney, from the Irish community of Philadelphia and a proud member of that city's heavily Celtic-Gaelic militia, rose to the fore at Princeton during the height of the crisis. Refusing to run before leveled bayonets of advancing British regulars, Mullowney "pounded out Yankee Doodle" on his drum with all his might to rally the hard-hit troops. While exposed out in the open on the snowy ground, the courageous Irish lad beat his little drum "with so much spirit and force that the waning courage of the [American] soldiers revived and forced the British to retreat."[9]

Some of the best-known Irish generals included Daniel Morgan, who led the finest rifle corps, consisting mostly of Irish and Scotch-Irish frontiersmen, in Washington's Army; Ephraim Blaine, born in Londonderry, Ireland, who hailed from Pennsylvania's fertile Cumberland Valley and led the Quartermaster Department of Washington's Army; and Cork-born Stephen Moylan, who served on Washington's staff from March 1776 to June 1776. Moylan first served as the Muster-Master General of the Continental Army and then as the Quartermaster-General by June 1776 after leaving Washington's staff. Moylan's last position was especially important to Washington because the Quartermaster-General worked closely with the commander in chief.

From beginning to end, the jovial Moylan demonstrated considerable leadership ability and presented a dashing appearance on the field of strife, where he led by example to inspire his men to greater exertions. Additionally, Moylan's distinct Celtic-Gaelic sense of humor, winning and polished ways, and good-natured affability easily won him the friendship of Washington and a good many Continental Army officers. After Washington presented this capable Son of Erin with a coveted colonel's commission to raise a regiment of Continental Light Dragoons on January 8, 1777, Moylan then commanded the elite cavalry unit, the Fourth Continental Light Dragoon Regiment. Appropriately, this fine command was also known as Moylan's Horse of Pennsylvania troopers. These hard-riding light cavalrymen were largely Irish troopers who hailed from the streets of Philadelphia, including the city's north part known as "Irish Town." The unit's principal players, like surgeon's mate Thomas H. McCawley, came from some of Philadelphia's leading Irish and Scotch-Irish families.

Of course, these young cavaliers were not all heroes; Irishmen Private Daniel McCarthy and Sergeant George Kilpatrick were charged with desertion. However, more from natural ability rather than political, military, or social connections as in the British Army, talented, highly motivated sons of lowly Irish immigrants and immigrants themselves often reached lofty positions of authority in the Continental Army. These mostly self-made men from the Emerald Isle, such as James McHenry and John Fitzgerald, held Washington's confidence. These two Irishmen served with distinction on Washington's personal staff.

When Washington took command of America's first ragtag New England army at Cambridge during the summer of 1775, he inherited a motley collection of top lieutenants with militia experience dating back to the French and Indian War. Unfortunately, some of these older high-ranking officers had already seen their best days. Four major generals, who had been promoted by Congress, knew relatively little about the art of war, and none distinguished themselves in upcoming years: French and Indian War-experienced Israel Putnam, known as "Old Put;" Artemas Ward, whom Washington replaced as senior commander; England-born Charles Lee, a fellow lucky survivor of Braddock's Massacre in July 1755; and wealthy Philip Schuyler, who hailed from the landed Dutch family of New York (old New Amsterdam).

America's aging top officer corps was eventually replaced by younger and more competent men of energy and enterprise. General John Sullivan provided the best example of one of these early timely replacements, joining Washington in time for the siege of Boston, where he played a key role. The end of the old social-military order and an anti-standing-army tradition inherited from England allowed a golden opportunity for younger men of natural ability from everyday American life to rise on their own, despite lack of military training, fancy educations, well-placed social connections, or aristocratic roots. More than any other ethnic group in America, Irish and

Scotch-Irish officers filled this gaping void, including at the highest levels, as the new American army evolved into an effective fighting force. Among this talented, dynamic group of new self-made Irish leaders who evolved into Washington's leading generals were Ireland-born Richard Montgomery, of New York; Daniel Morgan, of Virginia; and two highly capable descendants of Irish immigrants, John Sullivan, from New Hampshire, and Henry Knox, the army's commander of artillery from Boston.[10]

A self-made man, Knox's energy, intelligence, and drive won him the coveted position of the artillery commander of Washington's Army. Built like a bull, he commanded the army's artillery, both state and continental "long arm" commands, with masterful skill, especially at the battle of Trenton. General Anthony Wayne earned a well-deserved reputation for aggressiveness and fighting spirit when leading his mostly Irish and Scotch-Irish troops of Pennsylvania in offensive strikes that became legendary throughout the Continental Army. Both of these fine commanders and sons of Irish immigrants could be depended upon by Washington for the most challenging assignments. Clearly, Washington possessed an invaluable gift for recognizing military talent and potential.[11]

Perhaps no Continental general in Washington's Army was more consistently "willing to pick a fight with the British" than Anthony Wayne, who loved the Emerald Isle to his dying day. Always eager to vanquish opponents on the battlefield at the first opportunity, he commanded two veteran brigades (the First and Second Pennsylvania Brigades) of elite Continentals.[12] Wayne had been born the son of a farmer in Chester County, Pennsylvania, in 1745. Although he had attended the Academy of Philadelphia, he served in the Pennsylvania Legislature from 1774 to 1775 before buckling on his saber. Wayne possessed no prior military training, but evolved into one of Washington's finest combat commanders. Wayne's natural aggressiveness and studious attention to the art of waging war, including the ancient classics, paid dividends. More importantly, Wayne's leadership style and high discipline created Washington's finest troops, the Line of Ireland.[13] Wayne maintained strict standards, including for his Pennsylvania men to be well groomed with shaved faces. He also issued orders that his soldiers should "dress their hair."[14]

Because of his sheer aggressiveness in combat that occasionally caused Washington some concern, the sobriquet of General "Mad" Wayne (his nickname was for combat prowess, not mental instability) was well deserved. Wayne was the son of Irish immigrants from Northern Ireland, Ulster Province. He wisely emphasized that Washington should more often follow his own good judgment and common sense rather than deferring to the prevailing opinion of his long-winded Councils of War. With an audacity hardly matched by any other of Washington's commanders, he led the veteran troops of the Pennsylvania Line with a tactical skill and hard-hitting style rarely seen. Wayne's elite command of Pennsylvania Continentals served with distinction as "one of the largest units in the Continental army [and] was known as the Line of Ireland [because] well over half its officers and enlisted men were back country Irish" and Scotch-Irish from the western Pennsylvania frontier.[15] Because of the hard-fighting qualities and tactical opportunism of General Wayne and his Pennsylvania Line, a popular wartime axiom rang true year after year: "where Wayne went there was a fight—that was his business."[16]

Likewise, the capable General Sullivan also evolved into "one of [Washington's] best officers" who could be counted upon by Washington for tactical skill and aggressiveness.[17]

Like so many Irish commanders such as Sullivan, Wayne was a better commander at offensive rather than defensive warfare. In the early morning hours of a bloody Sunday morning on September 21, 1777, Wayne's encampment at Paoli, Pennsylvania, was attacked by a stealthy bayonet attack of British regulars, who promptly cut down scores of Irish and Scotch-Irish soldiers. One of the unfortunate victims of the sudden strike, Captain Andrew Irwin, a Scotch-Irishman of the Seventh Pennsylvania Infantry, suffered seventeen bayonet wounds.

While attempting to surrender, Irish Private John McKie, Eleventh Pennsylvania Infantry, was bayoneted and killed by a fellow Irishman in a bright red uniform, an experienced sergeant named Murphy.[18] What happened at Paoli, located just outside and north-west of Philadelphia, resulted in a one-sided British victory that made Wayne look bad as a commander because of his heavy losses. Destined to be hung as a spy on October 2, 1780, for his part as a secret agent in the Benedict Arnold betrayal to hand over the bastion of West Point to the British, aristocratic Major John Andre revealed his upper-class contempt for the Irish people, writing how "a great number were stab'd with bayonets or cut with broad swords [in defeating] General Wayne (a Tanner)."[19] After he married the daughter of a Philadelphia merchant, Wayne had opened a tannery for additional income while farming the land that he loved.[20]

Having been caught by surprise at the cost of fifty-two of his men, killed mostly by British bayonets, infuriated General Wayne. A recent immigrant from County Antrim, Northern Ireland, Private James Reed was bayoneted so many times that he "was left for dead" but survived. To reap revenge, "Washington's most audacious and hot-tempered commander" now wanted to deliver a devastating blow as never before. To fulfill his burning ambition, Wayne now relied on capable Irish officers like Major Michael Ryan, a faithful aide-de-camp who played a role in rallying troops to cover the withdrawal from Paoli, and Captain Thomas Buchanan. The opportunity finally came for him and his boys at the battle of Germantown, just outside Philadelphia, on October 4, 1777.[21]

Four of Wayne's Pennsylvania regiments led the attack up the Germantown Road and upon the isolated garrison with the rousing war cry of "Avenge Wayne's affair!" With grim satisfaction and a sense of pride, Wayne wrote how his mostly Celtic-Gaelic soldiers meet the enemy with a pent-up fury: "Remembering the Action of the Night [at Paoli] pushed on with their Bayonets—and took Ample Vengeance for that Nights Work."[22] Washington's most aggressive Irish general penned with obvious delight how the "Rage and fury of the [Pennsylvania] Soldiers was not to be Restrained for some time—at least not until Great Numbers of the Enemy fell by our Bayonets."[23] Basking in his success, Wayne concluded with contentment that "it was a Glorious day."[24]

Yet another tactical opportunity came for Wayne, as he still desired. Washington counted on him to regain one of the most formidable defensive points that had been recently captured by the British on June 1, 1779, and threatened the severing of Washington's communications to New England. In one of the most daring exploits of the war, General Wayne was given the daunting mission of capturing Stony Point, New York, a heavily fortified strategic bastion on the Hudson's west bank amid the Hudson Highlands, situated between British-held New York City and Canada, on July 16, 1779.

Wayne always seemed to rise to the stiffest challenge when the odds were greatest and chances for success were slim. Such was the tactical situation during the seemingly suicidal attack on the impregnable fortress at Stony Point, situated atop granite bluffs that jutted east in a narrow point to tower above the Hudson River. But as in regard to so many Celtic-Gaelic troops, Wayne's daring surprise attack would not have been possible without the initial contributions of an unsung Irishman. After the British began to focus their offensive efforts on conquering the South after experiencing years of frustration in attempting to crush rebellion in New England and the middle colonies, Washington needed to regain the initiative. The possibility that the imposing bastion of Stony Point might be captured by direct assault was first ascertained from a risky July 2 intelligence-gathering mission by Irishman Captain Allan McLane, one of Washington's best scouts and intelligence-gathering officers.

Nevertheless, a headlong attempt to capture this powerful fortress was one of the war's most difficult challenges. If General Wayne and his light infantry, consisting mostly of veteran Irish and Scotch-Irish soldiers who were known for their elite qualities, could not capture this natural bastion, then Stony Point simply could not be taken. By this time, Wayne commanded the battle-seasoned Continentals of the Light Corps, which he had skillfully led since July 1, 1779.

Despite the dangers, when Washington first informed General Wayne of his new assignment, the Irishman from Pennsylvania leaped at the opportunity: "General, if you only plan it, I'll storm Hell!" Washington responded to the Irishman's unbridled enthusiasm with a wry smile: "Perhaps, General Wayne, we had better try Stony Point first." Wayne possessed ample good reason to be supremely confident. With intense drill and iron discipline, Wayne had already prepared his troops, drawn from the companies of Washington's best regiments, for just such a risky assignment. Wayne emphasized the use of the bayonet in the assault, which made his well-trained troops of the Light Corps, a full brigade of hardy veterans, comparable to the effectiveness of professional British regulars and the Hessians in the deadly art of bayonet usage.

Washington's detailed battle plan, which he gave Wayne permission to tactically modify if necessary in a solid vote of confidence and wise delegation of authority, was calculated to launch a nighttime attack with only light infantry. Therefore, as ordered by Washington, Wayne prepared to rely upon the bayonet in unleashing a stealthy attack, just before daylight, of around 1,400 men of his Light Infantry Corps, representing six states, upon an almost impregnable fortress. Based upon McLane's thorough intelligence report, Washington's plan of unleashing a bayonet attack without firing a musket was a tactically good one. Precise timing and the high level of discipline of Wayne's troops were crucial elements in this bold tactical plan, but Washington was confident of a successful outcome.

In the sweltering blackness of July 16, 1779, elite Continental soldiers of two columns pushed up the steep slope with fixed bayonets in the haunting silence. As usual in leading by example, General Wayne personally headed the right attack columns inching up the commanding perch in the night. A volunteer band of soldiers were the foremost advancing American soldiers, who pushed relentlessly toward their greatest challenge to date. This "forlorn hope" was led by Irishman Lieutenant George Knox and consisted of other hardened Irish soldiers of the Ninth Pennsylvania Regiment, Pennsylvania Line.

Wayne's top lieutenant in the assault was Ireland-born Colonel Richard Butler, who was fated to die in fighting the Miami Indians along the Wabash River in early November 1791. He was formerly the top lieutenant of Daniel Morgan and his rifle command after having served with distinction as the colonel of the Fifth Pennsylvania Regiment, Pennsylvania Line. He now commanded the Ninth Pennsylvania Continental Regiment. Butler was born on July 1, 1743, in St. Bridget's Parish in Dublin. His father, Thomas Butler, a native of the town of Kilkenny, County Kilkenny, southeast Ireland, brought his family to Pennsylvania in 1748. Overlooking the River Nore that flowed southeastward, Kilkenny Castle had served as the Butler family home since 1391.

In this key situation, Wayne's iron discipline and endless training now paid dividends, with the troops maintaining a perfect silence during their advance. Colonel Butler encouraged his column forward on the north while General Wayne led the southern column toward the triangular-shaped fort atop the commanding heights. Meanwhile, a diversionary force progressed in timely fashion toward the British center. As the elite Continental light infantrymen neared the darkened network of fortifications, all hell suddenly broke loose. A sheet of flame from a British volley lit up the night. While his frantic troops tore through a thick abatis of felled timber as rapidly as possible under a hail of cannon and musketry fire, General Wayne was knocked down when a lead musket ball struck him in the forehead.

Nevertheless, the feisty Irish commander, with his fighting blood up, refused to relinquish his role in boldly leading the way up the slope. Instead of being taken to the rear to an infirmary like most wounded officers, General Wayne ordered his aides to carry him into the fort so that he could die at the column's head if that was his fate.

However, the bullet had only grazed Wayne's forehead, leaving a scar that he carried the rest of his life. In the pitch-black darkness, a rejuvenated Wayne again encouraged his troops onward into the hail of lead. Assisted by his young aides, Wayne entered the smoke-filled British fort just as his soldiers rushed into the bastion while a chorus of loud victory cheers cut through the smoke-laced night air. One of Washington's finest Irish generals captured Stony Point with relatively light losses, defying the odds and expectations. Wayne also stopped what might have been a massacre of some surrendered British troops in a war that had become increasingly merciless and ugly by this time.

General Henry Clinton, who had earlier declared that Washington's best troops were the Irish soldiers who fought harder than any other men, paid a fine compliment to Wayne: "The success attending this bold and well-combined attempt of the enemy procured very deservedly no small share of reputation to the spirited officer (General Wayne) who conducted it, and was [most] mortifying since it was unexpected" and a remarkable victory. Wayne's capture of the mighty citadel was important in raising the Continental Army's sagging morale while also lifting hope across the young nation engaged in a lengthy war at a time when American battlefield successes, especially in the South, were few. Once again at a critical low point in a nation's struggle, the ever-resilient Irish soldiers, officers, and reliable enlisted men had risen to the fore to achieve a remarkable success at Stony Point to inject new vitality into the revolutionary war effort as so often in the past.[25]

Wayne reported that his elite light infantry had "behaved like men who are determined to be free" and at any cost.[26] In a July 18, 1779, letter, Major Henry "Harry" Lee described the remarkable success at Stony Point in some amazement: "The troops rushed forward with a vigor hardly to be paralleled, and with a silence which would do honor to the first veterans on earth. A spirit of death or victory animated all ranks. General Wayne has gained immortal honor; he received a slight wound, one proof that Providence decreed him every laurel in her gift."[27]

Most importantly, Wayne's audacious strike that overran Stony Point had unnerved General Clinton, who considered himself a "sly bitch" in tactical terms thanks to a considerably inflated ego. Clinton had failed to draw Washington's Army from its New Jersey position and into a decisive stand-up battle in which the wary Virginian could be vanquished after Wayne took Stony Point and threatened other British forts that guarded the strategic New York Highlands on the Hudson.[28] Marveling at Wayne's amazing tactical accomplishment and skill, the Marquis de Chastellux described in his journal how the "affair of Stoney-Point has gained [for Wayne] much honour in the army [but] he is only a Brigadier-General!"[29] And General William Heath wrote with admiration how Wayne's nighttime assault at Stony Point "was done with great promptitude, the works being carried by assault, and the whole garrison made prisoners of war, with all the artillery, ammunition, stores, &c. This was a most brilliant affair."[30]

Wayne's dramatic victory at Stony Point dealt a significant blow to British morale and prestige, playing a role in Clinton tendering his resignation, which was rejected in London.[31] One dismayed British officer, Commodore George Collier, who now began to realize that decisive victory was impossible for British forces in America during this long war, scribbled in his journal: "The rebels had made the attack with a bravery they never before exhibited."[32] As the dramatic storming of Stony Point demonstrated, Washington's Army was growing more disciplined and finely tuned by intensive training under capable leaders, proving more than a match for even the toughest British regulars or the strongest defensive positions created by Europe's finest military engineers.[33]

Even without the colorful sobriquet of "Mad," General Sullivan possessed the same hard-hitting qualities as General Wayne did. Resourceful and resilient on the battlefield, Sullivan was a proud son of Limerick, which began as a Viking settlement on the Shannon River in 922 AD. As indentured servants from the Shannon River country of southwest Ireland, the Sullivan family arrived in America around 1723. Sullivan's Celtic-Gaelic aggressiveness on the field of strife became legendary on both sides. This highly respected general hailed from the ancestral O'Sullivan clan, of County Kerry, which possessed a breathtaking natural beauty and an almost mystical quality of enchantment, ensuring a sad departure for migrating Scotch-Irish and Irish Catholics heading for the unknown in faraway America.

Immigrants from County Kerry never forgot the natural beauty of the place. Dingle Peninsula jutted west like a dagger into the seemingly endless expanse of the blue Atlantic. Here, the Kenmare River's clear waters and the hazy blue mountains known as MacGillycuddy's Reeks presented pristine landscapes of beauty. The O'Sullivan clan of Ardea, which included Gaelic poets and harpists, who were revered by the Irish people throughout the past, defended their vast landholdings against the English invaders. Built of white-colored stone, the castle of the O'Sullivan clan loomed above the rich Cloonee Valley of County Kerry and overlooked Kenmare Bay before Cromwell's Puritan wrath destroyed it around 1643, along with a good many O'Sullivan clan members, who battled in vain against the English.

The distinguished and lengthy military tradition of battling against the odds was especially vibrant in the Sullivan family. An Irish Jacobite rebel, Sullivan's paternal grandfather had served in the French Army as one of the "Wild Geese" of exiled Irish warriors while his material ancestors fought "in defence of the [Irish] Nation against [William of] Orange [including one who] was killed in the battle of Airim." And a martial-minded cousin served on the staff of Bonnie Prince Charlie (Charles Stuart, the Young Pretender) who hoped to snatch the king's crown, venturing forth with his Scottish Highlanders in 1745 to almost conquer England until the bloody nightmare of Culloden's slaughter ended the ambitious Jacobite dream of nationhood.[34]

Sharing a history so unlike Washington with his English antecedents, the Irish general's great-grandfather was Owen Sullivan. John Sullivan Sr. had been born during the siege of Limerick in 1691 while his own father Philip (the general's grandfather) faced the Jacobite Catholic hordes at the city's stone walls. The Sullivan family was proud of a lineal descent from Dermod O'Sullivan. He was the chief of Bantry and Beare of County Kerry before he was killed by the English in defending his family's ancient castle at Dunboy in 1549.

As a young boy from the rich Irish oral tradition, John Sullivan learned all about the blood, sweat, and tears of the O'Sullivan clan that had so often confronted the English invaders. But the ultimate defeat of the O'Sullivan rebels ensured that future generations of the family were destined to exist as lowly tenant farmers on the same luxurious lands once owned by them when the clan had possessed a vast domain of seemingly endless bounty and natural beauty. The tragic fate of the Sullivan clan of County Kerry was never forgotten by General Sullivan. With a powerful blend of "energy, courage, and ambition," therefore, Washington's fiery Irish general waged his own personal holy war against the British on America's battlefields, as if attempting to avenge the many tragedies that had befallen his family in Ireland so long ago. Most of all, Sullivan knew that only decisive victory could save the infant American nation from sharing Ireland's dismal fate.

Sullivan's aggressive qualities and tactical skill were exactly what Washington most needed in a trusty top lieutenant during the crisis of the Battle of Trenton, when he gave Sullivan command of one of the two main attack columns (the First Division) while he led the other one (the Second Division) in person with General Nathanael Greene. What has been most often overlooked about Washington's dramatic victory over the well-trained Hessians at Trenton on December 26 was the large percentage of Irish and Scotch-Irish who served in the ranks, including a disproportionate number of officers. After General Charles Lee, who was not eager to link with Washington for both personal and strategic reasons, was captured in a cavalry raid, Sullivan had hurried south to reinforce Washington's diminutive army in the nick of time. Sullivan's troops had been recently led by America's second highest-ranking commander, Lee, before he was captured.[35]

General Sullivan also played key leadership roles in the Battles of Princeton and Brandywine in 1777. In fact, he initiated the opening phases of both hard-fought battles as directed by the commander in chief himself. In his diary, Lieutenant James McMichael, of the Pennsylvania Line, described a leading role at the Battle of Princeton that was repeated by the ever-unconventional Sullivan at Brandywine: "Gen. Sullivan with 1000 men were detached to bring on the attack. . . ."[36] When captured during the disastrous Battle of Long Island only after tenacious resistance against impossible odds (both British and Hessians) on August 27, 1776, Sullivan openly expounded upon his lowly Emerald Isle background, including indentured servitude, to the haughty, class-conscious Hessian officer captors. This surprisingly frank revelation shocked the aristocratic General Leopold Philip von Heister, who commanded all Hessian troops in America. With some disbelief, Heister described an ambitious Irishman's dramatic social climb up the ladder: "John Sullivan was a lawyer, and previously a domestic servant, but a man of genius, whom the rebels will much regret" his capture at Long Island.[37]

In the astonished Heister's words: "Among the prisoners are many so-called Colonels, Lieutenant Colonels, Majors, and other officers, who, however, are nothing but mechanics, tailors, shoe-makers, wig-makers, barbers, &c."[38] Some men in arms had been tavern owners or waiters, including perhaps at Lancaster, Pennsylvania, where the popular Irish tavern, operated by Irishman Tom Mahoney, was named the Sign of the White Horse, which appropriately stood on Donegal Street, named after County Donegal in Ulster Province, Northern Ireland.[39] America's homespun army, representing a hopeful democracy, especially when filled with so many young members of lower-class Irish and Scotch-Irish from rural areas, resembled the ancient Roman army in overall demographic terms during the late Roman period, which consisted of so many small farmers and peasants of the lower class.[40]

Generals Sullivan and Wayne gained widespread recognition for leading the troops of the legendary Line of Ireland. The elite Pennsylvania Line, consisting of mostly Irish and Scotch-Irish lower and middle-class soldiers, was known far and wide for its combat prowess and sterling qualities, earning distinction as the "corps d'elite in the American army. . . ."[41] For such reasons, distinguished historian W. E. H. Lecky concluded in his *History of England in the Eighteenth Century* that the Irish and Scotch-Irish "supplied some of the best soldiers of Washington's army."[42] Young Colonel Walter Stewart was one such promising Line of Ireland officer. Known as "the Irish Beauty" for his striking good looks, Stewart had been born in Londonderry (formerly Derry), Ulster Province, in Northern Ireland in 1756. He migrated to Philadelphia, where he began working for an Irish merchant firm around 1772. Wounded at the Battle of Monmouth, Stewart was destined for a general's rank before the war's end.[43]

Impressive tactical performances of Washington's Celtic-Gaelic generals were significant from the beginning to the end of the American Revolution. Ireland-born General Richard Montgomery led America's first offensive on foreign soil in the desperate attempt to overwhelm one of the strongest fortified positions in Canada at Quebec, which was defended by a force larger than his own during a miserable, ill-supported winter campaign in late 1775. With fifteen years of invaluable experience in the British Army before he resigned in 1772, Montgomery was one of America's rising stars in the Continental Army. Formerly a respected member of the Provincial Congress and well known for his keen sense of humor, he was also blessed with outstanding leadership ability. This dynamic Son of Erin was largely responsible for keeping a ragtag army of amateurs together during America's first foreign invasion of almost unbelievable hardship. In fact, the egalitarian-minded Montgomery came within a whisker of conquering Canada for, in his own words, the "Glorious Cause of America." Montgomery was beloved by his men, a natural liberator desiring to "rescue a province from the British yoke," as if battling for Ireland's own liberty on the Green Isle.

The first-ever British battle flags captured by American troops became prized trophies when Montgomery's troops took the British fort, commanded by the aristocratic son of an Irish earl, at Chambly, Canada. This impressive initial success was achieved early in the grueling Canadian campaign just before Montgomery captured his larger prize in Montreal. He then made his final descent upon Quebec. The gallant Irish general from County Dublin, Ireland, led his troops onward until killed by a British cannon blast at point-blank range in his last-ditch effort to make Canada the fourteenth colony and to eliminate this omnipresent northern strategic threat to America.

As sad fate would have it, Montgomery became America's first general to be killed in combat. Also fatally cut down at Montgomery's side was his trusty aide-de-camp, John McPherson. He was "a most promising young" Scotch-Irishman from Philadelphia, a College of New Jersey classmate of young Aaron Burr, who was a dashing officer of great promise. McPherson's red-uniformed brother now served in the Eighteenth Royal Irish Regiment. Tall and handsome despite a face left pockmarked by smallpox, Montgomery was a popular general who led the way by example: the quality that cost the Irishman his life. He was a member of a privileged Protestant family of career soldiers, who had long fought against Irish Catholics in the brutal struggle for Ireland's possession.

A strange fate followed Montgomery all the way to the frozen landscape of Quebec in his quest to vanquish the forces of his Ireland-born opponent, Governor Guy Carleton, whom he had served beside during the French and Indian War. His troubled wife, Janet Livingstone, feared the worst for her soldier-husband. With a heavy heart, Washington lamented "the unhappy Fall of the brave and worthy Montgomery" and so many of his Irish and Scotch-Irish soldiers in Canada's wintry wasteland.[44] During the revolution's most arduous campaign, Montgomery had inspired his troops by sheer force of character and willpower, leading by example until the very end. In the words of one admiring Pennsylvania rifleman: "General Montgomery was born to command [and] His easy and affable condescension to both officers and men . . . creates love and esteem . . . He is tall and very well made [and] a native of Ireland."[45]

The body of one of America and Ireland's best and brightest was found by the British victors on New Year's Day buried in a deep blanket of snow with a frozen arm extending stiffly above a mound of white on a blood-stained Quebec street, almost as if still beckoning for reinforcements to continue the attack or for personal salvation from the war's horrors.[46]

Daniel Morgan, who hailed from a poor Ulster family, also played a prominent leadership role throughout the audacious Canadian campaign, especially during the attack on Quebec. He and his westerners from the frontier were detached from Washington's Army. Morgan led the van of the invading force's left wing, under Colonel Benedict Arnold, north through the Maine wilderness. Commanding the three rifle companies, including two companies of high-spirited frontiersmen from the Pennsylvania Rifle Battalion of Ireland-born Colonel William Thompson and his own rifle company of "fine fellows" (mostly Irish and Scotch-Irish), Morgan proved to be Montgomery's most resourceful top lieutenant. Wearing liberty caps with the slogan "Liberty or Death," Morgan's frontiersmen, with inadequate clothing, half-frozen hands and feet, and few rations, battled against a stubborn opponent in frenzied desperation to somehow salvage victory from the jaws of defeat.

After reinforcing the floundering attack column under Arnold, who was cut down with a leg wound and fell into the snow, Morgan then took command of the few remaining Americans left standing in the bullet-swept street. By this time the Continentals were unable to fire muskets with firing-pans wet from blustery winds and heavy snowfall. Morgan, with his reliable frontier Virginia riflemen, continued to lead his ragged column through the blinding snowstorm and into the twisting maze of streets in Quebec's lower town, fighting whenever he met the enemy. At the first British defensive barricade bolstered by artillery, Morgan led by example in the headlong attack. He ordered the wooden ladders, carried on the shoulders of the burliest men, set up against the stone wall. When a British officer and his troops sallied forth to block Captain Morgan's men and demand surrender, the spunky Emerald Islander immediately snatched a flintlock from one of his soldiers and shot a very surprised Englishman in the head. Morgan's resurgent troops then drove the British soldiers rearward with their bayonets and musket-butts amid the freezing cold and falling snow.

The Irishmen from Virginia's untamed frontier now lingered on the verge of the war's most improbable victory, or so it seemed. Success in overrunning the lower town on December 31, 1775, seemed so close that Morgan's elated men yelled, "Quebec is ours!" But in the end, swarming reinforcements converged on Morgan and his band of isolated soldiers, who waited in vain for the column under Montgomery, now lying dead in a pile of blowing snow. Nevertheless, Morgan screamed to nearby British soldiers, who arrogantly requested his sword and threatened to shoot him on the spot, "Come take it if you dare!" The tough frontiersmen only finally gave up the fight when no possible alternative remained. But he decided to hand his sword to a Catholic priest, declaring, "I give my sword to you; but not a scoundrel of those cowards shall take it out of my hands!"[47]

But the desperate assault on Quebec was only the first of Morgan's remarkable exploits in this war for America's liberty. No commander of humble Irish origins more personified the feisty Irish fighting spirit and never-say-die attitude among so many Celtic-Gaelic troops than Morgan. In fact, this resourceful frontiersman from Virginia's virgin forests still carried reminders of past violent clashes with both the civilized and uncivilized worlds whose distinctions were often blurred in the horror of frontier warfare.

Morgan had lost all his teeth on one side of his mouth to an Indian bullet and the back of his imposing physique carried the scars from 499 lashes (he later described vanquishing British troops at Cowpens, South Carolina, on January 17, 1781, as administrating "a severe flogging") for striking an abusive British officer during the French and Indian War. This self-taught tactical genius from the school of hard knocks and wilderness warfare became one of "America's most gifted light infantry commanders" of the American Revolution.[48] Morgan's innovative tactics at the Battle of Cowpens were among the most brilliant of the American Revolution. The Marquis de Chastellux wrote with admiration how at Cowpens, this backwoods warrior "entirely defeated the famous Tarleton [and] This event, the most extraordinary of the whole war [nevertheless] The modesty and simplicity with which General Morgan gave the account of it, have been generally admired [but he succeeded by] one of the boldest stratagems [the double envelopment] ever employed in the art of war."[49]

General Nathanael Greene, one of Washington's top lieutenants, perhaps said it best: "Great generals are scarce—there are few Morgans around."[50] Besides the western frontier experience, the novel tactical skills and natural instincts of Morgan in part reflected the longtime utilization of guerrilla war waged by generations of Irish nationalists and revolutionaries against invading English armies and occupying forces. Even before the *Mayflower* sailed toward the Massachusetts coast, the earliest Virginia settlers and English soldiers benefited from combat experience gained from the brutal suppressing of Irish revolts. These veterans compared the Indians' style of fighting of ambush and hit-and-run strikes (essentially guerrilla tactics) to that of the "wild Irish," Catholics who fought to save their homeland from the English invader.[51]

Morgan early proved that his astute tactical insights and instincts were right on target. He had been convinced that the mighty fortress-city of Quebec could be overwhelmed with a bold rush when his army first reached the city's outskirts. But the Irishman's sound tactical advice to strike immediately was ignored, and this opportunity to win Quebec slipped away. In regard to the final attack on December 31, a frustrated Morgan later lamented about the inability to exploit his initial tactical success: "I was ordered to wait for General Montgomery; and a fatal order it was[.] It prevented me from taking the garrison, as I had already captured half the town."[52]

As late as June 1781 and horrified by the brutal warfare waged by the British and Tories in the South, Morgan was proud of how his troops had taken no revenge on captured soldiers, who had dealt harshly with the Southern populace, of the British Legion at the battle of Cowpens, South Carolina: "Had not Britons during this contest received so many lessons of humanity, I should flatter myself that this might teach them a little. But I fear they are incorrigible."[53] Clearly, Morgan understood the supreme importance of maintaining the moral high ground in an increasingly bitter struggle.

Morgan began his military career inauspiciously with the lowly rank of a Virginia frontier captain. In the exciting summer of 1775, Morgan organized one of the six elite frontier rifle companies called up by the Continental Congress from Maryland, Pennsylvania, and Virginia, which considerably enhanced the war-waging capabilities of Washington's rookie army of New Englanders, after a grueling march to Cambridge in only three weeks in broiling summer weather.

These nearly one hundred mostly Celtic-Gaelic riflemen were not only frontiersmen but also experienced Indian fighters, sporting Long Rifles and trademark white "hunting shirts with long [deerskin] breeches," in Washington's words. Generally taller and more physically imposing than New England's yeoman farmers and artisans or the British troops, these western riflemen wore the fluffy tails of white-tailed bucks in their slouch and tricorn felt hats of black and brown.[54]

After exchange from his capture at Quebec, newly promoted Colonel Morgan, whose exploits in Canada won him widespread fame, formed an entire regiment of riflemen in June 1776 upon Washington's direction. Once again, Morgan's command, the Eleventh Virginia Continental Regiment, became one of Washington's most dependable combat units, consisting of the best marksmen from different regiments. Morgan's new regiment was composed primarily of Irish and Scotch-Irish from the Virginia frontier counties of Frederick, Prince William, Loudoun, and Amelia. But Morgan's rifle regiment also included frontiersmen from the unruly Maryland and Pennsylvania frontiers and from both sides of the densely forested Blue Ridge Mountains.

Forty-six percent of the Eleventh Virginia Regiment consisted of Ireland-born and the sons and grandsons of Irish immigrants. Typical reliable fighting men in the ranks included such veteran Irish soldiers of Captain Michael Simpson's rifle company in the summer of 1779 as Lieutenant Thomas Boyd, the son of an Irish immigrant who was fated to die in this war in his early twenties; Sergeant Jonathan McMahon; Corporals John Kelly and John Ryan; and Privates Patrick McCaw, John McKenny, John McCreery, Daniel McMullen, and Robert McDonol.[55] John Marshall, Thomas Jefferson's cousin, was one of the most promising young Celtic officers in Morgan's elite regiment. At age nineteen, he became a member of the heavily Scotch-Irish Culpeper Minutemen. Consisting of an entire battalion known simply as the Culpeper Battalion, these young Blue Ridge country soldiers were legendary for their expert marksmanship. In the frontier style of the day, they wore lengthy hair, Indian-style hunting shirts, long knives, and tomahawks: appearances that considerably frightened the polite, refined gentry in Williamsburg.

Although only a teenager, Marshall was elected captain of a company of soldiers. Wearing large white-tails of bucks in their cocked hats, these young frontiersmen were known as the Fauquier Rifles, hailing from Fauquier County, Virginia. Some proudly wore the slogan "Liberty or Death" in large white letters across the front of buckskin hunting shirts. Marshall's company was assigned to Morgan's Eleventh Virginia in April 1777. This resourceful Celtic officer soon won promotion to a captain's rank. After the war was won, Marshall continued to excel, becoming the most famous Chief Justice of the United States Supreme Court.[56]

Marshall's father, Major Thomas Marshall, served as one of the leading officers in the Culpeper Battalion. The handsome colonel was an unrelenting ladies' man, leading to a degree of frustration for an equally romantically inclined but much less adept Captain John Chilton. A thirty-six-year-old Fauquier County slave owner, who was killed in less than two months at the Battle of Brandywine, Chilton wrote in a July 8, 1777, letter about his frolicking Ireland-born commander of the elite Third Virginia Regiment of Continental troops: "Col. Marshall has just come from Headquarters where he was dined with the finest ladies in [New] Jersey, feasting his eyes and his stomach[.] His eyes sparkle at the thought of it."[57]

With the capable Morgan in command, the Eleventh Virginia served as an effective first-strike, intelligence-gathering, and harassing force for Washington. Morgan's regiment also led the way in spearheading attacks. But Morgan soon took leadership over the elite unit of riflemen who then became known as Morgan's Rifle Corps consisting of Maryland, Pennsylvania, and Virginia marksmen. This dependable and highly flexible command was described by a thankful Washington with sense of admiration as a "corps of Rangers." It effectively gathered vital intelligence that was quickly funneled back to Washington's headquarters while also serving in key vanguard and rearguard roles for the army in advance and retreat.[58]

Red-haired and stoutly built Timothy Murphy was one of the most distinguished common Irish soldiers in Captain Michael Simpson's company. This rifle unit was Company B of Ireland-born Colonel William Thompson's First Pennsylvania Continental Regiment and consisted of Northumberland County men on detached service in Colonel Morgan's regiment. Born near Delaware Water Gap before his family moved farther west to the fertile Wyoming Valley, Murphy hailed from a lower-class Irish immigrant family and was apprenticed to a middle-class German family. Murphy's "Irish inheritance taught him [that] British oppression must always be resisted" at the first opportunity. When the American Revolution erupted to change his life forever, Murphy and his brother, with Pennsylvania Long Rifles on their shoulders, departed from the family's farm in the fertile Susquehanna Valley, of which the Wyoming Valley was a part. Doing their patriotic duty, they promptly enlisted during the heady summer of 1775.

With idealistic thoughts of embarking upon a grand adventure, the two Murphy boys joined the ranks of the Northampton County riflemen from the frontier region north of Philadelphia. Timothy served in the siege of Boston, where he demonstrated his long-distance marksmanship skill by picking off unwary British soldiers with his double-barreled Long Rifle. This weapon had been fashioned specially for him by a German gunsmith named James Golcher of Easton, which was located in the Lehigh Valley of eastern Pennsylvania. The young Irishman from Pennsylvania's frontier became the most legendary American sharpshooter not only of Morgan's command but also of Washington's Army.

Murphy gained a widespread reputation for shooting down more than forty British soldiers, mostly at long range. But these were no ordinary enemies of America who fell victim to Murphy's skilled marksmanship. As he repeatedly demonstrated, these finely uniformed leaders, especially officers mounted on horseback, made perfect targets in their bright red coats, epaulets, solid silver, brass, and copper gorgets, and shiny brass buttons and buckles, even in the dim light of early morning or late evening.

Washington's undying faith in what Morgan and his frontiersmen could accomplish on the battlefield was evident when he detached Morgan's command from the main Continental Army to meet the most serious threat to America's existence in 1777. When General John Burgoyne's British and Hessian Army advanced south through upper New York's dark forests along the Hudson River from Canada with a large force of Indian auxiliaries, Washington reasoned that Morgan's woodsmen and hunters were the ideal Continental marksmen to play a leading role in negating this combined European-Indian threat calculated to terrorize the colonists and cause widespread panic. Indeed, Washington was convinced that "no corps [was] so likely to check their progress" in attempting to sever the colonies in half by dividing north from south as Morgan's riflemen. Washington knew that Morgan and his frontiersmen could discourage and defeat the Indians by fighting them in their own way.

At the second Battle of Saratoga at Bemis Heights on October 7, 1777, when an increasingly desperate Burgoyne attempted to break through the lines of General Horatio Gates's formidable northern army, young Sergeant Timothy Murphy rose to the fore and made perhaps the most important contribution in marksmanship during the entire American Revolution. Enjoying his finest day as one of America's best military commanders, the offensive-minded General Benedict Arnold sought to exploit the day's success by emphasizing to Morgan that an especially courageous mounted British officer, Scotland-born General Simon Fraser, had to be stopped from mounting a counterattack at all costs. Morgan picked his best marksman for the task: Murphy, who scaled a tall tree that offered an excellent view of the smoke-laced field filled with scarlet figures. With his long shot, Murphy inflicted a mortal wound upon the dynamic Celtic general from Scotland.

Murphy then neatly dropped another vital target of opportunity, Sir Francis Clarke, at a range of three hundred yards. The deaths of these two leading British officers, especially General Fraser, shattered the already sagging morale of their troops, who withdrew to the relative safety of their fortified camp. Ireland-born British soldier Roger Lamb was stunned by the awful destruction caused by the barking Long Rifles of Morgan's frontiersmen at Saratoga. General Burgoyne experienced a number of close calls and brushes with death, including a bullet that zipped through his long waistcoat. Murphy then joined the even more heavily Irish ranks of General Wayne's Pennsylvania Line, the Line of Ireland. Despite considerable recognition for his wartime feats, Private Murphy remained a modest individual for the rest of his life. However, he became the American Revolution's most famous riflemen, much like Audie Leon Murphy, who became America's most decorated World War II hero.[59]

Other young Irishmen besides Timothy Murphy also gained legendary reputations with the deadly use of the Long Rifle. One of these was South Carolina frontiersman William Kennedy, who fought under General Morgan when the Irishman won his most tactically brilliant victory at a strip of pastureland known as the Cowpens. The sharp-eyed Celtic-Gaelic teenager was widely "considered one of the best shots in South Carolina."

Kennedy's superior marksmanship first rose to the fore in the protection of his Irish agrarian community known as Fair Forest Shoals, nestled along Fair Forest Creek in the Piedmont's rolling hills south of Cowpens, from Tory raiders.[60] A fellow comrade-in-arms, Scotch-Irish teenager Thomas Young, never forgot that "while we were fighting a man was seen running through an open field near us [when suddenly] he halted, wheeled round, and fired at us. Old Squire [William] Kennedy (who was an excellent marksman) raised his [Long] rifle and brought him down[.] We had but one wounded, William Kennedy, who was shot by my side" during this deadly clash with the Loyalists.[61] But these highly effective Irish frontier riflemen often exposed themselves in their eagerness to pick out targets. For instance, Irishman Michael Mahoney was killed at Kings Mountain on a balmy October day, dying far from his log cabin home.[62]

Lifting patriot spirits after a disastrous series of South Carolina reversals in ill-fated 1780, the key to the battle of Williamson's Plantation (known as Huck's Defeat in today's York County, South Carolina) was the deadly rifle shot that felled Loyalist commander Captain Christian Huck. One of Tarleton's top lieutenants, Huck was a terror to the patriots, both soldiers and civilians, across South Carolina. Scotch-Irishman Thomas Carroll, a frontier rifleman, killed Huck with a well-placed shot, leading to the collapse of Tory resistance and a victory. Huck had become a number one target of the Celtic-Gaelic frontiersmen because of "his intense hatred for the Scotch-Irish populace" and his ruthless actions, including burning down homes and killing civilians.[63]

The trusty Long Rifle of James Collins, of Scotch-Irish descent, proved deadly during the frontiersmen's attack, including the "South Fork boys" of Emerald Isle heritage from the Catawba, up Kings Mountain on October 7, 1780. He described the tenacious struggle from the point of view of a common soldier: "I took the precaution to conceal myself as well as I could, behind a tree or rock of which there were plenty, and take as good aim as possible."[64]

But the average Irish fighting man was not an unfeeling killing machine without remorse or pity while battling for his new nation's liberty. Born in Ireland and now a settler from the York District of South Carolina, John Copeland felt empathy for the wounded Loyalists after the capture of Kings Mountain. With a measure of sympathy and compassion, he described the wounded as "Poor Creatures," who had become victims of Long Rifle bullets.[65] Such Irish Presbyterian warriors across South Carolina were highly motivated because of destructive actions such as those of Major James Wemyss, Sixty-Third Regiment of Foot, who waged a merciless war and put the torch to the Indiantown Presbyterian Church with the cry, "A sedition shop!"[66]

With so many sturdy Celtic-Gaelic warriors like Private Murphy in the ranks, Morgan's riflemen were invaluable assets to Washington that proved vital for the army's survival. Year after year, Morgan's marksmen were almost "always in the vanguard of the army—the first to be deployed as skirmishers and the last to be called off" the battlefield.[67] Morgan's finest day in the northern theater, before taking independent command in the South, was witnessed in his decimation of Burgoyne's troops at Saratoga. Employing a rare blend of Indian, guerrilla, and conventional European tactics, he led multiple hard-hitting advances, striking aggressively at the enemy's flank and rear. Burgoyne learned to fear Morgan and his sharpshooting troops more than any other Continental soldiers in the late summer and fall of 1777. Here, at Saratoga, Morgan utilized a masterful blend of tactical skill and natural instincts about exactly when and where to strike a blow. He also deployed his marksmen in thick woodlands, including high in treetops, withdrew in stealth-like fashion when necessary to fight again at better advantage, and pressed the attack for maximum tactical advantage whenever the most inviting opportunity arose. Morgan and his rifle unit suffered more heavily in battle because of their leading roles, but they still inflicted more damage upon the foe than any other command in Washington's Army during the Saratoga campaign. This elite rifle command was almost always the first in the field and the last out of fight. Not the finely educated, conventionally minded General Gates, but the unorthodox and rough-hewn former wagon-driver Morgan was the one who rose magnificently to the challenge. He relied upon his own natural abilities and tactical instincts to make the most significant tactical contributions to victory at Saratoga after General Arnold's stirring battlefield role.

The dramatic victory at Saratoga ensured the signing of the important French Alliance of 1778. Morgan and Arnold were the true tactical architects of this decisive success at Saratoga; definitely not Gates, whose passivity dominated his lackluster performance. Not long after the surrender of thousands of British and Hessian troops on October 17, 1777, a chivalric Burgoyne, who was "too nice to smell gunpowder," in the words of a lampooning Irishmen in a British regiment, paid Morgan the ultimate compliment: "Sir, you command the finest regiment in the world."[68]

This was a rare tribute from an upper-class British gentleman to a hard-fighting Scotch-Irish leader and his largely Celtic-Gaelic command. During the Saratoga campaign, Burgoyne's survivors, including a good many Irishmen, felt fortunate to have escaped the "bloody slaughter," in the words of one Son of Erin, of the Twentieth Regiment of Foot. Like the fellow countrymen whom he fought, this fortunate Irishman in scarlet was known for "my strongest blarney," especially in seducing American country women.[69]

Other lesser-known, but no less distinguished, Ireland-born soldiers played leading roles off the battlefield. Dr. John Cochran was one such indispensable Irishman to Washington and his army who worked behind the scenes, performing his medical duties for little pay or public recognition like so many Irish revolutionaries. Born of immigrant parents from Northern Ireland, Dr. Cochran served as the surgeon-general of the Continental Army. With expert medical skill and a self-sacrificing sense of dedication, he managed to save a good many lives, including that of the future fifth president of the United States, Lieutenant James Monroe, who was a gangly teenager of Mercer's Third Virginia Continental Regiment. A graduate of William and Mary College in Williamsburg, Virginia, and a wealthy planter's son, Monroe was one of Washington's few casualties (the most serious) at the Battle of Trenton.

Other equally capable Irishmen combined prestigious medical educations with fighting skill. A future general, Edward Hand was one of the most gifted regimental commanders in Washington's Army. He was a Trinity College graduate and possessed a wide range of experience, military and civilian, before the revolution. Born in the quaint village of Clydruff, west of Dublin, he had served as a former surgeon of the Royal Irish Eighteenth Regiment that had been long stationed in America. Hand first came to the New World in 1767 when his regiment of Irish troops in redcoats was assigned to duty in the colonies. Like the vast majority of Irishmen who journeyed to America, Hand never saw Ireland again.

Refusing to go to war against America, Hand resigned his commission at age twenty-seven. He then commanded one of Washington's finest rifle commands, the First Continental Infantry Regiment, with skill and resourcefulness. After compiling an impressive record, Hand earned a general's rank in April 1777 and evolved into Washington's "favorite adjutant general" and a trusted confidant whom the Virginian relied upon for sound tactical advice.[70]

In a lengthy letter to his young wife, "My Dear Kitty" (Katharine Ewing) of Scotch-Irish descent, whom he had married in March 1775 and who became the mother of his daughter, "Little Sally," Hand described how he was motivated to fight against the British and

Hessians in large part because he was intoxicated by the egalitarian and Presbyterian "Spirit of Pennsylvania."[71] He never wavered in his firm conviction that "If confidence can be put in a good Cause, and Numbers of as Good Soldiers as I ever saw, we need not doubt success."[72]

As the foremost band of defenders, Hand's Pennsylvania boys harassed the initial British and Hessian advance into Long Island in August 1776. One Irish soldier in the British ranks on Long Island, Thomas Sullivan, described the murderous fire of Hand's marksmen, who hailed from York, Cumberland, Lancaster, Northampton, Bedford, Northumberland, and Berks Counties, Pennsylvania. With Hand effectively employing Indian-style tactics of stealth and harassment, Sullivan penned in his journal entry on August 22 that "they kept firing all night." Unseen by their opponent, the Pennsylvania marksmen shot down a number of unlucky Britons while their Hessian comrades were unable to rest that night from fear of an attack. From Dublin's cobblestone streets, this young soldier, who had once believed that war was nothing more than a romantic adventure, was learning about the horrors of war. Sullivan could not have imagined that he was facing the accurate gunfire of so many Irish and Scotch-Irish soldiers who were led by an aggressive Ireland-born commander named Hand.[73]

Ever-resourceful and highly capable, Hand also played a vital role in the defense of a small but strategically important spit of land known as Throg's Neck, a thin peninsula jutting into the East River where it met the Long Island Sound north of New York City. Colonel Hand and his homespun Pennsylvania boys were all that stood before ten thousand troops under Howe, who possessed complete command of the maze of waterways around the city, thanks to the powerful Royal Navy. In a bold tactical maneuver, Howe planned to gain the mainland and the vulnerable rear of Washington's Army in defensive positions on Harlem Heights to the south. Howe's clever landing of his forces at Throg's Neck on October 12, 1776, placed the American army in a most precarious position. Although facing a mighty invasion force, this lone Irish commander and 225 of his seasoned Pennsylvania riflemen stubbornly held their ground in a well-prepared defensive position. Against the odds, Hand and a relative handful of his Celtic-Gaelic marksmen, who unleashed a blistering fire from their Long Rifles, managed "to hold off the whole British army" by keeping them pinned down on the marshy peninsula north of Washington's Army and New York City.[74]

Demonstrating as much skill in offensive operations as in defensive actions, Hand and his Pennsylvania riflemen also contributed to Washington's one-sided victory by tactically frustrating and inflicting losses upon the Hessians with impunity at Trenton. Colonel Johann Gottlieb Rall was cut down in leading a daring counterattack back into Trenton all the way to King Street, where his headquarters were located. A marksman's bullet, perhaps fired from one of Hand's riflemen, ended Rall's shining military career and weakened Hessian resolve. The combination of Hand's firepower and skillful maneuvering of his regiment played a key role in forcing the surrender of the entire Hessian brigade.[75]

One factor that made the Irishman's Pennsylvania Regiment so valuable was the fact that so many Irish and Scotch-Irish served in the ranks. Lieutenant Samuel Brady was one such hard-fighting officer who led his mostly Celtic-Gaelic riflemen with skill.

Born near Shippensburg, Pennsylvania, located around 150 miles west of Philadelphia, in 1758, Samuel Brady was part of an effective Irish father and son fighting team, including at Trenton. Samuel's father and brother were "badly wounded" in a flurry of jabbing British bayonets in the vicious night attack at Paoli, Pennsylvania, at midnight on September 20, 1777.

The infamous Paoli Massacre (northwest of Philadelphia) resulted from the stealthy night attack of Major General Charles Grey's battle-experienced British regulars, who relied solely on the lengthy bayonet in the darkness. Samuel narrowly escaped death when a steel bayonet plunged and ripped through his uniform. More than three hundred of

Wayne's men, including Continentals trying to surrender or sleeping, were not so lucky and were killed and wounded with a ruthless employment of British bayonets and swords.[76] "Remember the Paoli" became the stirring battle cry of Wayne's revenge-seeking Pennsylvanians, not unlike the fierce war cry of the Irish exiles after the 1691 Treaty of Limerick when the Celtic-Gaelic Jacobite exiles unleashed a fierce bayonet charge that routed the British regulars at the Battle of Fontenoy (in today's Belgium) in mid-May 1745: "Remember Limerick!"[77]

During the late summer 1779 invasion of the Indian country in western New York during the Sullivan-Clinton campaign, General Hand also played a leading role in taking the war to the powerful Iroquois Confederacy, now allied with the British. This ambitious mission called for the dispatching of a sizeable expedition of Continental troops from the main army to the northwest to thoroughly punish England's Indian allies, who had been ravishing the western frontier of New York and Pennsylvania. Because this fertile region had long provided a flow of foodstuffs, including wheat for bread, to the Continental Army, Washington's bold decision was based on logistical as well as humanitarian and moral concerns to stop the massacres. Washington chose the ever-combative Sullivan to lead this risky expedition because he possessed the necessary aggressive qualities and experience that guaranteed that he would maintain the initiative against the British, Indians, and Tories. In turn, General Sullivan placed well-founded faith in his top lieutenant, Ireland-born General Hand, throughout the arduous campaign in a remote western region. The dynamic leadership team of Sullivan and Hand was an ideal choice for fulfilling Washington's ambitious strategic mission, if a proper degree of aggressiveness (as emphasized in his orders) was utilized to the fullest.

Therefore, Hand commanded the Continental "Light Infantry Corps" of Sullivan's invasion force. This expedition was America's largest independent offensive operation (around two thousand five hundred Continental troops who were augmented by another approximately one thousand five hundred militia) from the main army during the entire war. The capable Hand and his light troops led the army's vanguard into a pristine wilderness far from logistical support and reinforcements. On one occasion during the arduous trek, General Hand dismounted from his favorite horse to set the proper example of marching beside his men and fording a fast-moving stream on foot to encourage them onward. At this time, "no person in the Army has more," in his own words, love for his spirited warhorses than General Hand.[78]

A large number of Irish and Scotch-Irish (especially among the Continental troops of the Pennsylvania Line and also including General James Clinton's New York brigade) and quite a few of the top Celtic-Gaelic officers of Washington's Army served throughout Sullivan's far-flung expedition where he commanded more than a quarter of America's professional forces. Razing one Indian village after another, Sullivan and his men waged a war against a much-feared opponent, who had most recently devastated the settlements in the Wyoming Valley of northeastern Pennsylvania in July 1778 and then in the Cherry Valley in November 1778 along the Mohawk River in New York.

These veteran Irish and Scotch-Irish soldiers, with flintlock muskets and Long Rifles on shoulders, marched through the war-torn New York frontier devastated by Tory and Indian raids that had ravished the isolated communities without mercy. Sullivan and Hand's Celtic-Gaelic fighting men never forgot the horror of comparable Indian strikes on their own western frontier homeland in Pennsylvania and the deaths of Irish family members during the French and Indian War and thereafter. One American officer who marched on Sullivan's retaliatory expedition deep into the wilderness of western New York, situated just below Lake Ontario, described how the devastated farm lands along the Susquehanna River of central Pennsylvania, were inhabited "by an industrious sett of Inhabitants tho' Poor [and Irish and Scotch-Irish], yet happy with their situation, untill [sic] . . . the British Tyrant, let loose upon them, his Emissaries, the Savages of the Wood, who not only destroy'd & laid waist [sic] those Cotages [sic], but in cool blood masacred [sic], and cut of[f] the Inhabitants, not even sparing the gray locks or helpless Infant."[79] Clearly, Washington had found a perfect righteously destructive tool in General Sullivan, whose combat prowess and leadership abilities were first exhibited at the Battle of Long Island.[80]

Only one strategic battle of any significance developed during this lengthy campaign through Indian country. Near the base of a heavily timbered southeastern spur of the commanding ridge along the Chemung River and behind a camouflaged (with cut brush and trees) log breastwork, hundreds of Indians and New York Tories of Colonel John Butler's green-uniformed command lay in ambush. Here, Butler's Rangers, who had raided the Wyoming Valley and returned to Fort Niagara with 227 scalps, and a handful of redcoats made their most determined defensive stand in an attempt to stop the American invaders. Fortunately, a sharp-eyed American frontier scout from Daniel Morgan's rifle command, which led the advance as usual, perched atop a tree, ascertained the ambush carefully laid out amid the thick summer foliage, which had already begun to wither in the heat. Appraised of the danger just in the nick of time, Sullivan soon ordered fast-moving flanking movements on each side to turn the ends of the formidable defensive position and to the rear to cut off retreat of the combined Tory, British, and Indian force.

The Irishman's adroit flanking maneuver resulted in a running fight through the dense virgin timber and up the long slope of the towering ridge now known appropriately as Sullivan's Hill that overlooked Newton. Fleeing revenge-seeking Americans with fixed bayonets, hundreds of Indians fell back over the ridge that towered behind their abandoned fortified position while firing from tree to tree. With "our war whoop in the American style," Sullivan's veteran Continental troops, in ragged blue uniforms, continued to charge up the slope with the bayonet. At last, and much to Sullivan's delight, they finally pushed over the body-strewn ridge, routing their surprised opponent.

With pride, Washington wrote to "My dear Marquis" Lafayette, the French nobleman who was Washington's surrogate son, on September 12, 1779, that "General Sullivan who is now in the heart of their Country with 4000 Men and . . . he advanced to their Intrenchments [sic] at a place called Newtown, where the Warriors of Seven Nation's [and] some [British] regulars—& Tories [and their] position was well chosen and disposition well made but on finding themselves hard pressed in front and their left flank in danger of being turned they fled in great confusion & disorder," thanks to Sullivan's tactical skill and aggressiveness. American losses were relatively light, but included Irishman Lieutenant McCalley, who fell in the attack at Newton and soon died after his leg's amputation and the excessive loss of blood.[81]

Washington had orchestrated the defeat of the legendary Anglo-Irish ranger, Colonel John Butler, whose oldest son Walter served by his side. Washington was mindful of the fact that his own father, Augustine, had first married a Jane Butler of Irish heritage in 1715 before he married George's strong-willed mother, Mary Ball, in March 1731, after Jane's late 1729 death.[82] Augustine had named his son George "just like the king in London."[83] A hard-fighting American refugee and Loyalist born in New London, Connecticut, who had been forced from New York where he had resided, Colonel Butler was proud of the Irish heritage. His lineage extended back to the family of Ormond from County Tipperary, where the magnificent Ormond Manor House was built by the tenth Earl of Ormond. His father had first journeyed to America as a lieutenant of a British regiment and then settled in New York, where he became wealthy. His finely educated son, who was bitter because his extensive New York properties had been lost and his wife and family persecuted by Tory-hating rebels, had formed his hard-hitting ranger command in 1777. Butler's Rangers included a good many Scotch-Irish and Irish soldiers, such as one of his top lieutenants, Captain McDonnell.[84]

After Butler's defeat at Newton, Sullivan led his troops deeper into Iroquois country, drained by the Genesee River, and through scorching summer weather. Fueled by Washington's stern directive to ensure that the Indians' "cruelties are not to pass with impunity," Sullivan continued to unleash a swath of destruction.[85] Cornplanter, a Seneca chief of the Iroquois Confederacy who had joined with Butler's Rangers in raiding the Wyoming Valley during the bloody summer of 1778, later lamented the terrible effectiveness of Sullivan's expedition: "When your army entered the country of the Six Nations, we call you Town Destroyer; and to this day, when that name is heard, our women look behind them and turn pale and our children cling close to the neck of their mothers."[86]

Washington's orders were necessary under the circumstances because the commander in chief was fighting a war on multiple fronts, and the Indians posed the greatest threat to the rear. Pennsylvania and its mostly Celtic-Gaelic settlers had suffered more severely than any other state from this two-front war. While the Celtic-Gaelic troops of the crack Pennsylvania Line died on conventional eastern battlefields and from disease in encampments far from their families, log cabins, and rural communities, the home front along the western frontier often came under Indian, British, and Tory attack. The cruel devastation of the Wyoming Valley settlements in northeastern Pennsylvania is but one example.

A good many Scotch-Irish and Irish families were wiped out in forgotten raids and skirmishes amid the savagery of a brutal wilderness war while their soldier husbands, fathers, and brothers faithfully served in Washington's Army. An angry Ireland-born George Bryan, as acting head of the Pennsylvania government and a long-time advocate of the releasing of Washington's troops for a strike deep into the Iroquois heartland, had played a leading role in demanding stern retaliation that resulted in the Sullivan-Clinton Expedition. This belated campaign was only feasible in large part because the frustrated British had shifted their major effort to the southern theater of operations after years of stalemate in the middle colonies. Therefore, Washington was able to detach large numbers of troops from the Continental

Army in the lower Hudson region and far to the northwest to pay a destructive visit to the Indian homeland to settle old scores.[87]

After the resounding victory at Newton, Sullivan proved unstoppable in the continued march north into the uncharted depths of the Seneca and fertile Genesee River country. Waging a logistical-oriented war that was comparable to General William T. Sherman's infamous March to the Sea through Georgia in 1864, American troops surged across hundreds of miles deep into the Finger Lakes region, located just below Lake Ontario. Here, Sullivan's men systematically destroyed at least forty villages, 160,000 bushels of corn, and seemingly endless stretches of orchards and fields of Indian crops to fulfill Washington's strategic vision of total war.

Sergeant Timothy Murphy, the young marksman and hero of Saratoga, now served as a member of Ireland-born Colonel William Butler's Pennsylvania Continental Regiment. The fact that Colonel William Butler, from Pennsylvania, confronted the green-uniformed troops of another Colonel Butler (John) at Newton is yet another example of the forgotten civil war among the Irish that existed in all theaters of war in America. However, Sergeant Murphy's military career nearly came to an abrupt end not long after Sullivan's one-sided success at Newton. Murphy escaped through a surrounding band of Indians and Tories after his small scouting party under Lieutenant Thomas Boyd, the son of Irish immigrants and also a member of Butler's Pennsylvania regiment, was ambushed and cut to pieces by Little Beard's Seneca warriors on September 13, 1779. A promising young officer, Boyd was captured and then tortured in an especially horrifically imaginative way. A stretch of one end of Boyd's intestine, still attached to his midsection, was removed from his body and nailed to a tree trunk. The lieutenant was then forced to walk around the tree, wrapping the intestine repeatedly around the trunk in a grotesque display that delighted onlookers who relished such ritualistic torture.

Upon the conclusion of this lengthy expedition into the upper New York wilderness, young Irish soldiers like Murphy celebrated their victory with a lavish feast, which had been ordered by General Hand. Reflecting typical Irish "good humor" and well-honed wit so common among Emerald Island soldiers, the Pennsylvania boys joked and quipped for much of the night while drinking toasts to each other, their complete victory, and their new country founded upon the novel concept of liberty. One especially memorable toast was offered by the Ireland-born Hand himself, which only a relative few of his Pennsylvania boys remembered upon awaking the next morning with severe hangovers: "May the Enemies of America be metimorphos'd into pack-horses, and sent on a Western Expedition against Indians."[88]

But perhaps no expedition member celebrated more enthusiastically than Hand himself. He had been a leading player in the most successful punitive expedition yet launched by the new American army that was becoming more formidable with each passing month. Before the war's horrors had descended upon the land, Hand had loved good music, sleek and fast horses, socializing, and drinking with friends, especially as a younger man before his marriage to Kitty, and now led the way in the merry-making. In his journal, Lieutenant Erkuries Beatty scribbled how "two or three Indian Dances [were] led down" by General Hand himself.[89] Beatty might have been related to the Beattie, or Beatty, clan of Virginia, including Indian fighter Captain David Beattie. At Kings Mountain, the captain led his company, which included members of his Irish family, such as his two brothers, John, who was killed, and William.[90]

Besides Knox, Morgan, Wayne, Hand, and Sullivan, a host of other capable Irish generals included the following: Andrew Lewis, one of America's early heroes for having vanquished the western Indians at the Battle of Point Pleasant in 1774; William Thompson, a seasoned French and Indian War veteran from Pennsylvania; Richard Butler, of County Kilkenny in Leinster Province, who served along with his four brothers, including William Butler; Andrew Lewis, from County Donegal, one of five brothers who fought for independence as officers; young Walter Stewart, born in Londonderry and blessed with abundant personal charm, earning renown as the handsome "Boy Colonel;" William Irvine of Enniskillen, who received a fine education at Dublin University; the polished John Shee, who was born in Ardanagrah Castle, County Meath, and still spoke with a thick Irish brogue; tactically astute John Armstrong, a tough Indian fighter and "old Washington friend" from the French and Indian War; the innovative William Maxwell, or "Scotch Willie," a brilliant tactician and master of light infantry tactics; John Gibson, another Irish product of the Pennsylvania frontier experience; John Greaton, the enterprising son of a thrifty Irish trader; James Hogan or Hogun; Thomas Conway, an overly ambitious colonel in French service who volunteered to serve in America's struggle; James Potter, who was a French and Indian War veteran and a gentleman farmer of Cumberland County, Pennsylvania; and the personable, gifted Stephen Moylan.

In total, twenty-two generals of the Continental Army were either born in Ireland or descended from Irish parents or grandparents. Some evidence has indicated that perhaps the ever-politically savvy Washington made a determined effort to have such a large number of Irish generals to serve under him in part because he became concerned about losing support from less committed native-born and British-born generals, especially when his generalship was so severely criticized during the war's early years.

Unfortunately, General James Hogan (or Hogun) has remained so obscure that even the exact spelling of his last name has been elusive to researchers and historians for generations. Hogan led his troops at Brandywine in September and October 1777 at Germantown. He was taken prisoner at the May 1780 surrender of Charleston, South Carolina. This little-known Irish general died in captivity in squalid conditions and anonymity while jeered at by his Irish-hating British captors, who mocked the Irishman's unshakeable faith in America, in early January 1781. William Maxwell was another little-known general who served in Washington's Army with distinction. One recent historian, Edward G. Lengel, described Maxwell in unflattering terms as "an ugly, stubborn, hard-drinking but resourceful Scotsman." But Maxwell was actually Scotch-Irish; his family migrated to northwest New Jersey from Northern Ireland in 1747. Maxwell enlisted in the British Army at age twenty-two and served capably in a New Jersey militia regiment for the duration of the French and Indian War. Maxwell's colorful nickname, "Scotch Willie," indicated not only Maxwell's popularity with his men, but also distinctive, well-known Celtic-Gaelic characteristics as well as his Ulster accent. Unlike most of his high-ranking peers, Maxwell remained a lifelong bachelor and enjoyed merry-making and lively parties that went late into the night.

Like Generals Knox, Wayne, Morgan, Hand, and Sullivan, Maxwell's rise had been swift. Beginning in the spring of 1775, Maxwell demonstrated adroit political skills as a New Jersey provincial congressman and an influential chairman of the county committee of safety. Maxwell then gained a colonel's rank and raised the Second New Jersey Continental Regiment, which was authorized by Congress in October 1775 and consisted of eight companies of soldiers from Salem, Sussex, Gloucester, Hunterdon, and Burlington Counties. With its young men and boys, mostly middle-class yeomen, from the farmlands and hardwood forests located near the Pennsylvania line, this Garden State regiment was known as the Western Battalion, which complemented the Eastern Battalion—the First New Jersey Continental Regiment.

Beginning in early 1776 and along with his New Jersey regiment, this promising Irish officer served in the ill-fated Canadian campaign under General Sullivan. Maxwell garnered a general's rank in the autumn of 1776 after he and his Garden State regiment were ordered from Canada and rejoined Washington's army. When the commander in chief decided to form a much-needed light infantry command to enhance his army's flexibility, intelligence-gathering, and offensive capabilities, it became known as Maxwell's Light Infantry.

Washington took considerable pride in Maxwell's highly mobile unit and his "light Troops," boasting to the Continental Congress of its repeated successes. The intelligence-gathering missions were vitally important because Washington had long operated without a sufficient amount of cavalry.

Especially in the war's beginning, almost no leading American officers possessed sufficient military experience or educations to allow them to emerge from this struggle over America's destiny with enhanced reputations. Among these relatively few high-ranking officers who managed to maintain unblemished reputations were a host of Washington's top Irish general officers: Generals "Mad" Anthony Wayne, who was especially proud of his eastern Ireland roots and the fact that his grandfather had fought with distinction in the climactic Battle of the Boyne in 1690; Henry Knox, the son of humble Irish immigrants from County Derry, who became Washington's chief artillery commander; Daniel Morgan, who was already a "legendary figure" in Washington's army for his impressive list of outstanding battlefield performances, especially at Saratoga in 1777 and Cowpens in 1780; and John Stark, the ever-individualistic old Indian fighter and brilliant tactician from New England who led by audacious example to inspire his admiring men, who were more than ready to follow him to hell and back if necessary.[91]

French nobleman the Marquis de Chastellux was greatly impressed by General Wayne, whose command presence and accomplishments were outsized like some force of nature. The observant Frenchman wrote with some amazement of a situation that was simply an impossibility in the French Army, where the officer corps was based on wealth, social connections, and aristocratic roots, writing how Wayne "has served more than any officer in the American army, and his services have been more distinguished, though he is yet but young."[92]

Still another good indication of how thoroughly Washington depended upon a seasoned cadre of talented, resourceful high-ranking Ireland-born officers and commanders of Irish descent was revealed in June 1777, when British forces suddenly advanced toward the Delaware. Washington relied primarily upon his most experienced team of Celtic-Gaelic commanders—Morgan, Sullivan, Maxwell, and Wayne—to ascertain the enemy's intent, exploit any tactical opportunity, and meet the growing threat, if necessary. When it was determined that General Howe's forces were actually evacuating New Brunswick, New Jersey, Washington ordered one of Wayne's brigades, along with two other Continental infantry brigades, "to fall on the enemy's rear" while Sullivan and Maxwell threatened the flank and Morgan advanced in front.

With his usual aggressive style, Morgan unleashed his infantry attack, overrunning British redoubts, after Sullivan's troops arrived in the nick of time to bolster the spirited offensive effort that steamrolled onward. Sensing victory, Morgan continued to aggressively lead the vigorous pursuit, with Sullivan's unleashed soldiers following with loud cheers and clashing repeatedly with the stubborn British rear guard. Sullivan followed Howe's redcoats all the way to Piscataway. But the hard-won advantages gained by the skill of these tactically adept Irish commanders, in whom Washington had placed so much trust, working in unison together could not be fully exploited, or "the day would prove a disastrous one to General Howe."[93]

A year later, in June 1778, Washington once again relied on his Irish commanders and their seasoned troops in pursuit of Clinton's Army that headed northeast after evacuating Philadelphia to New York City. With British strategists shifting their efforts to the south and most troops having been transported off the mainland to protect the more economically valuable (thanks to sugar cultivation) British West Indies possessions, Clinton's lengthy column was vulnerable. Most of Washington's top commanders were content to see the enemy depart, but not the more aggressive young Celtic-Gaelic leaders. Wayne most of all wanted to strike a blow while the time was right. Washington was convinced of Wayne's tactical wisdom and moved his army in pursuit.

Clinton's redcoats and Hessians marched through the humid woodlands of New Jersey. Washington dispatched the light troops of Maxwell's Brigade to "impede their progress" as much as possible. He then reinforced Maxwell with "Colo[nel] Morgan with a select Corps of 600 Men."[94] Then Washington once again united Colonel Morgan and Generals Maxwell and Wayne for the express purpose of "tak[ing] the first fair opportunity of attacking the Enemy's Rear." Washington's bold directive led to one of the longest and hardest-fought battles in the northern theater during the war, Monmouth, New Jersey, on June 28, 1778.[95]

As Wayne had promised, Washington's aggressive plan was a good one. But unfortunately, Washington's lead units smashed into the rear guard under Lord Charles Cornwallis, the best fighting British officer in America. Reacting quickly to the threat, Howe's most capable lieutenant turned the army's finest units around and chastised the advance guard command under General Lee, who ordered a withdrawal hardly before the battle began. Fortunately for the Continental Army's fortunes, Washington's timely arrival on the field in the midst of the flight of his forces turned the tide. As never before, Washington's men stubbornly fought to a bloody standstill "the flower of the [B]ritish army."[96] One of Clinton's stunned captains wrote with some amazement, if not shock, that "Today the Americans showed much boldness and resolution on all sides during their attacks."[97]

One secret of General Wayne's repeated successes was that he was "utterly contemptuous of the enemy," in no small part because his family's tragic experiences on the Green Isle fueled strong urges to strike back whenever possible. And, of course, Wayne's well-known determination and unbridled aggressiveness directed at crushing the foe on the battlefield indicated as much, to Washington's delight.[98] Therefore, one British soldier, John Robert Shaw of the Thirty-Third Regiment of Foot, paid Wayne a rare compliment that was seldom given to any American commanders: "General Wayne paid a visit to Stoney Point [on July 16, 1779 and] woe to the simple commander of Stoney Point! [when] that undaunted hero general Wayne tickled their ears" with his daring surprise night attack on what was seen as an impregnable bastion.[99]

Wayne explained his method of reaping victories in a letter to Dr. Benjamin Rush, who was one of the foremost medical men in America, the surgeon general of the middle department, and a Declaration of Independence signer. Wayne emphasized his well-known penchant of employing typically aggressive Celtic tactics of attacking at close quarters, especially in ordering his troops to rely on the bayonet not only to cut down but also to terrorize the enemy. In Wayne's gleeful words, his seasoned troops delivered "a close fire [and they] then give them the bayonet under the cover of the smoke" of accurate gunfire that raked the British formations. General Wayne was fully convinced that his tough, reliable Irish "lads" could stand up to "any troops on earth," including the finest British soldiers in America.[100] No wonder that the Sons of Erin of the Line of Ireland served as the dependable "backbone of the American army."[101]

Therefore, Wayne rejoiced in the fact that his highly motivated Emerald Isle Continentals were determined to "conquer or die."[102] High opinion, if not awe, of the overall high quality of the average Irish soldier was widely shared by many other officers throughout Washington's Army. One of Wayne's top colonels of the elite Pennsylvania Continental Line, Colonel Francis Johnston was another fine Scotch-Irish commander of the Presbyterian faith. He was a former attorney who had been born in Chester County, Pennsylvania, in 1748. Johnston first led his troops of the Fourth Pennsylvania Battalion, consisting of mostly Chester Country men, in the Canadian campaign of 1776. He gained a promotion to colonel and took charge of the Fifth Pennsylvania Continental Regiment in February 1777.[103] With obvious pride, Colonel Johnston described the high caliber of the Pennsylvania troops in a October 20, 1776, letter to Richard Peters, the Secretary of Board of War: "It appears to me that the Pennsylvanians were originally designed for Soldiers, their Vigilance, assiduity & resignation to bad Usage, fatigue & ye strictest Discipline convinces me—their bravery too & enthusiasm in the Service are equally remarkable."[104]

Known for their combat prowess regardless of the odds, these hard-fighting Pennsylvania troops were proud to be esteemed members of the Line of Ireland.[105] Such unsurpassed martial qualities were common characteristics of the Irish fighting spirit that was well known on battlefields on both sides of the Atlantic. In the analytical words of a historian, who knew that the Irish character created an elite soldiery, "they have the most sunny dispositions [and are] able to make the best of a bad situation [and] Had this not been true, they would long since have perished from the face of the earth [and the Irish are most] responsible to higher appeals, patriotic, religious, or social."[106]

Indicating the powerful influence of the Irish experience and its long-lasting legacies on American soil, these Emerald Islanders of the Pennsylvania Line were armed with excellent muskets and sharp bayonets: quite unlike ill-trained and inexperienced ancestors, including Jacobites, who had long fought in vain across the Emerald Isle with swords and lengthy wooden pikes against English cannon and muskets. In a July 29, 1776, letter to his wife, a confident General Wayne revealed his considerable pride in the deadly effectiveness of his Celtic-Gaelic boys: "I have 1500 Hardy Veterans left who will push hard for Victory and Revenge."[107]

Like Generals Wayne, Sullivan, and Knox, Morgan emerged as an almost legendary figure. He especially loomed larger than life to the Irish teenagers in the ranks, representing a revered father figure. Perhaps no one in Washington's Army held a burning vengeance closer to his heart than the hard-fighting Morgan, who possessed plenty of old scores to settle. His combat prowess, tactical ability, and feisty Celtic-Gaelic temperament that made him excel in combat against the odds and in almost any battlefield situation became the talk of Washington's Army.

But the rough-hewn Morgan also possessed a softer side seldom revealed by historians. Historians have focused primarily on Morgan's battlefield accomplishments, especially at Cowpens, at the expense of other qualities that stemmed from the overall Irish experience: warm-hearted feelings for the welfare of his common soldiers and underprivileged civilians, especially women, although he possessed an exceptionally hardened frontier exterior, which shocked both friend and foe, that concealed these admirable empathetic qualities. Like other Irish soldiers from high-ranking generals to lowly privates, he possessed a seemingly paradoxical nature: combat ferocity on the battlefield that existed beside a distinct sense of Celtic-Gaelic compassion, humanitarianism, and warm sentimentality off the battlefield.

General Henry Knox's lofty reputation was not far behind that of the raw-boned Virginia backwoodsman from Virginia named Morgan. Knox still spoke with the slight traces of an Ulster brogue from his immigrant parents from County Derry combined with a Boston accent. Knox traced his ancestors back to the Scottish lowlands before they migrated in the northern midsection of Ulster Province. The Scottish lowlands were yet another bloody borderland where Scotsmen and Englishmen had often met in savage combat to continue their ancient feud between Celt and Anglo-Saxon (as from 1775 to 1783), which had been made more intense by a toxic brew of land, race, and nationalism.

Knox was an ideal leader to the large number of those who embraced the Protestant faith in Washington's ranks. Bright, inquisitive, and blessed with abundant abilities, Henry Knox was the son of a shipbuilder, hailing from a large Boston family of Scotch-Irish Presbyterians. He was related to Scotsman John Knox, who had spearheaded the Protestant Reformation. A natural intellectual with an insatiable curiosity and love of reading, especially ancient and military history, Knox became a self-taught expert on military strategy and tactics.

Knox had read everything about military strategy that he could possibly get his hands on, even borrowing books from the library at

Harvard College. Knox's endless pursuit of knowledge, including detailed military manuals and classical works about the campaigns of ancient Roman generals, had been relatively easy. After all, he owned his own Boston bookstore. The introspective, when not gregarious, Knox took considerable pride in his fashionable London Book Store patronized by the educated upper-class elite.

The popular bookshop, named specifically to target an educated clientele, was often visited by British officers, whom Knox had duly quizzed for additional information about the art of war. But Knox was hardly a stereotypical bookworm. The handsome, energetic son of Scotch-Irish immigrants was blessed with a Celtic can-do attitude from County Derry. Knox also learned how to use his fists as a rough-and-tumble teenage gang member on Boston's mean streets and notorious wharf section of town, toughening him up for the Continental Army's arduous campaigns. Knox gained additional practical military experience as a coveted member and later second in command of a militia corps known as "The Train." Formed in 1768, this volunteer corps later evolved into the Boston Grenadier Corps while the revolution drew ever nearer.

Like a holy warrior, Knox held the "most sacred regard to the liberty of my country" and was fully prepared to die for it, if necessary. With an unabashed confidence, the twenty-five-year-old Knox informed Washington that he could handle what was perhaps the new army's most demanding position despite his lack of experience. Knox backed up his optimistic words with bold action and skill, performing like a seasoned leader. When Washington first assigned Knox to take charge of the artillery at Cambridge, the commander in chief was surprised by the curt question of where the location of the army's non-existent artillery was.

The large, merry Scotch-Irishman, who thought as creatively as he fought, then presented an innovative idea to Washington: that he could transport to Washington's Army sixty tons of the vast artillery arsenal (dozens of guns) and two thousand three hundred pounds of lead for bullets that had been captured in May 1775 by Ethan Allen at the largest military fortress in North America, Fort Ticonderoga, three hundred miles north of Boston. The task of transporting so much artillery through upper New York's winter-draped wilderness and densely forested hills, including the imposing Berkshires, of western Massachusetts and all the way to the East Coast seemed an entirely impossible undertaking, especially in winter.

Military professionals, including experienced British officers, would have thought such an unprecedented mission at best folly or at worst sheer madness. Senior American officers voted the audacious plan down because of its sheer unorthodoxy and impracticality. But the commonsense Washington, who continued to be a very good judge of character, relied upon his best instincts. The crucial importance of obtaining so much invaluable artillery for the gathered throng of ill-trained New Englanders at Cambridge was well worth the risk. During an arduous fifty-six-day mission, Colonel Knox's "noble train of Artillery" of fifty-nine artillery pieces, drawn by more than forty oxen-drawn sleds that laboriously made their way through a hilly and timbered landscape covered in snow and ice, presented Washington's Army with dozens of cannon and mortars to face a superior British Army at Boston.

Knox's timely effort was invaluable. Scores of well-positioned cannon aligned across the fortified high ground of Dorchester Heights, overlooking the shipping lanes of Boston harbor and the congested, low-lying city below, forcing thousands of troops to evacuate Boston. Howe possessed the wisdom not to assault the heights crowned with Knox's artillery, especially after Bunker Hill's bloody lesson, sailing to Canada during the late winter of 1776.

But Knox's remarkable success was dampened by losses of a number of Washington's Irish soldiers. Twenty-three-year-old Dr. Enoch Dole, of Lancaster, Pennsylvania, was one of these Irish martyrs cut down not long before Howe evacuated Boston. He was killed by a cannonball on March 9, 1776, by "our cruel & unnatural Foes ye

British Troops," as inscribed on his tombstone.[108] David McCulloch correctly emphasized that "without Knox, there would have been no triumph at Dorchester Heights [. . .] Henry Knox, in sum, had saved the day."[109]

Washington's first military success in forcing the British to vacate Boston was also very much the first victory for Knox, forging a dynamic team for the war's duration.[110] Mark Puls also stated "no one played a more critical role in the triumph [at Boston] than Knox[.] The triumph remains one of the most significant military victories in U.S. history, for it boosted hopes for independence in that heady spring of 1776 when provincial congresses were deciding whether to authorize their delegates to the Continental Congress to support a break with England; it quieted claims that the British military could not be defeated [and] Without victory at Boston, support for nationhood would have seemed a hollow cry based on unrealistic expectations."[111]

Although not a general officer, the resourceful and free-thinking Scotch-Irishman possessed comparably high command responsibility throughout the 1776 New York campaign. He advocated for the establishment of a standing army of regulars, a military academy for the infant United States of America, and a regular "Corps of Continental Artillery" for Washington's Army. Knox excelled whenever the challenge was greatest and the odds against success were highest, as during the wintry crossing of the Delaware River. While other seasoned Continental officers doubted that Knox could transport his cumbersome eighteen artillery pieces across the eight-hundred-foot-wide, unruly Delaware, swollen by recent rains and melting snow, he continued to emphasize to Washington that they could succeed.

Irishman Thomas McCurry described how the bitter weather on Christmas night consisted of "the worst day of sleet that could be" possible, through which Knox supervised the precarious movement of the army's cannon across the Delaware River in wide, level ferry and flat boats manned by the fisherman and sailors of Colonel John

Glover's mariner regiment of hardy sailors and fishermen. Knox then made sure that his eighteen guns were hauled, pushed, and pulled during the nightmarish nine-mile march across a white-shrouded landscape to Trenton. When the Hessians attempted to rally from the surprise attack at around eight o'clock, they were rudely greeted by the unbelievable sight of a lengthy array of Washington's angry guns poised along the heights north of town, bellowing sheets of fire through the falling snow.

With so many American muskets unable to fire because of wet powder dampened by the stormy weather, Colonel Knox's iron and brass cannons were the true key to victory in subduing the Hessian brigade and its half-dozen artillery pieces. The amazing tactical success at Trenton provided Washington with his first real battlefield victory that essentially saved the revolution and shocked the world. Ireland-born Lieutenant Patrick Duffy was one of the zealous young artillerymen of Knox's command who described in a letter how Captain Thomas Forrest's guns from Philadelphia played a leading role in the battle: "I can assure you that the Battery got applause." Because of his imposing size, an authoritarian command presence, and inspirational leadership roles, the irrepressible Knox gained the complimentary sobriquet "the Ox."[112]

In the words of historian George Trevelyan, who unknowingly complimented the heroic actions of so many common Irish and Scotch-Irish soldiers in Washington's thinned ranks, "it may be doubted whether so small a number of men ever employed so short a space of time with greater and more lasting effects upon the history of the world."[113] And in the southern theater, this was certainly the case in regard to the largely Celtic-Gaelic victory at Kings Mountain. In a representative example at Kings Mountain, three Celtic brothers and leaders of the frontier clans, Major Micajah Lewis, Captain Joel Lewis, and Lieutenant James M. Lewis, were all wounded in the success that paved the way to Cornwallis's surrender at Yorktown.[114]

Largely Celtic-Gaelic contributions were instrumental in saving the revolution at Trenton and then leading the way to Yorktown by the Kings Mountain victory, when combined with Morgan's success at Cowpens. What Trevelyan failed to emphasize was the most significant fact that such a large percentage of this relatively small number of Washington's stalwart men (around fifteen hundred of the total main strike force) at Trenton were Irish and Scotch-Irish soldiers who dominated both the officer and enlisted ranks.[115]

In a September 5, 1776, letter to his charming wife Lucy, a prophetic Knox, who had been responsible for moving the army's tons of supplies out of New York City before America's most strategic city was lost to the British, revealed typical Irish steadfastness, even amid the gathering gloom of still another defeat suffered by an ill-trained army that had yet to win a single battle: "We want great men, who when fortune frowns will not be discouraged [and therefore] One or two drubbings will be of service to us" in the end.[116]

Providing unfailing support to Knox while he served at the front year after year, Lucy knew how to deftly handle her gregarious, dynamic husband, being as feisty and high-spirited as he in part because of her own Northern Ireland background. In a 1777 letter, she teasingly and gently cautioned her husband, to whom she was supremely devoted, "I hope you will not consider yourself as commander in chief of your own house . . . there is such a thing as equal command."[117]

Frontiersmen John Stark was another enterprising Scotch-Irish leader of men who rose to the fore not only in the French and Indian War but also during some of the American Revolution's most important showdowns. He became one of Washington's best fighting generals and possessed a brilliant tactical sense that meshed with a natural aggressiveness on the battlefield. Such characteristics made the unconventional Stark something of a Celtic renegade because he possessed the single-minded goal of winning independence at all costs. Indeed, year after year, "Stark's battlefield bravery and leadership redeemed a fierce independence that upset his superiors as much as it did the enemy."[118]

Born in the southeastern New Hampshire town of Londonderry, dominated by Scotch-Irish settlers and named after the Northern Ireland town, in August 1728, Stark was the son of Scotch-Irish immigrants. The Gaelic meaning of the name Londonderry was Doire Calgach, "fierce warrior," which perfectly described Stark when unleashed to fight on his own, especially when far from his military superiors. Other Scotch-Irish immigrants settled nearby frontier communities of New England, such as Antrim, named for County Antrim, northeast Ulster Province, and Dunbarton, named after a town in south Scotland and from the Scottish Gaelic words meaning "fort of the Britons." Like so many Emerald Isle immigrants, Stark's parents eventually turned their backs on city life, where opportunities were limited but prejudice was seemingly endless. After staying about a year in Boston, Stark's family then migrated north with a flood of other Scotch-Irish settlers into the vast pine and spruce forests of New Hampshire in 1720.

Here, amid New England's wilds and brutal winters not seen in Ireland, these hardy Celtic-Gaelic pioneers staked their futures on taming the pristine lands that lay along the clear waters of the Merrimac River, nestled in a fertile valley, around nearby Amoskeag Falls. Archibald Stark and his pioneer family erected the "Stark Fort" for relative safety against Indian attack. Stark had no time for the luxury of education or the finer things of life because simple survival was the foremost priority. He felt most at home in the heart of the New Hampshire mountains, a pristine natural world far from man's corrupting influences and civilizing ways that were decidedly uncivilized in some respects.

As an adventurous young man, he and his hunting companions once made the mistake of straying too far afield. On unfamiliar ground, they were captured by Indians and then taken far north to the Abenaki village of St. Francis on the St. Lawrence River. Stark feared a death sentence through ritualistic torture. However, in a seemingly no-win situation, he managed to gain a healthy dose of respect from the St. Francis Indians during the deadly game of running the gauntlet. With a spirited Irish feistiness, Stark fought back with an unprecedented effectiveness, measured in knocking down a number of stout warriors, that won him admiration among the native people and the title of the "young chief."

After his miraculous survival, Stark never forgot what he had learned (the good as well as bad) while a captive and then a respected warrior with the Native American people. He had grown to admire the Abenaki because of their honesty and simple dignity that he had often found missing in the white world. Stark became the reliable top lieutenant of Scotch-Irish Major Robert Rogers, whose New England Rangers consisted of many Scotch-Irish frontiersmen chosen for their wilderness savvy and marksmanship. Like no others, Rogers's Rangers excelled at waging war in guerrilla fashion in the northern wilderness.

Often serving beside his Ranger older brother, William, who was born in 1724, Stark early rose to prominence in successfully leading detachments of dark green-uniformed Rogers's Rangers against the hated French and Indians during the French and Indian War. He served as a daring Ranger leader (first as a lieutenant and then as a captain) who became well known for his innovative Indian-style tactics, raids, and combat skills across the New England frontier. The wearing of distinctive "Scots bonnets" as standard Ranger headgear clearly indicated the most dominant demographic of Rogers's Rangers.

After learning of Lexington and Concord, Stark immediately left his sawmill and proceeded to Cambridge. He then served as the no-nonsense colonel of the raw-boned New Englanders of the First New Hampshire Regiment. Possessing a lofty fighting spirit and feisty nature, Stark had often inspired his green-clad frontier soldiers to do the impossible against the French, Canadians, and Indians. He himself fought by the stoic motto that left no room for negotiation, retreat, or compromise with the enemy, red or white: "Live free or die—death is not the worst of evils." Stark was extremely proud that his "parents were Presbyterian Irish and he inherited their stern, uncompromising nature [. . .] the Irish in New Hampshire honored his ancestry by rallying to him" for the showdown between amateur colonial militias of Massachusetts and a well-trained army of British professionals just outside Boston.[119]

Colonel Stark's mostly Irish and Scotch-Irish soldiers of the New Hampshire frontier, wearing the homespun clothes of farmers, clerks, and tailors instead of proper military uniforms, were "the best troops in the amorphous American army" at this time, thanks in part to Stark's inspiring leadership. One of Stark's most trusted lieutenants was Irishman Major Andrew McClary, who was killed at the Battle of Bunker Hill (Breed's Hill). Like Colonel Stark, McClary had served with distinction in Rogers's Rangers, battling Native Americans across the northern frontier. He gained considerable combat experience in warfare against the rampaging Canadians, Indians, and French, ensuring that McClary displayed exceptional leadership qualities at Breed's Hill.

By the time of the Battle of Bunker Hill on steamy June 17, 1775, when he commanded the New England Army's largest regiment, Stark already possessed a well-deserved military reputation second only to Israel "Old Put" Putnam, who also gained fame during the French and Indian War. Here, just outside Boston with his fifteen-year-old soldier and son Caleb by his side, Stark orchestrated a clever ambush. Without receiving orders from a superior, Stark took the initiative and smartly shifted his New Hampshire troops to exactly where he sensed that the British regulars had targeted: the weak American left flank that could be easily turned to spell certain disaster for the hill's defenders who still lacked training and experience.

Bringing the ways of New England frontier warfare to the hill's defense in the nick of time, Colonel Stark ordered his New Hampshire boys to carefully conceal their flank position from prying British eyes by hurriedly erecting a stone fence. The now sturdy defensive line was also masked with clumps of hay hastily gathered from the nearby farmer's fields and with thick underbrush from along the river. Again relying on a trick not found in European military textbooks and manuals, Stack then set a series of stakes in the ground before his defensive line so that the exact range was established for his marksmen to open fire once the British advanced to reach the deadly point. Fairly lusting at such a splendid martial display of courage and discipline, Stark allowed his opponent to get as close to his position as possible before yelling at the top of his voice, "Boys, aim at their waistbands!"[120]

Behind his hastily built camouflaged wall of stone, Stark had carefully positioned his New England farm boys in three firing ranks: one standing, one kneeling, and one in the rear to guarantee an almost continuous rate of fire that proved devastating to the attackers. Then, after the defenders of the main redoubt ran out of ammunition after blasting two separate assaults to pieces, Stark and his men once again rose to the fore in splendid fashion by keeping the British at bay after Howe's third assault finally succeeded and waves of redcoats poured over the parapet. Here Stark's men bought precious time, saving a good many American lives. Stark then distinguished himself at the Battles of Trenton and Princeton during the arduous 1776–1777 winter campaign. In a "thundering charge," he led the surging vanguard of one of two of Washington's columns under General Sullivan (First Division), striking the lower town of Trenton and the vulnerable Hessian brigade from the southwest.

By this time, the hard-hitting Scotch-Irishman from the raw New Hampshire frontier burned with a greater sense of revenge than usual: Stark's second son, John, had only recently died of smallpox in upper New York while serving as his regiment's adjutant. Here, in the snows of Trenton, this resourceful ex-frontier Rogers's Ranger now led his hard-charging New Englanders into the fray as the commander of the First New Hampshire Continental Regiment (reorganized in January 1776 as the Fifth Continental Regiment) with consummate tactical skill.

Stark also proved every inch a tenacious fighter off the battlefield. When he grew sick of the self-serving backdoor politics that sabotaged America's war effort while so many good men were dying at the front, Stark resigned in disgust in late March 1777, taking off the uniform that he once loved as much as his son. In true citizen-soldier fashion, like Lucius Quinctius Cincinnatus of ancient Rome, he then went back home to his picturesque Merrimac River country in New Hampshire, retiring quietly to civilian life.

But additional inspiring leadership roles lay ahead. When General John Burgoyne's British, Hessian, Tory, and Indian army marched south down the Hudson River from Canada during the summer of 1777 to threaten New England from the west, northern New England issued the call to arms to defend the threatened homeland. Determined not to be "subject to any orders but his own," the independent-minded Scotch-Irish leader gathered a small army of citizen-soldier followers (mostly Scotch-Irish Presbyterians like himself) from New Hampshire and the Connecticut River Valley.

The Scotch-Irishman refused to serve under his less tactically astute and aggressive superior, General Benjamin Lincoln, the placid-faced son of a Massachusetts farmer-turned-politician. He had been ordered to take command of all gathering New England troops to meet the growing crisis posed by Burgoyne's invasion and his ambitious push south to reach Albany. Lincoln had directed Stark and his New Hampshire militia troops to march west and join the forming main army, but Stark would have none of it. Since he had been passed over by Congress for a well-deserved promotion long overdue and was now leading New Hampshire militiamen, not Continental troops, Stark refused to submit to any Continental authority. But he willingly served under the New Hampshire government in his efforts to defend his threatened homeland.

He was determined to wage war according to his own rules and frontier ways of fighting that had nothing to do with the Continental Army, military manuals, or the seemingly always interfering Continental Congress, because these requirements were now the key for success. With so much at stake in regard to this mighty British invasion from Canada, this seasoned Scotch-Irish leader was determined that no incompetent amateur politician back in Philadelphia or politically appointed superior without sufficient military or frontier warfare experience would dim America's prospects for victory.

Understanding the unorthodox, freewheeling style of Stark that had resulted in past victories, General Lincoln at least possessed the wisdom to ignore the Scotch-Irishman's flagrant insubordination. Instead, he merely turned this Irishman and his New England brigade loose to wage their own war as they saw most appropriate. Contrary to all military axioms and conventional wisdom, Lincoln's smart leadership decision paid off in the end. As usual, Stark thought for himself in both tactical and strategic terms, relying on his Rogers's Rangers experience, natural instincts, and own common sense. He planned to advance rapidly and strike the left-rear of Burgoyne's Army, which had pushed deeper south along the Hudson River. But before the tactically astute Irishman could attack Burgoyne, whose lengthy march south down the Hudson made the over-confident British and Hessian invaders more vulnerable with each passing mile, incredibly, a large portion of the enemy's force suddenly turned east toward Stark.

At the Battle of Bennington, Vermont, in mid-August 1777, Stark and around fifteen hundred of his New Hampshire militiamen, which included primarily Irish and Scotch-Irish veterans of Bunker Hill, prepared to descend upon a sizeable German raiding column that had been dispatched eastward by Burgoyne to secure horses, new Loyalist recruits, and much-needed supplies for the British Army. Hessian Lieutenant Colonel Friedrich Baum commanded the expedition. He was not expecting resistance from the few isolated frontier settlements and farms in the wilderness, so the expeditionary force was vulnerable during its push nearly thirty miles east of the Hudson while the main British army continued to march south.

Stark decided on a bold plan of attempting to encircle the unwary force of Hessians, now far from Burgoyne's main army, in order to immediately strike an overpowering blow. However, he was unable to ascertain that Baum was about to be reinforced by another eight hundred Hessian soldiers under Lieutenant Colonel Heinrich von

Breymann before he had time to unleash his attack. Sensing the golden tactical opportunity, Stark prepared to strike and yelled at the top of his voice, "Yonder are the Hessians. They were bought for seven pounds and ten pence a man. Are you worth more? Prove it. Tonight the American flag floats from yonder hill or Molly Stark sleeps a widow!" Here, on August 16, 1777, at Bennington and in masterful fashion, Stark was setting the stage for winning "one of the most spectacular and decisive successes of the Revolution."[121] Later, General Nathaniel Greene penned with astonishment that "seldom has such rank insubordination produced such excellent results."[122]

The aggressive Irishman's attack at Bennington was all the more remarkable because Stark led militiamen (long known to be the most unreliable troops and not well trained compared to Continental troops, who were regulars), although he was reinforced by Seth Warner's Continentals and two hundred Green Mountain Boys from the remote Vermont backcountry. Bennington was one of the rare battlefield successes in which mostly colonial militia not only triumphed over hardened professional soldiers but also American Tories and Canadians. This considerable battlefield feat was a testament to Stark's leadership ability, tactical skill, and sheer aggressiveness. After having moved with stealth to surround Baum's doomed troops, Stark utilized frontier tactics while Burgoyne's well-trained Hessians were handicapped by fighting conventionally in the eighteenth-century European tradition. As so often in the past, when Stark struck, he hit exceptionally hard. As usual, Stark led the way, encouraging his howling troops forward with the war cry, "There are the Red Coats, and they are ours, or this night Molly Stark sleeps a widow." Molly was Stark's wife, Elizabeth, whom he had married in 1758.

Like an unstoppable flood, Stark's cheering soldiers swarmed over the earthen breastworks, capturing four artillery pieces, colorful Hessian battle flags, and a good many German soldiers, who never knew what had hit them. Baum and his Hessians surrendered to the mostly Scotch-Irish troops just before Breymann arrived to reopen the contest. After his rawboned militiamen captured an iron six-pounder, not one of these young New Englanders possessed sufficient knowledge of how to work the gun. Therefore, amid a hail of zipping bullets, Stark dashed up and quickly dismounted. Shouting like a drill sergeant, he then taught his New Englanders how to load, aim, and fire the artillery piece upon the retreating Germans and Loyalists.

During what had evolved into two distinct battles (the first one fought against Baum and the second against Breyman) in which he emerged victorious, Stark had swiftly eliminated a full third of the German troops of Burgoyne's Army. He also inflicted heavy losses on the hated American Tories of the Queen's Loyal Rangers and Burgoyne's Canadians, who were mostly frontiersmen from wilderness regions located north of the Great Lakes. Skilled in frontier warfare, these Canadians, who had no desire to become part of America's fourteenth colony, were experienced bush fighters like Stark. While leading his disciplined German Brunswickers, Lieutenant Colonel Baum was mortally wounded, falling in a hail of gunfire from New Hampshire flintlock muskets.

Stark's victory cost General Burgoyne one-sixth of his total force: around one thousand Germans, Tories, and Canadians. These were well-trained veterans whom this aristocratic British commander could ill afford to lose, especially the dragoons and their horses when his isolated army was situated so deep in hostile country. Barely half a dozen dragoons survived the disastrous battle to rejoin Burgoyne, who had lost his intelligence-gathering "eyes and ears" at Bennington. The development boded ill for the eventual outcome of the British invasion. Stark's losses among his mostly Scotch-Irish boys at Bennington were relatively light by comparison. Only a red sunset over the hardwood forests lining the western ridges saved the survivors of the battered Hessian task force from destruction during Burgoyne's most serious reversal to date.

Stark's one-sided victory at Bennington not only lifted American morale across the thirteen colonies but also set the stage for General

Gates's upcoming decisive success at Saratoga. Here, Burgoyne's ill-fated British advance south toward Albany came to an inglorious end in no small part because Burgoyne, who was incapable of either prudence or tactical flexibility, so thoroughly minimized the seriousness of the Bennington defeat. Therefore, he continued to march south on the lengthy trek toward Albany as if nothing had happened.

In a scenario deemed impossible, therefore, the aristocratic Burgoyne, a victim of his own hubris and folly, was forced to surrender his army at Saratoga in mid-October 1777 to end the ambitious British bid to sever the colonies in half and end the war. For his outstanding performance in this all-important campaign that paved the way for the French Alliance of 1778, Stark won a well-deserved promotion to a general's rank only two months later. The jubilant Scotch-Irish commander proudly presented Bennington battlefield trophies of the vanquished Hessian troops to the government of New Hampshire and the Massachusetts legislature.

Burgoyne's surrender at Saratoga stunned England and its military because it seemed so improbable, in no small part because of the tactical skills of two little-known Scotch-Irishmen (Stark and Morgan) without professional military educations. One young German member of General Burgoyne's main force was astounded by the defeat's magnitude because it sprang from an unexpected uprising of so many ordinary "country people" (mostly Scotch-Irish) from a wide stretch of New England and without the Continental Army's assistance. But it had taken a dynamic leader of Stark's popularity and tactical ability to have made the decisive Saratoga victory possible by reaping such a remarkable success at Bennington.[123]

A thoroughly dismayed "Gentleman Johnny" Burgoyne explained in a private letter the true cause of this stunning defeat of his finest troops by writing how "the New Hampshire Grants, a country unpeopled and almost unknown in the last war, now abounds in the most active and rebellious race on the continent. . . ."[124] And without question and as demonstrated at obscure places in the middle of nowhere like Bennington, by far "most active and rebellious race" in all America was the Irish and the Scotch-Irish. A disillusioned Baum also complimented the combat prowess of so many never-say-die Celtic-Gaelic soldiers, who had so thoroughly crushed his forces at Bennington, while lying in anguish on his deathbed so far from his Germanic homeland: "They fought more like hell-hounds than soldiers."[125] This astute, if not pained, observation from the vanquished German commander of the Bennington debacle was most appropriate. After all, Stark himself had bedeviled and outsmarted not only the British and Hessians, but also his own superiors in order to orchestrate his victory at Bennington. Because of his independent streak and blatant disregard for authority at all levels, he was twice reprimanded by the Continental Congress for his outright refusal to link his troops to both Generals Gates and Benjamin Lincoln as ordered.[126]

Continuing to display open defiance toward Continental authority, Stark and his independent-minded New Hampshire soldiers marched away just before the first day's battle at Saratoga. With trusty flintlocks on shoulders and fully satisfied that they had entirely fulfilled their patriotic duties as required, they simply left the army because they believed that their two-month terms of enlistments had expired. With harvest time back home drawing near and families and farms in neglect because of their timely service to their country, these rustic victors of the dramatic success at Bennington went back to their farms and "home[s]—regardless of the consequences."[127]

Despite Stark's persistent flagrant insubordination, Washington praised the timely rising of the largely Scotch-Irish militia of New Hampshire and Stark's invaluable efforts. In an August 22, 1777, letter to General Israel Putnam, he lavished praise upon "the great stroke struck by Genl Stark near Bennington."[128] Having experienced Celtic-Gaelic wrath on the battlefield, an amazed German officer wondered, "With what soldiers in the world could one do what was done by these men, who go about nearly naked and in the greatest privation? . . . But from this one can perceive what an enthusiasm—which these poor fellows call 'Liberty'—can't do!"[129]

As Burgoyne, Washington, and Baum's words all revealed, British leadership, military and civilian, came to the shocking realization that their confident decision to attempt to subdue the rebellious colonists by brute force had proved badly misplaced and much too optimistic. The sheer determination of the Celtic-Gaelic fighting men to succeed can be readily seen in the words of one Scotch-Irish leader, who spoke to his mostly Scotch-Irish men from the western frontier: "appealing to them to stand by and die with him, if need be"—a stirring appeal that brought victory in South Carolina.[130]

Contrary to the popular stereotypes of Irish as drunks and devoid of morality, Stark's high moral standards were early exhibited during the French and Indian War. At a British fort, when its garrison of a good many Irish soldiers celebrated St. Patrick's Day with the usual heavy drinking on March 17, Stark refused to join in the activities to honor Ireland's patron saint. Stark ordered his Rogers's Rangers, including Irish and Scotch-Irish, not to join the festivities: an order that risked mutiny. Naturally, Stark's directive caused a great deal of disgruntlement among his green-uniformed rangers. However, Stark was devoted to improving the overall quality of his men and enhancing their combat capabilities: a focus that continued unabated during America's struggle for liberty.[131]

Bad Irish Seeds

Not all of Washington's tactically innovative and unorthodox leaders from Ireland who served as generals were as heroic as Stark, Wayne, and Morgan. Thomas Conway was one of the few Irish Catholic generals of the Continental Army, not unlike the solitary role of Maryland's Charles Carroll (O'Carroll) as the only Irish Catholic signer of the Declaration of Independence. With immense pride in playing the part of a true revolutionary, General Conway was early convinced that the Americans were entirely undeserving of the derogatory names of rebels. Instead, there was something uniquely laudatory in that much-ridiculed name to Conway's distinctive Celtic-Gaelic way of thinking.

This high-ranking Irishman with French Army experience emphasized that this common people's struggle for independence was in fact not a rebellion at all, as so often denounced by the British conservatives of King George III's government in London and by his solders across America. Conway stressed that "in 1715 was [the Jacobite] Rebellion; that in 1745 was a [Jacobite] Rebellion of the foulest and rankest kind." But the Irishman "was fully convinced that the present [struggle] of America was NOT REBELLION," because the British government had betrayed its own enlightened principles of freedom and self-government.[132] Conway also viewed America's struggle for liberty as a holy war, because "a great and good God has decreed that America shall be free. . . ."[133]

Born in Ireland in 1733, Conway was sent to France at age six by his parents to secure a high-quality education that had been denied him in Ireland by the British government, thanks to the restrictive Penal Laws, because of his Catholicism. Conway then excelled, serving as an officer in a French regiment and gaining solid military experience, rising to a colonel's rank. On the American Revolution's eve, Conway still served in the Anjou Regiment of the French Army. When war erupted, the republican-minded Conway received permission to join the rebel cause in faraway America. Inspired by lofty Enlightenment ideals and eager to join the colonist's liberation effort, he departed the French Army in December 1776.

Urgently needed by Washington's Army of novices unfamiliar with the finer points of European warfare, especially the importance of discipline and drill, this Roman Catholic Irishman brought valuable military experience to a new Continental Army short on experienced leaders. In early May 1777, Conway met with Washington, who was impressed with the Emerald Islander's considerable military knowledge. Not long thereafter, therefore, Conway gained a general's rank from Congressional members by mid-May, thanks in part to a "usually commendatory letter" from Washington to the Continental Congress.

Conway's case was only one example of the many instances in which Washington actively, if not enthusiastically, favored the Irish, regardless if Catholic or Protestant. Unlike many high-ranking Protestant military commanders of English descent and despite his aristocratic planter's background, Washington exhibited no personal biases or race- or religion-based prejudices toward the Irish. After all, they were another oppressed colonial people and a historic underdog who had suffered far longer and more severely than America's colonials dreamed possible.

Washington embraced these Celtic-Gaelic kindred spirits and revolutionaries like true brothers, and quite unlike any other Europeans, including even the French after they officially became allies in 1778. And unlike so many Protestant Americans, Washington was not known to discriminate against Irish Catholics or deny them promotions, if he ascertained that they deserved higher rank. Washington's Ireland-born staff officers—Fitzgerald, Moylan, and McHenry—proved as much.

From the beginning, this dignified gentleman planter demonstrated a distinct partiality toward both Irish Catholics and Irish Protestants in a day in which such open-mindedness was rare. In this sense, Washington hardly fit the common Anglo-Saxon stereotype of the provincial, conservative planter of Virginia's gentry class who was restricted by class consciousness and narrow-mindedness by embracing prevalent anti-Irish and anti-Catholic stereotypes. No evidence has revealed that Washington viewed the lowly Irish in general in a negative light during the war years. Moylan, an Irish Catholic like Fitzgerald, served with distinction not only on Washington's staff but also in obtaining higher command in the cavalry and in high-level "trusted positions" in the Continental Army, thanks to the Virginian's support.

General Conway demonstrated his leadership ability during the fighting at Brandywine and Germantown in 1777 (where Washington met with defeat on both fields), appropriately while command-ing General Sullivan's mostly Irish and Scotch-Irish troops of the Pennsylvania Line. One of the most reliable units in Washington's Army, Conway's brigade included the Third, Sixth, Ninth, and Twelfth Pennsylvania Regiments, Continental Line: men of the elite Line of Ireland. This highly ambitious Irish general also proved highly skilled in the art of political maneuvering behind the scenes with influential Congressional members and fellow high-ranking officers. Not surpris-ing when combined with his solid battlefield performances, therefore, that Conway won the lofty rank of major general before the end of 1777. In fact, he became the highest-ranking Irish Catholic general in Washington's Army that defended a largely Protestant nation, which was still anti-Catholic in many ways.

In time, Washington began to learn from his supporters, including staff officers like young Alexander Hamilton, what a for-midable personal enemy he possessed in this Irishman of limitless ambition. Conway won his coveted position of inspector-general from the Continental Congress, which had been originally advocated by Washington, to supervise the overall improvement of the Conti-nental Army's discipline. However, Conway was hardly alone in his anti-Washington sentiment that was growing in the army and Con-gress, thanks to the commander in chief's many losses that began with New York City and recently increased with the Brandywine and Ger-mantown defeats in less than a month in September-October 1777.

In fact, by this time, Washington's only clear tactical success was Trenton. Conway appealed to a number of Congressmen, emphasizing the liabilities of Washington's too "passive" ways of conducting war at Brandywine and Germantown compared to his own more shining battlefield performances, which had transformed him into "the idol" of many soldiers. Thanks to ample experience in the French Army, Conway was blessed with greater tactical skill than Washington, but considerably lesser leadership skills and moral character.

Conway could hardly be faulted in politically angling for Washington's job, an effort supported by former Congressman Dr. Benjamin Rush, because late 1777 was still another significant low point of America's fortunes, and the often-losing Continental Army was racked by seemingly endless intrigues and conspiracies at the highest levels. In fact, the Irishman's strong opposition to Washington's tactical ability paved the way for what the Virginian's protectors believed was the formation of the "Conway Cabal." In general, historians have overemphasized the existence of a powerful anti-Washington cabal that they believed was essentially an ambitious bid of the once-powerful New England faction of Congress to regain its foremost position in leading the revolution as in 1775.

The replacement of the Continental Army's commander in chief by Gates or Conway was advocated in part because Washington was a Southerner, not to mention a slave owner. Like Dr. Rush, Conway was fully convinced that he could perform more capably than Washington against the well-trained British and Hessians in a military showdown.

A good many influential people throughout the colonies were also convinced that Washington had become more of a liability than an asset by this time. Dr. Rush, like Washington's former aide Joseph Reed, who was of Irish antecedents, was disillusioned by Washington's inability to reap battlefield successes. The highly respected Dr. Rush, who believed that Conway could transform Washington's Army into an invincible force, was only another influential voice in a rising chorus championing Washington's replacement by Conway, especially after Gates's victory at Saratoga in October 1777.

A bright Princeton graduate from Pennsylvania, Rush was convinced that Conway, with extensive French Army experience on the European continent, could "yet save Washington's Army" by the autumn of 1777.

After all, Conway had performed quite well at the Battle of Germantown, Pennsylvania, on October 4, 1777. Just when it had appeared that the Americans were on the verge of victory at Germantown, the elated Irish Catholic general openly "wept with joy" in the belief that victory had been won. Conway's inspired battlefield performances did not go unnoticed by his division commander, General Sullivan, who was very proud of his own Ireland immigrant heritage. Never before encountering a general with a feisty Celtic-Gaelic fighting spirit as vibrant as his own, the "headstrong" Sullivan gained "a respect [for Conway] that amounted almost to awe" that was well deserved.

Besides possessing an abundant amount of arrogance that he failed to conceal, Conway was also high-strung, quarrelsome, and sarcastic and was known for emotional outbursts. He also possessed a legendary temper and an in-your-face confrontational style, even when dealing with Washington. But while Washington succeeded in taming his temper under a refined gentleman's proper guise, Conway proved a flat failure in this regard. During one incident when he took personal offense from General John Cadwalader, of Scotch-Irish descent and a die-hard Washington supporter, Conway promptly challenged the outspoken Pennsylvanian to a duel.

By his choice for settling a personal dispute, Conway adhered to a well-established custom of upper-class Irish society. Dueling to settle personal disputes among gentlemen first became socially acceptable among the Irish aristocracy in the sixteenth century, reaching its height in the eighteenth century among Europe's upper classes. At this time in Ireland, "virtually every major political name 'smelled powder'" to settle affairs of honor. Likewise, dueling became an accepted form of settling personal disputes at the highest levels of Washington's Army, except for the commander in chief, who was forbidden by army regulations to engage in dueling.

When Conway and Cadwalader turned to face each other, the over-anxious Irishman fired first, but missed his target entirely in his eagerness to get off his first shot. Conway stood tall to receive the return fire and yelled, "Why do you not fire, General Cadwalader?" Cadwalader replied that he was waiting for a slight breeze to pass. Now realizing that he faced an experienced marksman, Conway then declared, "You shall have a fair chance of performing it well." Holding his breath, the controversial general from Philadelphia took careful aim at his stationary Irish target. Clearly, Conway was no coward. Conway was hit in the mouth by the small-caliber lead ball from Cadwalader's pistol, which knocked him to the ground. Extensive damage was inflicted upon the unfortunate Irishman's tongue and teeth when the bullet passed through the fleshy part of his neck just under "his pigtailed hair."

Standing over Conway, who lay on the ground with blood dripping from his mouth and down the back of his neck, the Scotch-Irish Pennsylvania general, age thirty-four, declared, "I have stopped the damned rascal's lying anyway." Acknowledging a steady hand and good aim, the spunky Irishman complimented Cadwalader, "You fire, general, with much deliberation, and certainly with a great deal of effect." It has not been recorded in history, but Washington must have chuckled out loud in the privacy of his headquarters, or at least to himself, when he first learned that this Irishman's notoriously sharp tongue that had so often lashed out against him had been finally silenced by what he very likely considered an act of divine Providence.

Weary of America's sagging fortunes, Conway returned to the French Army in the summer of 1779. When he reached Europe's shores once again, the aristocratic Irish Catholic undoubtedly felt a good deal not only more humble but also much safer. After all, he had been dealt with harshly by these rough-and-tumble, honor-sensitive American revolutionaries, especially a fellow Irishman from Philadelphia, who knew how to take careful aim and shoot straight in affairs of honor.[134]

But Conway's sojourn in America was hardly a wasted effort. Fully appreciated by the commander in chief before he had become an ambitious personal enemy who hoped to replace him, Conway had been an esteemed member of a hard-hitting team of Irish,

Scotch-Irish, and Celtic commanders by the early autumn of 1777, when Washington took the offensive while Howe was content to occupy Philadelphia. Hoping to repeat his impressive Trenton success, Washington ascertained that the British garrison at Germantown was vulnerable. Therefore, he struck with the "divisions of Sullivan & Wayne, flanked by Conways Brigade [that] were to enter the Town . . . while Ireland-born General [John] Armstrong [who led the surprise attack on Kittanning during the French and Indian War] with the Pennsylvania Militia [should] get upon the Enemy's left and Rear [and] the Militia of Maryland & [New] Jersey under Generals Smallwood and Foreman [were] to fall upon the rear of their Right, while Lord Stirling with [Francis] Nash [who was the son of a Welsh immigrant] & Maxwell's Brigades was to form a Corps of Reserve," specified Washington in his October 5, 1777, battle report. Washington especially complimented Sullivan, the Scotch-Irish general, and the right wing "as they acted . . . with a Degree of Gallantry that did them the highest honor."[135]

As could be expected, Conway's antics off the battlefield had tarnished his battlefield reputation, proving to be his undoing. Washington's esteem for Conway quickly eroded when he concluded, as revealed in a December 31, 1777, letter to his good friend the Marquis de Lafayette, that "his ambition and great desire to being puffed off as one of the first Officers of the Age [meant] he became my inveterate Enemy."[136] After Congress appointed him to inspector general, Conway wrote a December 31, 1777, letter dripping in sarcasm by way of comparing "the great Washington" to Frederick the Great. After reading the letter, one of Washington's aides declared that the outspoken Irishman "deserved to be kicked." Deciding not to challenge Conway to a duel as some officers advocated, Washington merely concluded how the Emerald Islander was "a secret enemy [and] a dangerous incendiary."[137]

Far away from Washington's Army, other Ireland-born generals served in militia units or obscure Continental commands on behalf of their native states. Pierce Butler was one such Irishman who served as the adjutant general of South Carolina, beginning in 1799 with the rank of brigadier general. He was a key player in orchestrating guerrilla resistance across South Carolina against the invading British at the low ebb of the faltering American resistance effort in the South, after the capture of Charleston and its large garrison, including many veteran Continental troops, in May 1780. The loss of the strategic Atlantic port, the South's most important and wealthiest city, was still another fiasco for American arms that sent America's fortunes spiraling downward in the South, where the situation remained bleak for an extended period.[138]

But of course, the largest number of Ireland-born generals who had the greatest impact on the war's overall outcome served in Washington's Army. For instance, the First Continental Regiment, organized on January 1, 1776, was commanded by Ireland-born Colonel William Thompson. He was a hard-nosed Pennsylvania frontier commander and French and Indian War veteran. Personable Ireland-born Lieutenant Colonel Edward Hand was his capable second-in-command of the First Continental Regiment. Earning a reputation as one of the most distinguished combat units in the annals of United States military history, the First Continental Regiment was the first regiment of the United States Army and consisted of mostly Irish and Scotch-Irish soldiers from Pennsylvania.[139]

At the conflict's beginning, when the thirteen colonies were still without real war-waging capabilities, Robert Treat Paine, the son of an Irish immigrant and respected lawyer from southern Massachusetts, emerged to play a leading role in the budding revolutionary government. Innovative and imaginative, he was appointed by the Continental Congress as chairman of the munitions committee. Scotch-Irishman Henry Knox repeatedly bombarded Paine with urgent requests for additional cannon to strengthen the deficient "long arm" capabilities of Washington's Army.

In this crucial role, Paine was responsible for devising a practical system for purchasing saltpeter and sulfur to make countless tons of gunpowder and cannon. While other less-capable colonial leaders, including even some Founding Fathers, only spewed fiery political rhetoric or proved totally inefficient in making timely contributions, Paine took early decisive action and worked tirelessly behind the scenes in his own quiet, effective manner, doing whatever he could in liberty's cause, which was a great deal. In Paine's own words, America's national struggle for existence was nothing less than a great "decision for Liberty or Slavery."[140]

But far more than Paine, it was the forgotten common and ordinary Irish, both men and women, who sacrificed their lives, fortunes, and family members in the name of liberty and played unsung roles that spelled the difference between victory and defeat for America. A patriot soldier who paid a frightfully high price for supporting America's bid for independence, Andrew Jackson, the son of Scotch-Irish immigrant parents, certainly seemed to realize as much when he bestowed a heartfelt tribute to his fiercely patriotic mother, Northern Ireland-born Elizabeth, who died in her efforts in supporting America's determined bid for freedom and in the service of her adopted country so that this new land of promise would never become another Ireland: "There was never a woman like her. She was gentle as a dove and as brave as a lioness."[141]

Chapter VII

Washington's Close-Knit Irish "Family" and Other Hard-Hitting Irish Leaders

The Marquis de Chastellux wrote with great interest and almost amusement how he was introduced by Washington to his "aide-de-camp, adjutants and other officers attached to the general, from what is called his family."[1] This was no exaggeration, but revealed the familial and almost collegiate setting that Washington established at his headquarters. With a sense of affection, Washington wrote to the father of Anthony Walton White in late August 1775 about how he planned "to take Mr. White into my Family as an Ade [sic] de Camp."[2] Throughout the war years, in keeping with his penchant for favoring the Irish and partly reflecting his generally lower esteem held for German immigrants, Washington's closest circle was one that was early flavored by its distinctive Celtic-Gaelic roots. On the field of battle and in the tented encampment, year after year, Washington was faithfully attended by a number of promising, dependable Irish aides-de-camp of his personal staff, or his unofficial "family."

His staff was not exclusively Irish, but was heavily Celtic-Gaelic, including the brilliant Alexander Hamilton who possessed a Celtic (Scottish) background on his father's side. One young staff officer of Irish ancestry, Joseph Reed, considered Washington's tight circle of young, talented officers as consisting of "Gentlemen of the Family," who served their commander in chief in both mundane duties and in any crisis situation. For the most part, they were both supportive and protective (not only physically but also in terms of Washington's reputation) of their beloved commander in chief, who was not always easy to work for as a boss, as dashing Captain Hamilton discovered to his consternation. Henry Knox was one of the first of Washington's trusty members of his esteemed inner circle. Except for Joseph Reed, who became the Judas of Washington's staff, these dynamic young men of Irish and Celtic-Gaelic background were the commander in chief's longtime favorites, who became warm friends and trusted confidants.

These staff members repaid him in kind with their loyalty, including ascertaining those many conniving intriguers, both military and civilian, who sought to have Washington disgraced and ultimately replaced. These included protective, highly intelligent, and dependable officers like Ireland-born Colonel John Fitzgerald from County Wicklow, who was a successful merchant from Alexandria, Virginia, and known as the army's best horseman whose equestrian skill had been acquired in Ireland from where he had migrated in 1769; Peregrine Fitzhugh, born in 1759 as the son of Colonel William Fitzhugh; the personable, likeable Dubliner James McHenry, who benefited from a classical education earned at Dublin's Trinity College and left his medical profession to serve by Washington's side; the articulate Joseph Carey; Joseph Reed, the bright, amiable Princeton graduate; and handsome Tench Tilghman, an erudite, natural ladies' man who was born in a tobacco planter family in Talbot County, Maryland, and whose mother was the pretty daughter of an Irish immigrant.

Partial to the finest claret wines and pretty girls, young Tilghman's promising life and seemingly limitless possibilities were tragically cut short by an early death from the disease incurred amid the winters spent at Valley Forge. Tilghman, who served not only as Washington's aide-de-camp but also his personal secretary beginning in the summer of 1776, was proud to have been part of the Washington's military family of young, enthusiastic officers.

The aide-de-camp whom Washington had initially most admired gradually evolved into the most traitorous one. A gifted, hard-working Philadelphia lawyer blessed with a host of talents but too conniving and clever for his (and America's) own good, Joseph Reed early became Washington's favorite aide when he first took command of the colonial army outside Boston at Cambridge. In his private letters and in a manner seldom revealed by the ever-austere commander in chief, Washington repeatedly referred to Reed as his good friend. The intellectual grandson of an Irish immigrant from Ulster Province, he later became the president of the Pennsylvania provincial congress.

Washington had so much to learn when he first took command of the Continental Army, whose complexities and inherent problems seemed endless, that Reed's competent services as his military secretary were invaluable. The versatile, cosmopolitan Reed was no dour intellectual, but a man of action who possessed a great deal of personal charm, wit, and good humor. Washington first encountered Reed, who had received a high-quality education in London, at the turbulent meetings of the First and Second Continental Congress in Philadelphia. They formed a tight bond, with the childless Washington accepting the young man almost as a surrogate son. As a strange fate would have it, Reed was the son of a wealthy Irish immigrant merchant from Trenton, New Jersey, where Washington achieved his most surprising victory, reaping an unexpected success in late December 1776 that helped to turn the revolution's tide to ensure America's very life, when prospects never appeared darker for the new nation's fortunes.

At Philadelphia, Reed first joined Washington on his long journey to take command of the infant American army at Cambridge, leaving behind a wife, three children, and a thriving law firm. Without rank or position, he rode along the dusty road leading to Boston as part of his "honorary escort" for the newly appointed commander in chief, who had ridden all the way from Mount Vernon. Reed had initially only planned to ride with Washington as far as New York City. But after much convincing by the persuasive commander in chief, who knew that he needed expert assistance for the tough job that lay ahead, he decided to stay with Washington. The young attorney of Irish descent accepted the important headquarters staff position as Washington's secretary, a hasty decision that revealed an impulsive nature: a central character flaw that later came back to haunt the commander in chief in time and much to his shock.

Indicating his many years of experience as a demanding taskmaster of hundreds of slaves on his Virginia tidewater plantation, Washington demonstrated a rare talent for recognizing the most capable men whose organizational skills and abilities outmatched his own. During the war years, he depended upon a host of capable staff officers with superior educations and abilities to perform essential headquarters duties as he sternly demanded in a timely, precise manner.

Clearly, this largely unheralded talent pool of young Irish and Scotch-Irish officers was one forgotten secret of General Washington's success. In fact, Washington had early learned to appreciate the considerable talents of the Irish and Scotch-Irish officers and enlisted men, and this experience served him well throughout the war years. Irishman Henry Alexander Clark, who "lived by his wits and fits," had been a member of Washington's land surveying team in 1749. When Washington became the colonel of the First Virginia Regiment during the French and Indian War, Clark served as a trusty orderly sergeant. Washington relied upon him in battling the Indians, French, and Canadians in the lengthy struggle for a continent's possession, the French and Indian War. Clark had been born in the strategic port town of Newry, County Down, Ireland. The town had been burnt down during the fighting for the heart and soul of Ireland in 1689 before evolving into Ireland's fourth-largest port by the time of the American Revolution.

As no one else in the revolution's beginning, Reed became a virtual godsend to Washington, fulfilling Washington's urgent needs for an energetic organizer and intelligent administrator. Therefore, this hard-working son of an Irish immigrant became Washington's confidant and most esteemed member of "my family" during the war's early days. With seemingly effortless skill, Reed assisted "immeasurably" in the creation of an army out of the confused situation at Cambridge.

Based upon his demonstrated abilities and at Washington's urging, the handsome Reed was commissioned adjutant general by Congress by the summer campaign of 1776.[3]

When only in his mid-thirties, therefore, Reed gained a well-deserved reputation throughout the army as Washington's "top aid[e]" and most "indispensable" staff member (his first "military secretary") during the crucial period of 1775 and 1776. As Washington explained to Reed in a long letter, "You cannot but be sensible of your importance to me. . . ."[4] However, like so many other Americans in military and political circles, Reed eventually lost faith in Washington's generalship after New York City's loss and subsequent setbacks and allowed himself to become convinced that the more experienced General Charles Lee was more suitable to command the army. Once Washington learned of the depths of this lost confidence and shattered friendship, Reed no longer served as Washington's top aide after the winter of 1776, hastening his retirement early the following year.[5]

Also joining Washington at Cambridge, Ireland-born Stephen Moylan, age thirty-eight, was another of Washington's most trusted aides of considerable ability. However, the Irishman served only from March to June 1776. A devout Catholic, Moylan was not only older than Reed, but also far more faithful to the commander in chief. Clearly, even Catholicism, which was almost universally despised by Protestants across America, provided no obstacle to Washington's way of thinking in regard to choosing promising officers of merit. Washington's open-mindedness also applied to his personal guard that included Irish Catholic Robert Blair, who was born in Ireland in 1763, and Thomas McCarthy from County Cork.

Most of all, Moylan was an excellent choice to serve on his staff. As Washington seemingly realized, Moylan's strong religious faith only helped to fuel the Irishman's burning resolve and motivation to defeat his people's ancient enemy, who were the longtime masters of Catholic Ireland. A devout Catholic, Moylan's two sisters found spiritual meaning in life in serving as nuns at the Ursuline Convent, established in 1771, of the Roman Catholic Ursuline Order in Cork, Ireland. Because he was so much like an Irish Catholic revolutionary of old and for many of the same reasons, he waged his own holy war against the British, only finding time to marry the woman of his dreams after his adopted nation won its independence.

Born in 1743, Moylan was raised at the busy port of Cork (the Anglicized word for the Gaelic name of Corcaigh) in County Cork, Munster Province, in Ireland's south. Here, at the longtime strategic port of call for the British Navy, including during the American Revolution, the Moylan family, which was headed by business-savvy patriarch John Moylan of Cork, had prospered as merchants. The family business thrived off the heavy maritime traffic propelled by the Gulf Stream to Ireland and their astute entrepreneurial sense. As a young man and the revered son of the attractive "Countess of Limerick," Moylan basked in the natural beauty of the limestone valleys along the Lee River, which drained most of County Cork's emerald-hued landscape and flowed east to enter Cork Harbor's head, and the Caha Mountains in the county's northwestern edge located just north of Bantry Bay. The well-trained troops of some of the British Army's finest regiments (some eight thousand redcoats were still stationed on the Emerald Isle in 1776), which eventually faced the colonists on America's battlefields, had embarked from Cork Harbor, or the Cove of Cork.

Educated in Paris because Irish Catholics were denied the right of an education in Protestant-dominated Ireland, Moylan was a liberal, free-thinking Irish son of the Enlightenment. He completed his splendid education while enjoying the balmy Iberian Peninsula climate of Lisbon in Catholic Portugal, where his father had long enjoyed strong commercial ties, before migrating to America in 1768 and launching a new branch of the family merchant business centered in the bustling port of Philadelphia.

Moylan's merchant fleet of sailing ships roamed the high seas, especially benefitting from the lucrative West Indies trade. Therefore, blessed with a keen business sense, considerable Irish charm, and highly developed interpersonal skills, young Moylan gained an elevated place in the upper echelon of Philadelphia society. By 1770, the Irishman was a privileged member of the prestigious Gloucester Fox Hunting Club. A natural leader of the Irish community in the thriving port city, Moylan was one of the original founders of Philadelphia's Friendly Sons of St. Patrick. He became its first president in 1771 when the organization was formed amid the celebrations of St. Patrick's Day. Before the Revolutionary War erupted to change his life forever, Moylan had visited Washington's extensive Mount Vernon plantation, located just south of Alexandria. Here, the young Irishman met Washington for the first time at the stately mansion poised on the commanding bluff, on Virginia's eastern border, that overlooked the Potomac's wide waters.

Known for his jovial, fun-loving nature, unlike his more serious-minded brother who was the respected Bishop of Cork, Moylan wore a bright green uniform and a large bearskin hat on the numerous fields of strife, as if oblivious to British cannon balls and bullets that whizzed around him. Especially as the inspirational commander of the Fourth Continental Light Dragoons, Moylan's daring manner and aggressive leadership style imperiled his life, but risky behavior made no difference to the confident young Irishman. Specifically designed by him, Moylan's green uniform coat represented his love for that ancient homeland across the sea. This most promising Irish officer from County Cork possessed a distinctive cavalier style that was almost more European than American, reflecting his distinctive Celtic-Gaelic background, romantic mindset, and past experiences on the Green Isle.

Thanks to his well-honed skills as an able businessman and administrator, Moylan became "Muster-Master General" of the Continental Army on August 11, 1775. Given his sound business background as a merchant ship-master in charge of the family mercantile business in Philadelphia, Moylan's knowledge of shipping, maritime logistics, and naval-related matters resulted in his early role of outfitting a fleet of American privateers to raid British ships on the high seas.

Blessed with a keen mind for the intricate complexities of economics as the longtime owner of a vast Virginia Tidewater plantation that functioned like a well-oiled machine, Washington had determined to strike a blow at the British blockade to ensure the arrival of invaluable supplies that fueled America's nascent war effort. These commerce ships, both American and European (especially from France but also from Ireland), brought the war munitions that Washington needed. Sea commerce was the principal source of England's vast wealth and power, and this seemingly endless flow of sailing ships was vulnerable. The experienced Moylan was Washington's ideal man for the job of turning America's first navy out to sea.

In March 1776, the debonair Son of Erin joined Washington's personal staff of bright young men of promise whose revolutionary zeal and commitment to their commander in chief were boundless. Moylan served with competence and diligence as the general's hard-working personal secretary and aide-de-camp of the overtaxed staff. As revealed in a January 30, 1776, letter, an impatient Moylan lamented to Joseph Reed how it was time for all debating to cease and that independence should be immediately declared. Elected by the Continental Congress on June 5, 1776, thanks to his extensive business experience, Moylan became the first Quartermaster General of the Continental Army, gaining a colonel's rank and wider respect throughout the army.

Because this was a new army of an infant nation so poorly prepared for war, especially against a dominant world power, the Irishman met with repeated frustration in this new role. In fact, Moylan's true talents lay far beyond that of the mundane tasks of quartermaster responsibilities and a thankless bureaucratic position behind the scenes. Intelligent and shrewd, he possessed an abundance of tact and a natural talent that were essential for high-level diplomacy: worldly abilities learned from his dealings in the sophisticated business experiences with leading merchants and businessmen in the mercantile world on both sides of the Atlantic.

Most of all, Moylan desired a prestigious position as America's ambassador to Catholic Spain. Before he had migrated to Philadelphia, the free-spirited man had fallen in love with the mild Mediterranean climate, the warm-hearted Catholic people, and the rich urban culture of sophisticated Lisbon, Portugal. Here, he had been educated at a fine Catholic institution of higher learning. But Moylan was much more than a savvy businessman bent on reaping family profits or a fine-dressed diplomat plotting to outsmart his adversary in a political chess game. Despite his youth, the gifted Irishman also possessed impressive leadership and tactical abilities as a dynamic commander of men. Demonstrating additional versatility, the polished Moylan performed well as a gentleman mixing easily with the highest levels of colonial or European society or as a hard-nosed military commander who was tough as a common Irish seaman on an American privateer roving the seas.

After his service as one of Washington's faithful aides, the young Irishman from County Cork led the mostly Irish troopers (including Sons of Erin Captain John Craig, Lieutenant John Sullivan, and a good many others) of the elite Fourth Continental Light Dragoons into action. This excellent light horse unit of Pennsylvanians and Marylanders became known as "Moylan's Dragoons" or "Moylan's Horse," which had been authorized by the Continental Congress in early January 1777.[6] In the beginning, the troopers of the Fourth Continental Light Dragoons wore red coats until friendly fire incidents caused a concerned Washington to order Moylan to promptly address the problem. Naturally, Moylan chose the national color of Ireland for the new uniform of his hard-riding troopers.[7]

A lover of liberty motivated by the loftiest concepts of Age of Enlightenment ideology, Moylan was also an idealist in the republican mold, which was in keeping with his aspiring generation of revolutionaries who were driven by a youthful exuberance that reflected the lofty sentiments of a romantic age. As Moylan penned in one letter of the strength of his revolutionary faith and idealism, "I am very willing to Sacrifice my Life, when Calld upon, in the glorious Cause which from the noblest principle, I have voluntarily engaged in."[8] Moyan's words were not hyperbole because dying in the name of America's liberty was viewed as the most noble, if not coveted, sacrifice, since a heroic battlefield death guaranteed everlasting fame in the sacred annals of America.[9]

Hailing primarily from Philadelphia's cobblestone, tree-lined streets in the more fashionable part of town, these "light dragoons" commanded by Moylan were employed by Washington for scouting, courier service, and reconnaissance. Moylan and his troopers scoured the countryside to gather vital intelligence for a more precise formulation of Washington's strategy at headquarters. Moylan became an inspirational and popular leader. His hard-riding cavalrymen in emerald green were likewise highly motivated and reliable. Despite his colonel's rank, the Irishman from County Cork exhibited a "fine appearance" and a "merry nature," both on and off the battlefield. A good many Irishmen, like Captains Erasmus Gill and Craig, served among Moylan's dashing horsemen, especially in the officer corps.

Colonel Moylan was extremely proud of his durable cavalrymen, especially the Green Islanders, who fought as hard for America's liberty as they rode after fleeing Britons and cursed their people's tormentors from the Albion Island. The discipline of Moylan's command, especially on the battlefield where it counted the most, became legendary. As he wrote with justification and a great deal of pride, "no Regiment could be more orderly than the 4th Continental Light Dragoons." Thanks to the colonel's tireless efforts to create an elite command to fight for America and to simultaneously honor the Emerald Isle's memory, Moylan possessed a hard-riding regiment that gained a widespread reputation as Washington's finest cavalrymen. The Irish sentiments and backgrounds among these Pennsylvania and Maryland soldiers was represented not only in their green coats, trimmed in red, and cloaks, but also in their feisty fighting spirit.[10]

Much more than a typical administrative, diplomatic, or staff officer, Moylan was a dynamic leader of men and an enthusiastic fighter on the battlefield. He led by daring example and from the front, inspiring his troopers. In a revealing January 7, 1777 letter to Robert Morris, an elated Moylan, who had been well educated in the ancient classics and remained romantic-minded to the very end despite the war's surreal horrors, described the intoxicating thrill of Washington's early January 1777 victory at Princeton: "when pursuing the flying enemy; it is utterly inexpressible [and] I know I never felt so much like one of Homer's deities before [and] We trod on air. It was a glorious day."[11] With a sense of admiration for a fellow cultured and sophisticated republican in arms, the aristocratic Marquis de Chastellux described Moylan as a "very gallant and intelligent man, who had long lived in Europe [and] is an Irish catholic [who had] served in the army as aid-de-camp to the general, and has merited the command of the light cavalry[.] During the war he married the daughter of a rich merchant in the Jerseys. . . ."[12]

Like so many Irish soldiers who served in the Continental Army's ranks, Moylan possessed a keen, wry sense of humor. In Moylan's particular case, this well-known fact was evident when Washington's fleet of small privateers captured the British vessel Little Hannah. Unable to resist the temptation of poking satirical fun at an English lord, who was familiar with the king and the highest aristocratic circles in London, Moylan wrote with sly and mocking humor how the booty included "130 puncheons of rum, 100 cases of gin, limes and oranges to please the delicate appetite of Lord Howe."[13]

On March 20, 1778 and only three days after St. Patrick's Day was celebrated in America's armies, Moylan was given command of all of Washington's cavalry in a solid vote of confidence from the wise Virginian, who continued to believe fully in the Irishman's leadership abilities and to be rewarded in his trust. Clearly, the young man from faraway County Cork had made quite a name for himself by this time. The British and Hessians could have hardly imaged that the pugnacious Moylan, who liked nothing more than to lead his troopers in close-quarter combat with opposing cavalrymen, was the brother of the highly respected Catholic Bishop of Cork.

Once unleashed by Washington, Moylan's cavalrymen pursued Sir Henry Clinton's forces during their lengthy withdrawal northeast toward New York City after the battle of Monmouth on June 28, 1778. The success of so many of his fellow countrymen from Philadelphia prompted Ireland-born James McHenry, who served capably on Washington's staff and took pride in these Irish horse-soldiers, to write in a letter with admiration how "Colonel Moylan's dragoons are still hanging on the enemy['s rear during the retreat to New York City] and waiting to see them safely a-ship aboard."[14]

When not fighting on the battlefield, Moylan was making love in the bedroom, but only to one woman. Confident that he was destined to leave no widow to mourn a deceased husband and believing that God protected him in such a righteous struggle, the Irishman's aggressiveness on the battlefield was not altered even after he married a vivacious young woman, the educated daughter of a rich merchant, on September 12, 1778.[15]

With all the sacrifices finally paying off after so many years of selfless effort, Moylan and his hard-riding regiment of cavalrymen served in the final drama at Yorktown, when Sir Charles Cornwallis found himself bottled up at the small tobacco port of Yorktown on the Virginia Peninsula in the early autumn of 1781. When the British Army surrendered on October 17, a popular song, entitled "Moylan's Dragoons," was sung in honor of Colonel Moylan and his jaunty troopers, including a good many Scotch-Irish and Irish from Pennsylvania and Maryland. One most revealing line of the song appropriately emphasized how "Old Ulster well may warm with pride [at the performance of] Moylan's brave Dragoons!"[16] New Englander General William Heath also admired "Moylan's light dragoons" and their penchant of unleashing a typical Celtic-Gaelic punch when they "charged them vigorously" at the best tactical opportunity.[17]

But no Irishman played a longer or more important role on Washington's staff than Ireland-born Lieutenant Colonel John Fitzgerald. He was another invaluable aide-de-camp and secretary whom Washington had relied upon since the early days at Cambridge. Much more than the unpredictable Reed, who had early lost faith and proved traitorous when Washington's generalship was heavily criticized during the winter of 1777–1778, Fitzgerald remained faithful to his commander in chief to the end. This "gallant and warm-hearted" Irishman from the Potomac River port of Alexandria, Virginia, proved indispensable to Washington year after year. Fitzgerald apprised Washington of the rising tide of ugly slanders, especially those harsh criticisms flowing from the acid-tongued General Conway by way of a letter to General Horatio Gates.

Proud of his Irish heritage, Fitzgerald might have been related to famed Irish Catholic revolutionary and "arch-rebel," in English words, James FitzMaurice Fitzgerald, who raised the banner of rebellion. This nationalistic Irish Catholic had long waged a desperate war against the English interlopers among the rolling, forested hills of Munster Province, including guerrilla warfare distinguished by highly effective hit-and-run tactics. Fitzgerald had first rallied the Catholics of Ireland in 1569 to rise up against the "heretic queen of England" (Elizabeth I) and her Protestant minions. He struggled to the bitter end for "faith and fatherland," attempting to free his land and people of English invaders. Like so many other revolutionary leaders who were among Ireland's best and brightest for generations, Fitzgerald was a revered Irish Catholic martyr for the ever-elusive dream of a free Ireland.

A Catholic like Moylan from County Cork, this versatile Irishman from nearby Alexandria, Virginia, knew Washington very well. In fact, Washington and Fitzgerald were fast friends long before the thirteen colonies broke with the mother country. Fitzgerald joined Washington's staff with ample leadership skills, filling a void because his younger staff members lacked comparable experience, especially in wartime. In November 1776 and just before his regiment was engaged at the battle of Trenton, the Irishman left his position as a captain in Scotland-born Colonel Hugh Mercer's Third Virginia Continental Regiment, which had been organized in Alexandria and Dumfries (settled by Scotsmen and named after Dumfries, Scotland), located just north of Fredericksburg, Virginia, in March 1776. He then joined Washington's staff as an aide-de-camp in time for the army's greatest challenge to date of attacking the Delaware River commercial town of Trenton and its Hessian garrison. The commander in chief referred to the faithful Irishman as "my dear Colonel," indicating the extent of his deep affection and respect.

Along with so many other Irish who migrated to America's shores, the Fitzgerald family had departed their Ireland homeland in 1769, bringing their ancient animosities and grievances (and, of course, prejudices) against the British with them across the Atlantic. At Alexandria, which easily accommodated the largest ocean-going sailing ships that eased effortlessly north and up the Potomac's wide expanse after having entered the Chesapeake Bay's even broader waters, Fitzgerald had long thrived as the partner of the mercantile establishment Fitzgerald & Peers. But this Celtic-Gaelic gentleman of Virginia's mercantile class was anything but a bookish type who was only good at deciphering the complexities of economics and balancing ledgers and account books.

Very much a stylish dandy in the tradition of a true Virginia cavalier, Fitzgerald early acquired a reputation as one of the finest horsemen in Washington's Army. In fact, he was perhaps only second to the commander in chief in regard to superior horsemanship. Fitzgerald only became bolder, if not more reckless, on horseback, thanks in part to the popular sport of fox hunting across wide stretches of Virginia's farms, woodlands, and fields that well honed his equestrian skill. Riding and sleek racing horses were a lifelong passion and popular recreation that Fitzgerald shared with Washington.

Despite being a devout Catholic who faithfully observed Mass and revered the words of his favorite priest, the true blue Irishman of promise from Alexandria liked to enjoy himself to the fullest in the Irish tradition of merriment. Blessed with a shining personality that easily won friends and admirers of both sexes, the handsome Irishman proved irresistible to the ladies. In the words of one individual who was quite envious of the Irishman's irresistible charm, the dashing Fitzgerald, broad-shouldered and handsome, was most appealing to "the English maidens and Scotch lassies" of Alexandria. But there was much more behind the Irishman's light-hearted and merry facade of loving the ladies, drinking fine wines from Portugal and Madeira, and dancing far into the night to the Virginia reel—a popular dance that had its antecedents in an ancient Irish dance called the Rinnce Fada.

He was also an intelligent, calculating politician with considerable popular support. Fitzgerald mixed politics with merriment with a smooth grace as if they were one in the same. Not surprisingly, when elected to the Virginia legislature in early December 1770, he threw a festive formal ball that lasted the entire night, along with flirting, drinking, and merrymaking.[18]

During the height of the battle of Princeton in early January 1777, a mounted General Washington made the mistake of riding too far out in front of panicky soldiers, who were in flight. While galloping over slick, snow-covered ground, Washington was entirely exposed to the close-range musketry of both armies in attempting to rally his troops after they had been hit by the British attack in which Celtic General High Mercer (another Virginia resident) fell mortally wounded. Fitzgerald, who had been ordered to hurry rearward units as reinforcements to bolster the faltering line, was certain that Washington was about to be fatally struck down amid the hail of lead musket balls. In shocked horror and expecting the worst, the Irishman placed his hat over his eyes to avoid the dreaded sight of Washington's almost certain fall that might well have sealed America's fate.

However, Washington once again miraculously escaped injury at Princeton while so many bullets whizzed around him. Spurring his horse forward, the much-relieved Son of Erin from Alexandria greeted his beloved commander in chief with an undisguised amazement. Overcome by emotion, Fitzgerald actually broke down before Washington for the first time in his life. This mature Alexandrian, of hardened exterior but a sentimental Irish heart, now "cried like a child" at Washington's seemingly miraculous escape from what appeared certain death.[19]

Scotch-Irish James Fergus, a member of Pennsylvania militia, was part of the burial detail assigned to the grisly task collecting bodies on the field of Princeton. The men of the detail buried two officers properly and with "the honors of war," but they left the private soldiers unburied because of the frozen ground, despite breaking through the same for the officers. Instead the bodies of the common soldiers—no doubt including Ireland-born men—were thrown into a deep ditch before an earthwork in the hope that proper burials would be completed when "the ground thawed in the spring."[20]

Clearly, class distinctions counted not only in colonial society but also in the army. In his journal, Scotch-Irish Lieutenant William McDowell recorded the death of not only a fellow Pennsylvanian officer, but also a fellow Scotch-Irishman, Lieutenant McCulloch. McDowell wrote how the lieutenant was buried with the full honors of war and that he commanded the burial "party consisting of one sergt, one corporal, & 24 privates."[21] For America's most natural rebels, these representative examples reveal the high cost of America's freedom when such Sons of Erin were buried in the ground thousands of miles from their native Emerald Isle homeland.

Rivaling Fitzgerald, James McHenry was one of the most trusted and respected Ireland-born members of Washington's special "family." Born on the River Braid in the market and linen industry town of Ballymena, County Antrim in northeast Ulster Province, McHenry had migrated to America in 1771. By venturing forth with high hopes, he paved the way for his parents to follow him to the New World and its seemingly unlimited promise in the following year. The Dublin University (Trinity College, which was first officially known as The College of the Holy and Undivided Trinity of Queen Elizabeth near Dublin) graduate took full advantage of America's ample opportunities that were available to an enterprising Protestant immigrant from the Green Isle. McHenry shortly enrolled at the Newark Academy in Delaware. He then studied medicine under Dr. Benjamin Rush, perhaps America's most accomplished physician, in Philadelphia and dedicated his life to easing the suffering and improving the welfare of his fellow citizens.

Almost as soon as the Revolution erupted in full fury, however, McHenry volunteered as an assistant surgeon at Cambridge, Massachusetts, where the infant American army had been created. The well-educated Irishman then became the chief surgeon of the Fifth Pennsylvania Battalion in August 1776. As fate would have it, McHenry was captured with this command when Fort Washington, overlooking the wide Hudson at Manhattan Island's northern end, was surrendered to Howe's forces in mid-November 1776 in still another fiasco that befell Washington's Army around New York City.

After his fortunate exchange in March 1778, this versatile Son of Erin then joined Washington's staff in May 1778 with renewed vigor and enthusiasm, as if determined to avenge the humiliation of Fort Washington's debacle. Like Fitzgerald, McHenry had an eye for the pretty ladies who flocked around Washington's headquarters. Of course, these groups included free-spirited women who eagerly sought the commander in chief's undivided attention, which was occasionally repaid in kind. The natural lighting up of Washington's eyes when approached by these attractive admirers revealed his flirtatious nature and overall fondness for women that plagued him since his early infatuation for his alluring, but unobtainable, neighbor Sally Fairfax in the days of his youth. She was married to his neighbor and friend George William Fairfax (now a Loyalist) of his stately home named Belvoir and encouraged Washington's sincere interest, if not love. Impressed by the young ladies whom he saw and no doubt mirroring Washington's own unexpressed views, McHenry penned in his diary in the summer of 1778 that "here [in New Jersey] are some charming girls."[22]

The Marquis de Chastellux, a member of the upper-class elite of France's hierarchical and monarchical-based society of wide class differences, marveled at how the highly educated Irishman rose on his own merits and talents without an aristocratic birth or upper-class antecedents. Revealing a dramatic rise not seen in the French army or a society with such broad class divisions, the nobleman wrote with some amazement about the gregarious "aide-de-camp, Colonel MacHenry [sic], who the year before performed the functions of doctor in the same army."[23]

One especially promising officer, Ireland-born Samuel Smith, who might well have become Washington's most illustrious staff member, refused the much-coveted position. He preferred to lead his cavalrymen when offered the prestigious position of a staff member (an immediate increase in rank) by the commander in chief himself. Despite his many accomplishments in the struggle for independence, Smith has been virtually forgotten by historians: the fate of so many patriotic Irish men and women. Born in 1752 less than two years after his immigrant parents migrated to the western frontier settlement of Carlisle, Pennsylvania, west of the Susquehanna River, from Ulster Province, Smith refused this lofty position on Washington's staff precisely because he loved his men and combat so much.

Instead, this highly "unusual" (in consequence) Irishman, only in his mid-twenties and whose potential seemed limitless, wanted most of all to remain in the field beside his common soldiers in the ranks, including so many Celtic-Gaelic warriors from Maryland. In this ever-quarrelsome Continental Army of backbiting revolutionary officers driven by a toxic mixture of overinflated egos, Machiavellian priorities, and soaring ambitions that knew few bounds, Smith was indeed one of a rare breed who actually preferred fighting beside his men to the dark art of political maneuvering behind the scenes for advancement and more money.

Smith's aggressive instincts and tactical skill became well known throughout the Continental Army, earning a guaranteed degree of Washington's admiration. Like so many Celtic-Gaelic families across America, Smith's Irish family made multiple contributions to the Revolutionary War effort. His father's prosperous Baltimore mercantile firm of John Smith & Sons traded cargoes of flour from the wheat crops grown in the rich farmlands of the Piedmont of western Maryland, such as the fertile valley of the turbid Monocacy River, a Potomac River tributary flowing through the Piedmont. Tons of Smith's flour were then sent to the sprawling sugar plantations of the West Indies in exchange for tons of ammunition and weapons that were then funneled to Maryland's Continental and militia soldiers.

Like so many Irish officers in Continental uniforms of navy blue, Smith's greatest recognition stemmed from his battlefield accomplishments and aggressive leadership style. From the beginning, this young son of hopeful Irish immigrants displayed a typical Celtic-Gaelic fighting spirit, never-say-die attitude, and resourcefulness, which early rose to the fore in the heat of battle. As a young captain leading a volunteer company in Colonel William Smallwood's Maryland battalion, Smith demonstrated tactical ability during the unit's baptismal fire at the battle of Long Island, on August 27, 1776.

Saddled with the responsibility by the dictates of Congress of defending an indefensible New York City, and handicapped by inexperience and lack of military insights, Washington had stationed far too many troops on isolated Long Island (after committing the folly of having divided his forces) separated by the East River from Manhattan Island, where he was headquartered. Washington's divided forces were especially vulnerable because the powerful British Navy possessed complete control of the waterways surrounding New York City. Consequently, the American troops stationed on Long Island were suddenly all but doomed when Howe landed his formidable army of around seventeen thousand British and Hessian troops on the island's west end. With the tactical skill of a professional, he then struck the unwary Americans from the rear.

As could be expected, a rout resulted with the collapse of the American left and center as the befuddled amateurs in rebellion, including General Sullivan's Division, were caught completely by surprise by British boldness and tactical skill. When the Marylander Continentals were all but surrounded by an encroaching tide of red-coat (British regulars) and blue-uniformed (Hessians) soldiers under the capable Lord Charles Cornwallis, Scotland-born Lord William Alexander Stirling, brigade commander on the south, decided that the best defense was a good offensive. He possessed two battalions of well-trained Continentals with which to strike a blow in order to buy precious time for thousands of retreating Americans, who now sought desperately to gain the safety of the line of American defenses poised atop Brooklyn Heights.

Under the command of Major Mordecai Gist, the troops of the Maryland battalion, whose commander Colonel William Small-wood was now assigned to court martial duties in Manhattan, stood ready with fixed steel bayonets that sparkled in the bright summer sunshine of August 27, 1776. Not far from Captain Smith, Captain Nathaniel Ramsey, the son of Irish immigrants from Ulster Province, commanded his finely uniformed company of Marylanders. In addition, Ireland-born Colonel John Haslet's Delaware command, now under the command of Major Thomas McDonough, another determined Celtic warrior of outstanding ability, was prepared to launch the offensive.

This desperate offensive strike was about to be unleashed by the leadership team of Stirling and Gist in a final bid to buy precious time for the shattered American forces, including Sullivan's Division, to reach the safety of Brooklyn's fortifications. During the upcoming dramatic showdown on Long Island soil, the Delaware Continental battalion was "composed largely of Irishmen" from the Emerald Isle: a guarantee that the British and Hessians were about to meet an opponent who would have to be overcome with brutal force.

Then the Marylander Continentals, in neat uniforms of blue trimmed in red, unleashed the offensive against the odds in an attempt to save the day on Long Island. In conjunction with the Maryland battalion's remainder, Captain Smith ordered a headlong attack into the enemy legions. Smith and other Maryland company captains launched their audacious attack straight at the dense Hessian and British ranks aligned around the Old Stone House, built in 1699 by a Dutch settler originally from New Amsterdam (New York City). The Scots and Scotch-Irish serving in the Maryland and Delaware ranks now met their fellow Celtic countrymen of the Seventy-First Regiment of Highlanders from Scotland's mountains and under the leadership of Simon Fraser, who was destined to fall to Timothy Murphy's Long Rifle at Saratoga. With losses mounting but still determined to succeed in a true crisis situation, the Marylanders continued to unleash repeated blows against the stubborn British and Hessian formations, until ordered by their brigade commander Stirling to cease their relentless assaults.

Casualties among the Marylanders, who were considered "the very flower" of Washington's Army, were frightfully high. Relatively few of the Maryland Continentals survived the slaughter (although large numbers were captured) and escaped across the brackish, tidal waters of Gowanus Creek before gaining the safety of Brooklyn's defenses on the high ground. From his perch at the fortifications dominating the heights of Brooklyn, Washington watched the cruel decimation of Major Gist's gallant command while they battled against impossible odds. He was deeply affected by the heroic sacrifice and sadly exclaimed, "Good God! What brave fellows I must this day lose!" Captain Daniel Bowie, the ancestor of James Bowie who was killed at the Alamo on the early morning of March 6, 1836, hailed from the tobacco lands along the Upper Patuxent River at Upper Marlboro,

Maryland. Along with General Sullivan, who battled to the very end until overwhelmed, this hard-fighting Celtic warrior Bowie was captured before reaching the fortifications. The Bowie family of southern Maryland hailed from a band of Jacobite Highland rebels who had been defeated in the bitter struggle for possession of the heart and soul of Scotland. They then migrated to Northern Ireland, where the Celtic Bowie clan settled as part of England's Ulster Plantation Settlement, before journeying to America.

But Howe, of Irish heritage himself, was denied a complete, if not decisive, victory at Long Island, thanks in large part to the hard-fighting qualities of so many Irish and Scotch-Irish soldiers serving in the Maryland and Delaware Continental Battalions. In an honorary tribute for their tenacious fighting prowess and high sacrifice "with more than Roman virtue," Smallwood's Marylanders earned well-deserved sobriquets of the "Immortals" and the "Tenth Legion"—one of Rome's elite legions that once led to one conquest after another by Julius Caesar.

With tactical skill, Captain Smith then commanded the rear guard of what little remained of the surviving Maryland Continentals, who played a key role by not only standing firm for so long against the odds but also by repeatedly taking the offensive to buy additional time by ensuring the escape of the army's overwhelmed right wing under Stirling. After encouraging his men to continue battling against superior numbers as long as possible, Captain Smith was one of the few Maryland officers who escaped death or capture during Washington's first conventional battle that proved an unprecedented disaster.

Smith then won renown and a promotion to colonel for his successful defense of Fort Mifflin, which protected the young nation's capital, located on the Delaware just below strategic Philadelphia. This notable tactical accomplishment earned Smith praise from a thankful Washington and the Continental Congress. After he orchestrated Fort Mifflin's spirited defense that thwarted the British, Washington thereafter took deep personal interest in Smith and his rise. Continuing to demonstrate an uncanny ability to pinpoint talent and ability, Washington thoroughly recognized the Irishman's potential and superior leadership talents, especially on the battlefield where resourcefulness, fighting spirit, and strength of character was required. Clearly, young Smith was a rising star in the Continental Army.

However, Smith was no saint. His hot temper occasionally erupted against both friend and foe, depending upon whoever crossed him first. When commanding Fort Mifflin in the early fall of 1777, Smith clashed with the autocratic Commodore John Hazelwood. When the naval commodore, described as a "slovenly debtor," demonstrated timidity in attacking the British with his heavily armed naval vessels, Smith grew incensed. The commodore's warships had remained too far distant from a fortified British position, which was manned by only a single gun, to be effective. For good reason, therefore, Smith became even more infuriated. In a towering fit of rage, Smith departed Fort Mifflin's safety to personally address the problem before it was too late.

On his own, the outraged Irish Marylander waded out into the Delaware's swirling waters while his men looked on in startled amazement. Screaming at the top of his voice, Smith implored Hazelwood and his tentative gunboats to draw nearer to the British position on Province Island to maximize their firepower in order to score a relatively easy success over the lightly defended point. When Hazelwood complained that Colonel Smith's presence (he was now standing in waist-deep water) was only drawing additional British fire, Smith exploded in even more anger. With his "Irish" up against an inflexible, aristocratic former English naval officer who had nothing but contempt for Sons of Erin regardless of rank, this Ulster Presbyterian reached new heights of indignation. Meaning business, he angrily roared at Commodore Hazelwood that unless "he took his vessels and left immediately [to more closely engage the enemy then] he would order the cannon at Fort Mifflin to fire on them!"[24]

And, as his men fully realized, Smith meant every word of what he said. Even during the heat of combat against the common enemy, the Irishman's words that threatened to rake Hazelwood's gunboats with artillery fire were no idle threat. After all, he wanted not only to open fire but also to personally thrash the haughty commodore, whom he believed needed some good sense knocked into him. This fiery Irish officer from Baltimore on the Patapsco River was about to literally go to war with aristocratic Commodore Hazelwood.

For such reasons, Washington's young aide Tench Tilghman, from the tobacco country of Talbot County, felt a great deal of pride in fellow Maryland leaders like Smith and Smallwood and their elite Continental troops. In a September 3, 1776, letter that informed his family about the Maryland Continentals' stirring performance at the Battle of Long Island on August 27, 1776, Tilghman wrote with pride that "no Regular Troops ever made a more gallant Resistance than Smallwood's Regiment [and] If the others had behaved as well, if Gen. Howe had obtained a Victory at all it would have been dearly bought" with blood.[25]

Clearly, this analysis was no provincial exaggeration by Tilghman. One secret that explained the elite qualities and successes of Smallwood's Maryland command on the field of strife was its heavily Celtic-Gaelic composition: 40 percent of the men of Smallwood's regiment were foreign born, and the vast majority of this percentage consisted of Ireland-born Continentals.[26]

In a strange twist of fate, some of these war-weary Maryland men later abandoned not only their hero status but also their cause at a time when it seemed as if the war and its horrors would go on forever. After their capture at the Battle of Camden in mid-August 1780, some Maryland Continentals, including Irish soldiers, joined British service (of all units in the British Army, the infamous Tarleton's Legion!) in order to escape prison, which was virtually a death sentence for American captives. These Irishmen included Patrick Mooney and Patrick Carney, both of the Sixth Maryland Continental Regiment;

Michael Craig and John Corker, both of the Fifth Maryland Continental Regiment; Barney McManis, Seventh Maryland Continental Regiment; Benjamin Connolly, Third Maryland Continental Regiment; John Duffey, Fourth Maryland Continental Regiment. All of these Sons of Erin hailed from the east side of the Potomac River in Prince George's County, Maryland.[27]

But in fact far more (both in numbers and overall percentage) Irish served in Washington's Pennsylvania regiments of the famed Pennsylvania than in Smallwood's Maryland command. These Irish demographics that revealed such a high percentage of Irish members in the ranks explained in large part why these Maryland and Pennsylvania troops, especially the Line of Ireland, won renown as the most hard-hitting and steadfast combat troops of Washington's Army year after year.[28] Therefore, when young Tench Tilgman penned in an August 13, 1776, letter to his father, he was right on target with his analysis and estimation that was based upon the high percentage of Irish soldiers in the ranks: "The Pennsylvania and Maryland Troops are a prodigious thing for us—Even the Eastern people acknowledge their Superiority."[29]

Other Dynamic Irish Generals

Both on and off the battlefield, Washington's other Irish generals were almost as colorful and distinguished as Sullivan, Wayne, Stark, Morgan, Hand, and Smith. General William Irvine, a former British Army officer educated at Dublin University, was a commanding general of much promise. He had been born near Enniskillen, which was nestled at the narrows situated between the Upper and Lower Lough Erne, in County Fermanagh, Ulster Province, Northern Ireland. After retiring abruptly from the British army, Irvine migrated to America in 1764. Here he made his dreams come true at Carlisle, Pennsylvania, west of Philadelphia. With a colonel's rank, Irvine led his Sixth Pennsylvania Continental Regiment in the ill-fated invasion of Canada, where he was captured in the debacle. Upon release, he promptly reentered the fray and continued to perform exceptionally well, serving as a general and brigade commander in Washington's Army, including at the battle of Monmouth, New Jersey, during the summer of 1778.[30]

Like General Irvine, who retained the distinctive accent of Ulster Province like so many soldiers in the ranks, other Ireland-born colonels of Washington's Continental regiments who rose in rank to become generals were Walter Stewart, John Shee, and William Thompson. Born on the Emerald Isle, William Thompson also settled in Carlisle, Pennsylvania. He was a member of the audacious Kittanning expedition of Pennsylvania militiamen who crossed the forest-covered mountains to unleash a devastating surprise attack on the hostile Delaware and Shawnee village on the east bank (flood plain surrounded by hills) of the Allegheny River in September 1756. Like other participants of this daring dawn strike that took the war deep into Indian country, Thompson gained invaluable experience during the French and Indian War. Commanding the first troops authorized by the Continental Congress, he then led the first Pennsylvania rifle regiment that joined Washington's nascent army at Cambridge. Thompson earned a general's rank in March 1776. However, he was then captured in Canada along with General Irvine.[31]

John Shee, born in County Meath, Leinster Province, located in east central Ireland, migrated to America with his brother in the early to mid-1740s, settling near Philadelphia. He became the commander of the Third Pennsylvania Continental Regiment with the call to arms. Born in Londonderry at the windswept tip of Northern Ireland, Walter Stewart migrated to Philadelphia around 1756. Leading Pennsylvania troops, Stewart was an aggressive commander who was popular with his men. Stewart was destined for a general's rank and widespread recognition as a fine leader.[32] Despite his youth, Stewart was not to be underestimated, especially by his opponents on the battlefield. He was in the forefront in boldly demanding fair treatment for ragged, starving Continental soldiers from America's leaders in 1783, which even included threatening Congress, if a host of persistent evils—the lack of clothing, pay, supplies—were not addressed by America's governing body.[33]

James and George Clinton, two colorful Continental generals of Irish descent, hailed from Orange County, New York. Located just north of New York City in the picturesque Hudson River Valley, Orange County had been named in honor of William of Orange, the Protestant William III of England. He had smashed the Irish Catholic Jacobites at the Battle of the Boyne on the River Boyne, Ireland, in 1690. Orange County was the home of mostly Scotch-Irish settlers of the Protestant faith. Irish settlers and soldiers in Orange County still sang popular ancient songs that ridiculed Catholics and praised Orange Protestant leaders, who vanquished Irish Catholics in the seemingly endless struggle for Ireland's possession.

Orange County and appropriately named nearby Ulster County had been the recipients of a relatively recent large surge of immigration of Ulstermen and their Irish families by the time of the American Revolution. Not surprisingly, therefore, Irishmen from this region of fertile agricultural lands played leading roles in the fight for America's independence. Like other Irish leaders who have received little recognition from either local or national historians, Colonel James McClaughry led the Celtic-Gaelic soldiers of the Ulster and Orange County militia during the Hudson River Highlands campaigns.

With past experience as a wide-ranging privateer against French shipping on the open seas during the French and Indian War, a New York politician, and savvy attorney before the American Revolution, George Clinton was not only a Continental general, appointed in March 1777, but also New York's first governor, designated in the following month. This dynamic Irishman, who deftly mixed military and political roles, earned distinction from having been "the father of his state." The Clinton brothers had gained their first military experiences while serving as officers in the Ulster County militia regiment, which was heavily Scotch-Irish, commanded by their father during the French and Indian War.

Their father, Charles Clinton, who had been born in the busy market town of Longford in County Longford (located between Ireland's north midlands and the fertile grasslands of the Central Plain), Leinster Province, was no ordinary Irishman. Like so many other Irish immigrants, Charles had been forced to flee to America because Ireland was a subjugated homeland. At his own considerable expense, Charles had then chartered a sailing vessel that carried his friends, neighbors, and family members, including his wife Elizabeth, who also hailed from Longford, Ireland, and three children, to America. The ship had departed the wharf at Dublin on May 20, 1729, embarking upon the lengthy journey of more than three thousand miles across the Atlantic to Philadelphia. But the dictatorial captain, who already had been paid and garnered a handsome profit, was abusive toward his Irish passengers, taking full advantage of their vulnerability.

Unable to tolerate such abusive authority and injustice on either land or water, an indignant Charles rose up to end the abuse. He confronted the despotic captain with good old-fashioned brute force. Waging his own personal war against the unfair dictates of arbitrary authority on the Atlantic, the spunky Irishman then took command of the sailing vessel in a successful mutiny. Charles Clinton displayed a reactionary Irish spirit and intolerance toward injustice that were inherited by his sons, who often convincingly demonstrated the same resolve during America's long struggle for liberty.

Commanding a newly formed regiment, which was heavily Scotch-Irish, of the New York Continental Line, Colonel James Clinton embarked upon the tortuous march north through the New England wilderness during Ireland-born General Montgomery's attempt to capture Quebec in 1775. Clinton led the Third New York Regiment of young "Yorkers," who were eager to whip the British regulars, which they naively reasoned would be an easy task. This high-spirited New York Line command was appropriately named the "Ulster regiment" because of its largely Celtic-Gaelic composition and in honor of the native Northern Ireland homeland and the New York county from where most of its soldiers hailed.

Colonel Alexander McDougall, born in Scotland, led the First New York Continental Regiment. Always concerned about soldiers' rights, he later played a role in demanding justice for long-neglected, undersupplied Continental fighting men from an apathetic Congress in 1783. Clearly, McDougall was no ordinary Celtic leader, continuing the revolutionary traditions of Jacobite ancestors who fought and died on Irish soil. A versatile leader of varied experiences, he was a former privateer who had gained wealth and prestige by leading successful raids against French commerce vessels during the French and Indian War. Then McDougall early rose to the fore as a radical revolutionary and inspirational founder of the Sons of Liberty in a New York City heavily dominated by Tory sentiment, largely because of extensive commercial ties with the Crown. This dependable regiment consisted primarily of workmen and common laborers, mostly Irish and Scotch-Irish, from New York City on the wide Hudson. A believer in the righteousness of liberty's cause, with confidence in his "Yorkers," Colonel McDougall led his Continental Line regiment into the vastness of the Canadian wilderness in the ambitious bid to make Canada part of the new United States of America by force of arms. The colonel's two sons, John and Ranald, a distinctive Celtic name, were by his side during the arduous push north through the spruce and pine forests that seemed to have no end. However, misfortune first struck the family of Celtic warriors during General Montgomery's invasion of Canada, when Ranald McDougall was early captured in the campaign during November 1775. Then Lieutenant John McDougall was taken captive in the last-ditch attack to carry Quebec by storm at December's end, when Montgomery fell.

Having proved himself one of Montgomery's top lieutenants, Clinton won a promotion to a coveted general's rank during the summer of 1776 for an abundance of leadership and tactical skills demonstrated during the Canadian campaign, including the capture of the British stronghold of Fort St. Johns: an early success that seemingly boded well for American fortunes in regard to eventually overwhelming the city of Quebec and winning Canada. Montgomery had forced the powerful fort's surrender by a combination of skillful maneuvering and New York artillery firepower.

This accurate artillery fire was unleashed by well-trained New York artillerymen under Captain John Lamb. He was the aspiring son of a wine maker who had been exiled to America. An early agitator for independence and blessed with promise, Lamb had been trained in the artillery art by Dublin-born Christopher Colles. Having migrated to Philadelphia in 1771 and like other Irish cannoneers of Lamb's "long arm" unit, Colles evidently served in Lamb's artillery command that also proved as formidable against British warships as Fort St. Johns.

Revealing the extensive Celtic-Gaelic connection, Brigadier General James Clinton commanded Fort Montgomery on the Hudson, protecting the strategic Hudson Highlands. This imposing defensive bastion had been named in honor of the martyred Ireland-born General Montgomery. As mentioned, he had been killed by a blast of canister from British cannon while courageously leading the assault on Quebec and had become America's first high-ranking martyr. Meanwhile, Brigadier General George Clinton, who was senior to his brother James, commanded the overall defense of the strategic Hudson Highlands. Situated atop a cliff overlooking the Hudson like Stony Point to the south, Fort Montgomery was nestled in the middle of the Hudson River Highlands. This formidable defensive bastion was one of a series of Hudson River forts that guarded the river, which was the strategic artery leading to Canada.

With construction having begun in 1776, Fort Montgomery and its band of defenders were in an ideal defensive position to stop the British warships and Sir Henry Clinton's forces from ascending the Hudson from New York City to link with the British-Hessian Army under

"Gentleman Johnny" Burgoyne, who was pushing south through the dense wilderness from Canada along the Hudson and heading for Albany during the summer of 1777. Although Fort Montgomery, along with nearby Fort Clinton, was quickly surrounded and doomed to fall, General James Clinton remained defiant, and for sound strategic reasons. He knew that he had to buy precious time for General Horatio Gates, who faced Burgoyne's challenge to the north during his push south from Canada toward Albany, while Clinton protected the northern army's rear. Therefore, the Irishman in a blue Continental general officer's uniform refused the British summons to surrender in five minutes or "die by the bayonet." Clinton's defiant response to hold firm to Fort Montgomery was promptly returned by a colonel to Scotland-born Lieutenant Colonel Mungo Campbell. Brother Irish generals, James and George, now prepared to meet the inevitable onslaught upon Fort Montgomery.

In the fort's October 6, 1777, defense against an overpowering British attack by a soldiery enraged in part because Campbell had been killed by a sharpshooter's bullet through the head when he ordered the bayonet charge, James Clinton remained in the forefront to encourage his men to greater exertions. Without a chance to repel the attackers' overwhelming might in what could be described as the Alamo of the American Revolution, the defenders fought against fate, including hand-to-hand combat, when the attackers poured over the defenses with victory cheers that echoed over Fort Montgomery and the wide Hudson.

The first attackers over the fort's earthen walls were Tories, including Irish and Scotch-Irish soldiers, of a Loyalist regiment. These Loyalists wore green coats, which perhaps gave James Clinton some momentary pause, because emerald green was Ireland's nationalist color long worn by generations of Irish revolutionaries. During the confused melee inside the smoke-filled Fort Montgomery, James suffered a nasty bayonet wound, but escaped capture. The hard-fighting general was more fortunate than Colonel McClaughry, Second

Ulster County Militia Regiment, who was bayoneted and taken prisoner. To avoid an inevitable slaughter, George Clinton ordered his overpowered defenders to fall back before it was too late, because the British and Loyalists were now giving no quarter. Indeed, the howling tide of victory-intoxicated attackers became out of control, continuing to "kill our soldiers without pity" or mercy to avenge their losses, especially popular Colonel Campbell.

But in the end, the high sacrifice suffered by the stubborn band of defenders of Fort Montgomery, which overlooked the Hudson, was not in vain. In overall strategic terms, the defiant last stand by the men of Fort Montgomery and Fort Clinton bought precious time, denying much-needed reinforcements to bolster Burgoyne's Army. In this way, Fort Montgomery's garrison helped to set the stage for Burgoyne's entrapment and surrender at Saratoga in October 1777 while preventing the colonies from being split in two.

Born in 1733, General James Clinton also served with one of Washington's most aggressive generals of Irish descent, John Sullivan, during his 1779 campaign against the Iroquois in the Sullivan-Clinton expedition. At that time, he led a fifteen-hundred-man brigade of New York soldiers, who became experts in the harsh art of destroying Indian villages and hundreds of acres of rich land during the wide-ranging campaign in the unmapped wilderness of western New York. In October 1781, this dynamic son of an Irish immigrant witnessed Lord Cornwallis's surrender at Yorktown while commanding one of Washington's veteran brigades. Like so many other Irish in the liberty's ranks, Clinton was as satisfied with his vital mission of making the New York and Pennsylvania frontiers safer and in protecting so many Scotch-Irish and Irish settlers as with an ancient enemy's ultimate humiliation at Yorktown.[34]

Mirroring their success in civilian life and rise of educated countrymen in colonial society before the war, the Irish continued to excel in leading positions in the Continental Army's medical field year after year. Dr. John Cochran was the first and foremost among this group. The Irish surgeon's efforts ensured that Washington remained an active commander in chief from the war's beginning to the final showdown at Yorktown: one of the forgotten contributions to American success. He continued to make a name for himself while serving the cause of his country and humanity. Eager to demonstrate his patriotism, Cochran joined the army as a lowly volunteer civilian physician who had only wanted to help in any way that he could in order to assist the holy cause of America's liberation. But Cochran's most important contribution came when he served as Washington's own personal physician, garnering the Virginian's undying respect and perhaps even saving his life.

The invaluable Cochran was the son of Irish immigrant parents from Ulster Province. He gained a fine Presbyterian-influenced education under the instruction of Dr. Francis Allison. Although he had served as a surgeon's mate in a British regiment during the French and Indian War, Cochran remained proud of his Celtic-Gaelic heritage and ancestral roots. Born on the frontier of Chester County, Pennsylvania, located just west of Philadelphia, in September 1730, Cochran created a good life for himself in America by way of his hard work and dedication. Thanks to his unwavering commitment to America's cause, Cochran was another Irishman whose tireless efforts benefited not only Washington and his men, but also the overall war effort at a time when skilled physicians were relatively few.

Like other proven Irish officers in the Continental Army, especially among his own personal staff, Washington held a high opinion of this capable surgeon, who was the son of lowly immigrants from Northern Ireland. Knowing that the Irish were only following in the footsteps of generations of ill-starred ancestors who had been nationalistic Irish revolutionaries, Washington readily identified with the Irish people who had battled for so long against the same powerful opponent.

Washington almost certainly learned more intimately about the Irish experience from Cochran. Drawing upon extensive medical experience as a colonial officer during the French and Indian War, Cochran became the Chief Physician and Surgeon of the Continental Army in

October 1780 and then the Director-General of Hospitals in 1781. He was successful in all aspects of life. The Irishman had married the only sister, Gertrude, of General Philip Schuyler, Washington's northern army commander, of New York in December 1760. Cochran and his wife called New Brunswick, New Jersey, home. He early gained recognition as the founder of the New Jersey Medical Society, becoming its president in 1769. With the war's end, Washington displayed his high esteem for his dedicated Irish physician by presenting him with the commander in chief's own "camp furniture" used during active campaigning in the field.[35] Treating him like an esteemed staff member, Washington was excessively fond of the good Dr. Cochran, writing to him as "my dear Doctor."[36]

"Father of the United States Navy," Irishman John Barry

As could be expected among a fiercely patriotic Celtic-Gaelic citizenry, Washington heavily counted on the steadfast performances of the Irish far beyond the ranks of his own Continental Army. The service of Irishmen was as distinguished on the high seas as on land or at the economic, medical, and political fronts of this people's struggle for nationhood. The most impressive of these naval contributions came from a lowly Irish Catholic, the son of a humble tenant farmer from the Emerald Isle. In the beginning, this Irishman's prospects could not have seemed less promising. However, like no other seaman in America's service, John Barry not only rose to the challenge, but also excelled at warfare against the ancient enemy of his people on the high seas.

Barry had been born to James Barry and Ellen Kelly in a cottage with a thatched roof (the typical homes of the lower class across rural Ireland) in Ballysampson, County Wexford, Leinster Province, which bordered the cold waters of the Irish Sea, in 1739. Here, in southeast Ireland, the commercial town of Wexford was the busiest port in all

Ireland. Although now largely forgotten by Americans, John Barry emerged as America's foremost naval officer.

Because of his unmatched naval achievements and his combativeness so often demonstrated in action on the ocean's waters, he earned the well-deserved nickname of "Fighting Jack" Barry. An early hint of Barry's natural fighting abilities and feistiness was seen in the fact that his native County Wexford, located in the volatile, rebellious southeastern Ireland, had been long known as "one of Ireland's foremost fighting counties" during past revolutionary struggles against the British interlopers.[37]

Like so many Irish who attempted to scratch out a meager existence from the rocky soil of Ireland's north-south running coastline that bordered the windswept, notoriously rough Irish Sea, Barry's father had long languished as a poor tenant farmer. He was finally evicted from County Wexford's lands by his abusive British landlord, who kept raising the rents (the old formula for forcing tenants off the land and turning to more profitable stock-raising for the importation of meat to England) that the already-struggling Barry family, like so many other Irish, was simply unable to pay, as planned by the greedy landowner.

This sad, haunting memory of such a sudden reversal of fortune that had cruelly uprooted the Barry family, combined with the tragic memories of the slaughter of hundreds of his fellow Irish "subjects" of County Wexford by Oliver Cromwell's Puritan soldiers, played a role in transforming Barry into a zealous revolutionary long before he ever saw America's shores. Embodying a legacy that defined the course of his life, what Barry never forgot was the beauty of his southeast Ireland homeland and the Irish patriots who he admired since his youth. He, therefore, fought the British on the world's oceans with a passion that bordered on an all-consuming obsession, as if battling to avenge past wrongs among the long-suffering County Wexford people.

With so few other opportunities existing for a young Irish lad, Barry became a seaman at an early age, with his wanderlust satisfied by the call of the ocean. Leaving County Wexford from the bustling port of Wexford, Barry first went to sea as a cabin boy on his uncle's merchant ship. Appropriately, after performing his arduous duties as an ordinary seaman for around six years, the gangly teenager first reached America aboard an Irish vessel. He then settled down in Philadelphia, America's largest city that contained so many Irish, around 1760.

In a strange twist of fate, Barry had been the first mate on the vessel that also brought the future Declaration of Independence signer, Irish Catholic Charles Carroll of Maryland, back to America in 1765 from Europe, where he had studied Latin and the ancient classics in Catholic schools of high standards. Then, in 1766, the enterprising Barry became a successful ship master and owner. He then served as the captain of his own ship, charting his own course and prospering from the vigorous trade with the sugar islands of the West Indies, especially Jamaica.

Barry became the first Ireland-born and Irish Catholic appointed to a Continental Navy captain's rank during the American Revolution. Thereafter, he served as the American navy's senior and most experienced captain, who was most distinguished by his energy and boldness. Having learned about the mysteries of the sea from his youth in County Wexford, Barry served with distinction as the foremost commander in the United States Navy. Captain Barry's many exploits at sea even outmatched those of America's much better known and most famous Celtic revolutionary naval hero of the infant Continental Navy, Captain John Paul Jones. Another fanatical Celtic warrior fighting for America, Jones was Scottish, having been born in a little gardener's cottage at Arbigland in the Scottish lowlands.

Unleashed to wage his personal war when sailing near his own Scottish homeland, this daring Celtic commander gained infamy in the highest circles of London and the English government for audaciously raiding British commerce in the Irish Sea within striking distance of London. However, in part by overlooking the seedier aspects (including having been a "Scottish slaver") of his life, Jones's image has been popularized and romanticized by generations of American writers, historians, and filmmakers at Barry's expense to ensure his relative obscurity to this day. More than the Ireland-born Barry, therefore, the Scotland-born and Protestant Jones has garnered wider recognition as the "Father of the American Navy." In consequence, Jones has earned a shrine-like final resting place at the United States Naval Academy, Annapolis, Maryland. All in all, Barry has provided a most revealing example of how the Irish role in the American Revolution has been ignored and obscured for so long.

But before Captain Jones's meteoric rise to fame captured the American public imagination and earned England's bitter wrath for humiliating Briton sea power, the pride of the British Empire, Barry commanded the Continental ship, the sixteen-gun brig *Lexington*, that captured the first British vessel—the *Edward*—of the war after a close-range engagement. With this daredevil Irishman at the helm, Barry's warship was the first vessel of the young American Navy to acquire widespread recognition for its daring wartime exploits that inspired patriots across America. During an unparalleled career on the high seas, Captain Barry captured more than twenty British ships in total, wreaking havoc on the island nation's commerce fleet upon which its vast wealth and world empire was based.

Barry's hard-hitting strikes on the vulnerable English commerce vessels raised a great uproar among the British upper-class merchants and politicians, whose wealth and lofty social status rested largely upon Atlantic commerce, including the lucrative slave trade. In typical Barry fashion, he struck relentlessly at England's vast fleet. By such effective naval tactics that resembled the art of guerrilla warfare, this son of a poor Irish father became famous across America, known as "Big John" Barry of Philadelphia and the "Father of the United States Navy." But to his American sailors, including many Irish seamen, whom he affectionately called his "children" out of compassion for the plight of the long-suffering common seafarer, Barry was more like a father than a typical autocratic naval commander of the eighteenth century, especially in the Royal Navy. Seemingly contradicting his imposing physical and command presence at six foot, four inches, Barry demonstrated excessive care for his men's welfare, especially those humble sailors of the lowest rank.[38]

But Barry was much more than a typical one-dimensional naval hero. Versatile and talented, he would do anything not only at sea but also on land to achieve the great dream of America's independence. When unable to sail his own vessel at Philadelphia out of sea because of the thick ice clogging the Delaware River during the winter of 1775–1776, he volunteered to fight on land after Ireland-born Stephen Moylan (a fellow leading member of the Friendly Sons of St. Patrick of Philadelphia) brought word of the dire condition of Washington's Army in late December 1776.

Consequently, during the revolution's darkest days in this winter campaign when so much was at stake, Barry played an inspiring leadership role on land while serving as aide-de-camp to General John Cadwalader. He was with Cadwalader's column (below Washington's main column) that had been ordered but ultimately failed to cross the Delaware on December 25–26 to join in Washington's surprise attack upon the Hessian brigade at Trenton. Because of Cadwalader's aborted effort due to the severe storm and a river clogged by ice, Barry narrowly missed the Battle of Trenton. But he saw plenty of action with Cadwalader's troops at the battle of Princeton early in 1777.[39]

Barry was best known as America's foremost naval hero during the war years, even more than John Paul Jones and at an earlier date. The hard-fighting Irishman was heralded across the colonies for his daring sea raids that captured British supply ships that served as the primary logistical support system for British armies in America, gaining badly needed provisions and munitions for Washington's Army.

Both on land and at sea, Captain Barry waged his own brand of logistical warfare against his opponents, raiding and destroying provisions meant to supply British and Hessian forces around Philadelphia. In February 1778, Barry worked closely with Anthony Wayne, transporting his troops across the Delaware in his "fleet" and to the New

Jersey's shore to destroy provisions, especially forage. Barry created a clever diversion that attracted the attention of British leadership, allowing Wayne's men the opportunity to drive a herd of confiscated cattle to Washington's starving troops at Valley Forge: an invaluable and timely resupply for Washington's Army.

Thereafter, Washington's famished men survived on beef until spring and the opening of the next campaign in the ongoing struggle. Amid an expanse of fertile farmlands south of Philadelphia, Barry's well-conceived diversion and logistical strike along the Delaware's east bank in south New Jersey called for confiscating and burning tons of hay, including the crops of incensed Irish farmers like John Kelley. This strategy was important because the British cavalry were more numerous than Washington's diminutive cavalry arm and this was Washington's only way to reduce the significant capabilities of the enemy's wide-ranging "eyes and ears" in regard to gathering vital intelligence. Barry's effective raids drew a swift British response while Wayne and his precious cattle herd pushed north toward Valley Forge unmolested. With independent ways that created an ideal Irish leadership team, Barry and Wayne became close friends thereafter.

But Barry proved far more valuable when not burning four hundred tons of hay in the wide fields along the Delaware. He became much acclaimed as the "hero of the Delaware" for aggressively taking the war to the British along the vital river that led to Philadelphia. The following month, in early March 1778, Barry's bold performance with a mere seven American barges of his little river "fleet" lifted the morale of Washington's Army and the war-weary people of a new nation, which especially needed good news during this dark period. In a spirited naval engagement on the Delaware south of Philadelphia, with nothing more than little wooden "washtubs" (river galleys or barges) that required laborious rowing by experienced seamen, Barry audaciously attacked three British vessels, a schooner and two transports, which were part of a large convoy including a merchant ship filled with red-uniformed reinforcements from Ireland by way of Rhode Island.

Taking them by surprise after only slight resistance, Barry captured the schooner and two transports filled with invaluable provisions. As usual, Barry was in the forefront, boarding one ship with cutlass in hand and personally demanding the surrender of the stunned British captain. The rampaging Irishman then captured the formidable schooner *Alert*, with considerable tactical skill.

Barry inflicted a humiliating setback on the proud British Navy by capturing three vessels right under the British Army's nose in Philadelphia. Demonstrating that he was as masterful a politician as a naval tactician, the good-natured Irishman then sent choice spoils of war, a jar of pickled oysters, and the finest cheese for Washington to enjoy at his spare dinner table amid Valley Forge's cold gloom. For his audacity on both land and sea, this incomparable Celtic-Gaelic naval warrior, who had migrated to America as a humble "Irish boy" with the lowest of expectations, became America's most outstanding naval commander. On the turbid Delaware, Barry reaped "as gallant an action as any during the war," in Washington's words, earning the commander in chief's warmest thanks and those of his remaining band of ragged soldiers still suffering in the ice and mud of Valley Forge.[40] American newspapers shortly carried glowing tales of the Irishman's exploits, including the most recent success which was appropriately deemed as "gallant an action as any during the war."[41]

From his Valley Forge headquarters, Washington wrote a sincere note of thanks to the Irishman whose "Bravery" lifted the sagging morale and spirits of an army barely able to survive during the cruel winter of 1777–1778. As Washington wrote, "I congratulate you on the Success which has crowned your Gallantry and Address in the late Attack upon the Enemie's Ships [because of] the degree of Glory, which you have acquired."[42]

In the manner of Ireland-born Samuel Smith of Maryland, Barry fought almost as tenaciously against his fellow Americans as the British, especially when it came to matters of honor. Barry was hot-tempered, and his wrath sometimes could not be controlled. Because he despised

the excessive arrogance and sense of superiority that so character-
ized upper-class, elitist politicians, Barry naturally clashed with the
privileged members of Congress, the Navy Board, and those anti-Irish
individuals regardless of rank who held him in contempt because he
was an Irish Catholic, especially if they faltered in any way during
his war against Ireland's ancient enemy. One such especially arrogant
victim—a long-winded Congressman—suffered Barry's wrath because
he had failed to take Barry's expert naval advice into consideration.
Instead, the politician panicked and unnecessarily ordered the sinking
of the Irishman's ship that had struck ground. Barry strongly opposed
deliberately scuttling his own ship when he knew he could free her,
but he was out-ranked in regard to this final decision.

Consequently, this ever-defiant Irish captain, who commanded
the swift Continental ship *Effingham*, was called before Congress, "an ineffective debating chamber that had little power and
no money," for showing too much open disrespect toward a Congressman and a Navy Board member. Before one and all, Barry
vigorously protested the Congressman's abrupt decision while
mocking this inept, condescending civilian politician of the Navy
Board, who knew nothing of military or naval matters, to sink
his own ship. But this respected colonial official possessed sufficient political connections and support to bring up official charges
against Barry, who had challenged his authority and the hasty
decision to sink the *Effingham*.

Most of all, while brave men sacrificed and died for their country,
Barry detested these self-serving Navy Board officials, who "in their
supreme ignorance claimed to have superior knowledge" in naval matters of which he was the ultimate expert. Fortunately, Barry possessed
General Washington's full support at this time, as always. Displaying
his usual care and tact in dealing with a hypersensitive Congress, the
sage Virginian knew that such a capable Irishman could not be lost to
this sacred cause because of petty politics and inflated egos of arrogant
politicians. He, therefore, applied the necessary pressure upon the

politicians to desist in their persecution of America's best sea captain. In the end, Barry was exonerated of these unjust charges, winning personal satisfaction and a moral victory that cleared his good name and military record.[43]

This revolutionary struggle raging across America had caused the Barry family some unusual twists and turns that only exemplified the torment of so many American families who similarly suffered, especially the Irish, divided by America's first civil war. Barry's own widowed mother, Catherine Barry, had married an Ireland-born British soldier and widower, James B. Stafford, who had served in America during the French and Indian War. Switching loyalties, Stafford then became an American patriot and battled against the professional soldiers who looked so resplendent in the same scarlet uniform that he had once worn with pride. Like the Barry clan, the Stafford family hailed from County Wexford in southeast Ireland. Clearly, deeply implanted Celtic-Gaelic cultural ties bound these people together during the toughest times of America's struggle for existence.[44]

Throughout his life, Barry was as proud of his many naval achievements at sea and on the Delaware River as he was of having been born in the beloved ancestral homeland of the Green Isle. Like other Irish in America, he could never forget his Emerald Isle past, his heritage, or his family's experiences under British control of the troubled Emerald Isle, where so many dreams of the downtrodden people had died in bloody fashion.[45]

Even after the war, Captain Barry stayed in close contact with the people of Ireland, especially his own relatives in his native County Wexford. And naturally Barry's naval exploits were a great source of pride among the Irish people across Ireland during the war years and long thereafter: more so than even in America.[46]

President John Fitzgerald Kennedy, America's thirty-fifth chief executive and first Catholic president of Irish heritage that extended back to immigrants from County Wexford, kept Barry's "sword . . . in [his] office," as he told the Irish Parliament on June

28, 1963, to remind him of the pivotal role played by the Irish in America's struggle for liberty.[47] The artifact was for him a source of inspiration in troubled periods, such as during the Cuban Missile Crisis when the world perched on the brink of nuclear destruction by way of human folly

But Barry was only the best-known Irishman who rose on his own abilities and merits during the naval war against the British. Thousands of Irish sailors served on America's roving warships and merchant ships, including large numbers of lower-class Catholics, who manned merchant vessels that sailed out of the ports of Cork, Galway, Waterford, and Dublin to America and the West Indies. Many Irish seamen made the transition from the British to the American merchant fleet after deciding to battle on behalf of a new nation and an underdog people that included so many of their fellow countrymen. Like their comrades in Washington's Army, a distinct sense of radicalism and a longing to overturn arbitrary authority and monarchical abuses were part of a deeply entrenched egalitarian faith among the lowly Irish "Jack Tars," who fought under the United States flag.[48]

While the Irish struggled year after year by land and sea, these Sons of Erin battling for America's liberty hoped and prayed that Ireland would follow America's example and rise up in revolt against the British. In his journal entry at the beginning of March 1780, Sergeant Jeremiah Greenman, a Rhode Island Continental who went to war at age seventeen, wrote of an exhilarating rumor that so many soldiers, especially Irish fighting men of Washington's Army, had long hoped to hear: "We are informed by Credible Persons that the Irish is Revolted & denigh [sic] the British any Substance" or assistance in crushing America's rebellion.[49]

In this regard, Greenman was referring to the acceptance of Henry Grattan's free trade bill of 1779 in the Irish House of Commons. At this time Great Britain's leaders were worried that the people of Ireland might revolt because so many British regiments had been dispatched from Ireland to America in the determined attempt to stop the rebellion, that unprecedented rights and privileges were finally bestowed by London upon the people of Ireland out of a prudent necessity.[50]

Likewise hopeful about the pace of developments in Ireland as revealed in a March 17, 1780, letter, General Knox, the son of a County Derry, Ulster Province immigrant, wrote to General William Heath, "the affairs in Ireland will be a pretty addition to the embarrassment of England, and will, I hope, produce a speedy peace for America."[51] And as penned in a January 25, 1783, letter, Washington was likewise greatly encouraged by the prospects of "a rumoured [sic] revolt in Ireland."[52] Interestingly, Greenman became a lieutenant of the famed "Black Regiment" (the First Rhode Island Continental Regiment) of the Rhode Island Continental Line, when the unit was organized during the spring of 1778. But the later-day renown as the "Black Regiment," led by white officers like Greenman, was still another myth.

Representative of the Irish role at all levels and even in the most unlikely of places, a number of Irish Continentals of the First Rhode Island Continental Regiment served in the command side-by-side with former slaves, including Ireland-born Privates Charles McAfferty, a twenty-nine-year-old laborer from County Derry; Dennis Hogan, age thirty and born in the Viking-founded town of Limerick; Peter Burns, age forty-three; Barne McDarmet, from Philadelphia and age thirty-eight; John Huzzey, a fifty-year-old common laborer from Northern Ireland; Cornelius Driskill, a teenage "mariner" born in Kinsale, Ireland; Matthew Hendly, a thirty-year-old barber from Limerick; Michael Killey, age thirty-six and a barber; James King, a tailor from Dublin; Daniel Miller, a thirty-year-old weaver; twenty-five-year-old Charles Watson, distinguished by a dark complexion, an experienced weaver from Londonderry in Ulster Province; Edward Fitzgerald, a teenage laborer; forty-two-year-old Michael Wright, a "ribbon weaver" from County Queens, Ireland; Mark Barns, a "wine cooper" of twenty-eight from the port town of Waterford, southeast

Ireland; Michael Doherty, age twenty-two and from County Donegal, Northern Ireland; and twenty-five-year-old James Hays, who had been born in Cork.

But the most atypical Ireland-born soldier of the First Rhode Island Continental Regiment was Private Daniel Monks, who was a barber from Newport, Rhode Island. He had been born in the town of Longward, Ireland, near the turn of the century. Because of his desire to fight the ancient foe of his people and to faithfully serve his adopted country, sixty-five-year-old Private Daniel Monks, distinguished by gray hair, marched in the ranks beside rambunctious teenagers, yet to shave, from the green hills and valleys of Ireland. This situation emphasized how this Celtic-Gaelic people's struggle against the British was a multi-generational commitment and part of a long-lasting, common people's conflict that had no end until independence was won.[53]

Most of these occupations revealed the fact that these Irishmen of the First Rhode Island Continental Regiment probably had been indentured servants and migrated to America because their artisan skills were highly sought in the New World. Such useful services could be obtained much cheaper from Irish indentured servants than a free British citizen of America. Some of these Irishmen had learned these skills in America as apprentices during dreary years as indentured servants to pay off the high cost of their passage to America before gaining a long-awaited release after their terms of bonded service expired.[54]

As indicative of the pervasive and disproportionate Irish contribution while Emerald Islanders filled the ranks of Washington's "Black Regiment" and even his German Regiment (of Marylanders and Pennsylvanians) that first won fame during the Battle of Trenton, there was no so-called Irish regiment or Irish brigade that served in Washington's Army, although the numbers of Irish soldiers made that a feasible possibility in regard to entire divisions of Celtic-Gaelic troops.[55]

Most importantly, the First Rhode Island Continental Regiment served in Washington's Army during the final showdown at Yorktown.

Here, on a balmy October 19, 1781, at the little tobacco port of Yorktown on the low-lying Virginia Peninsula, the improbable happened. It was most appropriate that so many battle-hardened Irish and Scotch-Irish soldiers in threadbare, dirty uniforms stood silently in the neat lines of Washington's Army for the dramatic moment that they would never forget. Looking more like farmers than Continentals, these seasoned Celtic-Gaelic warriors stood at attention with their trusty flintlock muskets by their sides while thousands of sullen redcoats and Hessians of Cornwallis's Army trudged gloomily out of their defenses in the most humiliating experience of their lives. Then Great Britain's finest soldiers marched south in the early afternoon sunlight. In a formation that spanned for more than a mile, Washington's men were aligned on the east side of the Hampton Road while their French allies, in fancy white uniforms, stood on the road's opposite side.

These veteran troops now marched forth to lay down their arms in a sunlit meadow, surrounded by tall trees tinged in the first yellows and reds of the season, during the highly structured ceremonial surrender. A shaken Lord Charles Cornwallis, proudly Eton educated and a friend of King George III himself, conveniently pleaded illness to escape the shame of the capitulation ceremony. Consequently, he ordered Brigadier General Charles O'Hara to formally surrender the once-mighty British-Hessian Army to the ragged American victors and their finely uniformed French allies. As fate would have it, O'Hara was an Irishman and perhaps the most distinguished soldier in Cornwallis's Army.

As could be expected, this long-dreaded experience of the vanquished was a tortured one for the men of Cornwallis's Army. While young British fifers and drummers played a sad, dirge-like tune entitled "The World Turned Upside Down" to capture the gloomy mood and sense of disbelief, more than seven thousand of Cornwallis's soldiers slowly marched farther south and away from their shell-pocked earthen fortifications that had proved entirely insufficient to stave off decisive defeat at the hands of Washington's emboldened troops and their French allies. A mounted O'Hara, "a ruddy-faced

Irishman," led the column of finely uniformed British and Hessian soldiers toward the grassy meadow. Now lacking their usual jaunty and confident stride, the defeated men of the principal British Army in the south marched with discipline toward two parallel ranks of Americans and French soldiers, who were aligned in close ranks on opposite sides of the narrow, dusty road.

At the head of the vanquished redcoats and Hessians, a resplendently uniformed General O'Hara continued to lead the way to the grassy meadow that had been designated as the place where arms were to be laid down. A seasoned veteran of the brutal war in the southern theater (where so many one-sided British pyrrhic victories had been won) and a respected member of the Coldstream Guards, O'Hara had only recently recovered from a wound suffered at the bloody battle of Guilford Courthouse, North Carolina, on March 15, 1781. But the high-ranking Irishman was now experiencing an even greater pain and sense of anguish because he was still haunted by his favorite nephew's recent death on American soil.

On this beautiful October day under the bright sunshine of coastal Virginia, while a faintly salty breeze blew in from the nearby Chesapeake, O'Hara represented the large numbers of Sons of Erin who fought and died for Great Britain in a faraway foreign war. His family originated from County Mayo, located on the northwest coast in Connacht Province, like a large number of veterans who served in Washington's ranks: still another example of what was very much of a civil war among thousands of Irishmen who fought against each other with a savagery seldom seen during one of America's longest wars.

In the formal surrender ceremony according to the long-accepted European traditions of the day, O'Hara handed his saber to General Benjamin Lincoln, as directed by Washington, in part to compensate in a symbolic gesture for the New Englander's humiliating surrender of Charleston in May 1780. The shocking news of the surrender of Cornwallis's Army sounded the death knell of Great Britain's determined efforts to subjugate its thirteen wayward colonies—now a new nation—filled with so many Irish and Scotch-Irish settlers and fighting men who became Washington's crack soldiers. Washington's victors included a good many Emerald Islanders who still spoke a melodic Gaelic (although these Irish Catholics were mostly bilingual) or with thick Ulster brogues from Northern Ireland and were still considered "foreigners" by so many Americans.[56]

For the hundreds of Irish and Scotch-Irish soldiers who served in Washington's ranks, the dramatic victory at Yorktown was about to fulfill the greatest dream and ambition of the Irish people that was never obtained by generations of Irish revolutionaries. The ancient Gaelic words of the Irish revolutionary saying, *La ar bith feasa*, "any day now . . .", no longer applied to America's lengthy struggle and high sacrifice of the disproportionate numbers of Celtic-Gaelic warriors in the ranks of Washington's Continental Army at Yorktown and in other revolutionary armies, fighting forces, and guerrilla bands across America.[57]

In the end, a Presbyterian minister of Scotch-Irish heritage offered a solemn prayer of thanks to God for bestowing the long-elusive decisive victory on a generation of rustic revolutionaries, including so many recent Irish immigrants and former indentured servants: "Good Lord, our God who art in heaven, we have reason to thank Thee for the many favors received at thy thanks, the many battles we have Won. The great and glorious battle at Kings Mountain where we kilt the great Gineral [Patrick] Ferguson and took his whole army . . . and the every more glorious battle of Coopens [Cowpens] where We made the proud Gineral Tarleton run doon [sic] the road helter skelter."[58]

In regard to the specifics of his heartfelt prayer for God's blessing for battlefield successes on southern soil, this revered minister of the Scotch-Irish people on the frontier should have more properly given profound thanks to victory to two dynamic Scotch-Irish commanders, William Campbell and Daniel Morgan, for their amazing successes at Kings Mountain and Cowpens, respectively, which turned the tide of the American Revolution.[59]

But perhaps the hard-fighting Edmondson clan, from Ulster Province, Northern Ireland, best personified the true importance of the Irish experience and the disproportionate contributions of the Celtic-Gaelic people, not only in winning the American Revolution but also in conquering the West. Three of the Irish Edmondson clan paid a high price for securing victory at Kings Mountain in the South Carolina Piedmont: Captain William Edmondson, who was killed; Robert Edmondson Sr., who also fell with a fatal wound; along with his son, Robert Edmondson Jr., wounded in the intense combat that raged back and forth across the timbered slope. Members of the volunteer company, commanded by Irishman Captain William Beattie, of hardy frontiersmen, this Irish father-son team consisted of veteran Indian fighters. The son of Robert Edmondson Jr. then fought under Scotch-Irishman Andrew Jackson, a South Carolina partisan in the American Revolution who lost his family (mother and all his brothers who also fought for liberty) during the Creek War of 1813. Most significantly, the son then served under Jackson, who defeated England's finest veterans of the Napoleonic Wars at the battle of New Orleans in January 1815.[60] Quite simply, these forgotten Sons of Erin of lowly origins were the kind of men who fought and died to literally shape the destiny of a new nation while so far from their native homeland across the sea.

Conclusion:

Irish Odyssey

No chapter of American history has been more mythical than the American Revolution. Therefore, America's much-embellished creation myth left no revered or permanent place for the lowly immigrant Irish, especially Catholics, who were considered outsiders and foreigners. Nevertheless, these long-forgotten Celtic-Gaelic warriors played leading and disproportionate roles in every phase of America's struggle for liberty to ensure America's survival and ultimate success.

The extent of these widespread Irish contributions to success in the realm of conventional warfare was best represented by Pennsylvania's famed Line of Ireland of Washington's Army. Washington's ability to continue the struggle year after year in the middle colonies eventually forced the strategic stalemate that then led to the disastrous British attempt to conquer the south. Here, in the south, Sons of Erin rose to the fore at the remarkable victory at Kings Mountain and in mastering the art of irregular warfare across South Carolina while also serving in disproportionate numbers in guerrilla bands led by famed leaders like Francis Marion, the "Swamp Fox." The true secret of Marion's remarkable success that rekindled the failed resistance effort in South Carolina was that most of his guerrilla followers were drawn from settlers who were either immigrants or "of Irish parentage [because] They inherited, in common with all descendants of the Irish in America, a hearty detestation of the English name and author [and] This feeling rendered them excellent patriots and daring soldiers . . . the men generally of fearless courage, powerful frame, well-strung nerves, and an audacious gallantry that led them to delight in dangers [and] they were good riders and famous marksmen" who especially enjoyed shooting down the king's soldiers of Ireland's ancient foe.

The very antithesis of the New England yeoman-farmer soldier stereotype, America's most ethnically distinctive fighting men were very much Old World warriors. These Celtic-Gaelic soldiers still dreamed of the Green Isle's natural beauty, from Dublin Bay to Sheep's Head Peninsula, and ancient cultural ways while battling for lofty republican visions on American soil; still loved the melodic rhythms of the Gaelic language; still were deeply moved by the sounds of popular Irish musical instruments, including flutes, "war bagpipes," Irish harps that were revered symbols of resistance against the English for centuries, and drums of traditional music; still recalled the inspiring words of generations of idealized Irish revolutionary leaders and martyrs; still remembered what they had learned about the tragic course of Irish history as children; still hoped to be buried one day under a Celtic Cross; and most of all, the Irish who fought for America never forgot about the true spiritual meaning and essence of their beloved homeland that they never saw again after crossing the Atlantic.

Tens of thousands of young Celtic-Gaelic men and boys fought hard and long to fulfill the great dream of America's independence, succeeding in completing the loftiest vision of generations of Irish revolutionaries who had failed in a comparable quest to win liberty on the Green Isle. These Sons of Erin were in fact the very heart and soul of America's lengthy resistance effort on multiple levels (political, military, and economic) throughout the struggle for nationhood: an uncomfortable truth to generations of so many non-Irish, including historians. As mentioned, this disproportionate contribution largely developed because the enduring legacies of the Irish experience, especially in regard to the transference of vibrant Celtic-Gaelic revolutionary and cultural traditions, evolved and merged neatly into the overall American experience in a symbiotic relationship, which guaranteed that thousands of Irish soldiers played leading roles in America's creation story.

Consequently, the many disproportionate contributions of the Irish and Scotch-Irish have been one of the best untold stories and last remaining forgotten chapters of the American Revolution. The long-overlooked truth of the American Revolution in regard to the crucial role played by the Irish, especially in Washington's Army in such premier combat units as the elite Continental Line of Ireland, was verified in the words of Luke Gardiner, Lord Mountjoy (like so many other British officials and leaders, both military and civilian), who emphasized to the House of Commons that "the Irish language [Gaelic] was as commonly spoken in the American ranks as English."[1]

However, to this day, no markers, monuments, or memorials honor the countless Irish heroics and sacrifices on any of America's Revolutionary War battlefields, while a disproportionate number of Green Isle soldiers lie today in unmarked and unknown graves across America. Even the much-revered Irish hero of Charleston's 1776 defense and the American-French assault on Savannah in 1779, where he fell to rise no more, Ireland-born Sergeant William Jasper's body lies today in an unknown place without recognition. As one disbelieving American, in regard to one of the struggle's best-known Irish patriots, admitted in 1876 on the one hundredth anniversary of America's birth, the final resting "place of his sepulture is unmarked [and] He sleeps with the brave dead of the siege who lie beneath the soil of Savannah [and] no monumental shaft designates his grave" to this day.[2]

The only designation of a final resting place for some Sons of Erin came quite by accident, if they just happened to have been buried with an apple, cherry, or peach in a pocket, from which a fruit tree later grew over the unmarked grave. Ireland-born Elizabeth Jackson, the mother of teenage partisan Andrew Jackson, who became the seventh president, was just another one of the forgotten patriots who gave their lives for America. Elizabeth occupied an unmarked grave in Charleston far from her Waxhaws (a Scotch-Irish community) home while attempting to save American prisoners. Andrew, now left a grieving orphan, only received a "small bundle" of his mother's clothes as a final reminder of the high-spirited Irish woman who had helped to transform him into a fiery patriot.[3]

In regard to an unknown final resting place, Sergeant Jasper has only shared this same obscure fate with the vast majority of the Celtic-Gaelic soldiers, who fought and died from 1775 to 1783. However, what was never lost were the memorable words shouted by Sergeant Jasper that inspired the hard-hit garrison of South Carolinians, including a large number of Scotch-Irish soldiers, to stand firm in a crisis situation during the all-important defense at Fort Sullivan, later renamed Fort Moultrie, that protected Charleston and prevented the British invasion of the South for several years: "God save liberty and my country forever."[4]

While Sergeant Jasper's never-say-die sentiments have been preserved for posterity, the equally inspiring words of another equally defiant Scotch-Irish soldier, Sergeant James McDaniel, Second South Carolina Continental Regiment, who fell mortally wounded in Fort Sullivan's spirited defense are far less known: "Fight on my brave boys; don't let liberty expire with me to-day."[5]

The vital contributions of so many Irish and Scotch-Irish patriots and their unfailing commitment to the vibrant dream of liberty can provide the most forgotten and overlooked reason why America won its independence in the end. The Marquis de Chastellux, the aristocratic Frenchman of noble birth who learned firsthand this now-forgotten truth about America's unsung Celtic-Gaelic participants of mostly lower-class origins, was entirely correct in his final analysis: "Congress owed their existence, and America possibly her preservation to the firmness and fidelity of the Irish."[6]

For such valid reasons, Washington's admiration for America's Irish and Scotch-Irish, especially in his army's ranks at all levels, knew no bounds because the Irish and Americans were not only kindred spirits, but also the same people in regard to their longing for liberty and their ceaseless struggle against their mutual enemy. After the war, consequently, Washington emphasized that the common people's struggle for liberty on both sides of the Atlantic were actually one and the same, informing the Irish people with heartfelt sincerity that "your cause is like unto mine."[7]

A grateful Washington offered words that were part of his personal "Invocation to Ireland" on a memorable Independence Day to commemorate America's difficult birth in the fiery forge of a people's revolution that simply would not have been won without the disproportionate contributions and sacrifices of the Celtic-Gaelic people: "Ireland, thou friend of my country in my country's most friendless days . . . accept this poor tribute from one who esteems thy worth. . . ."[8]

What has been most overlooked in the annals of American Revolutionary War historiography was the fact that without the countless contributions and disproportionate achievements of so many Irish and Scotch-Irish, the infant republic would have succumbed to an early, untimely death. Without the all-important influence of the enduring, vibrant legacies of the Irish experience that fueled the disproportionate contributions and the sacrifices of the Sons of Erin, the United States of America almost certainly would have vanished into the trash bin of history.

Many distinguished men of the day realized this most forgotten truth that explained why Great Britain lost her thirteen colonies. Luke Gardiner (the future Lord Mountjoy) was entirely correct and right on target when he presented the true reason why Great Britain lost its North American colonies. In no uncertain terms, he informed the aristocratic members of the House of Commons in Parliament, who thought of the lowly, impoverished Irish people as little deserving of any kind of respect or even capable of any significant accomplishments whatsoever, of the true and most fundamental—but today's most forgotten—reason why England failed to prevail in regaining control of its wayward thirteen colonies was revealed in full when he declared, "You have lost America by the Irish."[9]

Notes

Chapter I

1. Richard Montgomery Biographical Sketch, Montgomery Collection, 1774–1775, Manuscript Division, William L. Clements Library, University of Michigan, Ann Arbor, Michigan; Hal T. Shelton, *General Richard Montgomery and the American Revolution: From Redcoat to Rebel*, (New York: New York University Press, 1994), pp. 1–3, 8–9,133–171; Richard Montgomery Manuscript, William Douglas Papers, New York Historical Society, New York, New York.

2. Shelton, *General Richard Montgomery and the American Revolution*, pp. 158, 161.

3. Richard Montgomery Manuscript, William Douglas Papers, NYHS; Shelton, *General Richard Montgomery and the American Revolution*, pp. 4–5, 163–164; Steven E. Siry, *Liberty's Fallen Generals: Leadership and Sacrifice in the American War of Independence* (Washington, DC: Potomac Books, 2012), pp. 22–23.

4. Shelton, *General Richard Montgomery and the American Revolution*, pp. 3–6; Siry, *Liberty's Fallen Generals*, p. 14.

5. Siry, *Liberty's Fallen Generals*, pp. 3–6, 163–164; Richard Montgomery Manuscript, NYHS; Jay P. Dolan, *The Irish Americans: A History* (New York: Bloomsbury Press, 2008), p. 1.

6. Shelton, *General Richard Montgomery and the American Revolution*, pp. 6, 173; Karl F. Stephens, *Neither the Charm Nor the Luck: Major-General John Sullivan* (Denver: Outskirts Press, Inc., 2009), pp. 1–2, 34–35, 49–53.

7. Stephens, *Neither the Charm Nor the Luck*, pp. ii, 3–4.

8. Ibid., pp. 1–2.

9. Edward G. Lengel, ed., *This Glorious Struggle: George Washington's Revolutionary War Letters*, (New York: HarperCollins Publishers, 2009), p. xiii.

10. Owen B. Hunt, *The Irish and the American Revolution: Three Essays* (Philadelphia: private printing, 1976), p. 101.

11. *The United States Miscellany*, Charleston, South Carolina, August 12, 1826.

12. Stephens, *Neither the Charm Nor the Luck*, p. 52; Tim Almaguer, *Baltimore's Patterson Park* (Charleston, SC: Arcadia Publishing, 2006), p. 11.

13. Stephen Brumwell, *George Washington: Gentleman Warrior* (New York: Quercus Publishing, Inc., 2012), p. 262.

14. John Dalling to Henry Clinton, July 30, 1780, Sir Henry Clinton Papers, vol. 113, item 39, William L. Clements Library, University of Michigan, Ann Arbor, Michigan.

15. *Maryland Gazette*, Annapolis, Maryland, March 20, 1777, and June 21, 1781.

16. Caroline Cox, *A Proper Sense of Honor: Service and Sacrifice in George Washington's Army* (Chapel Hill: University of North Carolina Press, 2004), pp. 1–8; Hunt, *The Irish and the American Revolution*, pp. 22–26; David Noel Doyle, *Ireland, Irishmen and Revolutionary America, 1750–1820* (Dublin: The Mercier Press, 1981), p. 109; Della Gray Barthelmas, *The Signers of the Declaration of Independence: A Biographical and Genealogical Reference* (Jefferson, NC: McFarland and Company, Inc., Publishers, 1997), pp. 3–304; Hunt, *The Irish and the American Revolution*, p. 101; Karen F. McCarthy, *The Other Irish: The Scots-Irish Rascals Who Made America* (New York: Sterling Publishing, 2011), p. 98; John Church Hamilton, *The Life of Alexander Hamilton* (2 vols., New York: 1834), vol. 1, p. 162.

17. Thomas J. Fleming, *Washington's Secret War: The Hidden History of Valley Forge* (New York: Smithsonian Books, 2005), pp. 141, 285; Doyle, *Ireland, Irishmen and Revolutionary America*, pp. xv–109; Noel Ignatiev, *How the Irish Became White* (New York: Routledge, 1995), pp. 35–38.

18. Thomas Fleming, *Liberty!: The American Revolution* (New York: Viking, 1997), p. 262.

19. Robert L. Tonsetic, *1781: The Decisive Year of the Revolutionary War* (Havertown, PA: Casemate Publishing, 2011), p. 11.

20. Brumwell, *George Washington*, p. 229.

21. Myles Dungan, *Distant Drums: Irish Soldiers in Foreign Armies* (Belfast: Appletree Press, 1993), pp. 1–41.

22. Marquis De Chastellux, *Travels in North-America in the Years 1780–81–82* (New York: n.p., 1828), p. 225–226, note; Brumwell, *George Washington*, pp. 381–407; Doyle, *Ireland, Irishmen and Revolutionary America*, p. 111.

23. Doyle, *Ireland, Irishmen and Revolutionary America*, p. 40.

24. Michael Foss, *Undreamed Shores: England's Wasted Empire in America* (London: Phoenix Press, 2000), pp. 101, 104–105.

25. Ibid., pp. 105, 108.

26. Ibid.

27. Peter F. Stevens, *The Rogue's March: John Riley and the St. Patrick's Battalion 1846–48* (Washington, DC: Brassey's Books, 1999), p. 13.

28. Brumwell, *George Washington*, pp. 24–26; Don Cook, *The Long Fuse: How England Lost the American Colonies, 1760–1785* (New York: The Atlantic Monthly Press, 1995), p. 315.

29. Brumwell, *George Washington*, pp. 84–117; Edith Moore Sprouse, *Mount Air, Fairfax County, Virginia* (Fairfax, VA: Fairfax County Office of Comprehensive Planning, 1976), pp. 1, 7–13.

30. Harrison Clark, *All Cloudless Glory: The Life of George Washington, Volume 1: From Youth to Yorktown* (Washington, DC: Regnery Publishing, Inc., 1995), p. 270; Paul Martin, "He saved George Washington's life . . . twice!," http://www.foxnews.com/opinion/2012/07/04/this-july-4-let-thank-forgotten-revolutionary-war-hero.html, July 4, 2012.

31. John F. Ross, *War on the Run: The Epic Story of Robert Rogers and the Conquest of America's First Frontier* (New York: Bantam Books, 2011), pp. 13–17, 81–288; Gary Zaboly, *American Colonial Ranger: The Northern Colonies 1724–64* (Oxford: Osprey Publishing, 2004), pp. 4–50.

32. Robert D. Bass, *Gamecock: The Life and Campaigns of General Thomas Sumter* (Orangeburg, SC: Sandlapper Publishing Company, 2000), pp. 21, 33–46; John Buchanan, *Jackson's Way: Andrew Jackson and the People of the Western Waters* (New York: John Wiley and Sons, 2001), pp. 22–38; Doyle, *Ireland, Irishmen and Revolutionary America*, pp. 79–83, 104–106, 118; James K. Swisher, *The Revolutionary War in the Southern Back Country* (Gretna, LA: Pelican Publishing Company, 2008), p. 28.

33. Ed Southern, editor, *Voices of the American Revolution in the Carolinas* (Winston-Salem, NC: John F. Blair Publishers, 2009), pp. 89–93, 97–100.

34. Buchanan, *Andrew Jackson's Way*, p. 36.

35. Brumwell, *George Washington*, p. 31.

36. Buchanan, *Andrew Jackson's Way*, p. 34.

37. Katherine Keogh White, *The King's Mountain Men: The Story of the Battle, with Sketches of the American Soldiers Who Took Part* (Santa Maria, CA: Janaway Publishing, Inc., 2010), p. 209.

38. Buchanan, *Andrew Jackson's Way*, p. 34.
39. Southern, ed., *Voices of the American Revolution in the Carolinas*, pp. 73–79.
40. Ibid., p. 78.
41. Shelton, *General Richard Montgomery and the American Revolution*, p. 35.
42. Ibid., pp. 36–41.
43. Ibid., pp. 133–169.
44. Fred B. Walters, *John Haslet: A Useful One* (Philadelphia, PA: New Horizons, 2005), pp. 6, 13, 19–384.
45. Stephens, *Neither the Charm Nor the Luck*, pp. 2–12.
46. McFarland, Robert W., "MacFarlane Clan in North America." Accessed January 5, 2004. http://scottish-clans.org/clans/mcfarlandclandraft.html#-ftn1.
47. Buchanan, *Andrew Jackson's Way*, p. 38.
48. Hunt, *The Irish and the American Revolution*, p. 41; Dolan, *The Irish Americans*, p. 8.
49. Hunt, *The Irish and the American Revolution*, pp. 41–42.
50. General John Armstrong, Archives of the Pennsylvania Center for the Book, Pattee Library, Pennsylvania State University, University Park, Pennsylvania; Brumwell, *George Washington*, pp. 149, 152–153, 318, 415; Fleming, *Washington's Secret War*, pp. 19, 199; Doyle, *Ireland, Irishman and Revolutionary America*, p. 122; Buchanan, *Andrew Jackson's Way*, pp. 29–35.
51. Buchanan, *Andrew Jackson's Way*, pp. 29–31; Swisher, *The Revolutionary War in the Southern Back Country*, pp. 21–51; Hunt, *The Irish and the American Revolution*, p. 42.
52. Swisher, *The Revolutionary War in the Southern Back Country*, pp. 212–213; S. Roger Keller, *Isaac Shelby: A Driving Force in America's Struggle for Independence* (Shippensburg, PA: Burd Street Press, 1999), p. 1.
53. Swisher, *The Revolutionary War in the Southern Back Country*, pp. 203–234; Robert M. Dunkerly, *The Battle of Kings Mountain: Eyewitness Accounts* (Charleston, SC: The History Press, 2007), pp. 9–99; Hank Messick, *King's Mountain: The Epic of the Blue Ridge "Mountain Men" in the American Revolution* (Boston: Little, Brown and Company, 1976), pp. 81–82, 101–106, 108–153; White, *The King's Mountain Men*, pp. 169, 202–206; Keller, *Isaac Shelby*, pp. 26–27, 39; Lyman C. Draper, *King's Mountain and Its Heroes: History of the Battle of King's Mountain, October 7, 1780, and the Events Which Led to It* (Johnson City, TN: The Overmountain Press, 1996), pp. 456, 460–461, 464–478.

54. Dunkerly, *The Battle of Kings Mountain*, p. 107.
55. John McQueen, Federal Pension Application (S30577), Revolutionary War Record, National Archives, Washington, DC.
56. Keller, *Isaac Shelby*, p. 43.
57. Major Patrick Ferguson to Robert Timpany, October 6, 1780, Kings Mountain National Military Park Archives, Kings Mountain, South Carolina.
58. Foss, *Undreamed Shores*, pp. 104–105.
59. Ibid., p. 110.
60. Draper, *King's Mountain and Its Heroes*, p. 70.
61. Messick, *King's Mountain*, p. 9.
62. Buchanan, *Andrew Jackson's Way*, p. 34.
63. Dolan, *The Irish Americans*, p. 19.
64. Shelton, *General Richard Montgomery and the American Revolution*, pp. 3–4.
65. Keller, *Isaac Shelby*, p. 46; Foss, *Undreamed Shores*, pp. 104–110.
66. Buchanan, *Andrew Jackson's Way*, p. 34.
67. White, *The King's Mountain Men*, p. 205.
68. Draper, *King's Mountain and Its Heroes*, pp. 127–128.
69. Ibid., pp. 126–127.
70. Ibid., p. 128.
71. Brumwell, *George Washington*, p. 268.
72. Extract of a Letter from Baltimore to a Gentleman in New-York, January 27, 1775, American Archives, Documents of the American Revolution, 1774 to 1776, Northern Illinois University Libraries, DeKalb, Illinois.
73. James McHenry Biographical Sketch, Center of Military History, Historical Research Center, United States Army, Washington, DC; Jon Latimer, *1812: War with America* (Cambridge, MA: Belknap Press of Harvard University Press, 2007), pp. 329–331.
74. Willard Sterne Randall, *Alexander Hamilton: A Life* (New York: HarperCollins Publishers, 2003), p. 9; Milton Lomask, *Odd Destiny: A Life of Alexander Hamilton* (New York: Farrar, Straus and Giroux, 1969), p. 48; Martin, "He saved George Washington's life . . . twice!," http://www.foxnews.com/opinion/2012/07/04/this-july-4-let-thank-forgotten-revolutionary-war-hero.html, July 4, 2012.
75. Dunkerly, *The Battle of Kings Mountain*, pp. 7–122; Fintan O'Toole, *The Lie of the Land: Irish Identities* (New York: Verso, 1998), pp. 18–30;

Buchanan, *Andrew Jackson's Way*, pp. 34–35; Dolan, *The Irish Americans*, pp. xi, 303.

76. Draper, *King's Mountain and Its Heroes*, pp. 124–125.

77. Ibid., p. 181.

78. Zaboly, *American Colonial Ranger*, pp. 4–50.

79. Douglas R. Cubbison, "Petite Guerre: Saratoga's Small War," *Patriots of the American Revolution*, vol. 4, issue 5 (September/October 2011), pp. 28–33.

80. Buchanan, *Andrew Jackson's Way*, p. 44; O'Toole, *The Lie of the Land*, pp. 18–30.

81. Buchanan, *Andrew Jackson's Way*, p. 45.

82. Zaboly, *American Colonial Ranger*, p. 26.

83. Messick, *King's Mountain*, pp. 99–101; James Corbett David, *Dunmore's New World: The Extraordinary Life of a Royal Governor in Revolutionary America—with Jacobites, Counterfeiters, Land Schemes, Shipwrecks, Scalping, Indian Politics, Runaway Slaves, and Two Illegal Royal Weddings* (Charlottesville: University of Virginia Press, 2013), p. 67.

84. Buchanan, *Andrew Jackson's Way*, p. 34.

85. Dolan, *The Irish Americans*, pp. xi, 303; John Copeland, Federal Pension Application (S30966), Revolutionary War Record, National Archives, Washington, DC.

86. Dunkerly, *The Battle of Kings Mountain*, pp. 62–63, Messick, *King's Mountain*, p. 101.

87. David Crockett Papers, Biographical Information, Tennessee State Library and Archives, Nashville, Tennessee; David Crockett Papers, Biographical Information, Briscoe Center for American History, University of Texas, Austin, Texas; Messick, *King's Mountain*, p. 104; White, *The King's Mountain Men*, pp. 164–165; McCarthy, *The Other Irish*, pp. 19–21, 56–57.

88. White, *The King's Mountain Men*, p. 185.

89. White, *The King's Mountain Men*, p. 173.

90. Draper, *King's Mountain and Its Heroes*, p. 469.

91. Southern, ed., *Voices of the American Revolution in the Carolinas*, pp. 86–87.

92. Woody Holton, *Forced Founders: Indians, Debtors, Slaves, and the Making of the American Revolution in Virginia* (Chapel Hill: The University of North Carolina Press, 1999), pp. 164–220; Hunt, *The Irish and the American Revolution*, pp. 40–43; Cox, *A Proper Sense of Honor*, pp. 1–8; Doyle, *Ireland, Irishmen and Revolutionary America*, pp. 51–74; Dolan, *The Irish Americans*, p. viii.

93. Holton, *Forced Founders*, p. 164.

94. Ibid., pp. 133–220.

95. *New York Daily Times*, New York City, June 21, 1852; Dolan, *The Irish Americans*, pp. x, 67–83.

96. Michael J. O'Brien, *A Hidden Phase of American History: Ireland's Part in America's Struggle for Liberty* (New York: Dodd, Mead and Company, 1920), pp. 100–117; Doyle, *Ireland, Irishmen and Revolutionary America*, pp. xv–151; Dolan, *The Irish Americans*, pp. xi, 22.

97. Wikipedia contributors, "Thomas Fleming (historian)," Wikipedia, The Free Encyclopedia, https://en.wikipedia.org/w/index.php?title=Thomas_Fleming_(historian)&oldid=667379839 (accessed January 10, 2003).

98. Shelton, *General Richard Montgomery and the American Revolution*, p. 167.

99. James Webb, *Born Fighting: How the Scots-Irish Shaped America* (New York: Broadway Books, 2004), pp. 9–327; Kenneth O. Morgan, *The Oxford History of Britain* (Oxford: Oxford University Press, 1993), pp. 1–7; David W. McCullough, *Wars of the Irish Kings: A Thousand Years of Struggle from the Age of Myth through the Reign of Queen Elizabeth I* (New York: Broadway Books, 2002), p. xxiv; Grady McWhiney, *Cracker Culture: Celtic Ways of the Old South* (Tuscaloosa: University of Alabama Press, 1988), pp. xxi–50; Billy Kennedy, *The Scots-Irish in the Hills of Tennessee* (Londonderry, Northern Ireland: Causeway Press, 1995); David S. Landes, *The Wealth and Poverty of Nations: Why Some Are So Rich and Some So Poor* (New York: W.W. Norton and Company, 1998), pp. 33–35; Doyle, *Ireland, Irishmen and Revolutionary America*, pp. xv–151; Brian Lalor, ed., *The Encyclopedia of Ireland* (New Haven, CT: Yale University Press, 2003), pp. 121–122; Dolan, *The Irish Americans*, pp. xi, 22, 303; Adrian Goldsworthy, *How Rome Fell: Death of a Superpower* (New Haven, CT: Yale University Press, 2009), pp. 12–14.

100. Fleming, *Liberty!*, p. 262; Kennedy, *The Scots-Irish in the Hills of Tennessee*, pp. 32, 95; Godfrey Hodgson, *The Myth of American Exceptionalism* (New Haven, CT: Yale University Press, 2009), pp. xvi–29; Hunt, *The Irish and the American Revolution*, p. 41; Doyle, *Ireland, Irishmen and Revolutionary America*, pp. 10–11, 106; Buchanan, *Andrew Jackson's Way*, pp. 32–35.

101. Doyle, *Ireland, Irishmen and Revolutionary America*, p. 62.

102. Doyle, *Ireland, Irishmen and Revolutionary America*, p. 106.

103. O'Toole, *The Lie of the Land*, p. 33; Dolan, *The Irish Americans*, 22.

104. O'Toole, *The Lie of the Land*, p. 33; Dolan, *The Irish Americans*, pp. 5–6; John Brendan Flannery, *The Irish Texans* (San Antonio: The University of Texas Institute of Texan Cultures, 1995), pp. 13–14.

105. Dolan, *The Irish Americans*, p. 7.

106. Ibid.

107. Stephens, *Neither the Charm Nor the Luck*, p. 17.

108. Ibid., pp. 13–14.

109. Flannery, *The Irish Texans*, p. 14; Henry Steele Commager and Richard B. Morris, editors, *The Spirit of 'Seventy-Six: The Story of the American Revolution as Told by its Participants* (New York: Bobbs-Merrill Company, Inc., Publishers, 1958), p. 306; Don N. Hagist, *British Soldiers, American War: Voices of the American Revolution* (Yardley, PA: Westholme Publishing, 2012), p. 23.

110. Messick, *King's Mountain*, pp. 41–43; Patrick O'Kelly, *Unwaried Patience and Fortitude: Francis Marion's Orderly Book* (West Conshohocken, PA: Infinity Publishing, 2006), p. 80.

111. Fleming, *Liberty!*, p. 262; McCarthy, *The Other Irish*, p. 96.

112. Brumwell, *George Washington*, p. 31.

113. Dolan, *The Irish Americans*, p. 25.

114. Buchanan, *Andrew Jackson's Way*, p. 34.

115. Doyle, *Ireland, Irishmen and Revolutionary America*, p. 110.

116. Ibid., p. 118.

117. Webb, *Born Fighting*, pp. 152–153.

118. Doyle, *Ireland, Irishmen and Revolutionary America*, pp. 51–151.

119. Lalor, ed., *The Encyclopedia of Ireland*, pp. 318, 1125; Doyle, *Ireland, Irishmen and Revolutionary America*, pp. 52, 83–87, 98, 106.

120. Webb, *Born Fighting*, pp. 152–153; David A. Wilson, *United Irishmen, United States, Immigrant Radicals in the Early Republic* (Ithaca, NY: Cornell University Press, 1998), p. 14; Kennedy, *The Scots-Irish in the Hills of Tennessee*, pp. 25, 32, 95; Hunt, *The Irish and the American Revolution*, p. 41; Doyle, *Ireland, Irishmen and Revolutionary America*, pp. 10–11, 106, 111–137; Dolan, *The Irish Americans*, pp. xi, 303; Holton, *Forced Founders*, pp. xiii–220.

121. Brumwell, *George Washington*, p. 269; Wallace Nutting, *Ireland Beautiful* (New York: Bonanza Books, 1972), pp. 9, 19; Dolan, *The Irish Americans*, p. 22; Fleming, *Washington's Secret War*, pp. 141, 285.

122. Nutting, *Ireland Beautiful*, p. 9.

123. David Hackett Fischer, *Liberty and Freedom: A Visual History of America's Founding Ideas* (Oxford: Oxford University Press, 2005), pp. 175–176; Fleming, *Liberty!*, pp. 49, 103, 262; Kennedy, *The Scots-*

Irish in the Hills of Tennessee, pp. 25, 32, 95; Hunt, *The Irish and the American Revolution*, pp. vii–41; Cox, *A Proper Sense of Honor*, pp. 1–8; Doyle, *Ireland, Irishmen and Revolutionary America*, pp. 10–11, 106, 109, 114–137; Stephens, *Neither the Charm Nor the Luck*, p. 17; Buchanan, *Andrew Jackson's Way*, pp. 32–38; Edwin G. Burrows, *Forgotten Patriots: The Untold Story of American Prisoners During the Revolutionary War* (New York: Basic Books, 2008), pp. 35–37; Dolan, *The Irish Americans*, p. 18.

124. Commager and Morris, eds., *The Spirit of 'Seventy-Six*, p. 2.

125. Stephens, *Neither the Charm Nor the Luck*, p. 18.

126. Brumwell, *George Washington*, p. 208.

127. Antonia Fraser, *Cromwell: The Lord Protector* (New York: Grove Press, 1973), pp. 326–357; Stevens, *The Rogue's March*, p. 13.

128. *New York Times*, July 30, 1862; Paul R. Wylie, *The Irish General: Thomas Francis Meagher* (Norman: University of Oklahoma Press, 2007), pp. 3–166; Thomas J. Craughwell, *The Greatest Brigade: How the Irish Brigade Cleared the Way to Victory in the American Civil War* (Beverly, MA: Fair Winds Press, 2011), p. 31.

129. Dungan, *Distant Drums*, pp. 5, 17–18.

130. Dolan, *The Irish Americans*, pp. 3–4; Stevens, *The Rogue's March*, p. 13.

131. Dolan, *The Irish Americans*, p. 10; Barthelmas, *The Signers of the Declaration of Independence*, pp. 38–40.

132. Stephens, *Neither the Charm Nor the Luck*, pp. 1–3, 13–24.

133. Frederick Cook, *Journals of the Military Expedition of Major General John Sullivan, 1779* (Ann Arbor, MI: University Microfilms, 1967), pp. 15, 34.

134. Fleming, *Liberty!*, p. 49.

135. Ibid., p. 103.

136. Commager and Morris, eds., *The Spirit of 'Seventy-Six*, pp. 14–15.

137. O'Toole, *The Lie of the Land*, p. 34.

138. Michael Rose, *Washington's War: The American War of Independence to the Iraqi Insurgency* (New York: Pegasus Books, 2008), p. 199; Webb, *Born Fighting*, pp. 9–327; O'Brien, *A Hidden Phase of American History*, pp. 1–372; Doyle, *Ireland, Irishmen and Revolutionary America*, pp. 111–137; Dolan, *The Irish Americans*, pp. xi, 303.

139. Stephens, *Neither the Charm Nor the Luck*, p. 19.

140. Dolan, *The Irish Americans*, p. 303.

Chapter II

1. McWhiney, *Cracker Culture*, p. 7; Hunt, *The Irish and the American Revolution*, pp. 33, 41–42; Doyle, *Ireland, Irishmen and Revolutionary America*, pp. 51–106, 109.

2. James M. McPherson, *Battle Cry of Freedom: The Civil War Era* (Oxford: Oxford University Press, 1988), p. 606; Wylie, *The Irish General*, pp. 5, 117–181.

3. Joseph McBride and Michael Wilmington, *John Ford* (New York: Da Capo Press, 1975), pp. 8–9, 17; Dolan, *The Irish Americans*, p. 22; Hunt, *The Irish and the American Revolution*, pp. 1–101; Ronald H. Nichols, editor, *Men With Custer: Biographies of the 7th Cavalry* (Hardin, MT: Custer Battlefield Historical and Museum Association, Inc., 2000), pp. 1–364.

4. Don N. Hagist, *A British Soldier's Story: Roger Lamb's Narrative of the American Revolution* (Baraboo, WI: Ballindalloch Press, 2004), p. 54; Doyle, *Ireland, Irishmen and Revolutionary America*, pp. xv, xvii–xviii; Cook, *The Long Fuse*, pp. 359, 386.

5. Terry Golway, *For the Cause of Liberty: A Thousand Years of Ireland's Heroes* (New York: Simon and Schuster, 2000), pp. 48–50; Hagist, *A British Soldier's Story*, p. 54.

6. *South Carolina and American General Gazette*, Charleston, South Carolina, August 2, 1776; Richard W. Hatcher III, National Park Service Historian, Fort Sumter National Monument, Charleston, South Carolina, email to author, March 31, 2014; Peter Horry and M. L. Weems, *The Life of General Francis Marion* (Winston-Salem, NC: John F. Blair Publisher, 2000), pp. 33–36, 46–51, 58–60; David K. Wilson, *The Southern Strategy: Britain's Conquest of South Carolina and Georgia, 1775–1780* (Columbia: University of South Carolina Press, 2005), pp. 52, 55, 167–168, 307, note 100; Swisher, *The Revolutionary War in the Southern Back County*, p. 91; Southern, ed., *Voices of the American Revolution in the Carolinas*, pp. xiii, 37–39; John G. Gallaher, *Napoleon's Irish Legion* (Carbondale: Southern Illinois University Press, 1993), pp. 1–65.

7. Cox, *A Proper Sense of Honor*, p. 14; Flannery, *The Irish Texans*, p. 3; *Famous Charleston Firsts* (Charleston, SC: First Federal Savings and Loan Association, 1976), p. 19.

8. David T. Gleeson, *The Irish in the South, 1815–1877* (Chapel Hill: University of North Carolina Press, 2001), pp. 143, 170.

9. Charles Colock Jones Jr., *Sergeant William Jasper* (Albany, NY: Joel Munsell Printer, 1876), p. 6.

10. Kennedy, *The Scots-Irish in the Hills of Tennessee*, p. 153.

11. Swisher, *The Revolutionary War in the Southern Back Country*, pp. 211–234.

12. Messick, *King's Mountain*, p. 38.

13. White, *The King's Mountain Men*, p. 143.

14. Ibid., pp. 207, 226.

15. Ibid., pp. 205, 211.

16. Ibid., p. 215.

17. Ibid., p. 147.

18. Ibid., p. 157.

19. Ibid., p. 174.

20. Ibid., p. 202.

21. Ibid., pp. 108–111; Dunkerly, *The Battle of Kings Mountain*, p. 133.

22. Swisher, *The Revolutionary War in the Southern Back County*, 241; Pension Records, Revolutionary War Records, National Archives, Washington, DC.

23. Thomas H. O'Connor, *The Boston Irish: A Political History* (New York: Back Bay Books, 1995), p. 1; Kennedy, *The Scots-Irish in the Hills of Tennessee*, pp. 32, 95; Michael Stephenson, *Patriot Battles: How the War of Independence Was Fought* (New York: Harper Perennial, 2007), pp. 3–35; Doyle, *Ireland, Irishmen and Revolutionary America*, p. 109; Wylie, *The Irish General*, p. 7–8; Wikipedia contributors, "Hubert Howe Bancroft," Wikipedia, The Free Encyclopedia, https://en.wikipedia.org/w/index.php?title=Hubert_Howe_Bancroft&oldid=665946713 (accessed April 15, 2004); Cox, *A Proper Sense of Honor*, pp. 1–8; Brumwell, *George Washington*, p. 269.

24. O'Connor, *The Boston Irish*, p. 2.

25. Doyle, *Ireland, Irishmen and Revolutionary America*, p. 109; Kennedy, *The Scots-Irish in the Hills of Tennessee*, p. 10.

26. Kennedy, *The Scots-Irish in the Hills of Tennessee*, p. 16.

27. Doyle, *Ireland, Irishmen and Revolutionary America*, p. vii.

28. Ibid., pp. 68–69; Webb, *Born Fighting*, pp. 10–11, 13–14; Kennedy, *The Scots-Irish in the Hills of Tennessee*, p. 25.

29. Hagist, *British Soldiers, American War*, pp. 60, 72.

30. Fischer, *Liberty and Freedom*, pp. 1–2; Kennedy, *The Scots-Irish in the Hills of Tennessee*, p. 25; Stephenson, *Patriot Battles*, pp. 3–35; Brumwell, *George Washington*, pp. 384–385; Doyle, *Ireland, Irishmen and Revolutionary America*, pp. 117–151.

31. Hagist, *British Soldiers, American War*, pp. 60, 66.

32. Brumwell, *George Washington*, p. 269.

33. Webb, *Born Fighting*, pp. 156, 161; Kennedy, *The Scots-Irish in the Hills of Tennessee*, pp. 32, 131–132; Doyle, *Ireland, Irishmen and Revolution America*, pp. 114–137.

34. Doyle, *Ireland, Irishmen and Revolutionary America*, p. 110.

35. Draper, *King's Mountain and Its Heroes*, p. 407.

36. Lalor, ed., *The Encyclopedia of Ireland*, pp. 121–122; Fischer, *Liberty and Freedom*, pp. 1–13; O'Connor, *The Boston Irish*, pp. 1–2, 4, 6–7, 19–20; McCullough, *Wars of the Irish Kings*, p. xxiv; Seumas MacManus, *The Story of the Irish Race: A Popular History of Ireland* (New York: The Devin-Adair Company, 1969), p. 337; Marian Broderick, *Wild Irish Women: Extraordinary Lives from History* (Madison: The University of Wisconsin Press, 2004), pp. 244, 248, 252–253, 340; Kennedy, *The Scots-Irish in the Hills of Tennessee*, pp. 32, 95–97, 131–132; Doyle, *Ireland, Irishmen and Revolutionary America*, pp. 10–11; Hunt, *The Irish and the American Revolution*, p. 41; Doyle, *Ireland, Irishmen and Revolutionary America*, pp. 114–115.

37. Doyle, *Ireland, Irishmen and Revolutionary America*, p. 110.

38. Max Dixon, *The Wataugans* (Johnson City, TN: The Overmountain Press, 1989), pp. 1–61; Kennedy, *The Scots-Irish in the Hills of Tennessee*, pp. 37–57; Doyle, *Ireland, Irishmen and Revolutionary America*, pp. 114–137; Swisher, *The Revolutionary War in the Southern Back County*, pp. 211–234; Messick, *King's Mountain*, pp. 137–156; Southern, ed., *Voices of the American Revolution in the Carolinas*, pp. 3–15.

39. Cook, *The Long Fuse*, p. 315.

40. O'Toole, *The Lie of the Land*, pp. 18–30; Mark Urban, *Fusiliers: The Saga of a British Redcoat Regiment in the American Revolution* (New York: Walker and Company, 2007), p. 55; Doyle, *Ireland, Irishmen and Revolutionary America*, p. 57; Barthelmas, *The Signers of the Declaration of Independence*, pp. 38–41.

41. Doyle, *Ireland, Irishmen and Revolutionary America*, p. 57.

42. Ibid., pp. 62–63, 68.

43. Doyle, *Ireland, Irishmen and Revolutionary America*, pp. 111–112, 114–137; O'Brien, *A Hidden Phase of American History*, pp. 98–117; O'Connor, *The Boston Irish*, pp. 1–2; Kennedy, *The Scots-Irish in the Hills of Tennessee*, pp. 16, 25, 95–97; Brumwell, *George Washington*, p. 204.

44. Doyle, *Ireland, Irishmen and Revolutionary America*, pp. 114–137.

45. Southern, ed., *Voices of the American Revolution in the Carolinas*, pp. 3–15.

46. Fred B. Walters, *John Haslet: A Useful One* (n. p.: News Horizons, 2005), p. v.

47. Doyle, *Ireland, Irishmen and Revolutionary America*, pp. 111–137.

48. *The Philadelphia Enquirer*, Philadelphia, Pennsylvania, February 21, 2003; Thomas Fleming (historian), Wikipedia.

49. Fleming, *Washington's Secret War*, pp. 141, 285.

50. Kerby Miller and Paul Wagner, *Out of Ireland: The Story of Irish Emigration to America* (Washington, DC: Elliott and Clark Publishers, 1994), p. 10; Webb, *Born Fighting*, pp. 10–11.

51. Miller and Wagner, *Out of Ireland*, p. 10; Draper, *King's Mountain and Its Heroes*, pp. 456–457, 460, 465–466.

52. Webb, *Born Fighting*, p. 162.

53. Doyle, *Ireland, Irishmen and Revolutionary America*, p. 51.

54. *Washington Post*, October 28, 1898; Ivan Musicant, *Empire By Default: The Spanish-American War and the Dawn of the American Century* (New York: Henry Holt and Company, 1998), pp. 9–658; Fleming, *Washington's Secret War*, pp. 141, 262.

55. Joseph Plumb Martin, *A Narrative of a Revolutionary Soldier: Some Adventures, Dangers, and Sufferings of Joseph Plumb Martin*. With an introduction by Thomas Fleming (New York: Signet Classic, 2001), p. x.

56. Fleming, *Washington's Secret War*, pp. 141, 285; Webb, *Born Fighting*, pp. 10–11; Kennedy, *The Scots-Irish in the Hills of Tennessee*, p. 10; Walter Edgar, *Partisans and Redcoats: The Southern Conflict That Turned the Tide of the American Revolution* (New York: Harper Collins Publishers, 2001), pp. 2–3.

57. Fleming, *Washington's Secret War*, pp. 141, 285; Robert and Isabelle Tombs, *That Sweet Enemy: Britain and France: The History of a Love-Hate Relationship* (New York: Vintage Books, 2007), p. 170; Edgar, *Partisans and Redcoats*, pp. 2–3; Doyle, *Ireland, Irishmen and Revolutionary America*, pp. 110–112.

58. Doyle, *Ireland, Irishmen and Revolutionary America*, p. 112.

59. Joseph G. Bilby and Katherine Bilby Jenkins, "The Woodwards Rise Up: Revolution as Civil War in Monmouth County, New Jersey, 1776–1777," *Patriots of the American Revolution*, vol. 4, issue 3 (May/June 2011), p. 46.

60. Cox, *A Proper Sense of Honor*, p. 14; Smallwood's Maryland Regiment, Muster Rolls and Other Records of Service of Maryland Troops in the American Revolution, vol. 8, Maryland State Archives, Annapolis, Maryland.

61. Brumwell, *George Washington*, p. 204.
62. Cox, *A Proper Sense of Honor*, pp. xv–16.
63. Hagist, *British Soldiers, American War*, p. 152.
64. Doyle, *Ireland, Irishmen and Revolutionary America*, pp. 64–65; Dolan, *The Irish Americans*, pp. 6–7; Cox, *A Proper Sense of Honor*, p. 14.
65. Shelton, *General Richard Montgomery and the American Revolution*, p. 169.
66. Doyle, *Ireland, Irishmen and Revolutionary America*, p. 99; Urban, *Fusiliers*, p. 55; Holton, *Forced Founders*, p. 176; Cox, *A Proper Sense of Honor*, pp. xv–14.
67. Doyle, *Ireland, Irishmen and Revolutionary America*, pp. 63, 111.
68. Stephens, *Neither the Charm Nor the Luck*, p. 126.
69. *New York Daily Times*, New York, New York, July 28, 1852; Doyle, *Ireland, Irishmen and Revolutionary America*, pp. 110–112.
70. Mark Mayo Boatner, *Encyclopedia of the American Revolution* (New York: David McKay Company, Inc., 1966), p. 1156.
71. Doyle, *Ireland, Irishmen and Revolutionary America*, p. 142.
72. *Washington Post*, August 31, 1902; Fleming, *Washington's Secret War*, pp. 141, 285.
73. *Washington Post*, October 28, 1898.
74. Arthur Herman, *How the Scots Invented the Modern World: The True Story of How Western Europe's Poorest Nation Created Our World & Everything in It* (New York: Three Rivers Press, 2002), p. 250; Webb, *Born Fighting*, p. 162.
75. Phillip Thomas Tucker, *George Washington's Surprise Attack: A New Look at the Battle that Decided America's Fate* (New York: Skyhorse Publishing, 2014), pp. 1–5; Donald N. Moran, "George Washington's Military Family," *Liberty Tree Newsletter*, December 1998; Whitaker, Carolyn. "LTC John Fitzgerald." Find A Grave. December 12, 2012. Accessed October 24, 2014. http://www.findagrave.com/cgi-bin/fg.cgi?page=gr&GRid=102078445.; National Park Service Historian, "Lt. Col. John Fitzgerald" Biographical Sketch, National Park Service, Valley Forge, Pennsylvania.
76. Randall, *Alexander Hamilton*, pp. 45–47, 49, 92, 121, 126, 132–133; Alexander Rose, *Washington's Spies: The Story of America's First Spy Ring* (New York: Random House, 2006), pp. 224–226; Martin, "He saved George Washington's life . . .twice!," http://www.foxnews.com/opinion/2012/07/04/this-july-4-let-thank-forgotten-revolutionary-war-hero.html, July 4, 2012.

77. White, *The King's Mountain Men*, p. 202.

78. Wade S. Kolb III and Robert M. Weir, *Captured at Kings Mountain: The Journal of Uzal Johnson, A Loyalist Surgeon* (Columbia: The University of South Carolina Press, 2011), p. 35.

79. Dolan, *The Irish Americans*, pp. 22–28; Webb, *Born Fighting*, p. 162.

80. Swisher, *The Revolutionary War in the Southern Back Country*, p. 176.

81. Southern, ed., *Voices of the American Revolution in the Carolinas*, pp. 89, 93.

82. Kennedy, *The Scots-Irish in the Hills of Tennessee*, p. 30.

83. Webb, *Born Fighting*, p. 162.

84. Ibid.

85. Joseph Lee Boyle, *From Redcoat to Rebel: The Thomas Sullivan Journal* (Westminister, MD: Heritage Books, Inc., 2004), p. 24.

86. Ibid., pp. 221–222.

87. Burrows, *Forgotten Patriots*, p. 45.

88. James H. Smylie, *Scotch-Irish Presence in Pennsylvania* (University Park: Pennsylvania Historical Association, 1990), p. 23.

89. Barbara J. Mitnick, editor, *New Jersey in the American Revolution* (New Brunswick, NJ: Rutgers University Press, 2005), p. 23; McCarthy, *The Other Irish*, p. 96.

90. Stephenson, *Patriot Battles*, p. 30.

91. *Washington Post*, March 17, 1911; Edward G. Lengel, *Inventing George Washington: America's Founder, in Myth and Memory* (New York: Harper Collins Publishers, 2011), pp. 33–34; Dolan, *The Irish Americans*, 22.

92. *Washington Post*, October 26, 1898.

93. Swisher, *The Revolutionary War in the Southern Back Country*, pp. 21, 27.

94. Piers Mackesy, *The War for America, 1775–1783* (Lincoln: University of Nebraska Press, 1993), pp. 30–31.

95. Ibid., p. 30.

96. Richard M. Ketchum, *The Winter Soldiers* (New York: Henry Holt and Company, 1973), pp. 144–145; Doyle, *Ireland, Irishmen and Revolutionary America*, p. 110.

97. Ketchum, *The Winter Soldiers*, pp. 144–145.

98. Dungan, *Distant Drums*, pp. 1–2.

99. Dolan, *The Irish Americans*, p. 22; Ketchum, *The Winter Soldiers*, pp. 144–145.

100. Mackesy, *The War for America*, p. 31.

101. Herman, *How the Scots Invented the Modern World*, p. 251.

102. Kennedy, *The Scots-Irish in the Hills of Tennessee*, p. 29.

103. Richard Brookhiser, *George Washington on Leadership* (New York: Perseus Books Group, 2008), p. 27.

104. Clark, *All Cloudless Glory*, p. 301.

105. Fleming, *Liberty!*, p. 262.

106. Draper, *King's Mountain and Its Heroes*, p. 409.

107. Doyle, *Ireland, Irishmen and Revolutionary America*, p. 112; Boatner, *Encyclopedia of the American Revolution*, pp. 746–748, 1136–1137; Dolan, *The Irish Americans*, p. 8.

108. Hunt, *The Irish and the American Revolution*, pp. 8–9; Cathleen Crown and Carol Rogers, *Trenton: Images of America* (San Francisco: Arcadia Publishing, 2000), p. 10; Brumwell, *George Washington*, pp. 149, 153, 201–202.

109. Dennis Clark, *The Irish in Pennsylvania: A People Share a Commonwealth* (University Park: Pennsylvania Historical Association, 1991), p. 9.

110. *Washington Post*, October 26, 1898.

111. David R. Higgins, *The Swamp Fox: Francis Marion's Campaign in the Carolinas 1780* (New York: Osprey Publishing, Ltd., 2013), pp. 20–21; Brumwell, *George Washington*, p. 415.

112. Henry Steele Commager, *The Spirit of 'Seventy-Six*, p. 1139; Swisher, *The Revolutionary War in the Southern Back Country*, p. 177.

113. Southern, ed., *Voices of the American Revolution in the Carolinas*, p. 135.

114. Southern, ed., *Voices of the American Revolution in the Carolinas*, p. xxi.

115. Bass, *Gamecock*, pp. 53–57, 60–62.

116. Ibid., pp. 62, 70.

117. Ibid., p. 56.

118. Jim Piecuch, *Cavalry in the American Revolution* (Yardley, PA: Westholme Publishing, 2012), p. 150.

119. Bass, *Gamecock*, p. 42; "Lachlan McIntosh (1727-1806)." New Georgia Encyclopedia. Accessed May 7, 2013. http://www.georgiaencyclopedia.org/articles/history-archaeology/lachlan-mcintosh-1727-1806.

120. Jim Piecuch, ed. *Cavalry of the American Revolution* (Yardley, PA: Westholme Publishing, 2014), pp. 168, 171.

121. Bass, *Gamecock*, pp. 20–21.

122. Ibid., p. 21.

123. Ibid., p. 33.

124. Ibid., pp. 74–75, 179.

125. Draper, *King's Mountain and Its Heroes*, p. 469.

126. Michael J. O'Brien, "South Carolina, Newberry—Some Account of the Irish Settlers and Revolutionary Soldiers," *American Irish Historical Society Journal*, vol. 12 (July 1913), pp. 167–175; William Dobein James, *Swamp Fox: General Francis Marion and his Guerrilla Fighters of the American Revolutionary War* (St. Petersburg, FL: Red and Black Publishers, 2009), p. 31; Lalor, ed., *The Encyclopedia of Ireland*, p. 66; W. Gilmore Simms, *The Life of Francis Marion* (reprint, New York: Dover, 2015), pp. 18, 35, 37.

127. Walters, *John Haslet*, p. 8.

128. Shelton, *General Richard Montgomery and the American Revolution*, p. 168.

129. Hunt, *The Irish and the American Revolution*, pp. 22–26; Fleming, *Washington's Secret War*, pp. 141, 285; Dolan, *The Irish Americans*, p. 22.

130. Fleming, *Washington's Secret War*, p. xi.

131. *Washington Post*, March 17, 1911; Fleming, *Washington's Secret War*, pp. 141, 285; O'Brien, *A Hidden Phase of American History*, pp. 98–117.

132. Fleming, *Washington's Secret War*, pp. 141, 285.

133. Dolan, *The Irish Americans*, p. 22.

134. Hunt, *The Irish in the American Revolution*, pp. 22–26; Doyle, *Ireland, Irishmen and Revolutionary America*, pp. 110, 142; Burrows, *Forgotten Patriots*, p. 45.

135. *New York Times*, November 1, 1861; Hunt, *The Irish and the American Revolution*, p. 62; Doyle, *Ireland, Irishmen and Revolutionary America*, pp. 146–150.

136. Marquis de Chastellux, *Travels in North-America in the Years 1780-1781 and 1782* (Reprint, London: G. G. T. and J. Robinson, 1787), pp. 225–226.

137. White, *The King's Mountain Men*, p. 194.

138. Southern, ed., *Voices of the American Revolution in the Carolinas*, pp. 138, 141.

139. Ray Raphael, *Founding Myths: Stories That Hide Our Patriotic Past* (New York: MJF Books, 2004), pp. 87–88; Doyle, *The Ireland, Irishmen and Revolutionary America*, pp. 10–11, 111–137; Hunt, *The Irish and the American Revolution*, p. 41; Cox, *A Proper Sense of Honor*, pp. 1–8.

140. Doyle, *Ireland, Irishmen and Revolutionary America*, pp. 10–11, 111–137.

141. Stephenson, *Patriot Battles*, pp. 3–4, 5–6, 20; Richard Holmes, *The British Soldier in the Age of Horse and Musket* (New York: W. W. Norton and Company, 2002), pp. 59–63; Cox, *A Proper Sense of Honor*, pp. 1–8.

142. Raphael, *Founding Myths*, pp. 85–104; Doyle, *Ireland, Irishmen and Revolutionary America*, pp. 11, 68; Brumwell, *George Washington*, pp.

249–250, 285; Cox, *A Proper Sense of Honor*, pp. 1–8; Dolan, *The Irish Americans*, pp. xi, 8, 22, 303.

143. Richard Hanser, *The Glorious Hour of Lt. Monroe* (Brattleboro, VT: The Book Press, 1975), p. 113.

144. Peter Haining, *Great Irish Humor* (New York: Barnes and Noble Books, 1997), pp.14–16; George P. Rawick, *From Sundown to Sunup: The Making of the Black Community* (Westport, CT: Greenwood Publishing Company, 1972), pp. 100–102; Nutting, *Ireland Beautiful*, pp. 60–62; Kennedy, *The Scots-Irish in the Hills of Tennessee*, pp. 25–26; Holmes, *Redcoat*, pp. 59–63; Doyle, *Ireland, Irishmen and Revolutionary America*, pp. 106–112; Hunt, *The Irish in the American Revolution*, pp. 22–26; Mackesy, *The War for America*, pp. 30–31; Joseph J. Ellis, *His Excellency: George Washington* (New York: Vintage Books, 2004), p. 86.

145. Chastellux, *Travels in North-America*, p. 37; Haining, *Great Irish Humor*, pp. 14–16.

146. Caesar A. Rodney, "Diary of Captain Thomas Rodney, 1776–1777," *Papers of the Historical Society of Delaware*, VIIL (1888), pp. 13, 31, 41, 43; David Hackett Fischer, *Washington's Crossing* (Oxford: Oxford University Press, 2004), pp. 115–159; Benson Bobrick, *Angel in the Whirlwind: The Triumph of the American Revolution* (New York: Penguin Books, 1997), pp. 222–226; Fleming, *Washington's Secret War*, pp. 141, 285; Walters, *John Haslet*, pp. 1, 653; Doyle, *Ireland, Irishmen and Revolutionary America*, pp. 110–112; Hunt, *The Irish in the American Revolution*, pp. 22–26; Dolan, *The Irish American*, p. 22.

147. Bruce Chadwick, *George Washington's War: The Forging of a Revolutionary Army and the American Presidency* (Naperville, IL: Sourcebooks, 2005), p. 143.

148. Phillip Thomas Tucker, *The Important Role of the Irish in the American Revolution* (Bowie, MD: Heritage Books, 2009), pp. 65–87; Brumwell, *George Washington*, p. 269; Fleming, *Washington's Secret War*, pp. 141, 285; John B. Trussell, *The Pennsylvania Line: Regimental Organization and Operations* (Harrisburg: Pennsylvania History and Museum Commission, 1993), pp. 249–250, 263–288; Edgar, *Partisans and Redcoats*, pp. 2–3; Hunt, *The Irish and the American Revolution*, pp. 22–26; Doyle, *Ireland, Irishmen and Revolutionary America*, pp. 110–112; Dolan, *The Irish Americans*, p. 22; Brumwell, *George Washington*, p. 262.

149. Brumwell, *George Washington*, p. 262.

150. Kennedy, *The Scots-Irish in the Hills of Tennessee*, pp. 161, 203–204; Lalor, ed., *The Encyclopedia of Ireland*, p. 611.

151. Messick, *King's Mountain*, p. 105.

152. Maureen O'Rourke Murphy and James MacKillop, editors, *Irish Literature: A Reader* (Syracuse, NY: Syracuse University Press, 1987), p. 128.

153. Ibid., p. 139.

154. Henry Whittemore, *The Heroes of the American Revolution and their Descendants: Battle of Long Island* (Salem, MA: Higginson Book Company, n.d.), pp. 119–120.

155. Messick, *King's Mountain*, p. 56.

156. Ibid., p. 97.

157. O'Connor, *The Boston Irish*, p. xvi; Webb, *Born Fighting*, pp. 12–14.

158. Flannery, *The Irish Texans*, pp. 29, 49; Lalor, ed., *The Encyclopedia of Ireland*, pp. 1022–1023.

159. O'Connor, *The Boston Irish*, pp. xvi, xvii–xviii.

Chapter III

1. Michael Lee Lanning, *Defenders of Liberty: African Americans in the Revolutionary War* (New York: Kensington Publishing Company, 2000), pp. 3–119; Dolan, *The Irish Americans*, p. 22; Fleming, *Washington's Secret War*, pp. 141, 285.

2. *Washington Post*, April 29, 1895; Boatner, *Encyclopedia of the American Revolution*, pp. 725, 736; Tucker, *George Washington's Surprise Attack*, pp. 128–130.

3. Thomas J. McGuire, *Battle of Paoli* (Mechanicsburg, PA: Stackpole Books, 2000), pp. 7, 46; Hunt, *The Irish and the American Revolution*, pp. 7–8.

4. McGuire, *Battle of Paoli*, p. 11.

5. Fleming, *Washington's Secret War*, p. 142.

6. Ibid., pp. 141–142, 285; Hunt, *The Irish and the American Revolution*, pp. 22–26.

7. Fleming, *Washington's Secret War*, p. xi.

8. Webb, *Born Fighting*, p. 162.

9. Stephenson, *Patriot Battles*, p. 29.

10. Webb, *Born Fighting*, p. 162; O'Brien, *A Hidden Phase of American History*, pp. 98–117; Fleming, *Washington's Secret War*, pp. 141, 285;

Edgar, *Partisans and Redcoats*, pp. 2–3; Brumwell, *George Washington*, p. 262.

11. O'Brien, *A Hidden Phase of American History*, pp. 98–117; Bobrick, *Angel in the Whirlwind*, pp. 222–226; Tucker, *George Washington's Surprise Attack*, pp. 1–558; Fischer, *Washington's Crossing*, pp.115–159; Edgar, *Partisans and Redcoats*, pp. 2–3; Hunt, *The Irish and the American Revolution*, pp. 22–26.

12. *Washington Post*, August 31, 1902.

13. David Power Conyngham, *The Irish Brigade and Its Campaigns* (New York: Fordham University Press, 1994), p. 253.

14. *Washington Post*, August 31, 1902.

15. Fleming, *Washington's Secret War*, pp. 6, 206–207.

16. Webb, *Born Fighting*, pp. 8, 10–11, 13–15; Hunt, *The Irish and the American Revolution*, p. 26.

17. J. P. Mayer and Max Lerner, editors, *Democracy in America*, by Alexis De Tocqueville (New York: Harper and Row Publishers, 1966), p. 27.

18. Ibid., p. 29.

19. David A. Wilson, *United Irishmen, United States: Immigrant Radicals in the Early Republic* (Ithaca, NY: Cornell University Press, 1998), pp. 1–152, 172–179; Fischer, *Liberty and Freedom*, pp. 61–67; Webb, *Born Fighting*, pp. 13–15; Doyle, *Ireland, Irishman and Revolutionary America*, pp. ix, xv–xvi, 10–11, 110–112, 114–137; Hunt, *The Irish and the American Revolution*, p. 41; Southern, ed., *Voices of the American Revolution in the Carolinas*, pp. 3–15, 89, 93; Dolan, *The Irish Americans*, pp. 26–27, 39; Mitnick, ed., *New Jersey in the American Revolution*, p. 90.

20. Fischer, *Liberty and Freedom*, p. 67; Doyle, *Ireland, Irishmen and Revolutionary America*, pp. ix, xv–xvi, 114–115.

21. Holton, *Forced Founders*, p. 193.

22. Doyle, *Ireland, Irishmen and Revolutionary America*, pp. ix, xv–xvi. 10–11, 114–115; Fleming, *Liberty!*, 47, 49, 103; John P. Reid, *In a Defiant Stance: The Conditions of War in Massachusetts Bay, the Irish Comparison, and the Coming of the American Revolution* (University Park: Pennsylvania State University Press, 1977), p. 13; Alfred W. Blumrosen and Ruth G. Blumrosen, *Slave Nation: How Slavery United the Colonies and Sparked the American Revolution* (Naperville, IL: Sourcebooks, Inc., 2005), pp. 15–143; Webb, *Born Fighting*, pp. 13–15; Fischer, *Liberty and Freedom*, pp. 61–67; Walter Isaacson, *Benjamin Franklin: An American Life* (New York: Simon and Schuster, 2003), p. 275; David, *Dunmore's New World*, p.

101; Michael A. McDonnell, *The Politics of War: Race, Class, and Conflict in Revolutionary Virginia* (Chapel Hill: University of North Carolina Press, 2007), pp. 2–527; Patrick Charles, *Washington's Decision: The Story of George Washington's Decision to Reaccept Black Enlistments in the Continental Army, December 31, 1775* (n.p.: Book Surge, LLC, 2005), pp. 17–18, 29, 44; Cox, *A Proper Sense of Honor*, pp. 1–8; Southern, ed., *Voices of the American Revolution in the Carolinas*, pp. 3–15; Mark M. Smith, editor, *Stono: Documenting and Interpreting a Southern Slave Revolt* (Columbia: University of South Carolina Press, 2005), p. xii; Edgar, *Partisans and Redcoats*, pp. 2–3.; Hunt, *The Irish and the American Revolution*, p. 41; Mitnick, ed., *New Jersey in the American Revolution*, p. 155.

23. Doyle, *Ireland, Irishmen and Revolutionary America*, p. 110.

24. Holton, *Forced Founders*, pp. 164–220.

25. White, *The King's Mountain Men*, pp. 113–115.

26. James Haltigan, *The Irish in the American Revolution, and Their Early Influence in the Colonies* (Washington, DC: Patrick J. Haltigan Publisher, 1908), p. 14; Fleming, *Liberty!*, pp. 47, 49, 103; Reid, *In a Defiant Stance*, pp. 12–13; Webb, *Born Fighting*, pp. 13–14, 20; Doyle, *Ireland, Irishmen and Revolutionary America*, pp. ix, xv–xvi.

27. O'Brien, *A Hidden Phase of American History*, p. xi.

28. Ibid., pp. xi–3; Haltigan, *The Irish in the American Revolution*, pp. 9–16.

29. Ron Field, *Buffalo Soldiers, 1892–1918* (Oxford: Osprey Publishing, 2005), p. 12–16; Peggy Samuels and Harold Samuels, *Teddy Roosevelt at San Juan: The Making of a President* (College Station: Texas A&M University Press, 1997), pp. 250–313.

30. Carl Bromley, editor, *Cinema Nation: The Best Writing on Film from The Nation, 1913–2000* (New York: Avalon Publishing Group, 2000), p. 155.

31. O'Toole, *The Lie of the Land*, p. 22.

32. Messick, *King's Mountain*, pp. 42–47; Webb, *Born Fighting*, pp. 138–139, 138–140, 150; Colin G. Calloway, *The American Revolution in Indian Country: Crisis and Diversity in Native American Communities* (Cambridge: Cambridge University Press, 1995), pp. 51–53; Doyle, *Ireland, Irishmen and Revolutionary America*, pp. 82, 103; Stephens, *Neither the Charm Nor the Luck*, pp. 1–3, 52, 97–126; Bass, *Gamecock*, pp. 34–41.

33. Ward Churchill, *A Little Matter of Genocide: Holocaust and Denial in the Americas, 1492 to the Present* (San Francisco, CA: City Lights Books, 1997), p. 206; Doyle, *Ireland, Irishmen and Revolutionary America*, pp. 47, 122, 221; Ray Raphael, *Founders: The People Who Brought You A Nation*

(New York: MJF Books, 2009), pp. 20–22; Dolan, *The Irish Americans*, pp. 26–27; Bass, *Gamecock*, pp. 34–41.

34. Raphael, *Founders*, pp. 21–22.

35. Doyle, *Ireland, Irishmen and Revolutionary America*, p. 11; Raphael, *Founders*, p. 20.

36. Raphael, *Founders*, p. 23.

37. O'Toole, *The Lie of the Land*, p. 23.

38. Stephens, *Neither the Charm Nor the Luck*, p. 124.

39. Southern, ed., *Voices of the American Revolution in the Carolinas*, p. xiii; Doyle, *Ireland, Irishmen and Revolutionary America*, pp. 122, 221.

40. Messick, *King's Mountain*, pp. 47, 82, 164–165; Bass, *Gamecock*, pp. 34–41.

41. White, *The King's Mountain Men*, p. 152.

42. Ibid., p. 156.

43. Southern, ed., *Voices of the American Revolution in the Carolinas*, p. 87.

44. "Searching for Molly Pitcher": An Exhibition, Monmouth County Library, Manalapan, New Jersey, October 2001, Monmouth County Archives, Manalapan, New Jersey; Theodore P. Savas and J. David Dameron, *The New American Revolution Handbook: Facts and Artwork for Readers of All Ages, 1775–1783* (New York: Savas Beatie, 2010), p. 136.

45. White, *The King's Mountain Men*, p. 232.

46. Bass, *Gamecock*, p. 59.

47. Reid, *In a Defiant Stance*, p. 14; Zaboly, *America Colonial Ranger*, pp. 9, 12, 46; Doyle, *Ireland, Irishmen and Revolutionary America*, pp. 111–137; Holton, *Forced Founders*, pp. 164–194; Raphael, *Founders*, pp. 86–88.

48. Zaboly, *American Colonial Ranger*, pp. 9, 12, 46.

49. Alexander Graydon, *Memoirs of His Own Time: With Reminiscences of the Men and Events of the American Revolution* (Philadelphia: Lindsay and Blakiston, 1846), p. 181; Lalor, ed., *The Encyclopedia of Ireland*, p. 866; Stevens, *The Rogue's March*, pp. x–244; O'Brien, *A Hidden Phase of American History*, pp. 119–121; Webb, *Born Fighting*, p. 20; Doyle, *Ireland, Irishmen and Revolutionary America*, pp. 65, 75.

50. Graydon, *Memoirs of His Own Time*, pp. 18, 181; Charles Lucey, *Harp and Sword: 1776 The Irish in the American Revolution*, (Washington, DC: The American Irish Foundation, 1976), pp. 43–44; Charles Royster, *Light-Horse Harry Lee and the Legacy of the American Revolution* (Baton Rouge: Louisiana State University Press, 1994), pp. 11–54.

51. Charles J. Stille, *Major-General Anthony Wayne and the Pennsylvania Line in the Continental Army* (Cranbury, NJ: The Scholar's Bookshelf, 2005), p. 248.

52. Bartlett and Jeffrey, *A Military History of Ireland* (Cambridge: Cambridge University Press, 1997), pp. 6–18; Grady McWhiney and Perry Jamieson, *Attack and Die* (Tuscaloosa: University of Alabama Press, 1984), pp. 174–191; Doyle, *Ireland, Irishmen and Revolutionary America*, pp. ix, xv–xvi, 11.

53. Fleming, *Washington's Secret War*, p. 285; Charles Lucey, *Harp and Sword: 1776* (Washington, DC: Colortone Press, 1976), in foreword; Fischer, *Liberty and Freedom*, pp. 61–67; Doyle, *Ireland, Irishmen and Revolutionary America*, pp. ix, xv–xvi.

54. Kerby A. Miller, Arnold Schrier, Bruce D. Boling, and David D. Doyle, editors, *Irish Immigrants in the Land of Canaan: Letters and Memoirs from Colonial and Revolutionary America, 1675–1815* (Oxford: Oxford University Press, 2003), p. 447; Boatner, *Encyclopedia of the American Revolution*, p. 605; Doyle, *Ireland, Irishmen and Revolutionary America*, p. 104; Dolan, *The Irish Americans*, p. 24.

55. Fleming, *Washington's Secret War*, p. 285; Boatner, *Encyclopedia of the American Revolution*, p. 605; Doyle, *Ireland, Irishmen and Revolutionary America*, pp. 11, 80, 92; Cox, *A Proper Sense of Honor*, pp. 1–65.

56. Hagist, *British Soldiers, American War*, p. 36; Dolan, *The Irish Americans*, p. 25.

57. James Graham, *The Life of General Daniel Morgan* (Reprint, New York: Derby and Jackson, 1856), pp. 135–175; Doyle, *Ireland, Irishmen and Revolutionary America*, p. ix.

58. McWhiney, *Cracker Culture*, pp. xiii–50; Hunt, *The Irish in the American Revolution*, pp. 22–26; Doyle, *Ireland, Irishmen and Revolutionary America*, pp. 83–87, 146–150; Savas and Dameron, *The New American Revolution Handbook*, p. 17; Fleming, *Washington's Secret War*, pp. 141, 285; Charles Murphy, *The Irish in the American Revolution* (Groverland, MA: Charles Murphy Publisher, 1975), pp. 59–64.

59. McWhiney, *Cracker Culture*, pp. xiii–xiv, 7, 28; Webb, *Born Fighting*, pp. 15, 18, 25, 32–41, 152–153; Doyle, *Ireland, Irishmen and Revolutionary America*, pp. 83–87, 114–137; Fleming, *Washington's Secret War*, pp. 141, 285; Flannery, *The Irish Texans*, pp. 29, 49; Lalor, ed., *The Encyclopedia of Ireland*, pp. 1022–1023; Dolan, *The Irish Americans*, pp. 25, 28.

60. Edwin Nott Hopson, Jr., *Captain Daniel Neil: A Short Biography* (Paterson, NJ: Braen-Heusser Printing Company, 1927), pp. 1–30.

61. *Daughters of the American Revolution Magazine*, vol. 11 (1897), pp. 619–620; Lalor, ed., *The Encyclopedia of Ireland*, p. 833; Wikipedia contributors, "Shane's Castle," *Wikipedia, The Free Encyclopedia*, https://en.wikipedia.

org/w/index.php?title=Shane%27s_Castle&oldid=623850243 (accessed December 1, 2004).

62. Dolan, *The Irish Americans*, pp. 25–26; Doyle, *Ireland, Irishmen and Revolutionary America*, pp. 96–97, 111, 149

Chapter IV

1. Doyle, *Ireland, Irishmen and Revolutionary America*, pp. 3–13, 106, 115, 118; Holton, *Forced Founders*, pp. 164–220.
2. Miller, Schrier, Boling, and Doyle, eds., *Irish Immigrants in the Land of Canaan*, p. 7; Doyle, *Ireland, Irishmen and Revolutionary America*, pp. 51–52, 58, 61, 70–71.
3. Stephenson, *Patriot Battles*, p. 30; Fleming, *Liberty!*, p. 262; Mackesy, *The War for America*, p. 29; Doyle, *Ireland, Irishmen and Revolutionary America*, pp. 51–52, 58, 61.
4. Miller and Wagner, *Out of Ireland*, p. 10; Fleming, *Washington's Secret War*, pp. 141, 285; Murphy, *The Irish in the American Revolution*, pp. 59–64; Doyle, *Ireland, Irishmen and Revolutionary America*, p. 52.
5. Fleming, *Washington's Secret War*, pp. 141, 285; Murphy, *The Irish in the American Revolution*, pp. 59–64.
6. Ibid; Hunt, *The Irish and the American Revolution*, pp. 26, 28,
7. Reid, *In a Defiant Stance*, p. 13; Fleming, *Liberty!*, pp. 47, 49, 103; Edgar, *Partisans and Redcoats*, pp. 2–3; Murphy, *The Irish in the American Revolution*, pp. 59–64; Stephenson, *Patriot Battles*, pp. 28–29.
8. Stephenson, *Patriot Battles*, p. 30; Brumwell, *George Washington*, pp. 384–385; Cox, *A Proper Sense of Honor*, pp. 1–8; Hunt, *The Irish and the American Revolution*, pp. 1–101.
9. Tonsetic, *1781*, p. 129.
10. Cox, *A Proper Sense of Honor*, pp. xv–xvii, 1–4, 8, 11–14.
11. McGuire, *Battle of Paoli*, p. 155.
12. Ibid.; McFarland, Robert W. "MacFarlane Clan in North America." Accessed January 5, 2004. http://scottish-clans.org/clans/mcfarlandclandraft.html#-ftn1; O'Toole, *The Lie of the Land*, p. 25.
13. James Thacher, *Military Journal During the American Revolutionary War From 1775 to 1783* (Cranbury, NJ: Scholar's Bookshelf, 2005), p. 121.
14. Burrows, *Forgotten Patriots*, p. 45.

15. O'Brien, *A Hidden Phase of American History*, pp. 103–105; Murphy, *The Irish in the American Revolution*, pp. 59–64.

16. Stephenson, *Patriot Battles*, p. 30; Fleming, *Washington's Secret War*, pp. 141, 285; Murphy, *The Irish in the American Revolution*, pp. 59–64.

17. O'Brien, *A Hidden Phase of American History*, p. xiii; Hunt, *The Irish and the American Revolution*, p. 26; Dolan, *The Irish Americans*, p. 22.

18. Smylie, *Scotch-Irish Presence in Pennsylvania*, pp. 34–35; Doyle, *Ireland, Irishmen and Revolutionary America*, p. 137.

19. Fleming, *Washington's Secret War*, pp. 39, 284–285; Anthony J. Scotti Jr., *Brutal Virtue: The Myth and Reality of Banastre Tarleton* (Bowie, MD: Heritage Books, 2002), pp. 13–16; Murphy, *The Irish in the American Revolution*, pp. 59–64; Jim Piecuch, *The Battle of Camden: A Documentary History* (Charleston, SC: The History Press, 2006), p. 17.

20. Fleming, *Washington's Secret War*, p. 285; Hunt, *The Irish and the American Revolution*, pp. 26, 28; Murphy, *The Irish in the American Revolution*, pp. 59–64.

21. Doyle, *Ireland, Irishmen and Revolutionary America*, pp. 122–123; O'Brien, *A Hidden Phase of the American History*, pp. 82–85; Boatner, *Encyclopedia of the American Revolution*, p. 409; Fleming, *Washington's Secret War*, pp. 58–59; Lawrence Leder, ed., *The Colonial Legacy, Loyalist Historians*, vol. 1 (New York: Harper and Row, 1971), pp. 60–61, 63; Isaacson, *Benjamin Franklin*, pp. 292–293; Murphy, *The Irish in the American Revolution*, pp. 59–64; Raphael, *Founders*, pp. 20–23, 157–158.

22. O'Brien, *A Hidden Phase of the American Revolution*, pp. 82–85; Leder, ed., *The Colonial Legacy*, p. 63.

23. Murphy, *The Irish in the American Revolution*, p. 99.

24. Stephenson, *Patriot Battles*, p. 30.

25. Clark, *All Cloudless Glory*, p. 270; Brumwell, *George Washington*, p. 337.

26. *Maryland Gazette*, March 20, 1777.

27. Doyle, *Ireland, Irishmen and Revolutionary America*, p. 110.

28. Fleming, *Washington's Secret War*, p. 285; Fischer, *Liberty and Freedom*, pp. 61–67; Doyle, *Ireland, Irishmen and Revolutionary America*, pp. 114–115, 123; Murphy, *The Irish in the American Revolution*, pp. 59–64.

29. Miller, Schrier, Boling, and Doyle, eds., *Irish Immigrants in the Land of Canaan*, p. 567; Hunt, *The Irish and the American Revolution*, pp. 22–26; Murphy, *The Irish in the American Revolution*, pp. 59–64.

30. Stephenson, *Patriot Battles*, p. 29; Murphy, *The Irish in the American Revolution*, pp. 59–64.

31. Doyle, *Ireland, Irishmen and Revolutionary America*, p. 92; Boatner, *Encyclopedia of the American Revolution*, pp. 570–571; Bobrick, *Angel in the Whirlwind*, pp. 192–193; Fleming, *Washington's Secret War*, p. 5; Kennedy, *The Scots-Irish in the Hills of Tennessee*, p. 25; Piecuch, *The Battle of Camden*, pp. 24–49; Horry and Weems, *The Life of General Francis Marion*, pp. 93–94.

32. Trussell, *The Pennsylvania Line*, pp. 222–226; Stephenson, *Patriot Battles*, pp. 30–31; Henry J. Retzer, *The German Regiment of Maryland and Pennsylvania in the Continental Army, 1776–1781* (Bowie, MD: Heritage Books, 2006), pp. v–161.

33. Southern, ed., *Voices of the American Revolution in the Carolinas*, pp. 16–19; William Tennent Biographical Sketch, South Carolinian Library, University of South Carolina, Columbia, South Carolina; Elias Boudinot, *Life of the Rev. William Tennent* (Trenton, NJ: E. B. Adams, 1833), p. 9.

34. Cook, *Journals of the Military Expedition of Major General John Sullivan, 1779*, pp. 42, 51; Retzer, *The German Regiment of Maryland and Pennsylvania*, pp. 28–34; Stephen, *Patriot Battles*, p. 30.

35. Chastellux, *Travels in North-America*, p. 289, note.

36. Trussell, *The Pennsylvania Line*, pp. 243, 249–250; Haltigan, *The Irish in the American Revolution and Their Early Influence in the Colonies*, p. 27; Trussell, *The Pennsylvania Line*, pp. 222–225; Retzer, *The German Regiment of Maryland and Pennsylvania*, pp. v–161; Fleming, *Liberty!*, p. 262; Murphy, *The Irish in the American Revolution*, pp. 59–64; Stephenson, *Patriot Battles*, p. 29; Southern, ed., *Voices of the American Revolution in the Carolinas*, pp. 16–19.

37. Clark, *The Irish in Pennsylvania*, p. 7; Justin Clement, *Philadelphia 1777: Taking the Capital* (Oxford: Osprey Publishing, 2007), p. 9; Edgar, *Partisans and Redcoats*, pp. 2–3; Murphy, *The Irish in the American Revolution*, pp. 59–64; Dolan, *The Irish Americans*, pp. 25–28, 39.

38. O'Toole, *The Lie of the Land*, p. 22.

39. Lucey, *Harp and Sword*, p. 28.

40. Fleming, *Liberty!*, p. 262.

41. O'Brien, *A Hidden Phase of American History*, pp. 275–276.

42. Dennis Clark, *The Irish in Pennsylvania, A People Share a Commonwealth* (University Park: Pennsylvania Historical Association, 1991), p. 5; Howard Zinn, *A People's History of the United States* (New York: Harper Perennial,

2005), pp. 76–77; Murphy, *The Irish in the American Revolution*, pp. 59–64; Doyle, *Ireland, Irishmen and Revolutionary American*, pp. 111–137.

43. Smylie, *Scotch-Irish Presence in Pennsylvania*, p. 6.

44. Stephenson, *Patriot Battles*, pp. 29, 31; Doyle, *Ireland, Irishmen and Revolutionary America*, pp. 110–112.

45. Doyle, *Ireland, Irishmen and Revolutionary America*, p. 150.

46. O'Brien, *A Hidden Phase of American History*, pp. 108, 285; Clark, *The Irish in Pennsylvania*, p. 9; Doyle, *Ireland, Irishmen and Revolutionary America*, pp. 1–2; Doyle, *Ireland, Irishmen and Revolutionary America*, pp. 1–2; Murphy, *The Irish in the American Revolution*, pp. 59–64

47. Cox, *A Proper Sense of Honor*, pp. 1–8; Doyle, *Ireland, Irishmen and Revolutionary America*, pp. 62–70, 143.

48. Franklin Folsom, *Give Me Liberty: America's Colonial Heritage* (New York: Rand McNally and Company, 1974), pp. 100–101; Hunt, *The Irish and the American Revolution*, p. 41; Doyle, *Ireland, Irishmen and Revolutionary America*, pp. 10–11, 111–137; Murphy, *The Irish in the American Revolution*, pp. 59–64.

49. Swisher, *The Revolutionary War in the Southern Back County*, p. 112; Doyle, *Ireland, Irishmen and Revolutionary America*, pp. 110–111; Boatner, *Encyclopedia of the American Revolution*, p. 1156; Bartlett and Jeffrey, *A Military History of Ireland*, pp. 13–16; Webb, *Born Fighting*, pp. 10–11; *New York Times*, November 1, 1861 and July 30, 1862; *New York Daily Times*, June 21, 1852 and July 28, 1852; Edgar, *Partisans and Redcoats*, pp. 2–3; Hunt, *The Irish and the American Revolution*, p. 26; Murphy, *The Irish in the American Revolution*, pp. 59–64.

50. Swisher, *The Revolutionary War in the Southern Back Country*, pp. 203, 211–234; Pension Applications, Revolutionary War Records, National Archives, Washington, DC.

51. Graydon, *Memoirs of His Own Time: With Reminiscences of the Men and Events of the American Revolution*, p. 122.

52. Higgins, *The Swamp Fox*, pp. 4–77; Swisher, *The Revolutionary in the Southern Back Country*, pp. 78–84; Doyle, *Ireland, Irishmen and Revolutionary America*, pp. 11, 135–137, 188; Edgar, *Partisans and Redcoats*, pp. 2–3, 8, 115; Hunt, *The Irish and the American Revolution*, pp. 33–34; Rod Gragg, *Forged in Faith: How Faith Shaped the Birth of the Nation 1607–1776* (New York: Howard Books, 2010), p. 90; Simms, *The Life of Francis Marion*, pp. 9–15, 18; William R. Reynolds, Jr., *Andrew Pickens: South Carolina Patriot in the Revolutionary War* (Jefferson, NC:

McFarland and Company, Inc., Publishers, 2012), pp. 7–15; Hugh F. Rankin, *Francis Marion: The Swamp Fox* (New York: Thomas Y. Crowell Company, 1973), p. 132; Southern, ed., *Voices of the American Revolution in the Carolinas*, pp. 96–97, 119–120, 127; Bass, *Gamecock*, pp. 50–62.

53. Higgins, *The Swamp Fox*, p. 48; Bass, *Gamecock*, p. 55; Swisher, *The Revolutionary War in the Southern Back Country*, p. 185; Southern, ed., *Voices of the American Revolution in the Carolinians*, pp. 15–19; Wikipedia contributors, "John Simpson (Presbyterian)," Wikipedia, The Free Encyclopedia, https://en.wikipedia.org/w/index.php?title=John_Simpson_(Presbyterian)&oldid=600880786 accessed June 23, 2015.

54. Doyle, *Ireland, Irishmen and Revolutionary America*, p. 137.

55. McWhiney, *Cracker Culture*, pp. xxxviii, 7, 28; Fleming, *Washington's Secret War*, pp. 141–142, 285; *Washington Post*, October 28, 1898; *New York Times*, November 1, 1861 and July 30, 1863; *New York Daily Times*, June 21, 1852 and July 28, 1852; Edgar, *Partisans and Redcoats*, pp. 2–3; Hunt, *The Irish and the American Revolution*, pp. 26, 31.

56. Doyle, *Ireland, Irishmen and Revolutionary America*, pp. 111–137; O'Brien, *A Hidden Phase of American History*, p. 285; Edgar, *Partisans and Redcoats*, pp. 2–3; Murphy, *The Irish in the American Revolution*, pp. 59–64.

57. T. H. Breen, *The Marketplace of Revolution: How Consumer Politics Shaped American Independence* (New York: Oxford University Press, 2004), p. 1.

58. Lucey, *Harp and Sword*, p. 49; Hunt, *The Irish and the American Revolution*, p. 31; Fleming, *Washington's Secret War*, pp. 141, 285; Doyle, *Ireland, Irishmen and Revolutionary America*, pp. 109–148; Murphy, *The Irish in the American Revolution*, pp. 59–64.

59. Lucey, *Harp and Sword*, p. 28; Webb, *Born Fighting*, pp. 10–11; Edgar, *Partisans and Redcoats*, pp. 2–3; Hunt, *The Irish and the American Revolution*, pp. 26, 31; Doyle, *Ireland, Irishmen and Revolutionary America*, pp. 110–148; Fleming, *Washington's Secret War*, pp. 141, 285; Murphy, *The Irish in the American Revolution*, pp. 59–64.

60. Fleming, *Washington's Secret War*, pp. 141, 285; Edgar, *Partisans and Redcoats*, pp. 2–3; Hunt, *The Irish and the American Revolution*, pp. 26, 31; Doyle, *Ireland, Irishmen and Revolutionary America*, pp. 110–112.

61. Stuart Reid and Marko Zlatich, *Soldiers of the Revolutionary War* (Oxford: Osprey Publishing, 2002), p. 107; Hagist, *British Soldiers, American War*, pp. x–xi; Webb, *Born Fighting*, pp. 10–11; David Smith, *New York 1776: The Continentals' first battle* (Oxford: Osprey Publishing Ltd., 2008), pp. 21–22;

Hunt, *The Irish and the American Revolution*, p. 3; Don Troiani, *Military Buttons of the American Revolution* (Gettysburg, PA: Thomas Publications, 2001), pp. 31, 79; Hagist, *British Soldiers, American War*, pp. 248–249; Lalor, ed., *The Encyclopedia of Ireland*, p. 754; Holmes, *Redcoat*, pp. 59–63; Edgar, *Partisans and Redcoats*, pp. 2–3; Doyle, *Ireland, Irishmen and Revolutionary America*, pp. 109–151; Murphy, *The Irish in the American Revolution*, pp. 59–64; Westvaco Corp., editor, *A Young Patriot in the American Revolution* (New York: Westvaco Corporation, 1981), p. 57, note 12.

62. Fleming, *Washington's Secret War*, pp. 141, 285; Mike Chappell, *Wellington's Peninsula Regiments: The Irish* (Oxford: Osprey Publishing, 2003), p. 5; *New York Daily Times*, June 21, 1852.

63. Brumwell, *George Washington*, p. 252.

64. Holton, *Forced Founders*, p. 170.

65. Ibid.

66. Commander and Morris, eds., *The Spirit of 'Seventy-Six*, p. 910.

67. Ibid., p. 151.

68. Troiani, *Military Buttons of the American Revolution*, pp. viii, 5.

69. *New York Times*, May 20, 1927; *New York Daily Times*, June 21, 1852; Catherine Clinton and Michele Gillespie, editors, *The Devil's Lane: Sex and Race in the Early South* (New York: Oxford University Press, 1997), pp. 5, 142; Hunt, *The Irish and the American Revolution*, pp. 26, 31; Doyle, *Ireland, Irishmen and Revolutionary America*, pp. 110–112; Murphy, *The Irish in the American Revolution*, pp. 59–64; Thomas J. Fleming, *1776: Year of Illusions* (New York: W. W. Norton and Company, Inc., 1975), p. 456.

70. Holton, *Forced Founders*, p. 41.

71. William J. Clinton, *Public Papers of the Presidents of the United States, 1995: Book I, January 1 to June 30, 1995* (2 vols, Washington, DC: United States Government Printing Office, 1996), p. 371.

72. Fleming, *1776*, p. 442.

73. *Washington Post*, October 28, 1898.

Chapter V

1. Zinn, *A People's History of the United States*, p. 38; Hunt, *The Irish and the American Revolution*, pp. 62, 31; Doyle, *Ireland, Irishmen and Revolutionary America*, pp. ix, xv–xvi, 110–137.

2. Stephen Saunders Webb, *1676: The End of American Independence* (Syracuse, NY: Syracuse University Press, 1995), pp. xv–141; Doyle, *Ireland, Irishmen and Revolutionary America*, pp. xv–151; Zinn, *A People's History of the United States*, pp. 38–42; Raphael, *Founders*, pp. 20–21.

3. Gordon S. Wood, *The Creation of the American Republic, 1776-1787* (Chapel Hill: University of North Carolina Press, 1998), pp. 83–85; Fischer, *Liberty and Freedom*, pp. 61–67; Webb, *Born Fighting*, pp. 142–144; Joseph S. Foster, *In Pursuit of Equal Liberty: George Bryan and the Revolution in Pennsylvania* (University Park: Pennsylvania State University Press, 1994), pp. xi–118; Isaacson, *Benjamin Franklin*, pp. 275; Zinn, *A People's History of the United States*, p. 80; Smylie, *Scotch-Irish Presence in Pennsylvania*, pp. 20–22; James R. Gaines, *For Liberty and Glory: Washington, Lafayette, and Their Revolutions* (New York: W.W. Norton and Company, 2007), p. 30; Hunt, *The Irish and the American Revolution*, pp. 26, 31, 41; Doyle, *Ireland, Irishmen and Revolutionary America*, pp. 10–11, 114–115, 120; Lalor, ed., *The Encyclopedia of Ireland*, pp. 121–122; Raphael, *Founders*, pp. 20–21; Eric Montgomery, *The Scotch-Irish and Ulster* (Belfast: Ulster-Scot Historical Society, 1965), p. 25; Fleming, *1776*, pp. 94, 268; Southern, ed., *Voices of the American Revolution in the Carolinas*, pp. 15–19.

4. Raphael, *Founders*, pp. 20–23.

5. Raphael, *Founding Myths*, pp. 125–141; Smylie, *Scotch-Irish Presence in Pennsylvania*, p. 22; Doyle, *Ireland, Irishmen and Revolutionary America*, pp. ix, 92, 110–115, 123–137; Fleming, *1776*, pp. 94, 268.

6. Doyle, *Ireland, Irishmen and Revolutionary America*, pp. 111–137; Fleming, *1776*, pp. 94, 268.

7. Raphael, *Founders*, pp. 20–23; Fleming, *1776*, pp. 94, 268; Doyle, *Ireland, Irishmen and Revolutionary America*, pp. 10–11, 115, 118, 122–127.

8. Chastellux, *Travels in North-America*, p. 234.

9. Doyle, *Ireland, Irishmen and Revolutionary America*, pp. 10–11, 115, 118, 122–127; Clifford Alderman, *Colonists for Sale: The Story of Indentured Servants in America* (New York: Macmillan, 1975), pp. 165–167; Fleming, *1776*, pp. 94, 145, 268.

10. Raphael, *Founding Myths*, pp. 125–141; 206–207; Southern, ed., *Voices of the American Revolution in the Carolinas*, pp. 151–169; Dolan, *The Irish Americans*, p. 39; Dunkerly, *The Battle of Kings Mountain*, pp. 135–136.

11. Raphael, *Founding Myths*, pp. 135–141, 206–207; Stephenson, *Patriot Battles*, p. 323; Messick, *King's Mountain*, pp. 99–101.

12. Southern, ed., *Voices of the American Revolution in the Carolinas*, p. 152; Dunkerly, *The Battle of Kings Mountain*, pp. 135–136.

13. Doyle, *Ireland, Irishmen and Revolutionary America*, pp. 114–115.

14. Wood, *The Creation of the American Republic*, pp. 84–85; Foster, *In Pursuit of Equal Liberty*, pp. xi–118; Smylie, *Scotch-Irish Presence in Pennsylvania*, p. 20; Doyle, *Ireland, Irishmen and Revolutionary America*, pp. 114–137, 194; Fleming, *1776*, pp. 94, 145, 268.

15. Foster, *In Pursuit of Equal Liberty*, pp. 13, 17, 31–33, 35–42; Doyle, *Ireland, Irishmen and Revolutionary America*, p. 194.

16. Foster, *In Pursuit of Equal Liberty*, pp. 44–46; Smylie, *Scotch-Irish Presence in Pennsylvania*, p. 20; Raphael, *Founders*, pp. 20–23.

17. Foster, *In Pursuit of Equal Liberty*, pp. 61–86; Smylie, *Scotch-Irish Presence in* Pennsylvania, p. 20; Doyle, *Ireland, Irishmen and Revolutionary America*, pp. ix, 114–137.

18. Smylie, *Scotch-Irish of Pennsylvania*, p. 20; Doyle, *Ireland, Irishmen and Revolutionary America*, pp. 10–11, 114–115; Hunt, *The Irish and the American Revolution*, p. 41; Doyle, *Ireland, Irishmen and Revolutionary America*, pp. 10–11, 118–137.

19. Lawrence H. Leder, *The Colonial Legacy, Vol. 1: The Loyalist Historians* (New York: Harper Torch Books, 1971), pp. 67, 69.

20. Ibid., pp. 60, 67, 84; Doyle, *Ireland, Irishmen and Revolutionary America*, pp. 10–11; Hunt, *The Irish and the American Revolution*, p. 41.

21. Wood, *The Creation of the American Republic*, p. 85; Doyle, *Ireland, Irishmen and Revolutionary America*, pp. 114–115, 123–124.

22. Wood, *The Creation of the American Republic*, p. 86; Fischer, *Liberty and Freedom*, pp. 61–67; Webb, *Born Fighting*, pp. 9–173; Foster, *In Pursuit of Equal Liberty*, pp. 78–83; Christopher Dawson, *Dynamics of World History* (Wilmington, DE: ISI Books, 2002), p. 351; Clark, *The Irish in Pennsylvania*, p. 9; Norman F. Cantor, *Alexander the Great: Journey to the End of the Earth* (New York: Harper Perennial, 2005), pp. 5, 15–17; John Buchanan, *Jackson's Way: Andrew Jackson and the People of the Western Waters* (New York: John Wiley and Sons, Inc., 2001), pp. 2–5; Brent D. Shaw, editor and translator, *Spartacus and the Slave Wars: A Brief History with Documents* (New York: St. Martin's, 2001), pp. 33–63; Hunt, *The Irish and the American Revolution*, pp. 26, 31, 41; Doyle, *Ireland, Irishmen*

and Revolutionary America, pp. ix, 10–11, 114–115, 123–137; Lalor, ed., *The Encyclopedia of Ireland*, pp. 121–122; Southern, ed., *Voices of the American Revolution in the Carolinas*, pp. 3–15.

23. Wood, *The Creation of the American Republic*, p. 87; Hunt, *The Irish and the American Revolution*, p. 41; Dolan, *The Irish Americans*, p. 39; Doyle, *Ireland, Irishmen and Revolutionary America*, pp. 10–11, 114–137.

24. Wood, *The Creation of the American Republic*, p. 88.

25. Ibid., pp. 88–89.

26. Foster, *In the Pursuit of Equal Liberty*, pp. 107–115; Doyle, *Ireland, Irishmen and Revolutionary America*, pp. ix, xv–xvi, 114–115.

27. Foster, *In the Pursuit of Equal Liberty*, p. 159.

28. Doyle, *Ireland, Irishmen and Revolutionary America*, pp. 10–11, 114–115, 118, 123, 132; Hunt, *The Irish and the American Revolution*, p. 41; Walters, *John Haslet*, pp. vi, 2, 43–45, 78, 111–119, 130–205.

29. Harlow Giles Unger, *Lion of Liberty: Patrick Henry and the Call to a New Nation* (New York: Da Capo Press, 2010), pp. 1–46.

30. Fleming, *1776*, pp. 135–145; Wikipedia contributors, "William Smith (South Carolina representative)," Wikipedia, The Free Encyclopedia, https://en.wikipedia.org/w/index.php?title=William_Smith_(South_Carolina_representative)&oldid=660404653 (accessed May 22, 2008).

31. Walters, *John Haslet*, p. v; Murphy, *The Irish in the American Revolution*, pp. 59–64.

32. Smylie, *Scotch-Irish Presence in Pennsylvania*, p. 24; Raphael, *Founding Myths*, pp. 107–124; Doyle, *Ireland, Irishmen and Revolutionary America*, pp. 114–115, 131; Murphy, *The Irish in the American Revolution*, pp. 15–64.

33. Doyle, *Ireland, Irishmen and Revolutionary America*, pp. 131–132.

34. Fleming, *Washington's Secret War*, pp. 141, 285; Webb, *Born Fighting*, pp. 10–11.

35. R. F. Foster, editor, *The Oxford History of Ireland* (Oxford: Oxford University Press, 1992), pp. 76–148; Seamas Mac Annaidh, *Irish History* (Bath, England: Parragon Publishing, 2005), pp. 70–133; MacManus, *The Story of the Irish Race*, pp. 319–469; Fintan O'Toole, *White Savage: William Johnson and the Invention of America* (New York: Farrar, Straus and Giroux, 2005), pp. 17, 22l; Fleming, *Liberty!*, pp. 47, 49; Reid, *In a Defiant Stance*, pp. 12–15; Webb, *Born Fighting*, pp. 9–173; Wikipedia contributors, "Fenian," Wikipedia, The Free Encyclopedia, https://en.wikipedia.org/w/index.php?title=Fenian&oldid=665432282

(accessed July 6, 2008); Hunt, *The Irish and the American Revolution*, pp. vii–viii, 41; Wylie, *The Irish General*, pp. 12–16; Dungan, *Distant Drums*, p. 4.

36. Isaccson, *Benjamin Franklin*, pp. 247, 251.

37. Herbert Asbury, *The Gangs of New York: An Informal History of the Underworld* (New York: Thunder's Mouth Press, 1998), p. 26; Webb, *Born Fighting*, p. 160; Hunt, *The Irish and the American Revolution*, pp. 3, 41; Doyle, *Ireland, Irishmen and Revolutionary America*, pp. 10–11, 111–137.

38. Reid, *In a Defiant Stance*, pp. 12–15; Fleming, *Liberty!*, pp. 47, 49, 262; Webb, *Born Fighting*, pp. 9–173; Hunt, *The Irish and the American Revolution*, p. 3; Doyle, *Ireland, Irishmen and Revolutionary America*, pp. 114–115; Murphy, *The Irish in the American Revolution*, pp. 59–64.

39. Fleming, *Washington's Secret War*, pp. 141, 285; Lucey, *Harp and Sword*, pp. 4–8; O'Brien, *A Hidden Phase of American History*, pp. 21, 98–117; Webb, *Born Fighting*, pp. 9–173; Miller, Schrier, Boling, and Doyle, eds., *Irish Immigrants in the Land of Canaan*, pp. 25–26; Reid, *In a Defiant Stance*, pp. 12–15; Fleming, *Liberty!*, pp. 47, 49, 262; Webb, *Born Fighting*, pp. 9–173; Hunt, *The Irish and the American Revolution*, pp. vii–3; Tonsetic, *1781*, p. 11; Doyle, *Ireland, Irishmen and Revolutionary America*, pp. 3, 114–115; Murphy, *The Irish in the American Revolution*, pp. 59–64.

40. McWhiney, *Cracker Culture*, p. xxxi; Fischer, *Liberty and Freedom*, pp. 61–67; Isaacson, *Benjamin Franklin*, pp. 249, 275; Murphy, *The Irish in the American Revolution*, pp. 59–64.

41. Stephens, *Neither the Charm Nor the Luck*, p. 27.

42. Haltigan, *The Irish in the American Revolution and Their Early Influence in the Colonies*, p. 14, 207–213; Barthelmas, *The Signers of the Declaration of Independence*, pp. 3, 262–266; Foster, *In Pursuit of Equal Liberty*, pp. 35, 43, 72–73, 102; Smylie, *Scotch-Irish Presence in Pennsylvania*, pp. 15, 23; Edgar, *Partisans and Redcoats*, pp. 2–3; Doyle, *Ireland, Irishmen and Revolutionary America*, pp. 114–115; Alderman, *Colonists For Sale*, pp. 165–167; Nutting, *Ireland Beautiful*, pp. 29, 59–62; Murphy, *The Irish in the American Revolution*, pp. 59–64; Dolan, *The Irish Americans*, pp. 25–26, 31; Boatner, *Encyclopedia of the American Revolution*, p. 409; Brumwell, *George Washington*, pp. 384–385; Messick, *King's Mountain*, pp. 105–106.

43. Barthelmas, *The Signers of the Declaration of Independence*, pp. 3–4.

44. Ibid., p. 263.

45. Foster, *In Pursuit of Equal Liberty*, p. 102; Boatner, *Encyclopedia of the American Revolution*, pp. 925–926.

46. Hagist, *British Soldiers, American War*, pp. 248–249; John T. Goolrick, *The Life of General Hugh Mercer* (New York: The Neale Publishing Company, 1906), pp. 11–75; Joseph M. Waterman, *With Sword and Lancet: The Life of General Hugh Mercer* (Richmond, VA: Garrett and Massie Incorporated, 1941), pp. 1–160; Herman, *How the Scots Invented the Modern World*, pp. 15–153; Fleming, *Liberty!*, p. 223; Boatner, *Encyclopedia of the American Revolution*, pp. 493–494; Fred Anderson, *Crucible of War: The Seven Years' War and the Fate of the Empire in British North America, 1754–1766* (New York: Vintage Books, 2000), pp. 67–68; Michael Fry, *How the Scots Made America* (New York: St. Martin's Press, 2004), pp. 2–20; Walters, *John Haslet*, pp. 3, 11–18; Rose, *Washington's War*, p. 84; Doyle, *Ireland, Irishmen and Revolutionary America*, pp. 92, 114–115; Frederick English, *General Hugh Mercer: Forgotten Hero of the American Revolution* (Lawrenceville, NJ: Princeton Academic Press, 1975), pp. 1–103; Varnum Lansing Collins, *A Brief Narrative of the Ravages of the British and Hessians at Princeton in 1776–1777: A Contemporary Account of the Battles of Trenton and Princeton* (Princeton, NJ: The University Library, 1906), p. 38.

47. Mike Cronin and Daryl Adair, *The Wearing of the Green: A History of St. Patrick's Day* (New York: Routledge, 2002), pp. xiii, xxix, 11; *New York Gazette and Weekly Mercury*, New York, New York, April 24, 1780; Alfred Hoyt Bill, *Valley Forge: The Making of An Army* (New York: Harper and Brothers, 1952), pp. 112–113.

48. Ibid., p. 11.

49. Draper, *King's Mountain and Its Heroes*, p. 87; Buchanan, *Jackson's Way*, pp. 2–5.

50. Draper, *King's Mountain and Its Heroes*, pp. 86–87.

51. Ibid., pp. 145–146

52. Ibid., p. 146.

53. *Maryland Gazette*, October 17, 1776.

Chapter VI

1. Walters, *John Haslet*, pp. v–379; Rodney, "Diary of Captain Thomas Rodney," Papers of the Historical Society of Delaware, pp. 34, 52; Fleming, *Liberty!*, pp. 223–224; Boatner, *Encyclopedia of the American Revolution*, pp. 493–494; Troiani, *Military Buttons of the American Revolution*, pp. 111–112.

2. Fleming, *Liberty!*, p. 224.

3. Rodney, "Diary of Captain Thomas Rodney," Papers of the Historical Society of Delaware, pp. 43–44.

4. Colonel John Haslet to Caesar Rodney, October 5, 1776, American Archives, Documents of the American Revolution, 1774–1776, Northern University Libraries, DeKalb, Illinois.

5. Walters, *John Haslet*, pp. 206–207; Collins, *A Brief Narrative of the Ravages of the British and Hessians at Princeton in 1776–1777*, p. 35, note 1; Elisha Bostwick Memoir, Yale University Library, Manuscripts and Archives, Yale University, New Haven Connecticut.

6. Walters, *John Haslet*, p. 381; "Ancestors and Relatives of William L. Hinds' Grandchildren," Rootsweb, Ancestory.com, wc.rootsweb.ancestry.com/cgi-bin/igm.cgi?db=GET&db=killion&id=142945 accessed January 10, 2003.

7. Colonel John Haslet to Caesar Rodney, October 5, 1776, American Archives, Documents of the American Revolution, 1774–1776, Northern University Libraries, DeKalb, Illinois.

8. Walters, *John Haslet*, pp. 10, 383.

9. Martin I. J. Griffin, *Catholics in the American Revolution*, vol. 2 (Reprint, Philadelphia: published by author, 1909), p. 375.

10. Ibid., p. 283; *American Daily Advertiser*, Philadelphia, Pennsylvania, April 6, 1835; Brumwell, *George Washington*, pp. 199, 238; Hunt, *The Irish and the American Revolution*, pp. 26, 31; Murphy, *The Irish in the American Revolution*, pp. 59–64; Dolan, *The Irish Americans*, p. 25; Stephens, *Neither the Charm Nor the Luck*, pp. 1–3, 27–31; Donald N. Moran, "George Washington's Military Family," Liberty Tree Newsletter, December 1998, Newsletter of the Sons of Liberty Chapter of the Sons of the American Revolution, Louisville, Kentucky.

11. Lucey, *Harp and Sword*, pp. 18–49; Burt Garfield Loescher, *Washington's Eyes: The Continental Light Dragoons* (Fort Collins, CO: The Old Army Press, 1977), pp. 97–120, 134–137; Brumwell, *George Washington*, pp. 277–279; O'Brien, *A Hidden Phase of American History*, pp. 210–240; Fleming, *Liberty!*, p. 262; Fleming, *Washington's Secret War*, pp. 141, 285; Raphael, *Founding Myths*, p. 127; Mark Puls, *Henry Knox: Visionary General of the American Revolution* (New York: Palgrave MacMillan, 2008), p. 2; Rose, *Washington's War*, p. 146; Hunt, *The Irish and the American Revolution*, pp. 26, 31.

12. McGuire, *Battle of Paoli*, pp. 17–18; Tonsetic, *1781*, pp. 16–17; Hunt, *The Irish and the American Revolution*, p. 7.

13. Tonsetic, *1781*, pp. 16–17.
14. Ibid., p. 16.
15. Ibid., p. 17; Brumwell, *George Washington*, pp. 328–329, 341; Fleming, *Liberty!*, p. 262; Glenn Tucker, *Mad Anthony Wayne and the New Nation: The Story of Washington's Front-Line General* (Harrisburg, PA: Stackpole Books, 1973), pp.13, 20.
16. Tucker, *Mad Anthony Wayne and the New Nation*, p. 13.
17. Brumwell, *George Washington*, pp. 276–283; Rose, *Washington's War*, p. 146.
18. McGuire, *Battle of Paoli*, pp.129–130.
19. Ibid., p. 133.
20. Tonsetic, *1781*, p. 16.
21. McGuire, *Battle of Paoli*, pp. 142, 146, 155, 167–174, 204–205.
22. Ibid., pp. 170–171.
23. Ibid., p. 171.
24. Ibid., p. 174.
25. Tucker, *Mad Anthony Wayne*, pp. 143–163; Brumwell, *George Washington*, pp. 328–329, 350, 399; Hunt, *The Irish in the American Revolution*, p. 63; Lalor, ed., *The Encyclopedia of Ireland*, pp. 588–589; Boatner, *Encyclopedia of the American Revolution*, pp. 1062–1067, 1156; Trussell, *The Pennsylvania Line*, p. 117; Bruce E. Burgoyne, compiled, edited, and introduction, *Enemy Views, The American Revolutionary War as Recorded by Hessian Participants* (Bowie, MD: Heritage Books, 1996), p. 329; Tonsetic, *1781*, p. 226; Lengel, *This Glorious Struggle*, pp. 183–185, 188–189.
26. Brumwell, *George Washington*, p. 350.
27. Henry Lee, *The American Revolution in the South* (New York: Arno Press, 1969), p. 20.
28. Brumwell, *George Washington*, pp. 340, 350
29. Chastellux, *Travels in North-America*, pp. 71–72.
30. William Heath, *Memoirs of Major-General William Heath by Himself* (New York: William Abbatt, 1901), p. 193.
31. Brumwell, *George Washington*, pp. 350–351.
32. Boatner, *Encyclopedia of the American Revolution*, p. 1066.
33. Brumwell, *George Washington*, pp. 350–351.
34. Boatner, *Encyclopedia of the American Revolution*, pp. 1070; Gerald Lyne, "Background of the Irish Family of Major General John Sullivan," Paper Presented at the O'Sullivan/Sullivan Seminar, Florida Historical Society,

Melbourne, Florida, February 1994; Lalor, ed., *The Encyclopedia of Ireland*, pp. 474, 630–631; Carolly Erickson, *Bonnie Prince Charlie* (New York: William Morrow and Company, 1989), pp. 1–195.

35. Michael Grant, *The Fall of the Roman Empire* (New York: Barnes and Noble, 2005), pp. 39–44; O'Toole, *The Lie of the Land*, pp. 21–23; Lyne, General Sullivan, His Irish Family Background; Bobrick, *Angel in the Whirlwind*, pp. 231–232; Haltigan, *The Irish in the American Revolution and Their Early Influence in the Colonies*, p. 69; Clark, *All Cloudless Glory*, pp. 222, 301; Hunt, *The Irish and the American Revolution*, pp. 24–26, 31; Fleming, *1776*, p. 225; Stephens, *Neither the Charm Nor the Luck*, pp. 1–2.

36. James McMichael, "Diary of Lieutenant James McMichael, of the Pennsylvania Line, 1776–1778," *The Pennsylvania Magazine of History and Biography*, vol. XVL, no. 2 (1892), pp. 140, 150.

37. *New York Times*, December 27, 1880.

38. Ibid.

39. Hagist, *British Soldiers, American War*, p. 45.

40. Grant, *The Fall of the Roman Empire*, pp. 37–38.

41. Tucker, *Mad Anthony Wayne and the New Nation*, 13; Stille, *Major-General Anthony Wayne and the Pennsylvania Line in the Continental Army*, pp. 2–4; Haltigan, *The Irish in the American Revolution*, pp. 213–214; Boatner, *Encyclopedia of the American Revolution*, pp. 1070–1071; Tucker, *Mad Anthony Wayne and the New Nation*, pp. 11–14; Tonsetic, *1781*, p. 11; Stephenson, *Patriot Battles*, pp. 3–35.

42. Lucey, *Harp and Sword*, foreword.

43. "Colonel Walter Stewart." National Park Service. Accessed March 15, 2013. http://www.nps.gov/yonb/learn/historyculture/stewartbio.htm.

44. Shelton, *General Richard Montgomery and the American Revolution*, pp. 2–174; Brendan Morrissey, *Quebec 1775: The American Invasion of Canada* (Oxford: Osprey Books, 2003), pp. 7–62; Fleming, *Liberty!*, pp. 153–158; Thomas A. Desjardin, *Through a Howling Wilderness: Benedict Arnold's March to Quebec, 1775* (New York: St. Martin's Press, 2007), pp. 6, 119–185, 203; Nancy Isenberg, *Fallen Founder: The Life of Aaron Burr* (New York: Penguin Books, 2007), pp. 13, 24–28; Lengel, *This Glorious Struggle*, p. 34; Chastellux, *Travels in North-America*, p. 385, note; Charles Royster, *A Revolutionary People at War: The Continental Army and American Character, 1775–1783* (New York: W.W. Norton and Company, 1996), pp. 120–123.

45. Desjardin, *Through a Howling Wilderness*, p. 158.

46. Isenberg, *Fallen Founder*, p. 27.

47. Fleming, *Liberty!*, p. 158; Michael Cecere, *An Officer of Very Extraordinary Merit: Charles Porterfield and the American War for Independence* (Westminister, MD: Heritage Books, Inc., 2004), pp. 13–14, 19–30; Desjardin, *Through a Howling Wilderness*, pp. 18–19, 50–51, 55, 94, 170–185; Peter Green, *Alexander the Great* (New York: Praeger Publishers, 1970), pp. 228–229; Graham, *The Life of General Daniel Morgan*, pp. 63–108, 464–466.

48. Jean Edward Smith, *John Marshall: Definer of a Nation* (New York: Henry Holt and Company, Inc., 1996), p. 52; Graham, *The Life of General Daniel Morgan*, p. 228.

49. Chastellux, *Travels in North-America*, pp. 235–237.

50. Desjardin, *Through a Howling Wilderness*, p. 202.

51. Ivor Noel Hume, *Martin's Hundred: The Discovery of a Lost Colonial Virginia Settlement* (New York: Dell Publishing Company, 1982), p. 235.

52. Graham, *The Life of General Daniel Morgan*, pp. 84–88, 98–99, 106–108.

53. Ibid., p. 467.

54. Richard B. LaCrosse Jr., *Revolutionary Rangers: Daniel Morgan's Riflemen and Their Role on the Northern Frontier* (Bowie, MD: Heritage Books, Inc., 2002), pp. 4–10; Smith, *John Marshall*, pp. 41, 45–46; Cecere, *An Officer of Very Extraordinary Merit*, pp. 2–4; Graham, *The Life of General Daniel Morgan*, pp. 53–55, 464.

55. LaCrosse Jr., *Revolutionary Rangers*, pp. 9–10, 86, 189; Robert K. Wright, *The Continental Army* (Washington, DC, United States Government Printing Office, 1983), pp. 289–290; Graham, *The Life of General Daniel Morgan*, pp. 116–123.

56. Smith, *John Marshall*, pp. 21–23, 44–53, 67; Michael Cecere, *They Behaved Like Soldiers: Captain John Chilton and the Third Virginia Infantry, 1775–1778* (Bowie, MD: Heritage Books, 2006), pp. 2–3.

57. Cecere, *They Behaved Like Soldiers*, pp. 6–7, 26, 45, 53, 64, 103–104.

58. Cecere, *An Officer of Very Extraordinary Merit*, pp. 35–46; Graham, *The Life of General Daniel Morgan*, pp. 124–132.

59. LaCrosse Jr., *Revolutionary Rangers*, pp. 79, 190; Chris Kyle with William Doyle, *American Gun: A History of the U.S. in Ten Firearms* (New York: William Morrow, 2013), pp. 1–12; Fleming, *Liberty!*, pp. 259, 262; Boatner, *Encyclopedia of the American Revolution*, pp. 397, 754–755; Webb, *Born Fighting*, pp. 11, 229; Hagist, *A British Soldier's Story*, p. 53;

Thacher, *Military Journal During the American Revolutionary War From 1775 to 1783*, p. 103; Trussell, *The Pennsylvania Line*, pp. 27, 34; Brendan Morrissey, *Saratoga 1777: Turning Point of a Revolution* (London: Osprey Publishing Limited, 2000), pp. 76–77, 80; Graham, *The Life of General Daniel Morgan*, pp. 140–175; Rose, *Washington's War*, p. 128; Charles F. Haywood, *Minutemen and Mariners: True Tales of New England* (New York: Dodd, Mead and Company, 1963), pp. 76–88; Brumwell, *George Washington*, pp. 312–313.

60. Thomas J. Fleming, *"Downright Fighting:" The Story of Cowpens* (Washington, DC: United States Government Printing Office, 1988), p. 60; Bass, *Gamecock*, p. 75.

61. Southern, ed., *Voices of the American Revolution in the Carolinas*, p. 88.

62. Draper, *King's Mountain and Its Heroes*, p. 303.

63. Swisher, *The Revolutionary War in the Southern Back Country*, pp. 184–188.

64. Dunkerly, *The Battle of Kings Mountain*, p. 34; Draper, *King's Mountain and Its Heroes*, p. 232

65. John Copeland, Federal Pension Application (S30966), Revolutionary War Record, National Archives, Washington, DC.

66. Bass, *Gamecock*, p. 89.

67. Smith, *John Marshall*, p. 52; Graham, *The Life of General Daniel Morgan*, pp. 140–175.

68. Graham, *The Life of General Daniel Morgan*, pp. 140–175; Hagist, *British Soldiers, American War*, p. 63.

69. Hagist, *British Soldiers, American War*, pp. 63., 69; Lalor, ed., *The Encyclopedia of Ireland*, p. 97.

70. O'Brien, *A Hidden Phase of American History*, pp. 210–240; Lucey, *Harp and Sword*, pp. 4–50; Michel Williams Craig, *General Edward Hand: Winter's Doctor* (Lancaster, PA: Lancaster County Foundation, 1984), pp. 1–111; Boatner, *Encyclopedia of the American Revolution*, pp. 244–245, 484–485, 725–727; Stuart Gerry Brown, editor, *The Autobiography of James Monroe* (Syracuse, NY: Syracuse University Press, 1959), pp. 25–26; Edward Hand, *The Unpublished Revolutionary Papers of Major-General Edward Hand of Pennsylvania, 1777–1784* (New York: George H. Richmond, 1907), pp. 7–8.

71. Craig, *General Edward Hand*, p. 37.

72. Tucker, *George Washington's Surprise Attack*, p. 461.

73. Boyle, *From Redcoat to Rebel*, p. 49; Brumwell, *George Washington*, pp. 222–224; Boatner, *Encyclopedia of the American Revolution*, pp. 484–485; Tucker, *George Washington's Surprise Attack*, p. 461; Rose, *Washington's War*, p. 86.

74. Brumwell, *George Washington*, p. 255; Clark, *All Cloudless Glory*, p. 290.

75. Craig, *General Edward Hand*, pp. 41–45; Boatner, *Encyclopedia of the American Revolution*, p. 911; Tucker, *George Washington's Surprise Attack*, pp. 271–415.

76. *Daily Intelligencer*, Lancaster, Pennsylvania, September 25, 1886; Brumwell, *George Washington*, pp. 306–307; Hagist, *British Soldiers, American War*, p. 28.

77. Dungan, *Distant Drums*, p. 5.

78. Trussell, *The Pennsylvania Line*, pp. 15–16, 71; Clement, *Philadelphia 1777*, p. 17; Cook, *Journals of the Military Expedition of Major General John Sullivan, 1779*, pp, 5–279; Hand, *The Unpublished Revolutionary Papers of Major-General Edward Hand of Pennsylvania, 1777–1784*, pp. 11, 23–24.

79. Trussell, *The Pennsylvania Line*, p. 159; Raphael, *Founding Myths*, pp. 236–237; Robert A. Mayers, *The War Man: The True Story of a Citizen Soldier Who Fought from Quebec to Yorktown* (Yardley, PA: Westholme Publishing, 2009), pp. 107–122; Cook, *Journals of the Military Expedition of Major General John Sullivan, 1779*, pp. 5–279; Wikipedia contributors, "James Potter," Wikipedia, The Free Encyclopedia, https://en.wikipedia.org/w/index.php?title=James_Potter&oldid=666425729 accessed November 15, 2009; Benjamin M. Nead, "A Sketch of General Thomas Proctor," *Pennsylvania Magazine of History and Biography*, vol. 4, no. 4 (1880), p. 454; Griffin, *Catholics and the American Revolution*, vol. 2, p. 201; Savas and Dameron, *The New American Revolution Handbook*, p. 12.

80. Brumwell, *George Washington*, pp. 353–354.

81. Ibid., pp. 353; Lengel, ed., *This Glorious Struggle*, p. 189; Mayers, *The War Man*, pp. 117–118; Cook, *Journals of the Military Expedition of Major General John Sullivan, 1779*, pp. 5–279; Stephens, *Neither the Charm Nor the Luck*, pp. 97–114.

82. Brumwell, *George Washington*, pp. 17–18.

83. Ibid., p. 18.

84. E. A. Cruikshank, *The Story of Butler's Rangers and the Settlement of Niagara* (Welland, Canada: Tribune Printing House, 1893), pp. 11–12, 31–35; Lalor, ed., *The Encyclopedia of Ireland*, pp. 842–843.

85. Brumwell, *George Washington*, p. 355.

86. Ibid.

87. Foster, *In Pursuit of Equal Liberty*, pp. 44, 98–100; Brumwell, *George Washington*, pp. 351, 353–355.

88. Trussell, *The Pennsylvania Line*, p. 162; Clement, *Philadelphia 1777*, p. 17; Boatner, *Encyclopedia of the American Revolution*, pp. 1072–1076; Mayers, *The War Man*, pp. 107–122, 225–226; Cook, *Journals of the Military Expedition of Major General John Sullivan, 1779*, pp. 5–279; Peter Meyler and David Meyler, *A Stolen Life: Searching For Richard Pierpoint* (Toronto: Natural Heritage Books, 1999), p. 54; Lalor, ed., *The Encyclopedia of Ireland*, pp. 1022–1023.

89. Cook, *Journals of the Military Expedition of Major General John Sullivan 1779*, pp. 5–279; Brumwell, *George Washington*, pp. 351, 354–355.

90. Draper, *King's Mountain and Its Heroes*, p. 405.

91. Lucey, *Harp and Sword*, pp. 4–50; O'Brien, *A Hidden Phase of American History*, pp. 228–230; Boatner, *Encyclopedia of the American Revolution*, pp. 276–277, 432–433, 449–450, 508–509, 686–689, 1059–1060, 1098–1099; Fleming, *Washington's Secret War*, pp. 6, 19, 29; Tucker, *Mad Anthony Wayne and the New Nation*, pp. 11–14, 20–21; Brumwell, *George Washington*, pp. 78–82; Fleming, *Liberty!*, pp. 158, 246–249; Wright, *The Continental Army*, pp. 255–256; Cecere, *An Officer of Very Extraordinary Merit*, pp. 55–56, 58, 64–65, 66–67, 79–80; Christopher Andrew, *For the President's Eyes Only: Secret Intelligence and the American Presidency from Washington to Bush* (New York: Harper Collins Publishers, 1995), pp. 6–9; Moran, "George Washington's Military Family," LTN, Edward Lengel, *General George Washington: A Military Life* (New York: Random House, 2005), p. 214; Hunt, *The Irish and the American Revolution*, pp. 24–26, 31, 75–76, 92–93; Cook, *Journals of the Military Expedition of Major General John Sullivan, 1779*, pp. 5–279; Fleming, *1776*, pp. 155, 222; James Potter, Wikipedia; Willard Sterne Randall, *Alexander Hamilton: A Life* (New York: HarperCollins Publishers, 2003), pp. 9, 123–124, 128–133, 185–187.

92. Chastellux, *Travels in North-America*, p. 71; Lalor, ed., *The Encyclopedia of Ireland*, p. 1137.

93. Graham, *The Life of General Daniel Morgan*, pp. 124–129.

94. Lengel, *This Glorious Struggle*, p. 156; Brumwell, *George Washington*, pp. 340–342.

95. Ibid.

96. Brumwell, *George Washington*, pp. 340–344.

97. Ibid., p. 344.

98. Brumwell, *George Washington*, pp. 340–341; Tucker, *Mad Anthony Wayne and the New Nation*, p. 35; Fleming, *Washington's Secret War*, p. 22; McWhiney and Jamieson, *Attack and Die*, pp. 172–191; Barlett and Jeffrey, *A Military History of Ireland*, pp. 13–16.

99. Hagist, *British Soldiers*, p. 28.

100. Brumwell, *George Washington*, pp. 340–341; Tucker, *Mad Anthony Wayne*, pp. 55–163; Stille, *Major-General Anthony Wayne and the Pennsylvania Line of the Continental Army*, p. 54; Bartlett and Jeffrey, *A Military History of Ireland*, pp. 13–16; McWhiney and Jamieson, *Attack and Die*, pp. 172–191; Clark, *All Cloudless Glory*, pp. 239–241.

101. Tonsetic, *1781*, p. 11; Fleming, *Liberty!*, p. 262.

102. Stille, *Major-General Anthony Wayne and the Pennsylvania Line of the Continental Army*, p. 42.

103. Francis Johnston Obituary, *Poulson's American Daily Advertiser*, Philadelphia, Pennsylvania, February 28, 1815; Tonsetic, *1781*, p. 11; Fleming, *Liberty!*, p. 262.

104. Johnston Obituary, *Poulson's American Daily Advertiser*, February 28, 1815; Stille, *Major-General Anthony Wayne and the Pennsylvania Line of the Continental Army*, p. 43; Francis Johnston Obituary, *Columbian Centinel*, Boston, Massachusetts, March 4, 1815.

105. Fleming, *Liberty!*, p. 262; Tonsetic, *1781*, p. 11; Murphy, *The Irish in the American Revolution*, pp. 1–64; Dolan, *The Irish Americans*, p. 22.

106. Nutting, *Ireland Beautiful*, p. 62.

107. Dolan, *The Irish Americans*, p. 303; Fleming, *Liberty!*, p. 262; Stille, *Major-General Anthony Wayne and the Pennsylvania Line of the Continental Army*, p. 36.

108. Brumwell, *George Washington*, pp. 215–216; Nutting, *Ireland Beautiful*, pp. 60–62; Fleming, *Liberty!*, pp. 153–154, 164–165, 314–316; Boatner, *Encyclopedia of the American Revolution*, pp. 586–588, 735–736; Fleming, *Washington's Secret War*, p. 238; Clark, *All Cloudless Glory*, pp. 238–239; Puls, *Henry Knox*, pp. 2–43; Murphy, *The Irish in the American Revolution*, pp. 49–65.

109. David McCullough, *1776* (New York: Simon and Schuster, 2005), p. 111.

110. Fleming, *Washington's Secret War*, pp. 141, 285; Murphy, *The Irish in the American Revolution*, pp. 49–54; Dolan, *The Irish Americans*, p. 22.

111. Puls, *Henry Knox*, pp. 45–46.

112. Ibid., pp. 47–78; Chadwick, *George Washington's War*, pp. 13–16; Griffin, *Catholics and the American Revolution*, vol. 2, pp. 201–202; Hunt, *The Irish and the American Revolution*, pp. 24–25, 52–53.

113. Chadwick, *George Washington's War*, p. 36; Fleming, *Washington's Secret War*, pp. 141, 285; Hunt, *The Irish and the American Revolution*, pp. 22–26; Murphy, *The Irish in the American Revolution*, pp. 59–64.

114. Draper, *King's Mountain and Its Heroes*, pp. 260–261.

115. Fleming, *Washington's Secret War*, pp. 141, 285; Fischer, *Liberty and Freedom*, p. 115; Murphy, *The Irish in the American Revolution*, pp. 59–64.

116. Puls, *Henry Knox*, p. 61.

117. Savas and Dameron, *The New American Revolution Handbook*, p. 5.

118. Morrissey, *Saratoga 1777*, p. 14; Hunt, *The Irish and the American Revolution*, pp. 26, 31; Ben Z. Rose, *John Stark: Maverick General* (Waverley, MA: TreeLine Press, 2007), pp. xi–160.

119. Thomas J. Fleming, *Now We Are Enemies: The Story of Bunker Hill* (New York: St. Martin's Press, 1960), pp. 208–209; Boatner, *Encyclopedia of the American Revolution*, pp. 1052–1053; Henry Whittemore, *The Heroes of the American Revolution and Their Descendants: Battle of Long Island* (Salem, MA: Higginson Book Company, n.d.), pp. 42–43; Gary Zaboly, *American Colonial Ranger: The Northern Colonies 1724–64* (Oxford: Osprey Publishing Ltd., 2004), pp. 9, 12; Stephen Brumwell, *White Devil: A True Story of War, Savagery, and Vengeance in Colonial America* (New York: Da Capo Books, 2006), pp. 11–131, 277.

120. Fleming, *Now We Are Enemies*, pp. 208–209, 249; Fleming, *Liberty!*, p. 138; Boatner, *Encyclopedia of the American Revolution*, pp. 1052–1053; John R. Cuneo, *Robert Rogers of the Rangers* (New York: Richardson & Steirman, 1987), pp. 18, 34, 45–46, 50, 52–53, 61–62, 65, 79; Whittemore, *The Heroes of the American Revolution and Their Descendants*, p. 43; Rose, *John Stark*, pp. xii, 52–65.

121. Whittemore, *The Heroes of the American Revolution and Their Descendants*, p. 45; Boatner, *Encyclopedia of the American Revolution*, pp. 69–76, 635–636,1052–1053; Fleming, *Liberty!*, pp. 246–249; Wright, *The Continental Army*, p. 197; Morrissey, *Saratoga 1777*, pp. 49–52; Rose, *Washington's War*, pp. 113–114; Rose, *John Stark*, pp. xi—160; Savas and Dameron, *The New American Revolution Handbook*, p. 3.

122. Boatner, *Encyclopedia of the American Revolution*, p. 69–76; Morrissey, *Saratoga 1777*, pp. 52–53.

123. William L. Stone, translator, *Letters of Brunswick and Hessian Officers During the American Revolution* (Cranbury, NJ: Scholar's Bookshelf, 2005), pp. 100–101; Lalor, ed., *The Encyclopedia of Ireland*, p. 1159.

124. Bobrick, *Angel in the Whirlwind*, pp. 260–261.

125. Whittemore, *The Heroes of the American Revolution and Their Descendants*, p. 45.

126. Morrissey, *Saratoga 1777*, p. 14.

127. Rose, *Washington's War*, p. 132.

128. Lengel, *This Glorious Struggle*, p. 107.

129. Brumwell, *George Washington*, p. 410.

130. Draper, *King's Mountain and Its Heroes*, pp. 148–149.

131. Robert W. Black, *Ranger Dawn: The American Ranger from the Colonial Era to the Mexican War* (Mechanicsburg, PA: Stackpole Books, 2009), pp. 62–63, 78.

132. *Maryland Gazette*, October 31, 1776; Brumwell, *George Washington*, pp. 329–330; Barthelmas, *The Signers of the Declaration of Independence*, pp. 38–40.

133. Brumwell, *George Washington*, p. 330.

134. Gaines, *For Liberty and Glory*, pp. 78–92, 100; Brumwell, *George Washington*, pp. 331–333; Lawrence S. Kaplan, *Alexander Hamilton: Ambivalent Anglophile* (Wilmington, DE: Rowman & Littlefield Publishers, 2002), p. 2; Hunt, *The Irish and the American Revolution*, p. 101; Boatner, *Encyclopedia of the American Revolution*, pp. 276–279, 925; Fleming, *Washington's Secret War*, pp. 90, 93, 96–97, 120–125; Lalor, ed., *The Encyclopedia of Ireland*, p. 324; Thacher, *Military Journal During the American Revolutionary War From 1775 to 1783*, pp. 457–458; Trussell, *The Pennsylvania Line*, p. 9; Graham, *The Life of General Daniel Morgan*, pp. 172–173; Moran, "George Washington's Military Family," *LTN*; Randall, *Alexander Hamilton*, pp. 139–140; Tonsetic, *1781*, p. 11; Rose, *Washington's War*, p. 131; Piecuch, *Cavalry of the American Revolution*, pp. 4–5; Tim McGrath, *John Barry: An American Hero in the Age of Sail* (Yardley, PA: Westholme Publishing, 2011), p. 106.

135. Lengel, *This Glorious Struggle*, pp. 112–114; Boatner, *Encyclopedia of the American Revolution*, pp. 767–768.

136. Lengel, *This Glorious Struggle*, p. 131.

137. Ibid., pp. 137–139; Brumwell, *George Washington*, p. 333.

138. Robert K. Wright Jr. and Morris J. MacGregor Jr., *Soldier-Statesmen of the Constitution* (Washington, DC: Center of Military History, 1987), pp. 76–78.

139. Craig, *General Edward Hand*, p. 17; Robert K. Wright Jr., *The Continental Army* (Washington, DC: United States Government Printing Office, 1984), pp. 259–260; Boatner, *Encyclopedia of the American Revolution*, p. 1098.

140. O'Brien, *A Hidden Phase of American History*, p. 245; Haltigan, *The Irish in the American Revolution and Their Early Influence in the Colonies*, p. 216; Puls, *Henry Knox*, pp. 19, 58; Robert V. Remini, *Andrew Jackson and His Indian Wars* (New York: Penguin Books, 2002), pp. 12–13.

141. Remini, *Andrew Jackson and His Indian Wars*, p. 13.

Chapter VII

1. Chastellux, *Travels in North-America*, p. 62.

2. Piecuch, *Cavalry of the American Revolution*, p. 107.

3. Ibid., pp. 4–5; Craig, *General Edward Hand*, pp. 85–103; Brumwell, *George Washington*, p. 31; Boatner, *Encyclopedia of the American Revolution*, pp. 485, 925–926, Wright and MacGregor, *Soldier-Statesmen of the Constitution*, pp. 106–108; Haltigan, *The Irish in the American Revolution*, pp. 47–48, 228–229, 493; Arthur S. Lefkowitz, *George Washington's Indispensable Men: The 32 Aides-de-Camp Who Helped Win American Independence* (Mechanicsburg, PA: Stackpole Books, 2003), pp. 10–11, 19–24, 59, 81–82, 140–142; McCullough, *1776*, pp. 44, 56–57, 132; Clark, *All Cloudless Glory*, pp. 240–241; Kennedy, *The Scots-Irish in the Hills of Tennessee*, pp. 156–157; Puls, *Henry Knox*, p. 30; Lengel, ed., *This Glorious Struggle*, pp. 35–36, 145–146; Hunt, *The Irish and the American Revolution*, p. 38; Doyle, *Ireland, Irishmen and Revolutionary America*, pp. 90, 196; Randall, *Alexander Hamilton*, pp. 121–122, 124; Tench Tilghman, *Memoirs of Lieutenant Colonel Tench Tilghman, Secretary and Aid to Washington* (Albany, NY: J. Munsell, 1876), pp. 2–175; Lalor, ed., *The Encyclopedia of Ireland*, p. 778; William Gardner Bell, *Secretaries of War and Secretaries of the Army: Portraits and Biographical Sketches* (Washington, DC: Center of Military History, 1982), p. 24; Fleming, *1776*, p. 414; Moran, "George Washington's Military Family," *LTN*; Brumwell, *George Washington*, pp. 332–333; Kaplan, *Alexander Hamilton*, p. 2.

4. McCullough, *1776*, p. 56; Lengel, *This Glorious Struggle*, p. 25.

5. Fleming, *Washington's Secret War*, p. 164.

6. *American Daily Advertiser*, Philadelphia, Pennsylvania, April 16, 1811; Piecuch, *Cavalry of the American Revolution*, pp. 4–7; Haltigan, *The Irish in the American*

Revolution, pp. 186–189; Lefkowitz, *George Washington's Indispensable Men*, pp. 29–31, 41, 50, 53, 102; Loescher, *Washington's Eyes*, pp. 97–120; Fleming, *Liberty!*, p. 262; Boatner, *Encyclopedia of the American Revolution*, pp. 751–752; Wright, *The Continental Army*, pp. 346–347; Lalor, ed., *The Encyclopedia of Ireland*, p. 617; Boyle, *From Redcoat to Rebel*, pp. 8–11; Gurn, *Commodore John Barry*, pp. 6–7; Hunt, *The Irish and the American Revolution*, pp. 82–84; Wikipedia contributors, "Ursulines," Wikipedia, The Free Encyclopedia, https://en.wikipedia.org/w/index.php?title=Ursulines&oldid=664878502 accessed December 8, 2009; Doyle, *Ireland, Irishmen and Revolutionary America*, p. 196; Kenneth Baker, *George Washington's War in Caricature and Print* (London: Grub Street Publishing, 2009), p. 171; Moran, "George Washington's Military Family," *LTN*; Griffin, *Catholics and the American Revolution*, pp. 217–218, 220, 227–275, 341.

7. Piecuch, *Cavalry of the American Revolution*, p. 7.

8. Griffin, *Catholics and the American Revolution*, vol. 2, p. 267.

9. Gregory D. Massey, *John Laurens and the American Revolution* (Columbia: University of South Carolina Press, 2000), pp. 168–169.

10. Griffin, *Catholics and the American Revolution*, vol. 2, pp. 276–277, 305, 337; Trussell, *The Pennsylvania Line*, pp. 212–218; Piecuch, *Cavalry of the American Revolution*, pp. 4–6.

11. Gurn, *Commodore John Barry*, pp. 48–49.

12. Chastellux, *Travels in North-America*, pp. 74–75

13. Robert Ellis Cahill, *New England's Naughty Navy* (Peabody, MA: Smith Publishing House, Inc., 1987), p. 27; Nutting, *Ireland Beautiful*, pp. 61–62.

14. Griffin, *Catholics and the American Revolution*, vol. 2, pp. 291, 302, 337; Bill, *Valley Forge*, pp. 112–113; *New York Gazette and Weekly Mercury*, April 24, 1780.

15. Ibid., p. 309.

16. Ibid., pp. 347–348.

17. Heath, *Memoirs of Major-General William Heath by Himself*, p. 197.

18. Lefkowitz, *George Washington's Indispensable Men*, pp. 81–82; Brumwell, *George Washington*, p. 382; Haltigan, *The Irish in the American Revolution*, p. 493; O'Brien, *A Hidden Phase of American History*, pp. 228, 246, 364; Wright, *The Continental Army*, pp. 285; Fleming, *Washington's Secret War*, p. 188; Gurn, *Commodore John Barry*, pp. 46–47; Lalor, ed., *The Encyclopedia of Ireland*, pp. 394–395; Shelley Klein, *The Most Evil*

Pirates in History (New York: Barnes and Noble, 2006), p. 21; Wikipedia contributors, "Virginia reel," Wikipedia, The Free Encyclopedia, https://en.wikipedia.org/w/index.php?title=Virginia_reel&oldid=340484812 accessed June 21, 2011; Griffin, *Catholics and the American Revolution*, vol. 2, pp. 366–368, 387; Foss, *Undreamed Shores*, pp. 105, 108.

19. Joseph Gurn, *Commodore John Barry: Father of the American Navy* (Cranbury, NJ: Scholar's Bookshelf, 2005) pp. 46–47; Hunt, *The Irish and the American Revolution*, p. 38.

20. Cox, *A Proper Sense of Honor*, p. 187.

21. Ibid.

22. Bell, *Secretaries of War and Secretaries of the Army*, p. 24; Lengel, *Inventing George Washington*, pp. 50–51; Brumwell, *George Washington*, pp. 31, 120; Lalor, ed., *The Encyclopedia of Ireland*, p. 66.

23. Chastellux, *Travels in North-America*, p. 43.

24. Frank A. Cassell, *Merchant Congressman in the Young Republic: Samuel Smith of Maryland 1752–1839* (Madison: The University of Wisconsin Press, 1971), pp. 3–4, 12–35; Samuel Smith Papers, Library of Congress, Washington, DC; Burgoyne, ed., *Enemy Views*, p. 236; Fleming, *1776*, p. 135; Tucker, *The Important Role of the Irish in the American Revolution*, pp. 32–64; Royster, *Light-Horse Harry Lee and the Legacy of the American Revolution*, pp. 24–25; Brumwell, *George Washington*, pp. 239–240; Jerry J. Gaddy, *Texas In Revolt: Contemporary Newspaper Account of the Texas Revolution* (Fort Collins, CO: The Old Army Press, 1973), p. 49.

25. Tilghman, *Memoirs of Lieutenant Colonel Tench Tilghman*, p. 135.

26. Stephenson, *Patriot Battles*, p. 29.

27. Piecuch, *Cavalry of the American Revolution*, pp. 183–200.

28. Stephenson, *Patriot Battles*, pp. 29–30; Tonsetic, *1781*, p. 11; Hunt, *The Irish and the American Revolution*, p. 7–8; Fleming, *Liberty!*, p. 282.

29. Tilghman, *Memoir of Lieutenant Colonel Tench Tilghman*, p. 131

30. Hunt, *The Irish and the American Revolution*, p. 75–76; Lalor, ed., *The Encyclopedia of Ireland*, p. 357.

31. Hunt, *The Irish and the American Revolution*, pp. 75–76, 94–95; Brumwell, *George Washington*, p. 149.

32. Hunt, *The Irish and the American Revolution*, pp. 92–94.

33. Brumwell, *George Washington*, pp. 149, 201–202, 413–414

34. Ibid., pp. 221, 413; Whittemore, *The Heroes of the American Revolution and Their Descendants*, pp. 25–28; Boatner, *Encyclopedia of the American Revolution*,

pp. 235–236, 240–241, 594–595; Morrissey, *Saratoga 1777*, p. 68; Lalor, ed., *The Encyclopedia of Ireland*, pp. 645–646, 838; Boatner, *Encyclopedia of the American Revolution*, pp. 594–595; Shelton, *General Richard Montgomery and the American Revolution*, p. 82; Doyle, *Ireland, Irishmen and Revolutionary America*, pp. 132, 203; Mayers, *The War Man*, pp. 19, 25, 28–32, 52, 56–93; Randall, *Alexander Hamilton*, pp. 46, 91, 95, 106.

35. Lengel, *This Glorious Struggle*, p. 127; Boatner, *Encyclopedia of the American Revolution*, pp. 245–246; Haltigan, *The Irish in the American Revolution*, p. 176; Hunt, *The Irish and the American Revolution*, pp. 65, 101.

36. George Washington to John Cochran, August 31, 1785, George Washington Papers, National Archives, Washington, DC.

37. McGrath, *John Barry*, pp. 4–7; Boatner, *Encyclopedia of the American Revolution*, pp. 60–61; *Washington Post*, August 31, 1902; Gurn, *Commodore John Barry* (Cranbury, NJ: Scholar's Bookshelf, 2005), p. 4; Doyle, *Ireland, Irishmen and Revolutionary America*, pp. 132, 144.

38. McGrath, *John Barry*, pp. 8–501; Haltigan, *The Irish in the American Revolution*, pp. 165–168; Boatner, *Encyclopedia of the American Revolution*, pp. 60–61; O'Brien, *A Hidden Phase of American History*, pp. 229, 246; Lucey, *Harp and Sword*, pp. 36, 41–43; Gurn, *Commodore John Barry*, pp. 4–5, 6, 10, 19–26, 291, 296–298; Samuel Eliot Morison, *John Paul Jones* (New York: Time Incorporated, 1964), pp. 1, 3; Baker, *George Washington's War in Caricature and Print*, pp. 140, 143.

39. McGrath, *John Barry*, pp. 107–109; Gurn, *Commodore John Barry*, pp. 43–46.

40. McGrath, *John Barry*, pp. 150–166; Gurn, *Commodore John Barry*, pp. 71–98, 299–300.

41. *Pennsylvania Gazette*, Philadelphia, Pennsylvania, March 21, 1778.

42. McGrath, *John Barry*, pp. 165–166.

43. Gurn, *Commodore John Barry*, pp. 54–70; Baker, *George Washington's War in Caricature and Print*, p. 209.

44. Gurn, *Commodore John Barry*, pp. 146–147.

45. Ibid., pp. 191, 292.

46. Ibid., p. 193.

47. John Fitzgerald Kennedy Address of Irish Parliament, June 28, 1963, John Fitzgerald Kennedy Library, Boston, Massachusetts; Edward Klein, *The Kennedy Curse: Why America's First Family Has Been Haunted by Tragedy For 150 Years* (New York: St. Martin's Press, 2003), pp. 33–34.

48. Doyle, *Ireland, Irishmen and Revolutionary America*, pp. 48–49.

49. Robert Bray and Paul Bushnell, editors, *Diary of a Common Soldier in the American Revolution, 1775–1783* (DeKalb: Northern Illinois University Press, 1978), pp. xiv–xv,169

50. Golway, *For the Cause of Liberty*, p. 51.

51. Murphy, *The Irish in the American Revolution*, p. 93.

52. Ibid., p. 94.

53. Bruce C. MacGunnigle, *Regimental Book: Rhode Island Regiment for 1781 &c* (East Greenwich: Rhode Island Society of the Sons of the American Revolution, 2011), pp. xi, xv, 4, 8–11, 14–15, 20, 22, 26, 30, 39.

54. Doyle, *Ireland, Irishmen and Revolutionary America*, pp. 63–64, 96–97.

55. MacGunnigle, *Regimental Book*, pp. xi, xv, 4, 8–11, 14–15, 20, 22, 26, 30, 30; Retzer, *The German Regiment of Maryland and Pennsylvania*, pp. 1–153.

56. Swisher, *Revolutionary War in the Southern Back Country*, pp. 32, 137–141, 312. 315, 325–326; Dolan, *The Irish Americans*, p. 22; Brumwell, *George Washington*, pp. 406–407; Doyle, *Ireland, Irishmen and Revolutionary America*, p. 150; "Fort Pitt and Letters from the Frontier." USGenWeb Archives Pennsylvania. Accessed August 25, 2005. http://www.usgwarchives. net/pa/1pa/1picts/darlington/fp4.html.; Tonsetic, *1781*, pp. 11, 203–205.

57. McGuire, *Battle of Paoli*, p. 156; Tonsetic, *1781*, p. 11; Dolan, *The Irish Americans*, p. 22.

58. Swisher, *The Revolutionary War in the Southern Back Country*, p. 173.

59. Ibid; pp. 173, 203–272.

60. Draper, *King's Mountain and Its Heroes*, pp. 405, 407–408; Remini, *Andrew Jackson and His Indian Wars*, pp. 7–19.

Conclusion

1. Doyle, *Ireland, Irishmen and Revolutionary America*, p. 150; Lalor, ed., *The Encyclopedia of Ireland*, pp. 754, 1022–1023; Tonsetic, *1781*, p. 11; Simms, *The Life of Francis Marion*, pp. 18, 35.

2. Jones, *Sergeant William Jasper*, p. 36; Cox, *A Proper Sense of Honor*, p. 187.

3. Draper, *King's Mountain and Its Heroes*, p. 93; Buchanan, *Jackson's Way*, p. 5.

4. Jones, *Sergeant William Jasper*, p. 19.

5. Ibid., pp. 20–21; Rick Hatcher, Fort Sumter National Monument, Sullivan's Island, South Carolina, email to author, March 31, 2014.
6. Jones, *Sergeant William Jasper*, p. 111.
7. Murphy, *The Irish in the American Revolution*, p. 12.
8. Hunt, *The Irish and the American Revolution*, p. 101.
9. John Fitzgerald Kennedy Address to Irish Parliament, Dublin, Ireland, June 28, 1963, John Fitzgerald Kennedy Library, Boston, Massachusetts.

Index